LOUISIANA STATE UNIVERSITY STUDIES

*Number 33*

# AMERICA IN ENGLISH FICTION
## 1760-1800

# AMERICA IN ENGLISH FICTION

## *1760 : 1800*

### THE INFLUENCES OF THE AMERICAN REVOLUTION

ROBERT BECHTOLD HEILMAN

1968
OCTAGON BOOKS, INC.
*New York*

*Reprinted 1968*
*by special arrangement with Louisiana State University Press*

OCTAGON BOOKS, INC.
175 FIFTH AVENUE
NEW YORK, N. Y. 10010


LIBRARY OF CONGRESS CATALOG CARD NUMBER: 68-28261


*Printed in U.S.A. by*
NOBLE OFFSET PRINTERS, INC.
NEW YORK 3, N. Y.

# CONTENTS

# PREFACE

I am glad to acknowledge here various obligations which I have incurred in completing this study.

I am especially indebted to Dean Charles W. Pipkin, Director of the Louisiana State University Studies, and to Professor Marcus M. Wilkerson, Director of the Louisiana State University Press, for making possible the publication of the study.

Professor C. N. Greenough of Harvard University suggested the subject to me and gave me much generous aid in the treatment of copious material. He has given me unlimited access to his invaluable Catalogue of Prose Fiction (hereinafter referred to as Professor Greenough's Catalogue), on which I have been dependent for lists of works, dates of first editions, authorship of books published anonymously, and a great deal of other information which I have acknowledged, as far as possible, in the notes. Dr. Frank G. Black, formerly Professor Greenough's assistant, let me draw constantly on his detailed knowledge of the Catalogue, and, in reading my manuscript, he has, with characteristic generosity, placed at my disposal his immense knowledge of eighteenth-century prose fiction.

Various colleagues and fellow-students have contributed information and suggestions. Dr. A. J. Bryan has not only read the manuscript and made valuable criticisms but has also shown the kindest interest in the progress of the work. Mr. Fred H. Fenn has generously done the diagrams which appear in Chapter II.

The staff of the Harvard College Library have shown me their customary helpfulness and courtesy and have permitted me to rely extensively on inter-library loans. Mr. Robert Haynes has been unfailingly kind to me, whether I have been resident student or visitor. The New York Public Library has permitted me to consult volumes in its Rare Book Room.

My wife, Ruth Champlin Heilman, has been patient in the long drudgery of checking references, correcting manuscript, and reading proof, and I have adopted many of her suggestions about form and style.

R. B. HEILMAN

CHAPTER I

# PRELIMINARIES

i

What use the English novel made of the American Revolution is partly a matter of journalism in prose fiction, partly a question of literary recognition of the potentialities of history, partly an aspect of the much larger problem of the relation of America to five centuries of old-world thought. The literature of the English-speaking peoples has always had a sharp eye on current events, witness the apparatus necessary for complete understanding of the works of any period, and today, for example, the crop of novels generated by the World War and the depression. At no time did the borrowing hand follow the sharp eye more consistently than in the latter eighteenth century:

All kinds of bastard products, whose home would now be the columns of the sensational press, appeared on the library shelves. Contemporary scandals and *causes célèbres*, lightly dished up in "two curious *open-worked* volumes"; fictitious or semi-fictitious biographies of statesmen, actresses, and prostitutes; secret histories; travels and memoirs of uncertain value; these and other obscure blends of fact and fiction counted as "novels" in the book lists of the day.[1]

Like current events, past events have paid tithes to the novel, which today often becomes a mammoth remembrance of earlier epochs. The quasi-veracious historical romance was just muddling into existence when Burke was denouncing the policies of North and economists debated the nexus between war and the national debt, between war and trade. General Wolfe soon

[1] J. M. S. Tompkins, *The Popular Novel in England 1770-1800* (London: Constable, 1932), p. 4.

1

occupied a whole shelf of the stock-in-trade, and twelve years after the Treaty of Paris the American fracas was already far enough in the past to provide the framework for a five-volume novel, Mrs. Eliza Parsons' *The Voluntary Exile* (1795).

But beyond the mere turning of battles into books, beyond the trailing of the sword by the pen, lies a broader field, that of the changing ideas of which imaginative literature is only one expression. That the eighteenth century, in its politics, its ideas, and its culture, was a period of transition is a truism; even to the superficial student there is a patent distinction between the days of Robert Walpole and those of Burke, between Whiggish placidity and the vociferousness of Jacobin societies, between the Augustan quest for symmetry and "Gothic" experiment and longing, between orderly Addisonian gardens and the "picturesque" landscaping neatly ridiculed by Peacock. Perhaps most commonly bandied about in essay and tome are the shifts in literature—the decline of the drama and the rise of the novel; the waning of the couplet, and all that it implied, and the waxing of the lyric; the passing of "propriety" and the elevation of "the real language of men"; the tumbling-down of the Graeco-Roman hierarchy and the apotheosis of a new hodge-podge of ideals, beliefs, and prejudices conveniently labeled Romanticism. At the height of the *ancien régime* Pope dogmatized:

> But critic learning flourish'd most in France;
> The rules a nation born to serve obeys,
> And Boileau still in right of Horace sways.

It was in these dead days, Keats retorted, that

> A thousand handicraftsmen wore the mask
> Of Poesy . . . [and] went about,
> Holding a poor, decrepid standard out,
> Mark'd with most flimsy mottoes, and in large
> The name of one Boileau!

The fumbling, tacking progress from *Vive Boileau* to *À bas Boileau* became a firm march as the century rushed out in a

2

conflicting tumult of liberty, fraternity, and inevitably, the last snorts of reaction. Between Quebec and Waterloo the world changed its spots. The drawing-room was jostled by the country, London by the Lakes, Rome by Camelot and the Border, Sense by Sensibility, Complacency by Dissent; as rebels questioned the infallibility of Johnson, the Georgian dispensation was more fiercely heckled by abolitionists, Wesleyans, and reformers, by East Indians, Irish, and Americans. Only to the third of the Hanoverians did the noise become positively painful; before, there may have been subterranean rumblings, like those stimulated by the Bubble and by the Foundry in Moorfields, but only now was there a real eruption, and with it the first symptoms of a retreat from the pleasant heights of prerogative. Toward century-end the transition moved rapidly. Earlier, things were too comfortable, even with signs and portents admitted; in the days of docks and counting-houses, with the alert Walpolean plays to the purse, change was an enemy. These we can pass over, since a limited study of an era of flux naturally stresses the years of most rapid action; hence we focus attention on the actual reign of the monarch thus described by his mock-elegist:

A better farmer ne'er brush'd dew from lawn,
A worse king never left a realm undone!

Whether or not the realm was undone, it was assuredly done over. Likewise its dependencies and neighbors. France disburdened itself of a royal line and got a dictator; the Irish were troublesomely indisposed to acquiescence in autocratic mismanagement; parvenu Nabobs so flaunted spoils as to irk the whole country and produce an investigation of Indian affairs; Quakers and Methodists joined hands to attack the treatment of the African; and, most decisively, America went off and set up shop on its own. New work for cartographers was one vivid objectification of the results of transition. In examining the multifold changes, political and literary, one can satisfy the

3

quest for unity with many a theory, and the ingenious man in search of a synthesis can find unlimited entertainment in striving to assemble, on some basic pattern, the diversity of the fall of the Bastille, the efforts of Wilberforce, *Tam O'Shanter, Baratariana,* the trial of Hastings, the *Book of Thel,* and the Declaration of Independence. I have no intention of replaying here the old game of diagnoses and labels, or of justifying or debating conclusions already current. Whatever name one gives the essential temper of the times, it is sufficiently clear that America and American history are of decided importance in the complete story of the period. Here we are concerned chiefly with that relationship, and with literary interpretations of it.

The significance of the American Revolution—or, as contemporaries called it, the American War—in English history needs no elaboration. But just as social change was not a solely English but a European phenomenon, so transatlantic events are bound up, in one way or another, with both British and continental evolution. The complex of spiritual modulations most easily summarized in *Romanticism* was "a great international movement,"[2] with constant interaction and intercourse of ideas and attitudes. These the three great European powers were exchanging more effectively than they had ever exchanged bullets, for the mutual influences of the various literatures, partially personified by the ubiquitous Mme. De Stael, are commonplace knowledge.[3] In the growth of a new *Weltan-*

[2] Irving Babbitt, *Rousseau and Romanticism* (Boston and New York: Houghton Mifflin, 1919), p. ix.

[3] One need only mention German influences on the English novel and the English drama, the exploration of German literature begun by Mackenzie and Scott and amplified by Coleridge and Carlyle. For the other side of the picture, see L. M. Price, *English> German Literary Influences* (University of California Publications in Modern Philology, Vol. 9, Nos. 1 and 2, Berkeley, 1919-1920) and Mary Bell Price and Lawrence Marsden Price, *The Publication of English Literature in Germany in the Eighteenth Century* (University of California Publications in Modern Philology, Vol. 17, Berkeley, 1934). French influence in England is demonstrated by the vogue of French novels, especially the works of Rousseau and Marivaux. Conversely, there is the popularity of Richardson in France.

4

*schauung*, America figures especially in political thought, with the most obvious liaison that between her revolt and the French Revolution:

. . . the world at large begins to consider with admiration the United States, who on a virgin soil are building an ideal and Arcadian republic; then, with a mixture of alarm and fervor, it sees France establish a democratic form of government in the place of the oldest monarchy of Europe. Therefore it is truly in America and France that we find the stronghold of revolutionary ideas at the end of the eighteenth century.[4]

Derivative from the republican idea is a whole host of aspirations, later to be traced; America as the land of promise excited visions in both France[5] and Germany, where even the seer of Königsberg manifested enthusiasm for American liberty.[6] He was not alone:

The Revolutionary War awakened a keen interest in America all over Germany. . . . At the close of the century America is no longer a "terra incognita" to Germans; an abundance of literary material gives extensive information about conditions prevailing in the New World. . . . The prevailing conception of America is that of the land of liberty, young and active, promising a prosperous future. Great masses of the German people, discouraged in the midst of wretched political and economic conditions at home, magnify the good news from across the sea, and pin their last hopes for mankind on America.[7]

To these belonged Goethe, according to one student, who points out that at the end of *Faust* the hero wins salvation

in wresting from the sea a free country for a free people. That Goethe

---

[4] Bernard Faÿ, *The Revolutionary Spirit in France and America*, tr. Ramon Guthrie (New York: Harcourt Brace, 1927), p. 472. For instances of the interpenetration of American, French, and English affairs and feelings, see pp. 368, 402, 426.

[5] For an account of the hopes and ideals of French travelers to America, see H. M. Jones, *American and French Culture 1750-1848* (Chapel Hill: University of North Carolina Press, 1927), pp. 124 ff.

[6] Paul C. Weber, *America in Imaginative German Literature in the First Half of the Nineteenth Century* (New York: Columbia University Press, 1926), p. 3.

[7] *Ibid.*, p. 41. Weber goes on to point out that another class of Germans decried American "lack of culture and ideals," while many German men of letters ignored America entirely.

5

had America in mind is made certain by the conclusion of his last novel. . . .[8]

Any study of the literary treatment of America cannot totally ignore such facts as these because of the close-knit intellectual and spiritual fabric of the period; what France and Germany thought about America both reflects and influences what England thought about America.

Of course it is primarily in the English attitude to the new world that we are interested, though what the islanders thought be never wholly separable from a continental point of view comprising, it already appears, a large measure of idealization. Of this one might expect less in England, naturally. While she was in the throes of cultural desquamation, her offspring was having rather considerable growing pains, a combination of circumstances conducive neither to fixity of attitude nor to a continuance of maternal complacency. America, too, managed to have a finger, whether unconsciously or no, in every outburst or row that challenged the comfortable old order—in "republicanism," Gallic or British; Hibernian resentfulness; Oriental furore; parliamentary reform—and hence remained steadily in the English line of vision. So England might be expected to feel not the same sensations she felt in the satisfying days of Wolfe.

The rebellion transformed the colonies into the United States, and with the change in name went a subtler one in character. Whatever the personality that appeared to a sufficiently bedeviled Old World, new arrangements were necessary; there were new international relationships, beginning somewhat unhandily with a war,[9] and the work of American diplomats "consisted in bringing other nations to a realization

8 O. E. Lessing, *Brücken über den Atlantik* (Stuttgart, etc.: Deutsche Verlags-Anstalt, 1927), p. 157.

9 Regretted by John W. Graham, *Britain and America: The Merttens Lecture, 1930* (London: Hogarth, n.d.), p. 10. Another commentator stresses "the growing appreciation of identity of interests"; see Andrew C. McLaughlin, *America and Britain* (New York: Dutton, 1919), pp. 39-40.

that America existed politically."[10] Here is evidence of a novel situation, matrix of ideas. England was no longer able to gaze with possessive fondness at "both th' Indies of spice and Myne." Imperial imagination turned to the East again, altering the whose politico-economic pattern,[11] and probably, as we shall see, influencing literary trends. There was less room, for instance, for the casually inevitable union of the two Indies, sneered at by the anonymous hack reviewing Mrs. Woodfin's *The History of Miss Harriot Watson:*

The father, Sir John, hates his daughter's lover Mr. Howard . . . and . . . hires a fellow . . . to trepan him on board a ship, and carry him, not, gentle reader, to the East or West-Indies, but to one of the small islands of Scilly. . . .[12]

And the Nabobs, the returned Anglo-Indians, began to cut a considerable figure in literature.[13]

So the question arises: What impact did a shifting world make on popular literature? Although measurements can be taken and descriptions drawn at any point of impact or contact, it is my purpose to investigate especially the American influence, both in itself and through its association with important contemporary movements. For one thing, how did the picture of America change as that of the world changed? What happened to the connotation of such words as *America* and *the new world* as the dust began to clear away and the new order to seem permanent? There is an *a priori* expectation that we are at a focal point in international attitudes and even cultural concepts. There may be hands across the sea, here and there, but there

[10] Robert E. Spiller, *The American in England during the First Half Century of Independence* (New York: Holt, 1926), p. 103.

[11] For a partial attribution of the decline of the slave-trade to the shifting of the British Empire from the West to the East, illustrating the interweaving of the political, social, and territorial matters of the time, see Frank J. Klingberg, *The Anti-Slavery Movement in England* (New Haven: Yale University Press, 1926), pp. vii-viii.

[12] *Critical Review*, XV (1763), 63.

[13] For a partial bibliography of illustrative works, see James M. Holzman, *The Nabobs in England* (New York, 1926), pp. 173-174.

are also stares and frowns. What England thought, or appeared to think, remains to be recorded; in the meantime, pertinent data appear in French views:

Since the days when this hemisphere [America] was 'El Dorado,' a land of mystery with somewhere in it the very fountain of youth and happiness, a land where all was different from the Europe where men suffered want, and hate, and age; for France at least this land had always continued to be in some sort a Utopia, where the weary search for the philosopher's stone was not requisite to set one above the misery of his fellows in the Old World, or where he should find brothers and not enemies among men. Since the conception was an ideal, no toil and disappointment were of sufficient force to shake it; and we find it growing still up to the time of our Revolution in the enthusiastic interest in our cause. And it expressed itself even more sincerely no doubt, even into the following century, in the charming conception, the "man of nature," the "good savage."

The interest in the American Revolution and in the subsequent political system, is the turning-point, however, where that old ideal, being as it were attached to the American soil, must, if it were not to be abandoned, find its way henceforth among men and their works, and no longer range unhindered where nature and her unspoiled children were living out the Golden Age. The "good savage" and the inspiring world where he moved had disappeared, giving way to European settlers who would soon make it all over into the banal city and country Europe knew too well.[14]

The American Revolution, it is to be noted, is the "turning-point," and, without implying a complete parallel between France and England, we may assume that the same is true of English opinion and that we are studying a historical axis on which turn the human feelings evoked by changes in a land and a society. At Philadelphia more was written than a Declaration.

Considerations of quality and quantity are often inseparable, especially here. Ideas about America are by no means the sole subject of study, for they cannot be divorced from reference to the number of writers who used the new world. If no eyes had

[14] Harold E. Mantz, *French Criticism of American Literature Before 1850* (New York: Columbia University Press, 1917), pp. 2-3.

turned to the West, no pens would have written about it, and hence it is important to count the pens. At the simplest, how many authors, or, more specifically, how many novelists, wrote about America at all? Then, how many found material in the American War? Was it as important to the English as we easily assume it to have been? What did they think about it, where did they distribute plaudits, where lay patriotism? And along trails an array of cognate issues—economics, humanitarianism, politics. Here is the preliminary problem.

Before arithmetic, however, there is need for further history. Filling in historical outlines with literary pictures is not a new game, but there is something to be said for this sort of illuminating process in a period which, as has already been sufficiently emphasized, is one of flux. That the transitional character of the age is to be found also in the old world's view of the new has been suggested as an inevitable consequence of political events. To turn suggestion into fact, it is necessary to glance at English opinion of America before and after the eighteenth century. If there is sharp divergence between the earlier and later periods, then the epoch under consideration will definitely represent a turning-point. To repeat, our particular investigation is inseparable from the problem of America's position in five centuries of old-world thought.

ii

In the Renaissance, Lewis Mumford has said, "the new world of exploration" brought Europe "within sight of a new world of ideas."[15] And he has headed a section of his book: "How something happened to utopia between Plato and Sir Thomas More; and how utopia was discovered again, along with the New World."[16] Another student has elaborated the European impression which held in Tudor days:

New continents inhabited by unheard of and unthought of races of people; conditions of life never before known to the civilized world, or if

[15] *The Story of Utopias* (New York: Boni and Liveright, 1922), p. 64.
[16] *Ibid.*, p. 57.

9

known, forgotten through centuries of artificiality; men living in freedom, without extreme or noticeable restrictions of law, and yet in reasonable harmony or order—these were the new conceptions which, though they by their suddenness struck hard and with stunning effect, yet cleared a new and immeasurably broader horizon, and brought out the contrast between the degenerating artificiality of civilization and the natural, original condition of man. . . . The fountain of eternal youth became a healthy climate, fresh air, and cool springs; the fabulous rivers of gold took the form and shape of cultivated fields and limitless stretches of timber; and the phantastical, mythical race of beings resolved itself into a simple people, an example of human life close to nature.[17]

So the initial view had been all freshness and bloom. After it had been splotched by several centuries of imperial conflict, a rebellion, and the growth of the grandsons of a few thousand farmers into internationally powerful industrialists and financiers, what happened to the Renaissance idyl? The sixteenth-century Garden of Eden has dwindled, in the twentieth, into the none-too-well-kept backyard of Uncle Shylock. Late in 1933 Bernard Faÿ sums up:

The United States is no longer what it was up to the middle of the nineteenth century, a sort of wild garden where thousands of fruits and millions of flowers flourished at random and the children were let loose to gather and eat to their heart's content. The flowers are spoiled, the fruits are becoming rare, and a gardener is needed to put things in order.[18]

As for the specific English view, J. D. Whelpley states:

To the casual American visitor America and American affairs do not appear to have a good Press in England. . . . There is a full appreciation of American energy, resource, vitality, and accomplishment. There is always an under-estimate of the spiritual forces at work in America and an over-estimate as to the importance with which material things are regarded in that country.[19]

[17] Felix E. Held, in his introduction to *Christianopolis: An Ideal State of the Seventeenth Century, Translated from the Latin of Johann Valentin Andreae* (New York: Oxford, 1916), p. 4.
[18] *Roosevelt and his America* (Boston: Little, Brown, 1933), pp. 317-318.
[19] *British-American Relations* (Boston: Little, Brown, 1924), pp. 27, 34.

Here there is little left of the dream; for vision has been substituted interpretation, or at least an effort at interpretation.

For a century and a half Europe and America have been eyeing each other and endeavoring to find out wherein their likenesses and differences consist. A host of personalities, as different as Franklin and Crèvecoeur and Tocqueville and Dickens and Matthew Arnold and Waldo Frank have contributed to this discussion; and since the war, with the appearance of observers like André Siegfried, Lucien Romier, and Herman Keyserling, the literature on the subject has become vast, not to say flatulent.[20]

The "literature" is not merely that of professional students, for novels, the drama, and poetry often play about issues of statecraft. A few instances will show how belles-lettres mirror the transformation of ideas. Faÿ's summary, for example, is not unlike that of Shaw's *Apple Cart,* which pokes fun, among other things, at the American commercial spirit which finds a material advantage in rejoining the British Empire. America is embodied in Ambassador Vanhattan, who, loquacious, self-confident, crass, announces to King Magnus of England:

. . . the Declaration of Independence is cancelled. The treaties which endorsed it are torn up. We have decided to rejoin the British Empire.[21]

Magnus doubts the advantages, but the Queen simultaneously expresses her approval and a traditional point of view about Americans:

I think it is a very good thing. You will make a very good emperor. We shall civilize these Americans.[22]

More balanced, if less clever, is the portrayal in Somerset Maugham's *Our Betters,* which harshly indicts the degeneracy of British society, and, more than that, the superficiality, affectation, and futility, if not actual viciousness, of expatriate

---

[20] Lewis Mumford, "American Condescension and European Superiority," *Scribner's Magazine,* LXXXVII (1930), 518.

[21] G. B. Shaw, *The Apple Cart* (New York: Brentano, 1931), p. 93.

[22] *Ibid.,* p. 100.

11

Americans who become hangers-on of English plutocracy and aristocracy, even though, as one of the more realistic of them says,

Good Heavens, when you've known England as long as I have you'll realize that in their hearts they still look upon us as savages and Red Indians. We have to force ourselves upon them.[23]

The speaker is Pearl Grayston, an unscrupulous climber; in her coterie are Arthur Fenwick, a crooked industrialist; the Duchesse de Surennes, of parvenu origin and character; and Thornton Clay, vain, effusive, and overdressed. These make up one panel in the picture of Americans. In the other, meant to be more representative, are Elizabeth Saunders, Pearl's younger sister, and Fleming Harvey, who take one glance at the expatriates and, repelled, return home. Elizabeth, honest and direct, flutters before a title for a moment, but ultimately is won by Fleming, who, distinguished by what the eighteenth century called "conscious virtue," yet manages to be more attractive than priggish. In them Maugham makes an unusually favorable interpretation of American character.

The balance between Maugham's two groups of characters illustrates a critical tendency in which, if there is not actual disillusionment, at least doubt sheds a grey light on fields once irradiated by Utopian hopefulness. The doubt is traceable backward to the eighteenth century. Before the immediate present, one stops first with Arnold, whose exposé of cultural imperfections was not limited to England, and whose exceptions are well remembered, perhaps because "bitterly resented."[24] Speaking in and to this first "representative democracy," the prophet of Hellenism dared to question its all-embracing virtue, expressing the fear that

23 Thomas H. Dickinson, ed., *Chief Contemporary Dramatists, Second Series* (Boston: Houghton Mifflin, 1921), p. 87.

24 William B. Cairns, *British Criticisms of American Writings 1783-1815* (University of Wisconsin Studies in Language and Literature, No. 1, Madison, 1918), p. 44 note.

. . . in a democratic community like this, with its newness, its magnitude, its strength, its life of business, its sheer freedom and equality, the danger is in the absence of the discipline of respect; in hardness and materialism, exaggeration and boastfulness; in a false smartness, a false audacity, a want of soul and delicacy.[25]

With the same temperateness, but without any effort at the same analysis, Thackeray makes Sir George Warrington, successively English citizen, American Loyalist, and English peer, say, in mellow retrospection:

Against the British in America there were arrayed thousands and thousands of the high-spirited and brave, but there were thousands more who found their profit in the quarrel, or had their private reasons for engaging in it. I protest I don't know now whether mine were selfish or patriotic, or which side was in the right, or whether both were not? I am sure we in England had nothing to do but fight the battle out; and, having lost the game, I do vow and believe that, after the first natural soreness, the loser felt no rancour.[26]

The "sporting spirit" and the balance are less in evidence as one goes back further in the century, and proportion yields to the rancor of *Martin Chuzzlewit*. Starting with the premonitory irony of the caption, "Chapter XV. The Burden whereof is Hail, Columbia!"[27] Dickens proceeds explicitly to categorize the coarseness, vulgarity, bumptiousness, rowdiness, and even brutality of American life, satirizing land-boom frauds with uncompromising bitterness, and viciously caricaturing a southern "Walley of Eden":

Rain, heat, foul slime, and noxious vapour, with all the ills and filthy things they bred, prevailed. The earth, the air, the vegetation, and the water that they drank, all teemed with deadly properties. Their fellow-passenger had lost two children long before; and buried now her last.[28]

It is not a question, here, of whether he is within legitimate

[25] Matthew Arnold, *Discourses in America* (New York: Macmillan, 1902), p. 66.
[26] W. M. Thackeray, *The Virginians* (London, 1869), II, 352.
[27] Charles Dickens, *Martin Chuzzlewit* (London: Macmillan, 1892), p. 237.
[28] *Ibid.*, p. 506. For a full account of the "Walley," see pp. 328 ff.

13

bounds, but of what could be written and accepted, and it is important that this is a description of a country to which the term *Eden* could once be applied literally.

Dickens' book, and of course his *American Notes,* belongs to the body of travel-literature which is important in shaping the opinion which novels and drama both represent and cater to, and which, beginning with early voyagers' accounts and such a satire of pre-voyage hopes as *Eastward Ho,* becomes over-abundant in recent years.[29] But it was not lacking a century ago, and there, if one accepts Dickens as typical, fiction and fact, or what purported to be fact, were at one. Allan Nevins terms 1825-1845 the period of "Tory condescension," when travelers were "men from the upper and professional classes" who came to learn and left to scorn:

Immoral, irreligious, illiterate, brutal, dirty—this was the character of the Americans, and it was "the natural consequence of that spirit of republicanism on which she prides herself."[30]

Earlier, however, opinions represented less bias, for, from the war to 1825 "the predominant motive of the British traveller . . . was utilitarian inquiry."[31] There were many matters to be investigated—questions about emigration, commerce, manufacturing, politics, the navy, society, all answered, it was insisted, with fidelity to fact, but with divergency of views at times difficult to reconcile.[32] Important, however, is the quest for truth, successful or not. Before the turn of the century Henry Lemoine found the states adequately supplied with "professors in every Art and Science,"[33] although others, among them

29 Of books and essays by tourists there is no end. Of the latter, one of the most frequently reprinted is H. W. Nevinson's "Farewell to America," *The Nation* (London), XXX (1922), 820-821.

30 *American Social History as Recorded by British Travellers* (New York: Holt, 1923), p. 112.

31 *Ibid.,* p. 10.

32 Jane Louise Mesick, *The English Traveller in America 1785-1835* (New York: Columbia University Press, 1922), pp. 1-17, *passim.*

33 *Gentleman's Magazine,* LXVI² (1796), 915.

Harriet Martineau, were more dubious of American letters.[34] Of formal literary criticism there was a good deal after 1815, ranging "from the extremes of panegyric to the most bigoted condemnation," but perhaps motivated most largely by the spirit of the fact-finder:

Not only did most critics aim to be fair, but many of them showed an eagerness to welcome American writings, based in part on mere curiosity as to what things could come out of the wilderness, but in part on higher motives.[35]

Earlier, between the two wars, there was a good deal of interest. Even then, when war-time emotions had not altogether cooled,

The great majority of English readers were disposed to be fair, though they were unable to restrain the expression of their own feeling of superiority, and were likely to adopt a paternal, if not a patronizing manner.[36]

Miss Martineau is quoted as saying that "there is the greatest hope for a people that can cherish high ideals,"[37] and, in thus taking the long view, she perhaps best represents the judicial spirit that, however successfully, struggles through the last century and a half of comments. Though brevity may lead to over-simplification, and although for the evidence presented it can be claimed not that it is conclusive but only that it represents major trends, it seems possible to affirm that there is one essential similarity in all the writings here quoted—the determination to make fact exclude illusion, to make positive data produce the interpretative summary. Whether a present-day Frenchman points out, in botanical metaphor, American decay, or a nineteenth-century schoolmaster weighs democracy; whether a nettled humanitarian caricatures a land-boom, or a magisterial reviewer sneers at republican gaucherie—the basic

[34] Mesick, op. cit., pp. 218 ff.
[35] William B. Cairns, British Criticisms of American Writings 1815-1833 (University of Wisconsin Studies in Language and Literature, No. 14, Madison, 1922), pp. 20, 296.
[36] Cairns, British Criticisms 1783-1815, p. 93.
[37] McLaughlin, op. cit., p. 47.

15

spirit is realistic. There is realism in either the narrow modern sense of willingness to suspect motives and impugn intentions, or in the wider meaning of seeing "things as they are." It is as if there had been an overdose of things as they are not, as if some prior force—visionaries enchanted by novelty, dreamers devoted to "Nature," radicals fervid about revolution—had foisted a grand pretense on reasonable but too unsuspicious people, and mature but deluded men needed a purge for fancies. Facts they were to have: this is one's central impression as he skims English conceptions of America and Americans from the present drama to the first traveler's jottings by an Isaac Weld or a Thomas Cooper. For detailed examination there remain the ideas of the eighteenth century, when the grand entity of the original unbounded new world was defined first by a wavering line of English outposts and then by congressional districts. In the meantime, what did England think before territorial lines reduced the illimitable? Were sixteenth- and seventeenth-century attitudes to America different from those of the nineteenth? Here is the next part of our preliminary investigation. If there is a demonstrable difference, then the eighteenth century marks the more clearly the transition we have presupposed for it, and we are definitely at a crisis in the history of an idea.

### iii

O brave new world
That has such people in't!

wonders Miranda[38] about a land of which the multifold charms and potentialities could be expressed only in the incantatory magic of *El Dorado, Eden,* and, as we have seen, *Utopia.* "Such people" might refer to the inhabitants of New England, which, according to Carew's masque *Coelum Britannicum,* "hath

[38] The modern Miranda, Aldous Huxley, scarcely echoes the tone of the original in his *Brave New World,* most appropriate title for a satire of a modern kind of Utopia. One might mention, also, his title *Beyond the Mexique Bay,* derived from a line in Marvell's poem on the Bermudas.

purged . . . virulent humours from the politic body";[39] to the

> Condemned wretches,
> Forfeited to the law.
> . . . Strumpets and bawds,

whom Massinger's *City Madam* mentions as typical of Virginia;[40] or to the poor tenants, whom, according to the scourging Bishop, Joseph Hall, their landlord evicts and "ships . . .to the new nam'd *Virgin-lond."*[41] But actually here is recognition of the fascination of the Indian, growing ultimately to idealization, although as yet he has not yet progressed far toward becoming the later "Noble Savage." Early poets tend either to shudder or to scorn, a typical attitude being that of Sir George Sandys, who was the only one to know anything of the Indian firsthand, and who thanks God because

> Thou sav'dst me from the bloody massacres
> Of faithless Indians; from their treach'rous wars.[42]

Shakespeare's Caliban is soundly interpreted as a commonsense answer to the deluded imaginings of Montaigne.[43] The Indian, however, had a considerable imaginative appeal, especially to the contrivers of spectacular masques; Chapman made full use of this new-world novelty in *The Masque of the Inns of Court* (1613), presenting "Virginian priests" in

[39] Thomas Carew, *Poems,* ed. Arthur Vincent (Muses Library, London and New York, n.d.), p. 205. Carew is making a thrust at the Puritans rather than a reference to the new world.

[40] William Massinger, *Plays,* ed. William Gifford (3rd ed., 1840), p. 403. In this connection should be recalled the rascals who were planning the voyage in *Eastward Ho,* Wycherley's dedication of *The Plain Dealer,* and the experience of Gibbet, in Farquhar's *Beaux' Stratagem,* in the plantations.

[41] Konrad Schulze, ed., *Die Satiren Halls* (Palaestra CVI, Berlin, 1910), p. 92. In George Herbert's *English Works,* ed. George Herbert Palmer (Boston and New York: Houghton Mifflin, 1905), II, 25, there is a reproachful reference to parents who do not rear their children adequately, but "ship them over, and the thing is done."

[42] *Poetical Works,* ed. the Rev. Richard Hooper (London, 1872), II, 406.

[43] Sir Sidney Lee, "The American Indian in Elizabethan England," *Elizabethan and Other Essays,* ed. F. S. Boas (Oxford, 1929), p. 301.

minutely described ornateness of costume.[44] And there is one unmistakable case of noble savagery—in *The Coxcomb* (1610), in which Ricardo, bewailing the misdeeds of Valerie and himself to Viola, says,

> How rude are all we men
> That take the name of *Civil* to ourselves!
> If she had set her foot upon an earth
> Where people live that we call barbarous;
> Though they had had no house to bring her to,
> They would have spoil'd the glory, that the spring
> Has deckt the trees in, and with willing hands
> Have torn their branches down, and every man
> Would have become a builder for her sake.[45]

So the savage is on his way to becoming a gentleman of nature. In the meantime his soul is to be improved, and the endowing of that soul with Christianity was a powerful motive in the minds of many who looked westward. John Rastell started the evangelical chorus as early as 1517 in his educational morality, *The Four Elements;*[46] Chapman ended *The Masque of the Inns of Court* by Christianizing his Indian priests, willy-nilly;[47] the plot of Massinger's *City Madam* hinges upon the introduction into an English family of several Indians (in this case, pseudo-Indians) who are to be converted.[48]

When Christianity and America, however, were united in men's minds, what is more important—in tracing the concept of America—than missionary zeal is the fact that America came to be regarded as the proper and inevitable inheritor of the

[44] *The Comedies and Tragedies of George Chapman* (London, 1873), III, 92 ff. The Priests are also referred to as Princes. In view of this masque, not to mention others, it is difficult to understand Professor H. N. Fairchild's assertion, in *The Noble Savage* (New York: Columbia University Press, 1928), p. 41, that the North-American Indian first appeared in John Dennis's *Liberty Asserted*, 1704.

[45] Francis Beaumont and John Fletcher, *Works,* edd. Arnold Glover and A. R. Waller (Cambridge: University Press, 1908 ff.), VIII, 366.

[46] J. S. Farmer, ed., *Six Anonymous Plays, First Series* (London, 1905), p. 26.

[47] *Comedies and Tragedies*, III, 115-116.

[48] *Plays*, pp. 392-394.

Christian church and tradition. While Phineas Fletcher and Andrew Marvell hail the westward march of the Protestant church,[49] Sir William Alexander interprets the phenomenon as due to the more favorable environment of the new world:

> In this last age Time doth new worlds display;
> That Christ a Church over all the earth may have,
> His righteousnesse shall barbarous Realmes array,
> If their first love more civill Lands will leave,
>   *America* to *Europe* may succeed,
>   God may of stones raise up to *Abram* seed.[50]

But the most emphatic and fiery prophet of the theme is George Herbert, whose *Church Militant* elaborates the idea of the progression of religion from a decadent to a healthy land; everyone is familiar with

> Religion stands on tiptoe in our land
> Readie to pass to the *American* strand.

From this point Herbert goes on to a bitter summation of the vices of the land that Christianity will desert, and concludes,

> Then shall Religion to *America* flee;
> They have their times of Gospel ev'n as we.[51]

This chorus of praise for the spiritual excellence of America indicates the general trend of English thought about the new world, particularly the concept growing up in English literature; most noteworthy is the tendency to idealize, to find advantages alien to Europe. The urge to illusion—to what we now perceive as illusion—was predominant in the make-up of those fascinated by visions of the West.

[49] Giles and Phineas Fletcher, *Poetical Works,* ed. F. S. Boas (Cambridge: University Press, 1908), I, 136; Andrew Marvell, *Poems and Letters,* ed. H. M. Margoliouth (Oxford, 1927), I, 17.

[50] *Poetical Works,* edd. L. E. Kastner and H. B. Charlton (Manchester: University Press, 1921-1929), II, 50. William Davenant carries the idea further in *Gondibert* by picturing the arts also as fleeing westward; see his *Works* (1673), p. 119.

[51] *English Works,* III, 377.

Illusions, however, need not be spun from abstractions; gold and all things material, as well as religious hopes, make dreams. Rastell, far ahead of his time in viewing American matters, was first to appreciate the value of American products:

> Great abundance of woods there be,
> Most part fir and pine-apple tree,
> Great riches might come thereby. . . .
> Now Frenchmen and other have found the trade,
> That yearly of fish there they lade
> Above a hundred sail.[52]

Three quarters of a century passed before Rastell's amplitude of suggestion finally flourished in a wide and avid interest that produced complete literary catalogues of American fecundity.[53] Typical is Drayton's *To the Virginian Voyage,* with almost an index of resources, including fowl, venison, fish, the vine, cedar, cypress, pine, and sassafras.[54] America combined utility and pleasure. Of all the sensuous stimulants for which it was responsible, none was so exciting as tobacco, which, viewed as stinking weed or heavenly nectar, kept the nation in a furore until the apologists finally won. There was no more spirited encomiast than Sir John Beaumont, whose ecstasy could describe the Graces as seduced to residence in Virginia, and could finally apostrophize:

> Thrice happie Isles, which steale the world's delight,
> And doe produce so rich a Margarite![55]

America was not merely the home of rarities titillating to smell and taste, but the storehouse of gold, endless gold, and a genuine gold-fever that swept the times made more than a flicker in literature. Wealth, opulence, value of any kind—these were verbally allied with the Occident as with the Orient until

---

[52] Farmer, *op. cit.,* pp. 26-27.
[53] See Robert R. Cawley, *The Influence of the Voyagers in Non-Dramatic English Literature between 1550 and 1650, with Occasional References to the Drama* (Dissertation, Harvard University, 1921), pp. 386 ff.
[54] *Works,* ed. J. W. Hebel (Oxford, 1931-1933), II, 363.
[55] *Poems,* ed. the Rev. A. B. Grosart (n.p., 1869), p. 305.

Cleveland could berate rhymesters for excessive use of "both
the Indias," a "bastard phrase . . . common as your mistresses."[56] Few poets could avoid letting some lines depend on
the glint of the yellow metal. Chapman thought of Indians as
filling English coffers with gold,[57] and some reference to
American gold appears, either directly or in comparison, in the
works of Spenser, Barnfield, Drayton, Peele, Lyly, Greene, and
Marlowe.[58] Shakespeare made obeisance to the convention; *As
You Like It* has the well-known lines in the note to Rosalind:

> From the east to Western Ind,
> No Jewel is like Rosalind.

And Congreve followed suit in *Love for Love* (1695), in which
Sir Sampson Legend says to Angelica:

> If I had Peru in one hand, and Mexico in t'other, and the Eastern
> Empire under my feet; it would make me only a more glorious victim
> to be offer'd at the shrine of your beauty.[59]

The non-dramatic poets of the seventeenth century were similarly fertile in the reproduction of these old verbal tags, for,
among others,[60] Donne, Cleveland, Davenant, and Cowley
pulled forth, as if from a convenient *Gradus ad Parnassum,* the
illuminating power of western wealth. Even Milton fell into
line, suggesting that, in reference to Adam's view of the world
provided by Gabriel in *Paradise Lost,* XI,

> . . . in spirit perhaps he also saw
> Rich Mexico, the seat of Montezume,
> And Cusco, in Peru, the richer seat

[56] George Saintsbury, ed., *Minor Poets of the Caroline Period* (Oxford, 1905
ff.), III, 21.

[57] *Works* (London, 1875), II, 52.

[58] To introduce all the evidence would take disproportionate space in what
is only a preliminary sketch, and figures must suffice. In some three hundred
plays and masques, almost all of them between 1600 and 1660, I have found
fifty-nine such references, whether brief passages, extended speeches, or adapta-
tions of the theme as part of the plot.

[59] William Congreve, *Comedies* (New York: Macmillan, 1927), p. 272.

[60] In the works of fifty poets I have found sixty references of the sort here
described.

21

Of Atabalipa, and yet unspoiled
Guiana, whose great city Geryon's sons
Call El Dorado.

Such unanimity of literary opinion outlines pretty clearly the early concept of America.

From get-rich-quick visions it is only a step to the imperialistic temper, and the "bigger England" began to stimulate poets. Again Rastell started the game with a sigh for the lost English opportunity to establish "a memory perpetual."[61] It was some time before Fulke Greville could speak soberly of

Planting new colonies in savage parts,
There to spread wisdom, pow'r, laws, worth and arts;[62]

before Samuel Daniel could make his familiar cultural prophecy in *Musophilus:*

And who, in time, knowes whither we may vent
The treasure of our tongue, to what strange shores
This gaine of our best glory shall be sent,
T'inrich vnknowing Nations with our stores?
What worlds in th'yet vnformed Occident
May come refined with th'accents that are ours?[63]

and before Chapman could urge Elizabeth, in *De Guiana:*

So let thy sovereign Empire be increased,
And with Iberian Neptune part the stake,
Whose trident he the triple world would make.[64]

Most enthusiastic of all was Drayton, who adjured the first Virginia expedition to *"Heroes* bring . . . foorth" and to "plant Our name" under new stars.[65]

[61] Farmer, *op. cit.,* p. 25.

[62] *Works in Verse and Prose,* ed. the Rev. A. B. Grosart (Privately Printed, 1870), I, 178.

[63] *Complete Works,* ed. the Rev. A. B. Grosart (London and Aylesbury: Spenser Society, 1885), I, 255.

[64] *Works,* II, 51.

[65] *Works,* II, 364. "Plant a nation" was a popular phrase; for further examples see Alexander Brown, ed., *The Genesis of the United States* (Boston and New York, 1890), I, 424; Hyder E. Rollins, ed., *The Pepys Ballads* (Cambridge: Harvard University Press, 1929-1932), I, 24 ff.

With lust of empire stronger than its literary evidence shows, with imagination warmed by a country of unlimited gold and invaluable products, it is impossible that some souls weary of the old world should not have transformed the hope of material gain into a vision of ideal surroundings, less physically than emotionally or spiritually, less as a homestead than as an ivory tower. Furthermore, perdition and paradise have an amusing way of being only different aspects of the same place. It was in the same country to which England nonchalantly dispatched convicts that Chapman could hope for, literally,

A golden world in this our iron age,

and proceed to sketch an existence of unequalled satisfaction for body, mind, and soul. In this Renaissance paradise Learning was rewarded, Valour honored, Beauty virtuous; Youth enjoyed honorable and happy matrimony founded on wealth, and practiced "healthful recreations"; palaces and temples rose to the skies.[66] Drayton relished the same theme:

> To whose, the golden Age
> Still Natures lawes doth give,
> No other Cares that tend,
> But Them to defend
> From Winters age
> That long there doth not live.

He rejoiced that, since plenty of laurel grew there, no doubt poets would flourish.[67] In the seventeenth century the wistful gaze at the neighbor's garden continued, especially among the non-dramatic poets, no doubt less restrained by the demands of verisimilitude than the brethren of the stage. Though by no means a dreamer, Marvell in *Bermudas* released an envy of softer scenes, of islands which, kinder than his own, were a land of refuge, where an "eternal Spring . . . enamells every thing."[68] Waller, of a totally different stamp, also idealized the isle of hogs, though with stress on physical ease:

[66] *Works*, II, 50-52.
[67] *Works*, II, 364.
[68] *Poems and Letters*, I, 17.

Oh! how I long my careless limbs to lay
Under the plantain's shade, and all the day
With amorous airs my fancy entertain,
Invoke the Muses, and improve my vein![69]

Love is to be the only passion, music the only activity. Irresponsibility, freedom, languorousness, and the absence of unpleasant material obstacles to the love-life—here is a perfect précis of the softer transformations of America made by romantic fancy. Going on to Abraham Cowley, we find that his yearning for little things did not exclude a big voyage when his dreams conquered his more suburban desires. He has always yearned, he says in the preface to the 1668 edition of his works,

. . . to retire myself to some of our *American Plantations*, not to seek for *Gold*. . . . But to forsake this world for ever, with all the *vanities* and Vexations of it, and to bury my self there in some obscure retreat (but not without the consolation of *Letters* and *Philosophy*).[70]

The transatlantic ivory tower also lures Davenant, who longs to get away from it all and who, in the preface to *Gondibert*, tells "Mr. Hobs" that the envy of his contemporaries is driving him to America.[71]

The potentialities of the little-known lead to its glorification; myth-making is at least partly a function of distance. The vastness of the Atlantic thrilled the Elizabethan and gave him a handy symbol for use on any occasion that needed an expression of distance or great space. Hence America could evoke an exuberant and resounding rhetoric, as when Tamburlaine promised to extend his kingdom "Even from Persepolis to Mexico";[72] or when the closing passage of *Henry VIII*, glorifying James I, prophesied,

[69] Edmund Waller, *Poems*, ed. G. Thorn-Drury (Muses Library, London, [1904]), I, 68.
[70] *Poems*, ed. A. R. Waller (Cambridge, 1905), p. 8.
[71] *Works*, p. 20.
[72] Christopher Marlowe, *Tamburlaine the Great*, ed. U. M. Ellis-Fermor (London: Methuen, 1930), p. 135.

Wherever the bright sun of heaven shall shine,
His honor and the greatness of his name
Shall be, and make new nations;[73]

or when even Milton once glanced "south as far Beneath Magellan."[74] This exhilarating vastness of the new-formed world was due to the explorers, who received continual literary salutes; briefly in such works as Drayton's *To the Virginian Voyage*, Peele's *Farewell* to Morris and Drake, Whitney's "emblem" on Drake, Cowley's *Sitting and Drinking in the chair, made out of the Reliques of Sir Francis Drake's Ship* and *Upon the Chair made out of Sir Francis Drake's ship;* with true epic spirit in Fitzgeffry's *Sir Francis Drake*, Drayton's *Poly-Olbion*, Warner's *Albion's England*, and Heywood's *Troia Britannica*. Exploration could be used indirectly, too, in amorous verse such as Donne's *Elegie XIX* and religious poetry such as his *Hymn to God*. The men of the sea provided great stimulus to letters, especially as an outlet for patriotism, and thus part of the concept of the new world is that it contributes to the glory of the old.

So much for a brief survey of an actually much larger aspect of literary history.[75] Sixteenth and seventeenth century English literature shows only faint traces of the later idealization of the Indian, but a strong desire to save his soul. The land on which he lived, and the society which it promised, would provide a new home for a more flourishing and deeper Christianity. But this new dwelling of the spirit also contained hundreds of products of both sensuous and commercial value, and endless gold of which the glitter filled Europe with mirages of material

[73] William Shakespeare, *Complete Works*, ed. W. A. Neilson (Student's Cambridge ed., Boston: Houghton Mifflin, 1906), p. 804.

[74] *Paradise Lost*, X, 686-687.

[75] The most complete compendia of references to America in English literature will be found in Professor R. R. Cawley's Harvard dissertation, previously referred to, and in his forthcoming book, *The Voyagers and English Drama, 1558-1642, With Some Reference to the Non-Dramatic Literature*. My own study has been entirely independent of these.

well-being. There was the challenge of empire. And in it were the potentialities of a new golden age marking a return to virtues long stripped from man by vicious society. To reach the scene, intrepid sailors covered vast distances and added a vibration to the thrills evoked by the new land.

In all this there is no fact-finding urge, but freshness and bloom, leading to excitement, exuberance, and endless hope. America was an offering of the Renaissance; a new surge of this-worldly interest disclosed new potentialities for life, and, inevitably, new hope for its excellence. A newly curious eye caught America, and its strangeness and fertility gave new impetus to the hopes of a people intensely conscious of the here-and-now. The splendid unknown had endless significance for human happiness and excellence. It brought forth new bravery in adventure. It produced rarities of magical sense appeal, rich savors that added to the variety and piquancy of life. Its wealth led to hope for a new economic millennium. It was untouched and unspoiled. There was no limit to the hopes for the life to be lived there.

iv

Clearly this was not the same country whose swamps, advertised as oases, could stir the wrath of a novelist; whose culture could distress a penetrating classicist; whose fervor for "Business First" could give a pungent scene to a dramatic satirist. From youthful hope and enthusiasm we have come to latter-day fact-finding and skepticism, to an often pejorative scrutiny. Original tales of magic have been rationalized, imagination has been curbed by experience, and legend discounted by fact. Such realities as imperialistic struggles and economic disputes, with their concomitants of death and debt, have helped dull the bloom of the new land so boundless in its original promise for the enrichment of the material and spiritual life. The age in which light dispersed through the prism of hope illumined a land in many colors has given way to the age in which an X-ray,

26

providing no brilliant panorama, outlines inner facts for diagnosis. The X-ray operators may be fumble-fingered, but their aim is to penetrate obscuring appearances.

The transition from the ancient to the modern is what concerns us here, the pivotal point. Roughly it is the eighteenth century, specifically the last several decades of it. These were the excited rapidly-changing years when the international situation revolved about the constant opposition of Burke and Pitt, the scorn of Fox for the schemes of the gradually declining North, the return of Burgoyne from failure as a general to success as a dramatist, the reports of battles and the parliamentary wrangles which drew many an amused observation from the master of Strawberry Hill, the debates on Indians and Hessians, the petitions of merchants and "radicals" who for once found common cause—opposition to the war, the constant warnings of the Rev. Richard Price on the budget and the colonies' invitation to Price to become their financial adviser, the outbursts of the ubiquitous Paine, the productive ambassadorships of the urbane Franklin, the influx of the American Loyalists and their subsequent indemnification by Parliament, the not quite credible news of Yorktown. From this confusion of forces—military, political, economic, personal—came whatever impress America made on literature. And she was bound up with the aftermath, with subsequent influences on literature until Wordsworth, hierophant of another sect of the new religion, was recollecting daffodils in solitude.

In treating the new faith, it is more convenient to adopt the conventional term *Romanticism* than to argue about its applicability. The political books of the most recent bible dealt with a reforming idealism which America followed at home and furthered abroad. In England the idealists were the "radicals," among whom the colonists found their chief champions.[76] Radicalism and belles-lettres most nearly achieved union in

[76] Dora Mae Clark, *British Opinion and the American Revolution* (New Haven: Yale University Press, 1930), pp. 152-180.

27

Blake, especially in his *French Revolution* (1791), *A Song of Liberty* (1792), and *America* (1793). The latter two are "interpretations of the American revolutionary movement" and the consequent European unrest, in which Blake "perceived the signs of an impending moral emancipation."[77] *America* develops the primal conflict between Restraint and Passion.

. . . in Blake's view political emancipation was but one, and not the greatest result of the American Revolution. Not the tyranny of the monarchical government alone, but that of all creeds and conventions was to end when men should rise and will their own freedom.[78]

Thus did America enter the literature of Romanticism, seen through the same vision which several years later created the Pantisocracy dream.

An allied subject is the new importance of the "common man," in which America obviously figures, since, after all, democracy and *Michael* are spiritually of the same paternity. All Europe viewed the practicing democracy of the United States, its liberty and equality, with concern.[79] There is not only Tory suspicion; German feelings exemplify the other attitude:

The poets of Storm and Stress, such as Klinger and Lenz, were influenced by the revolt of the colonies. Schiller, Herder, Wieland, Voss, Leopold von Stolberg, Schubart, Klopstock, Gleim and others exalted in the glory of Franklin and Washington, denounced the disgraceful soldier-traffic of German princes, and strongly supported the liberal aspirations of the Americans. It was, to be sure, not the political events as such that awakened this overwhelming sympathy for Americans in the hearts of these poets, but the humanitarian ideals which they saw realized in the victorious struggle of the colonies.[80]

All this is identical with the devotion to humankind which led on one hand to naïve and sentimental poetry and on the other to industrial reform.

[77] D. J. Sloss and J. P. R. Wallis, edd., *The Prophetic Writings of William Blake* (Oxford, 1926), II, 82.

[78] *Ibid.*, I, 44-45.

[79] William A. Dunning, *The British Empire and the United States* (New York: Scribner, 1914), p. 5.

[80] Weber, *op. cit.*, p. 3.

Humanitarianism, also, was the alma mater of emancipation, and the negro, if not often made the mouthpiece of wisdom like his newly-discovered white brother in simplicity, at least had as much sentiment lavished on him as any other species of the common man. It was late in the century that abolition of the slave trade, sought by Wilberforce, approached actuality. Then the state of slavery existing in the West Indies and America became a matter of growing interest to the English, as travelers' accounts show.[81] And English fiction, gorging itself on "problems," gobbled up slavery with the rest.[82]

It appears then that the coastal strip west of the Atlantic, not merely a lost child to one European country but also a sort of young hopeful to two other nations, was entwined in the interwoven affairs and ideas of the three of them, inseparably jostling along in the new literary and intellectual surge, the Romantic Movement. Its inclusive sweep gathers in such diverse elements as political idealism, interest in the "common man," humanitarianism, and its concomitant of abolitionism. There are many American ingredients in the formula; to the very existence of some of the elements America must have made measurable contribution. Whether before or after the Revolution one can declare a judicial "more" or "less" is a matter for further examination. And whether prose fiction mounted the bandwagon of progress remains to be seen.[83]

The function of literature in clarifying an estimate of a period or in influencing non-literary relationships need not be argued. James Bryce remarks on the disadvantage of two nations' possessing the same language, since each can understand the other's abuse and consequently tends to make too much of it.[84] Whelpley comments on the weight carried by such transitory and pseudo-literary efforts as "cartoons, paragraphs, jibes"

[81] Mesick, *op. cit.*, pp. 122-142.

[82] Tompkins, *op. cit.*, pp. 71, 184.

[83] Cf. Miss Tompkins' chapter, "New Life in the Novel," pp. 172 ff.

[84] In his introduction to Dunning, *The British Empire and the United States*, pp. xxv-xxvi.

29

and on present-day English and American misconceptions, especially the misunderstanding of America by Englishmen.[85] One wonders how much greater this must have been in the years when the English conception of America depended to a great extent on writers, political or not, who had never been west of Land's End. Right or wrong, however, the conception illuminates the times. The British historian, Sir George Trevelyan, in his six-volume history of the American Revolution, makes various allusions to the literary representation of different aspects of the struggle.[86] Hence it is easy to expect a considerable body of war-literature, and in America, indeed, there was some fulfillment of the prophecies of Daniel and Drayton, echoed, unconsciously, by an anonymous contemporary reviewer who began by remarking that as yet poetry was not

highly cultivated in that soil [America]. But great events will produce great poets. Homer, perhaps, had never immortalized himself in song, had the siege of Troy never taken place.[87]

One recalls immediately Trumbull, Barlow, Hopkinson, and Freneau; it took Professor Tyler two packed volumes to record the occasional writings between 1763 and 1783; and other compilations exhibit American productivity.[88]

The question then arises whether the "stirring times" equally stimulated English letters. Although there are to be found

[85] British-American Relations, pp. 9-14.
[86] Sir George Otto Trevelyan, Bart., The American Revolution (London and New York, Part I, 1899; Part II, 1903; Part III, 1907); George the Third and Charles Fox: The Concluding Part of the American Revolution (New York: Longmans Green, 1912-1914). See, for instance, Part I, 105, 234; Part II, I, 175, 253-255, 293.
[87] Monthly Review, LXII (1780), 389. The comment is made in a review of A Poetical Epistle to his Excellency George Washington, Esq .... from an Inhabitant of the State of Maryland.
[88] Moses Coit Tyler, The Literary History of the American Revolution (New York and London: Putnam, 1897); Frank Moore, ed., Songs and Ballads of the American Revolution (New York, 1856); Winthrop Sargent, ed., The Loyal Verses of Joseph Stansbury and Doctor Jonathan Odell Relating to the American Revolution (Munsell's Historical Series, No. 6, Albany, 1860); William Leete Stone, ed., Ballads and Poems Relating to the Burgoyne Campaign (Munsell's Historical Series, No. 20, Albany, 1893).

30

conflicting statements about the English concern over the war,[89] and although we unconsciously impute to the English a sense of crisis equal to our own, the blunt fact is that the war did not make much of a stir in the upper literary levels. The *Cambridge History*, although its Volume XI is entitled "The Period of the French Revolution," does not devote even a chapter to the American Revolution, and of its 125 indexed references to America and the United States, less than a dozen, and these in the most fleeting fashion, concern the war.[90] Other histories are still briefer,[91] and only in a study of popular circulating-library literature, largely unknown today, do we find some discovery of direct American influences.[92] One can think of few men of letters whose writings reflect the current political drama. Such men as Burke and Wesley do not belong primarily to belles-lettres; Johnson's blasts on taxation are perhaps his least known and least felicitous efforts, as are the pamphlets of the Macpherson who created Ossianic reveries; of Shebbeare, a minor novelist; and of Henry Mackenzie, creator of the lachrymose Harley, who did anything but shed tears over the colonies.[93]

Among other literary figures of the time, one thinks perhaps first of Sheridan, whose major works all appeared during the '70's, but whose only suggestion of the war occurs in Puff's

[89] See McLaughlin, *America and Britain*, pp. 44 and 55. Miss Clark concludes that by 1776 controversial writings had practically ceased and that by 1778 attention was directed largely to the European war (*British Opinion and the American Revolution*, p. 280).

[90] The writers concerned are Horace Walpole (X, 284); Burke (XI, 6 ff); Fox (XI, 58); Bentham (XI, 78-79); Smollett (i.e., his "prophecy," X, 48); Blake (XI, 209-210); Paine (XI, 52-53). These and all other citations are from the American edition.

[91] Elton's and Saintsbury's general histories offer negligible material, as do Cross's and Baker's histories of the novel.

[92] Tompkins, *The Popular Novel*, pp. 13-14, 69, 184-185.

[93] For a discussion of Mackenzie's political writings, see H. W. Thompson, *A Scottish Man of Feeling* (London and New York: Oxford University Press, 1931), pp. 258 ff. For notes on the pamphleteers, see Trevelyan, *American Revolution*, Part II, II, 259-279; Clark, *op. cit.*, p. 213.

memorandum, in *The Critic,* "To take Paul Jones."[94] Then there are General Burgoyne's three comedies, pretty china so far removed from the strenuous scenes of northern New York that the last two, at least, might have been written "to forget."[95] As for the novel in this period—the interim between the great four and Edgeworth, Austen, and Scott—the leading practitioner was Miss Burney, whose chief works, *Evelina* and *Cecilia,* appeared during the war-years. They have no concern at all with foreign affairs, an indifference apparently reflecting the author's own attitude.[96] If we look at the *Spectator* tradition for a moment, we find that Boswell's *Hypochondriack,* which appeared from 1777 to 1783, ignored the war. No. 3, *On War,* December 1777, draws no example from contemporary events.[97] That Henry Mackenzie's *Mirror* likewise abstains from the topical is perhaps explained by an editorial note in No. 38, June 5, 1779:

This paper (as the London *Gazetteer* says) it [*sic*] *open to all parties;* with this proviso, however, which is exactly the reverse of the terms of admission into the *Gazetteer,* that my correspondents do *not* write politics.[98]

Essayists, and, for that matter, many editors, fed alternately a longing for didactic generalization, decidedly divorced from immediate actuality, and a weakness for odds and ends of conjecture, often amusing in their impotent isolation. As for the poets, Goldsmith, Gray, and Chatterton were dead before swords were drawn in earnest; Johnson was writing the *Lives,*

94 R. B. Sheridan, *Plays and Poems,* ed. R. Crompton Rhodes (Oxford, 1928), II, 214.
95 The drama needs further investigation, a problem which I hope to undertake in the future.
96 An apparently thorough index to her *Diary and Letters,* ed. Charlotte Barrett; Preface and Notes by Austin Dobson (London and New York: Macmillan, 1904-1905), records no direct reference to transatlantic scenes or events.
97 James Boswell, *The Hypochondriack,* ed. Margery Bailey (Stanford University Press, 1928), I, 118-126.
98 *The Mirror: A Periodical Paper Published at Edinburgh in the Years 1779 and 1780* (2nd American ed., Philadelphia, 1793), I, 177-178.

and Cowper hymns. Cowper, "not deeply interested in politics," at first thought the Americans "simply rebels against the cause of God"[99] but later modified the prejudice.[100] But there is no literary evidence of either state of mind. Blake, already mentioned, became later the only poet really to make much of the situation, but he is recollected in terms rather of "Tiger, Tiger" than of his political prophecies. Burns's revolutionary sympathies got him into temporary embarrassment in the best Scotch literary circles, where Mackenzie was aping an Addisonian rule, but his bibulous and amorous expressions practically blot out knowledge of The Dream, the fourth and fifth stanzas of which express his feelings about America. And in the same years Edward Gibbon and Adam Smith were opening new fields of scholarship; Malone was working on Shakespeare, Tyrwhitt on Chaucer; Hume was doing philosophy, Priestley theology; Bentham discussed government, Lord Kames education, William Kenrick divorce; Potter was translating Aeschylus and Euripides. Economics, history, criticism, science, theology, translation, and travel—all had enough devotees to make regular and even frequent publication possible.

The great, then, appear to have turned elsewhere for subjects and themes, and so we too must turn elsewhere to find the literary fate of America, the American war, and the American connection with the whole body of general and special developments which as we have already seen are characteristic of the period. How broad the entire field is, even with the exceptions already made, is apparent from the number of studies which have already plowed individual fields contiguous to our own and which need to be carried further to bring out all the data for a complete history of the period and its culture. If we are studying the interpretation or the concept of America, we have in France the works of Gilbert Chinard tracing French thought

[99] David Cecil, The Stricken Deer (London: Constable, 1929), p. 173.
[100] Trevelyan, George the Third and Charles Fox, II, 249, 389.

33

about America, important in the study of Romanticism.[101] The German attitude is traced by Weber's *America in Imaginative German Literature* and Wadepuhl's *Goethe and America*, the English by Nevins' and Miss Mesick's studies of travelers' accounts and Cawley's studies of the voyagers' influence. Here also must be classed Fairchild's and Bissell's investigations of the eighteenth-century romantic primitivism,[102] which achieved its best-known expression in Pantisocracy.[103] English interest in America is further demonstrated by Cairns' studies of literary criticism, by Tuckerman's early account of commentators on America,[104] by a collection of English poetry of which America is the theme,[105] by a study of Horace Walpole's opinion on American matters.[106] As for the interest evoked by the war-period, that is discussed by Miss Clark's *British Opinion and the American Revolution*, Hinkhouse's *The Preliminaries of the American Revolution As Seen in the English Press 1763-1775*, and Fraser's *English Opinion of the American Constitution and Government 1783-1798*.[107] The Revolution in literature has been treated most fully in the German field, having attracted the attention of various scholars and been summed up in King's

[101] Most significant for this period is *L'Amérique et le rêve exotique dans la littérature française au XVIIᵉ et au XVIIIᵉ siècle* (Paris: Hachette, 1913).

[102] H. N. Fairchild, *The Noble Savage;* Benjamin Bissell, *The American Indian in English Literature of the Eighteenth Century* (Yale Studies in English, No. LXVIII, New Haven, 1925).

[103] See J. L. Lowes, *The Road to Xanadu* (Boston and New York: Houghton Mifflin, 1927), pp. 554-555; Sister Eugenia, "Coleridge's Scheme of Pantisocracy and American Travel Accounts," *P. M. L. A.*, XLV² (1930), 1069 ff.; Maurice Kelley, "Thomas Cooper and Pantisocracy," *M. L. N.*, XLV (1930), 218, and "A Pennsylvania Land Sale Project," *Western Pennsylvania Historical Magazine*, XIII (1930), 202, for notes on influences and bibliography.

[104] H. T. Tuckerman, *America and Her Commentators* (New York, 1864).

[105] Sir Charles Firth, ed., *An American Garland* (Oxford, 1915).

[106] Ruth W. Tucker, *Horace Walpole and British Imperialism* (Master's Thesis, University of Maine, 1928), pp. 110-177.

[107] Fred J. Hinkhouse, *The Preliminaries of the American Revolution As Seen in the English Press 1763-1775* (New York: Columbia University Press, 1926); Leon Fraser, *English Opinion of the American Constitution and Government 1783-1798* (New York, 1915).

*Echoes of the American Revolution in German Literature.*[108]
Finally, if it is a question of the general field of politics and
fiction, we have Allene Gregory's *The French Revolution and
the English Novel,* which illustrates the unity of the period by
its dealing at different times with America in the novel.[109]

Obviously, what remains to be done is to search some untouched corners, to dust them out for a moment and cull what
stray ends of history and politics may have fallen there. In
themselves, the stray ends are insignificant, but they are valid
evidences of the whole economy. The notes on America in
long-dead novels, in their day flutteringly borrowed from the
nearest library, may illuminate that once-dearest of subjects,
"the state of the nation."

V

This introductory chapter has thus far epitomized British
thought about America, from the sixteenth to the twentieth
centuries, as the background against which the late eighteenth
century is to be placed; it has outlined the political, social, and
literary trends with which America was in some way connected;
it has named writers who did not show, and historians who
have investigated, the literary influence of the American Revolution. It now remains to indicate the types of influences to be
studied and the method to be followed.

The evidence which the novels present tends to answer two
broad questions: To what extent does a given phenomenon
occur? Of what kind are the thoughts either inspired or affected
by the events under consideration?

The first question has three subdivisions. In the first place,
what was the effect of the war upon the production of novels?
The search for an answer demands study of the annual variation
in the output of novels and of the other channels into which

[108] Henry Safford King, *Echoes of the American Revolution in German
Literature* (University of California Publications in Modern Philology, Vol. 14,
No. 2, Berkeley, 1929). For a list of works in the field, see pp. v-vi.
[109] (London and New York: Putnam, 1915), pp. 135-144, 213-222.

35

the interest of the average novel-reading public might be diverted during a political upheaval. In the second place, in how many novels did America provide the background or important plot-elements, and how did this number vary during and after the war? Here comes up the relationship between empire and literature, for one cannot spend much time in circulating-library thrillers without realizing that when authors needed or wanted foreign scenes, they laid hold of America, the West Indies, or the East Indies (a loose term generally meaning India) in many ways very similar. In the third place, in how many novels did the American Revolution itself provide the background or plot-elements, and how did this number vary during and after the actual hostilities?

Around this center cluster several related points. Since the eighteenth-century novel felt no compulsion to stick to narrative but could be unabashed in exposition, the Revolution appears not only in story but also in homilies. Outright discussions, pro and con, occur regularly to the end of the century, a fact which introduces the problem of whether time cooled enthusiasm and the decades nourished a sense of proportion. Criticism, also, means occasional efforts at interpretation. The modernity of the verdict of history that the Revolution was in essence a civil war becomes a trifle dimmed when one realizes that the same conclusion was being written at English novel-readers— and not the most intelligent of the reading public—before Yorktown. Then, it was perhaps the peculiar intimacy of a civil war which led to understanding of and admiration for the temper of war-time Americans, though, to detractors, American spirit often appeared as craven, self-seeking, or merely stubborn. When there was sympathy for the "oppressed," it produced some violently anti-militaristic rhetoric. Pacifism can hardly be thought to have originated before 1776, but here we find some of the earliest outbursts against the cruelty of war. More immediate are such related subjects as taxes; indeed, a running commentary on the events from the first quarrel to the final

36

separation appears in various extended allegories or obiter dicta on transatlantic affairs. Colonies and colonization, taxes and other economic matters such as trade, investment, and loss of property—all had their expositors in a fiction of unparalleled inclusiveness.

The second major problem is conceptual: What did the English think about America, and how did their ideas vary during and after the war? Here, of course, one must guard against the *post hoc* danger, since it is easy to attribute an attitude of 1785 to events of 1781. But one can at least establish probabilities, which will gain credence if they coincide with tendencies manifested in the preceding and following centuries. Hence it is important to relate the materials of this section to the ideological backgrounds previously sketched.

The concept of America is partly built up from the varying beliefs about the excellence of primitive life. Back-to-nature cultists effervesced; we find the last bubbles of a draught that had been intoxicating for two centuries. Substantial volumes of prose, however, stuck to reason—if often a quite specious reason—long after Burns and Blake had shaken the thrones of the coupleteers. Against illusion there are powerful attacks, in which logic, humor, and realism replace sentimentality. So, as idealization of a rustic habitat, innocent and uncorrupted, passes, we see the final flickers of fond dreams about an American Golden Age. As the dream faded, however, hope did not die but established itself on more realistic ground. The visionary became a man of the world, and the ivory tower was transformed into a counting-house. The Golden Age was decked out with new wings and backdrop and became the Land of Promise—a country where farmers, artisans, tradesmen, and professional men would find security, advancement, and even wealth. "Go west, young man" was good pre-Greeleyan dogma. In their grosser versions, plots appealing to the acquisitive instinct turned America into a mere locale for the operation of get-rich-quick schemes. Especially for the army did the innocent

37

expect America to produce a rapid rise in the world; booty and bounty would finance a few comfortable years.

Exaggerated praise of America, on whatever grounds, meant that it possessed virtues with which the vices of the old world could be most unfavorably compared. Hence it could become a medium for criticism and satire of Europe, with a method like that of the semi-fictional genre known as Letters of a Foreign Visitor. But the three-thousand-mile distance which was a necessary factor in the device also produced, on the other hand, an unpleasant sensation that going to America was going to the end of the world, to an uncomfortable, uncouth, savage wilderness where there was an absence of everything that made life tolerable; epistolary groans, long-drawn, anticipated many a projected voyage. Too, if one did not like to go to America himself, he considered America a very suitable place for people whom he did not like. He calmly shipped undesirables of all kinds across the Atlantic. The government transported convicts, or prospective convicts beat the government to it; others, in any kind of personal difficulty, fled across the sea. And all the types appeared in fiction.

All contributed somewhat to shaping the character of "the American," of whom there was considerable discussion. A few individuals, such as Franklin and Washington, appeared in novels, but the interest was largely in establishing the type; even manners, dress, and speech came in for attention. Here the novel was purveying information, as it did in many fields— geography, commerce, science.[110] After the war, subjects of a different sort appeared for investigation—American institutions. Slavery evoked many outcries. Democracy secured little mature deliberation but equally vociferous attacks and defenses. Religion excited at least curiosity—about missionary work, the episcopacy, an establishment, toleration.

From comments on such diverse subjects—the Golden Age in

[110] For the importance of the new world to science, see the footnotes to Erasmus Darwin's versified treatises, which are full of references to America.

PRELIMINARIES

America, the commercial and scientific aspects of America, American character, and American institutions—must be put together, if possible, a unified concept of America. To complete a study of the influence of the war, variations during and after the war must be checked. The process involves the old mechanics of counting instances and noting frequencies. And that brings us to a final word on method.

The period treated, 1760-1800, including approximately the same number of years before and after the war, permits an ample glance at the antecedent and subsequent situations and hence a more satisfactory measurement of the impact of the war on the fiction of the period. To continue a detailed study beyond 1800 would result in an unmanageably ponderous compilation, while a superficial study is made unnecessary by the lists in Baker's *Guide to Historical Fiction*. Generally, in checking developments, we can divide the forty years into the pre-war period, the war period, and the post-war period, although occasionally, for the sake of detailed accuracy, it is desirable to proceed by half-decades.

Now and then it is possible to make illustrative references to periodical literature, essays, drama, and poetry.[111] Fiction, however, is the main object of attack, and conclusions are based on an examination of approximately four hundred and fifty novels, which seem to be a representative cross section of the total output.[112] These have been so selected throughout the period as to provide a practically constant percentage of the total

[111] Such comparisons, though brief, may be quite illuminating. Mackenzie's treatment of slavery in the novel, for instance, is quite different from his treatment of the subject in his essays.

[112] The forty years produced about two thousand novels, according to my own count of the titles in Professor Greenough's Catalogue, the most complete record of the period. The great majority of these have not survived. E. A. Baker's *The History of the English Novel* (London: Witherby, 1924-1936), V, 12 note, refers to Miss H. W. Husbands' Master's Thesis at the University of London, *The Lesser Novel, 1770-1800*, as surveying "more than thirteen hundred novels." Although the reference is not explicit, it appears that the examination depended on "a methodical study of the contemporary reviews."

published in each year. A prior canon of selection, however, has been the existence in a novel of any material at all about America, insofar as this was ascertainable from titles, reviews, advertisements, or secondary sources.

The method of deducing a set of ideas from a broad survey of the fiction almost automatically limits one to studying the contents of the books rather than the author's background. At best the latter method would be unproductive, since countless novels are anonymous, and scores of authors are merely names. Similarly restricted must be historical annotation, often impossible because of the vagueness of the stories, but occasionally demonstrating an aspect of the writer's technique.

Finally, the subject does not imply a mere epitomizing of all plots involving America, but rather a record of all uses of America, which fall into three divisions: the verbal reference, the anecdote or episode, and the major plot-element. These serve rather to facilitate the presentation of material, however, than to classify the evidence. The real topics have already been outlined—stories about the war, criticism of the war, influence of the war on the concept of America. These provide the channels through which ultimate conclusions are to be reached. In using this topical method it is seldom possible to discuss novels as units; *The Ants* (1767), for instance, deals with problems of colonization and with taxation, and exemplifies the use of America as a medium of satirizing the English government, and hence it must be discussed under three heads. This note should explain apparent repetitions.

The topical method partially insures against isolated conclusions by providing for a logical introduction of earlier and later ideas. It is virtually impossible, for instance, to discuss America as the background of a new Golden Age without referring to prior manifestations and succeeding variations of the idea. Thus is gained a necessary perspective. The panorama qualifies, amplifies, and in a measure justifies the period-study.

CHAPTER II

## THE PRODUCTION OF NOVELS, 1760-1800

i

At first glance the last forty years of the eighteenth century
do not seem to be a fair field full of fiction. Fielding and
Richardson had completed their work; Sterne died in 1768,
Smollett in 1771. Jane Austen, although she wrote her major
works before the turn of the century, did not publish until 1811,
and it was three years more before *Waverley* aroused a buzz of
conjecture. In the meantime a dull horizon had been lighted by
only two bright figures—Frances Burney, star of the '70's and
'80's, and Maria Edgeworth, whose *Castle Rackrent* appeared in
1800. Lesser luminaries were those of the new Gothic school—
Walpole, Clara Reeve, Mrs. Radcliffe, Lewis, and a host of
mediocre imitators. Dimmer still were the members of the
Oriental school, known chiefly through the *Vathek* of the lord
of Fonthill.

These were a negligible percentage of the novelists who
entertained, thrilled, and lectured a gradually increasing audience. Not that there are wide expanses of unsuspected excellence in this field of literature. There were, however, large
numbers of fiction-writers who, now unknown, were very important to their times. Hundreds of novels—and a few decidedly
readable ones, such as *Berkeley Hall* and *Jonathan Corncob*—
were anonymous, but familiar to most readers of the day were
Robert Bage (1728-1801), Mrs. Frances Brooke (1724-1789),
Henry Brooke (1703?-1783), the Rev. Richard Graves (1715-
1804), Thomas Holcroft (1745-1809), Charles Johnstone
(1719?-1800?), Dr. John Moore (1729-1802), Mrs. Charlotte

41

Smith (1749-1806), Mrs. Agnes Maria Bennet (d. 1808), Mrs. Elizabeth Bonhote (1744-1818), Peter Henry Treyssac de Vergy (d. 1774), Mrs. Susanna Gunning (1740?-1800), Mrs. Hedgeland (fl. 1790-1800), Elizabeth Helme (fl. 1785-1800), William Hutchinson (1732-1814), Mrs. Eliza Parsons (d. 1811), Samuel Jackson Pratt (1749-1814), Mrs. Mary E. Robinson (1758-1800), and Arthur Young (1741-1820). I list only those who produced three or more novels; there were literally scores of others whose pens were worn out after a novel or two. By 1800 the new genre had arrived, and its two chief characteristics were "its popularity as a form of entertainment and its inferiority as a form of art."[1]

ii

Our first question has to do with fluctuations in this ascending curve of popularity. Miss Tompkins raises the issue:

> The output of novels, which moralists found so sinister and so formidable, slackens unaccountably in the half-dozen years at the end of the 'seventies and the beginning of the 'eighties. In 1771, designated by the *Critical* "this prolific, scribblerian year," the *Monthly* and *Critical* dealt between them with some sixty novels, though some of these were reprints and a few translations, while one or two may have escaped the critical net. After 1775 the numbers drop rapidly; 1776 can muster but sixteen in all. . . . There was, then, a real shortage, which first made itself felt soon after the outbreak of war in America, and continued until within a few years of the French Revolution.[2]

Despite the *unaccountably,* reasons suggest themselves, for it is striking that the years of depression coincide rather closely with those of military activity. Perhaps there is only coincidence, but several other possible factors are to be considered. First, however, figures will show more specifically how the war-period

---

[1] Tompkins, *op. cit.,* p. 1. The first chapter has an excellent account of the book-business of the day.

[2] Page 13.

sent fiction into a decline. The following table lists the number of new novels produced each year from 1761 to 1800[3]:

| Year | Novels | Year | Novels |
|------|--------|------|--------|
| 1761 | 26 | 1781 | 24 |
| 1762 | 19 | 1782 | 31 |
| 1763 | 17 | 1783 | 32 |
| 1764 | 20 | 1784 | 29 |
| 1765 | 24 | 1785 | 72 |
| 1766 | 32 | 1786 | 48 |
| 1767 | 40 | 1787 | 62 |
| 1768 | 40 | 1788 | 81 |
| 1769 | 48 | 1789 | 82 |
| 1770 | 53 | 1790 | 77 |
| 1771 | 52 | 1791 | 83 |
| 1772 | 44 | 1792 | 58 |
| 1773 | 42 | 1793 | 60 |
| 1774 | 27 | 1794 | 59 |
| 1775 | 39 | 1795 | 60 |
| 1776 | 18 | 1796 | 84 |
| 1777 | 31 | 1797 | 65 |
| 1778 | 18 | 1798 | 77 |
| 1779 | 26 | 1799 | 86 |
| 1780 | 40 | 1800 | 117 |

The significance of these figures is more vividly indicated by the graph in Figure I following. No attempt can be made to account for annual variations, but the general trend is clear enough: in the mid-'seventies there is a gradual decline reaching a nadir in 1778, the year in which France entered the war; after that there is a faint rise which gains unmistakably after the signing of the peace treaty. With the decline in production of novels went a similar decline in the attention paid them by

[3] The count, which is my own, is based on the year-file in Professor Greenough's Catalogue. It includes only first editions, excluding, as far as they are identifiable, reprints and translations. Complete accuracy is impossible, since for many titles so little information is available that it is not definitely determinable what they represent. Naturally, I have made every effort to count only full-length novels; in a few instances the quantitative and psychological equivalent of a novel, such as a collection of several of what would now be called "novelettes" or of prose miscellanies, seemed logically admissible.

43

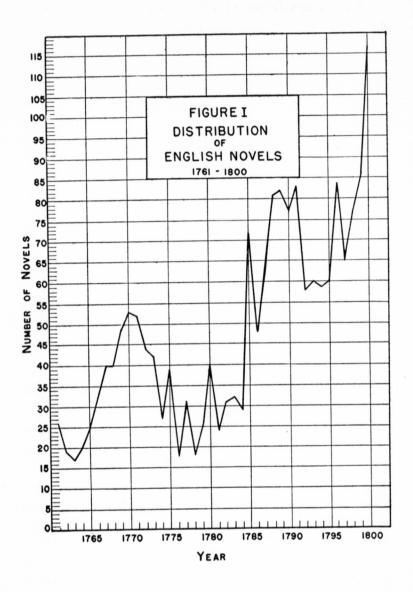

FIGURE I
DISTRIBUTION
OF
ENGLISH NOVELS
1761 - 1800

the contemporary reviews. The following columns indicate the number of novels reviewed or listed in three leading periodicals during the two decades in which we are chiefly interested:

44

| Year | Gentleman's Magazine | Monthly Review | Critical Review |
|------|------|------|------|
| 1770 | 17 | 34 | 30 |
| 1771 | 43 | 43 | 51 |
| 1772 | 26 | 41 | 39 |
| 1773 | 25 | 35 | 29 |
| 1774 | 9 | 23 | 17 |
| 1775 | 16 | 25 | 18 |
| 1776 | 3 | 15 | 12 |
| 1777 | 3 | 18 | 11 |
| 1778 | 10 | 18 | 12 |
| 1779 | 0 | 10 | 5 |
| 1780 | 0 | 11 | 6 |
| 1781 | 0 | 13 | 17 |
| 1782 | 1 | 18 | 13 |
| 1783 | 1 | 22 | 20 |
| 1784 | 1 | 25 | 25 |
| 1785 | 25 | 27 | 37 |
| 1786 | 35 | 30 | 29 |
| 1787 | 53 | 44 | 36 |
| 1788 | 35 | 38 | 52 |
| 1789 | 15 | 43 | 55 |
| 1790 | 2 | 47 | 49 |

The curves, as represented in Figure II following, show the same general rise and fall that we have already seen, except for the odd variation in the *Gentleman's* due to editorial policy.[4]

Was there causation or coincidence? If we insist on the former, we run the risk of approving some such generalization as that the sterner spirit of the war period reduced the frivolity of reading novels. This would be an absurdity, not to mention the previous admission that the war did not exclusively absorb Great Britain between 1776 and 1783. There is, however, a more plausible interpretation: that the decline of novels may have been due to a diversion of the normal, and growing, interest in them. Fiction demanded, as vivaciously described by Miss Tompkins in her chapter, "Didacticism and Sensibility,"

---

[4] The *Gentleman's* reviewed novels rather infrequently but listed them in its "Catalogue of New Publications," which appeared with unexplained irregularity. After 1788 it began to be crowded out by the "Index Indicatorius," which today

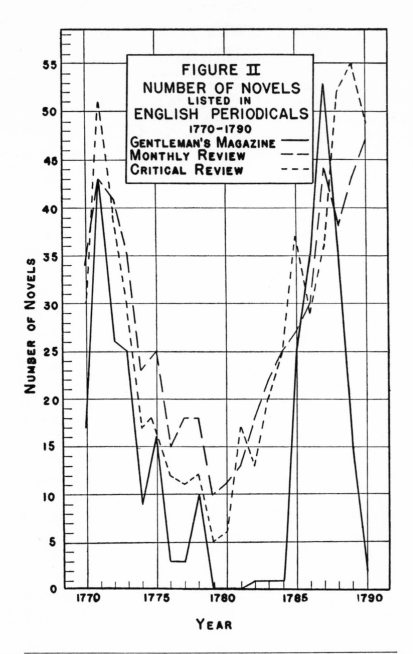

FIGURE II
NUMBER OF NOVELS
LISTED IN
ENGLISH PERIODICALS
1770-1790
GENTLEMAN'S MAGAZINE ———
MONTHLY REVIEW ———
CRITICAL REVIEW ----

NUMBER OF NOVELS

YEAR

might be called "Our Mailbag." By 1790 the "Catalogue" was gone entirely, and consequently all forms of literature were slighted.

46

a thorough dose of information and morality and a sugar-coating of emotional titillation:

The church-going, sermon-reading middle classes liked a good plain moral at the end of a book. . . . Critics and novelists of the sterner breed scouted mere "amusement" as waste of time: the business of the novelist was to teach. . . . To this end, not only must the novel always show life subservient to moral law, but in addition a little solid information, on whatever pretence inserted, was always favourably received—at least by the critics. . . . No reviewer ever complains of irrelevance in face of the interpolated sermons, dissertations on slavery, Greek music, the penal laws, and the like. . . . The digressions might not be strictly germane to the story, but they were welcome superfluities, and would, it might be hoped, instil a little information, willy-nilly, into the class, already formidable in size, that read nothing but novels.[5]

Later came sensibility—weepiness, "pleasing distress," hypersympathetic commiseration. But even before the tender heart became a fad, a decadent emotionalism was rampant: morality was always trimmed out with dueling, seduction, adultery, elopement, and bawdy-house scenes that must have kept the susceptible on tenterhooks for hours on end.[6]

This combination of fodder for the brain and assault upon the nervous system was duplicated, or at least approximated, I submit, in the occasional literature of the day, the pamphlets which briefly, emphatically, and with strong-arm methods rather than incisiveness, dealt with every sort of problem and event that occurred. Pamphlets, of course, always professed to be informative, but during the war-years their informativeness had the especial intensity conferred by immediate association with rapidly moving history. Even the slightest interest in colonial affairs must have increased the sense of virtuous performance of duty, of character-building acceptance of instruction, which accompanied perusal of printers' daily offerings of journalistic

[5] Op. cit., p. 71.

[6] The pattern derives from Clarissa, which, whatever its intent, shares much with the relatively unpretentious shilling-shocker.

and argumentative sheets. What England was doing across the sea might not have seemed exclusively important, but still it was an aspect of that English policy, an emanation of that English constitution which was peculiarly every man's property and which could always accelerate the heart and magnify the voice. And if the average reader was oblivious of the metaphysical, he at least knew what taxes meant, and the outbursts of Richard Price on the war and the budget could not have failed to catch his eye. Hence it is not impossible that in the stress of unusual times, even though they were not the object of a general absorbed interest, the receptivity toward didacticism may have been taken up by effective journalism rather than by the moralistic fiction which satisfied the mind in the calm of normal years.

The possibility becomes stronger through the fact that the sugar-coating of the homiletic pill was not unlike the seductive sweets of the novel. The pamphlet could hardly thrill with the novel's grotesque medley of forbidden fruit and horrible example, but it was not without its emotional quality. The American War was a controversial issue. Fervor of advocacy, violence of denunciation, vigor in vituperation and invective,[7] which took the place of unity, coherence, and emphasis, could not have failed to warm the blood and stir the appetite. Any palate could find its sauce. If one's taste ran to personal animosity, he would find ample condiment in such works as *The constitution defended and pensioner exposed, in remarks on the False Alarm*[8] [*The False Alarm* was by Samuel Johnson] . . . (1770) ;

[7] "Officials failed to suppress the attacks of opposition writers; and in the period of the American Revolution the administration suffered from the liberty, not to say license, of the British press. . . . Even the laws concerning libel could not check the pamphleteers, and no one may expect to find in the pamphlet literature of the eighteenth century an unbiassed statement of facts. The contemporary reader was happy to see his own views corroborated, or angry to see them refuted" (Clark, *op. cit.*, pp. 2, 4-5).

[8] Titles are abbreviated and are in lower-case throughout; the originals are often interminable and show wide typographical variations. These selections are from a long list compiled from the Harvard College Library collection and from the previously cited works of Clark, Hinkhouse, and Fraser.

William Jackson's *Reply to Johnson's Taxation No Tyranny* (1776); hymn-writer Augustus Montague Toplady's sneering exposé of Wesley's borrowings from Johnson—*An old fox tarred and feathered* (1776); and *A letter to the most insolent man alive* (1789). A reader who would smack his lips over governmental follies could try *On the abuse of unrestrained power, an historical essay* (1778) or *The cabinet conference, or tears of ministry* . . . (1779). One who craved a dash of violence might dip into *The Crisis* (1775-1776), which was "to be continued weekly during the present bloody Civil War in America." A liberal would be well served by Richard Price's *Observations on civil liberty and the justice and policy of the war with America* (1776); Richard Watson's *The principles of the revolution vindicated* (1776); and a work typical of the new radicalism, *Necessity for the associations now forming generally* . . . (1780). For one who considered the colonials a gang of upstarts whose theories ought to be knocked on the head, there was satisfying sustenance in *Civil liberties asserted and the rights of the subject defended against the anarchical principles of the Rev. Dr. Price* (1776); similar defenses by John Lind and "Ossian" Macpherson; Alexander Gerard's *Liberty a cloack of maliciousness* . . . (1778); and the pious pronouncement, *Dr. Price's* . . . *civil liberty shown to be contradictory to reason and scripture* (1777). A more reserved taste would find ample stimulus in Gilbert Wakefield's *A calm address to the inhabitants of England* (1777). And no doubt many, weary of it all, blessed Matthew Robinson-Morris for *Peace the best policy* . . . (1777). But if the reader was still avid of excitement, and if obvious bias did not sufficiently vivify such pages as have been listed, there was still a steaming dish in accounts of battles and Indian activities.[9]

To summarize: pamphlets, whether on the war or on govern-

[9] The controversy over the employment of Indian auxiliaries reached a height with Burke's famous speech in 1778. For an account of the whole subject see Trevelyan, *George the Third and Charles Fox*, I, 81 ff.

49

mental or financial questions evoked by the war, not only contained sufficient meat for systems trained to prefer solid substance, but furthermore, through their uncompromising, angry, and fiery tones, provided enough emotional spice to seduce even a sluggish reader. In this fact lies some probability that journalism, with its variety and immediacy, may have gained some extra adherents from the novel-reading public. It seems much more plausible that the new volume of pamphlets[10] evoked by new and sensational subjects would have caused a diversion of reading interests, than it would have called forth a new reading-public from those for whom books and papers had previously been too tough a pabulum.

Why a diversion from novels, one may ask, instead of from other forms—essay, drama, poetry? The answer is of course that the novel was still an unproved form, generally considered little more than frivolous:

As a new and rather shapeless literary kind, with little discipline and no classical tradition, its foothold in critical esteem had always been precarious. . . .[11]

Hence it was least stable, most subject to influence or even eclipse. The essay was established, it fed the cultivated taste for didacticism, and, as a type, it included the very political pamphlets of which we have spoken. Drama and poetry had a tradition of such length and durability that they would absorb rather than yield to passing political upheavals.[12] Poetry had

[10] In the "Catalogue of New Publications" of the *Gentleman's* there was a regular subdivision captioned, "Proceedings of the American Colonies." The *Monthly* had a similar section of its booknotes reserved for Americana; often appearing first was "American Controversy," which once in 1776 included ten pages of reviews (LIV, 325-334). As early as 1769 the *Critical,* which also listed many titles on America, reviewed a sermon, *Shall I go to War with my American Brethren?* (XXVII, 239). Besides, these magazines, as well as the *Universal,* the *Scots Magazine,* and others, were enlivened by "controversies over colonial affairs" (Clark, *op. cit.,* p. 5).

[11] Tompkins, *op. cit.,* p. 3.

[12] For instance, Miss Gregory is able to list 57 plays produced between 1789 and 1812 that show the influence of the French Revolution (*The French Revolu-*

long been a medium of political expression,[13] and the reader of poetry had no need to feel that he was being inattentive to current events. He might have come across such lyrics as *Ode on the Expedition to America* and *Albion Triumphant;*[14] Miss Seward's *Monody on Major André;*[15] *America. An Ode to the People of England; Desolation of America;* John Farrer's *America; The American War, a Poem;* and David Humphreys' *A Poem. On the Happiness of America; addressed to the Citizens of the United States.*[16] These titles alone should afford conviction that the war was not likely to reduce the supply of verse.

If the decline of novels is attributable to the war, we have further evidence of the truth of Professor Draper's dictum that

The American War also turned the public attention to sterner things than the cultivation of the emotions through the fine arts. Mason, the true barometer of his age, to some extent reflects this reaction.[17]

Whether or not Mason's bibliography is an efficient *speculum*

*tion and the English Novel,* pp. 311-317). See also Charles Cestre, *La Révolution Française et les Poètes Anglais (1789-1809)* (Paris: Hachette, 1906).

[13] See C. W. Previté-Orton, *Political Satire in English Poetry* (Cambridge: University Press, 1910).

[14] *Gentleman's Magazine,* XLVI (1776), 178, and LII (1782), 444, respectively.

[15] The *Monthly* gives it a five-page review—LXIV (1781), 371-376, generally favorable except for a remarkably judicious objection to the anathema on Washington, who "could not . . . have acted otherwise than as he did" (p. 373).

[16] The anonymous *America* and the four following were all named in the *Critical:* XLII (1776), 73; XLIV (1777), 391; L (1780), 470; LII (1781), 146-147; and LXI (1786), 361, respectively. In reference to the third (Farrer's *America*), the reviewer objects to the title, although the poem exhibits "Britain's indulgence" and "America's insolence." *The American War* inspires the complaint that one of the evils of the war is the "multiplicity of bad productions, both in verse and in prose, which it has occasioned"; the reviewer wonders how the author of the poem, which describes "every battle and skirmish," could "prevail on himself to publish such intolerable jargon." Concerning Humphreys' poem it is stated that his ideas of the future grandeur of the United States are "so brilliant and dazzling, as to render his meaning scarce perceptible."

[17] John W. Draper, *William Mason: A Study in Eighteenth-Century Culture* (New York: New York University Press, 1924), p. 95.

*mundi,* we find a momentary desertion of mere entertainment. Then novels regain their strength and go on to a position of ascendancy. Furthermore, they increase in variety and they develop new types—the historical and the Gothic. These two, very strikingly, began to achieve prominence after the world had quieted down from its first eighteenth-century revolution. Along with this emergence of new types there is observable a development of new literary interests. The new Scandinavian influence, after a decline in the '70's, shows a remarkable resumption of strength in the '80's. In the same decade the Celtic revival goes on apace, reaching previously untouched heights. The whole antiquarian movement seems to reach its peak about the same time, and the Oriental influence also becomes stronger. Here is not the place for a detailed discussion of these literary phenomena,[18] but some mention of them is relevant. One receives a fairly strong impression that the war may have been a barrier against literary progress, at least in new fields. Of course, no proof is possible. One might argue, on the contrary, that all the aspects of literary evolution mentioned are phases of the Romantic Movement, that the war was part of the political expression of the same movement, and that the chronological relationship between them is of negligible import; he might contend that all are symptoms of an underlying condition which would naturally achieve such utterances, of which the dates and terms are largely a matter of accident. Still it seems no unreasonable conclusion that an exhausting war which brought increasing international involvements and complexities until eventually matters military and political became paramount—that such a war so absorbed national strength as to leave less energy than usual for literature, less, especially, of the creativity requisite for the pursuit of innovations; that, further, the coming of peace, the ending of tension, and the renewal of economic balance released ener-

18 See Appendix A for further chronological evidence on the development of the types and movements here mentioned.

gies that were devoted, whether by reading, writing, or criticism, to the renewed practice of old literary exercises, or to experimentation with novelty, both in form and in content.

We are, of course, in the realm of conjecture. But it is a definite fact that novels went into a decline during the war period and then gradually reasserted their power as military activity decreased. The figures are clear, as are those which demonstrate that the periodicals of the time temporarily lost interest in fiction as political affairs became not only more important but more sensational. It is not impossible to assume, therefore, that the war had an adverse effect on fiction. The assumption gains weight from the fact that the novel, of all forms of literature, was most insecurely established and was therefore most liable to damage from external causes. The assumption gains further weight from the fact that the war and all attendant matters gained a consequential place in journals and pamphlets, and that such pamphlets, through their substance making a didactic appeal, and through their color and force an emotional appeal, were somewhat the psychological equivalents of fiction. It is impossible to go beyond that, to assert definitely that the war temporarily delayed the upsurge of the novel to an ultimate position of prime importance. The evidence does, however, establish a strong probability that such was the case.

CHAPTER III

# AMERICA IN THE NOVEL

i

Discussion from now on will proceed in a direction opposite from that heretofore taken: while Chapter II dealt with what the war may have taken away from the novel, the present chapter and those following will attempt to show what the war added. Temporarily the approach will continue with statistics and chronology, which are necessary in an attempted measurement of the occurrence of various phenomena. Since variations are important, it has been necessary to divide the forty-year period into manageable units. A year-by-year investigation would be too detailed and would becloud rather than clarify the issues; to proceed by whole decades would be inexact, since the war covered parts of both the '70's and the '80's. Hence a division into five-year blocs gives a workable mean.

The subject to be measured by means of these eight periods is the use which the novel made of America, particularly as a background for all or a major part of the action, and also as a topic for discussion or occasional reference. The increase or decrease of such use as the century goes on will provide the clue to a second possible influence of the war on prose-fiction.

First, there is at least mild significance in negative results, that is, the record of those novels which made no mention whatever of either America or the West Indies and East Indies. The latter two must receive some attention at least for the moment, since the years were important in the reshaping of empire, and we constantly are looking at a tri-cornered map of political and economic affairs. There follows a record of those

54

novels which were purely European in their geographical interests:[1]

| Period | Novels Examined | Negative Results | |
|--------|:---------------:|:----------------:|:---:|
| | | Number of Novels | Percentage |
| 1761-1765 | 22 | 6 | 27% |
| 1766-1770 | 49 | 21 | 42% |
| 1771-1775 | 42 | 8 | 19% |
| 1776-1780 | 38 | 8 | 21% |
| 1781-1785 | 43 | 8 | 18% |
| 1786-1790 | 78 | 19 | 24% |
| 1791-1795 | 72 | 12 | 16% |
| 1796-1800 | 94 | 25 | 26% |

Outstanding is the fact that so small a percentage—the figures in the third column are the really significant ones—of novels was restricted to the domestic scene; approximately three-quarters of the total in some way brought in America or the Indies.[2] More to our purpose is the peak of interest shown in the distant parts of the world from 1771 to 1785, when American troubles were at their height, and again from 1791 to 1795, when the Hastings affair and the French Revolution were dictating the directions in which the public eye turned. Here is apparent corroboration of Miss Tompkins' suggestion, "No doubt the war in America and the trial of Warren Hastings quickened interest in our distant dependencies. . . ."[3] It seems natural enough that the general excitement aroused by events

[1] The novels examined are always in the same proportion to the number originally turned out in any year. The totals, which are given only here, are the basis for the calculation of percentages in all the following tables. See Appendix B.

[2] Because of the variation in the number of novels published each year, the percentage method is needed to provide a common denominator. Since many novels have disappeared, the results are naturally representative, not absolute. Reading of more novels would probably raise the low percentages, since I have naturally tried to gather in all works reflecting colonial interests.

[3] *Op. cit.*, p. 181.

in America, and the consequent growth of attention to other colonial problems, should have evoked a response from a fiction still not too remote from journalism. In the early '90's, the probable influence of the Hastings furore is clear enough. And the French Revolution, through popular association and through such agencies as the work of the cosmopolitan Paine, naturally turned many an eye westward again.

Advancing to positive results, we find that all uses of America by the novel—plots, episodes, discussions, and mere references— are distributed according to following tabulation:[4]

| Period | Number of Novels | Per- centage |
|---|---|---|
| 1761-1765 | 7 | 31% |
| 1766-1770 | 20 | 40% |
| 1771-1775 | 21 | 50% |
| 1776-1780 | 18 | 47% |
| 1781-1785 | 22 | 51% |
| 1786-1790 | 44 | 56% |
| 1791-1795 | 45 | 62% |
| 1796-1800 | 48 | 51% |

It is illuminating, to say the least, to see in the fiction of this period, which one thinks of chiefly in terms of sensibility, medieval history, haunted castles, and later the manners of Austen and Edgeworth, so wide a concern, even if only in isolated passages, with transatlantic scenes and affairs. Here it is that we really learn what was going on in the popular mind—much more clearly than in the works now labeled "major." The discrepancy is sharp.

We must, however, observe the variations, and there our attention is caught by the increase of interest from the time of the Stamp Act to that of the Declaration of Independence, and the subsequent maintenance of that interest at a uniformly high level—fifty per cent or over. Allowing for the *post hoc* fallacy, as always, and conceding the absence of a demonstrated causal

[4] For a complete list of the titles recorded here numerically, see Appendix C. For totals on which percentages are based, see table of Negative Results, *ante.*

56

relationship, we can still safely defend, I think, the proposition that the war acted as an advertiser of America, which had certainly not been ignored before, but which afterward made a far deeper imprint on letters. The war served to focus attention on what had before been only a convenient appendage of the Empire, a property casually accepted after a century and a half of relatively comfortable possession, and to renew its imaginative stimulus. Then the drama inherent in the development of a new social order held the attention, which grew almost into devotion in the first half of the '90's. This final high point in the curve, significantly, is the time of the French Revolution, always associated, in the minds of both professors and populace, with the American experiment. And the final mild decrease of the interest in America is coincidental with the century-end heightening of tension in continental affairs. The whole pattern of events suggests strongly that the war and other developments growing out of it made England "America-conscious," not only in journalism and factual dissertation, but also in such nominally artistic literature as the novel.

It is not entirely irrelevant to continue briefly with related phenomena, the treatment accorded the Indies by prose fiction, or, in broadest possible terms, the subject of empire and art. The West Indies fared as follows at the hand of the novelists:[5] One notes first, possibly, that the West Indies, though remain-

| Period | Number of Novels | Per- centage |
|---|---|---|
| 1761-1765 | 7 | 31% |
| 1766-1770 | 9 | 18% |
| 1771-1775 | 11 | 26% |
| 1776-1780 | 6 | 15% |
| 1781-1785 | 12 | 27% |
| 1786-1790 | 26 | 33% |
| 1791-1795 | 25 | 34% |
| 1796-1800 | 29 | 30% |

[5] For a list of the titles, see Appendix D. See preceding note.

ing British, never achieved the place in fiction accorded America. Second, there are no major variations except for the marked decline in the war-period, which seems to indicate that momentarily the melodrama of continental America eclipsed interest in a less extensive dependency. With the resumption of normal economic relations there was restored the average prior interest, which thenceforth remained virtually static. Novelists using the West Indies had two main themes: the study of the returned plantation-owner, usually regarded with the highest disfavor, but best known through a rare defense, Richard Cumberland's play, *The West Indian;* and the success of the adventurer, who, as Robert Burns planned to do, went to the islands to make his fortune.[6]

Passing on to India and the East Indies, we can chart their contributions to the novel as follows:[7]

| Period | Number of Novels | Percentage |
|---|---|---|
| 1761-1765 | 6 | 27% |
| 1766-1770 | 10 | 20% |
| 1771-1775 | 21 | 50% |
| 1776-1780 | 17 | 44% |
| 1781-1785 | 16 | 37% |
| 1786-1790 | 37 | 47% |
| 1791-1795 | 31 | 43% |
| 1796-1800 | 43 | 45% |

[6] See Lewis Melville, *The Life and Letters of Tobias Smollett* (London: Faber and Gwyer, 1926), p. 23, for a bit of personal history which could have been the basis of many a West-Indies plot. After the Carthagena expedition, Smollett was landed at Jamaica, where occurred "his meeting with a very good-looking Creole girl, Anne (Smollett called her Nancy) Lascelles, with whom he fell in love. She was an heiress, owning houses and slaves, and her fortune was estimated to be about £3000. When Smollett left Jamaica in 1743, it was understood that she would presently follow him to London and marry him there, when he had had an opportunity to establish himself as a surgeon. At the moment, apart from his pay, he had no means whatever." In the stories the lady's fortune would have solved all problems.

[7] For a list of the titles, see Appendix E. For totals on which percentages are based, see table of Negative Results, *ante.*

Here again one is struck by the fact that the general average is
lower than that of the interest in America. Generally, the curve
varies uncertainly enough to make conclusions dubious, although one cannot ignore the sharp rise in the early '70's, when
colonial problems were much to the fore, and the gradual drop
during the years when America held the center of the stage.
Whatever the relationship here, there is a periodic association
of America and India in the minds of both novelist and reviewer; while the former, mercenary in intent, would artlessly
shift a plot or literary device from Oriental to Occidental
setting, or vice versa, the latter was quick to catch him up.
Speaking of *The Disinterested Nabob* (1787), one reviewer
limits himself to severe understatement: "The story . . . is not
uncommon; and . . . is not very different from the 'Liberal
American' [1785]."[8] Another reviewer finds a similar liaison
as he takes down *Gilham Farm* (1780):

. . . [It is] fabricated to introduce some seemingly original accounts
of India. Allured by the success of Emily Montague [by Mrs. Brooke,
1769], and the pleasing descriptions of Canada in that agreeable novel,
the Author hath followed his original with unequal steps.[9]

Undiscriminating dislike for the children of all imperial corners
appeared in the *Public Advertiser* of September 13, 1774, which
mentioned " 'Africans,' Americans, Nabobs, and Scotchmen"
"in the same unfriendly newspaper paragraph."[10] Later Henry
James Pye, scarcely more impressive as novelist than as laureate,
made a Southampton jack-of-all-trades complain, "We are eat
up by a number of East and West Indians, who live in all those
fine houses you see above bar."[11] Usually, however, the highest
order of antipathy was reserved for the Nabobs.[12]

[8] *Critical Review,* LXIII (1787), 309.
[9] *Monthly Review,* LXIV (1781), 71.
[10] Holzman, *op. cit.,* p. 16. Cf. Horace Walpole's *Letters,* ed. Mrs. Paget
Toynbee (Oxford, 1903-1905), V, 376: "My next assembly will be entertaining;
there will be five countesses, two bishops, fourteen Jews, five papists, a doctor
of physic, and an actress; not to mention Scotch Irish, East and West Indians"
(in a letter to George Montagu, October 3, 1763).
[11] *The Democrat* (New York, 1795), I, 22.
[12] For a most violent, and almost continuous philippic against the Nabobs,

A return to the figures is a reminder that, whatever the attitudes expressed, America occupied more space in the English novel than either of the dependencies which remained under the British aegis. Obviously not empire alone created the interests exemplified in novelists' use of foreign scenes. The drama of war, likewise political experiments, would provide a partial explanation. And it may be not too far off the track to suggest an economic influence—this will seem at least plausible in an era when economics is popularly believed to provide an *Open Sesame* to all truth—on literary interests. England's trade benefited by the war. Her mercantilists had always been against it, they opposed it with increasing vigor, and they were responsible for the favorable terms for the new Anglo-American trade.[13] Immediately after the war Lord Sheffield prophesied that England would have as much trade as she could handle and would benefit from the occurrence of the break then instead of later.[14] By 1793 Jeremy Bentham could advise the French on a basis of English experience—in *Emancipate Your Colonies.* The generally felt advantages were pointed out statistically by George Chalmers, an observer who had a keen eye for economic facts. Using what he called a "six years average," he presented the following figures for English exports for the periods ending 1774 and 1792:[15]

|  | To 1774 | To 1792 |
|---|---|---|
| American Colonies (U. S.).... | £2,216,824 | £2,807,306 |
| West Indies............... | £1,209,265 | £1,845,962 |
| East Indies.............. | £ 907,240 | £1,921,955 |

see Sir Samuel E. Brydges, *Arthur Fitz-Albini* (1798), especially I, 13-14, 52-53, 109, 246, 250-251, 258 ff., 271-272; II, 95-96, 100-101, 109, 118, 125.

13 Clark, *op. cit.,* p. 118.

14 *Observations on the Commerce of the American States* (2nd ed., 1783), pp. 78, 108.

15 *An Estimate of the Comparative Strength of Great Britain; And of the*

There is a rather suggestive set of parallels between literary and economic interests: America was ahead of the two Indies, the West at first led the East Indies, and by the end of the century the latter were in the van. In the novel the East Indies were proportionately more important than in their economic position, a fact no doubt to be accounted for by the greater publicity attendant upon, and consequently the greater imaginative value attaching to, the returning Nabobs.[16]

It would be ingenuous to argue that since England had more trade with America, *ergo,* England wrote more novels about America. But it is conceivable that satisfactory economic relations were a factor in the whole situation, basically political, which kept America a continual object of English attention. If commerce increased, and there was a resultant greater "prosperity," the consciousness of the material improvement—and of its sources—would permeate the middle classes. It was they for whom the novelists wrote, and they, presumably, who began exercising the prerogative of determining what should be written for them. Hence if there was a general comfortable awareness of American contributions to commercial growth, the popular moods which can be assumed to have existed would find some reflection in fiction, or at least would stimulate the treatment of American subjects which, for whatever reason, were already there. In other words, money probably "talks" here no less than in other phases of experience, though in different tones. And the money, that is, the new increases in trade, it is to be remembered, was indirectly a product of the war, so that we are not too far from our primary subject of war influences.

While politics and economics may contribute to the new high

---

*Losses of her Trade from Every War Since the Revolution; With an Introduction of Previous History* (New ed., Corrected and Continued to 1801; 1802), p. 285.

[16] See Holzman, *op. cit.,* pp. 17, 131-168. Besides the spectacular quality of the returned Nabobs, there was the Hastings trial, which had a tremendous repercussion in popular imagination.

level of interest in America shown by the novel, a matter of solely psychological import is the influence of the American war on the increase of the attention paid by the novel to the East Indies. Halving the empire, the war was the most significant single event in the history of imperial development. Thenceforward, to relish the panorama of broad possessions, English eyes could turn only to the East. Circumstances magnified many times the importance of India, for she was now the only major resting place of the spirit of expansion. That spirit was a strong force in England. Novelists felt it—or attacked it; at least they were not indifferent to it. So, paradoxically, while the war advertised America, it also advertised India; without it, America might have been the place where young Englishmen, still remaining Englishmen, went out to make their fortunes. Kipling might have written of army posts on the Mississippi.

But there was the war with its concomitant difficulties. During times of stress, English fiction showed wider exotic interests; in the periods of the American and French Revolutions, novels offered fewer purely domestic scenes and subjects than in the quieter intervals. America first rose to major importance in the '70's, and it retained its position for the rest of the century; battles, and then democracy, and then trade kept people constantly alive to its existence. The final proposition is this: first the war advertised America, and then it brought about a changed political and economic world which influenced the tastes of the reading public. Here is a second possible influence of the war on the English novel.

ii

A subject growing naturally from this preceding one is the contents of the novels in which the background is America or in which a large part of the action takes place either across the Atlantic or as a result of transatlantic events. Again chronology, the pre-war and post-war development, comes to the fore.

Neither whole plots nor half-plots, discussions or references, are the sole indices of the place which America came to have in the novel. The outside of a book, in fact, may prove just as much as the inside; titles, the sign and the lure by which readers were induced to stop, look, and enter, throw a good deal of light on popular reactions. In considering titles by which publishers strove to allure the public, we find some twenty-five in which occur such words as *America* or *American,* a sum which perhaps poorly rivals the stock magic of *history, adventures, romance,* and *castle,* but which is none the less notable. Further, it is greater than the combined titles which were intended to appeal to interest in the East and the West Indies.[17] The list follows:[18]

1760—*Memoirs of the Life of a Modern Saint . . . in England, Scotland, and America*

1766—*The Adventure of a Bale of Goods from America in Consequence of the Stamp Act*

1767—Arthur Young—*The Adventures of Emmera, or the Fair American*

1767—*The Female American*

1767—Edward Thompson—*Sailor's Letters . . . in Europe, Asia, Africa, and America*

1769—*Private Letters from an American in England to his Friends in America*

1769—*The American Traveller. . . .*[19]

[17] I have found five titles using the West Indies: Sir John Hill, *The Adventures of Mr George Edwards, a Creole* (3rd ed., 1788); *The Peregrinations of Jeremiah Grant, Esq; a West Indian* (1763); *The West Indian; or the Memoirs of Frederick Charlton* (1787); Samuel J. Arnold, Jr., *The Creole* (1796); *The Life and Wonderful Adventures of Henry Lanson . . . of . . . the West Indies* [1800?]. There are ten for the East Indies: *The Orientalist* (1774); *The Indian Adventurer* (1780); H. F. Thomson, *The Intrigues of a Nabob* (1780); H. Scott, *Adventures of a Rupee* (1782); *The Nabob* (1786); *Rajah Kisna, an Indian Tale* (1786); *The Disinterested Nabob* (1787); Capt. John Walsh, *Ship's Husband . . . to the East India Company* (1791); Mary J. Young, *The East Indian* (1794); Elizabeth Hamilton, *Translation of the Letters of a Hindoo Rajah* (1796).

[18] Titles are assembled from works read, from reviews, and from Professor Greenough's Catalogue. All the works, of course, are fictional or semi-fictional; doubtful works are included on a basis of Professor Greenough's Catalogue.

[19] An instance of the value of suggesting that the writer had been in America.

1772—*Memoirs of an American* ("from the French")
1777—*A Letter from an Officer at New-York to his Friend in England*[20]
1778—Mrs. Phoebe Gibbes—*Friendship in a Nunnery; or, the American Fugitive*[21]

1781—*The Revolution*[22]
1783—*The American Wanderer . . . by a Virginian*
1785—*The Liberal American*
1786—*Letters Written by an American Spy*
1786—James Buckland—*Remarkable Discovery of an American Hermit*
1786—*The Cacique of Ontario*
1787—*Adventures of Jonathan Corncob, Loyal American Refugee*
1787—*The Algerine Spy in Pennsylvania*
1788—*The American Hunter*[23]
1789—*The American Spy, Written after the Manner of the Turkish Spy*[24]

1790—*Louisa Wharton. A Story . . . during the Bloody Contest in AMERICA*
1792—*Life and Adventures of Joseph Enim, an American*[25]

---

The *Gentleman's* says the work might have been written by someone "who never went out of his counting house" (XXXIX, 399).

[20] Here is a clear-cut case of the writer's adopting the American background for publicity value, for the *Gentleman's* comments sharply: "A performance evidently fabricated on this side of the Atlantic . . .stuffed with some private corporation politics (not American), with which officers of the army, and the public in general, have no more concern than they have with the gallantries of Otaheite" (XLVII, 237).

[21] Once again the title appears to be an advertising stunt. The *Critical* notes that the war "never presumes to approach the parties concerned in this novel" (XLVI, 300).

[22] The title certainly suggests the influence of contemporary events, although the long summary of the action in the *Monthly* indicates no connection with the war (LXV, 390-391).

[23] This work survives in the edition of 1789, which was renamed *Fanny Vernon, or the Forlorn Hope; . . . Containing Scenes of Horror and Distress that happened during the War in America.*

[24] An interesting example of a truckling to fashion very familiar today. If primary interest was in the spy, it appears that America was the most popular locale for the follow-up.

[25] This is the title of the B. M. copy. In Professor Greenough's Catalogue *Armenian* replaces *American*. The existence of two forms is as indicative as would be that of *American* alone.

1793—*Anonymus's Travels from Europe to America* . . .

1793—Imlay—*The Emigrants* . . . *Written in America*

1800—*Life of Rolla, a Peruvian Tale*

1800—*Singular Sufferings of Two Friends Lost in an American Forest*

The frequency of *America* and *American* and of other terms suggesting America, especially when their use was in no way justified by the contents, is noteworthy; there is no better index of the popular appeal of the new world. In the second place it is clear that titles become more numerous just after times of greatest stress in American affairs, that is, in the three years just after the Stamp Act and its attendant furore, and in the decade after the war. The regular succession in this latter period leads up to an outburst of five titles in the years of the French Revolution. In other words, the evidence completely harmonizes with data already presented; titles fall into the general stream of presumptive American war influences.[26]

More fictional works than used America on the title-page gave to America, either directly or indirectly, a major role in their action. The distribution of these works follows:[27]

| Period | Number of Novels | Percentage |
|---|---|---|
| 1761-1765 | 0 | 0 |
| 1766-1770 | 7 | 14% |
| 1771-1775 | 1 | 2% |
| 1776-1780 | 1 | 2% |
| 1781-1785 | 5 | 11% |
| 1786-1790 | 7 | 8% |
| 1791-1795 | 7 | 9% |
| 1796-1800 | 11 | 11% |

[26] Non-fiction reacted similarly; tax troubles and the subsequent uproar produced a storm of books about America. For a good discussion of the new public interest and the publishers' endeavor to satisfy it, see Clark, *op. cit.*, pp. 3-4. Even biography followed the trend of the times. The *Apology* of the arch-mendicant, B. M. Carew, appeared in 1749, in the edition of the following year the title was expanded to include the fact of his having been in America, a renovation which held throughout the numerous editions of the rest of the century (see Professor Greenough's Catalogue).

[27] A list is omitted, since all these works are discussed individually later in the chapter. For the totals on which the percentages are based, see the table of Negative Results, *ante.*

65

Attention will probably be first attracted by the high percentage of novels about America even before the war started, a phenomenon due to several causes. First, two of the novels (here the term is by courtesy, as often), *The Adventure of a Bale of Goods from America* (1766) and *The Ants* (1767), are directly the result of the Stamp-Act controversy and hence are, in the broadest sense, a product of the war-influence; with them may be classed Smollett's *Adventures of an Atom* (1769), which, in the parts with which we are concerned, grew out of the Seven Years' War. Personal experience, plus the accident of a return to England and consequently to publishing facilities, accounts for two others—Mrs. Brooke's *History of Emily Montague*[28] (1769), and the *History of Charles Wentworth* (1770), probably by Edward Bancroft.[29] This latter, too, as well as *The Female American* (1767) and Arthur Young's *Adventures of Emmera* (1767), are in the specialized tradition of the Noble Savage which had been established long before. Hence, when special influences are considered, the number of novels about America in the late '60's is not disproportionately large, nor is there evidence of a strong general American tradition before the war.

The low figures during the '70's, I think, show nothing but a preoccupation with less imaginative pursuits. The important thing is the increase at the end of the war and the maintenance of a steadily high level to the end of the century, both in number of novels and in percentages; in the twenty-year period ending with 1780, there were only nine novels devoted mainly to America, whereas in the following twenty years there were

[28] Mrs. Brooke spent several years in Canada when her husband was chaplain of the forces at Quebec (Baker, *History of the English Novel*, V, 146.)

[29] Edward Bancroft, M.D., summarizes his experiences and observations in Dutch Guiana in *An Essay on the Natural History of Guiana* . . . (1769), reviewed at length by the *Gentleman's* (XXXIX, 145-149) and the *Monthly* (XL, 198 ff., 276 ff.). In the following year (1770) appeared anonymously the *History of Charles Wentworth*, which the *Monthly* in 1770 attributed to Bancroft (XLIII, 67). Miss Tompkins makes an excellent case for the attribution (*op. cit.*, p. 29).

thirty. The war seems clearly to have played an important part in determining the contents of fiction.

If one should expect a drop in the '90's and demand explanations, he would find several matters to take into account. In the first place, the Revolution had now become a subject for historical treatment,[80] which appears in Mrs. Parsons' *Voluntary Exile* (1795), George Walker's *Cinthelia* (1797), and in large portions of Harriet and Sophia Lee's *Canterbury Tales* (1797-1799), and the *Tales of Truth* of E. H. (1800). Second, the French Revolution was associated with the American Revolution, as indicated in Mrs. Charlotte Smith's *Old Manor House* (1793) and *Young Philosopher* (1798), and in George Walker's *Vagabond*[81] (1799). Third, through the medium of Rousseau, the French Revolution revived interest in the primitive, discussed, either pro or con, in *Berkeley Hall* (1796), Bage's *Man As He Is Not* (1796), Eugenia De Acton's *Disobedience* (1797), *Henry Willoughby* (1798), and Walker's *Vagabond* (1799). Fourth, visits of inspection to America were now popular, and there was a flood of travelers' accounts to stimulate further curiosity.[82] Finally, other causes were giving America good press notices. Prominent and well-publicized liberals fled there—William Cobbett in 1792 and J. B. Priestley in 1794. Imlay's *Emigrants* (1793) had been written "to promote American settlement and easy divorce."[83] The former received more attention than the latter, for land-agents were peddling their wares assiduously. Imlay, in his *Topographical*

[80] Miss Tompkins notes that the war made a slow entry into fiction (*op. cit.,* p. 69).

[81] On Mrs. Smith and Walker see Miss Gregory's chapters in *The French Revolution and the English Novel,* pp. 213 ff. and 135 ff., respectively.

[82] Such accounts appeared by Thomas Anburey in 1789, W. Matthews in 1789, Thomas Coke in 1792 and 1793, P. Campbell in 1793, William Winterbotham in 1795, Henry Wansey in 1796, Isaac Weld in 1799, and William Priest in 1802. For discussions, see Mesick, *op. cit.*

[83] Tompkins, *op. cit.,* p. 184.

*Description* (1792), and Thomas Cooper, in his *Some Information Respecting America* (1794), were "rival auctioneers."[34] Whatever the causes, novels made no inconsiderable use of America in the latter part of the century. Except for the important increase after the war, the details of the distribution are of less moment than the existence of the works and the nature of the contents. A brief survey of the latter will give some indication of the major uses to which writers of fiction put the new world.

The title of *The Adventure of a Bale of Goods from America, in Consequence of the Stamp Act* (1766) is a fairly complete betrayal of the author's ideas; the bale and its shipper have hard luck. The writer uses the ancient technique of posing as the "editor" of some papers that fell into his hands. Exactly the same trick is used by the author of *The Ants* (1767), probably by Philip Withers,[35] which is a political satire also evoked by the Stamp Act. One Eugenio, the observer, is aided by a familiar sylph to watch the goings-on of the ant-world, an allegorical representation of Europe and America; the red ants are the English, the white the French, and the black the Indians. Watching the ant "assembly," obviously Parliament, Eugenio hears the deliberations, which soon give way to an account of imperial conflicts in America.[36] This is roughly the first half of the story, the second part of which deals clearly enough with the Stamp Act from passage to repeal, and finally goes off into a long exhortation on good government.[37] The reviews agreed in hearty condemnation of the allegory.[38] Still another pungent

---

[34] Lowes, *Road to Xanadu*, p. 555. Professor Lowes's notes contain much information on writings about America.

[35] Attribution by Harvard College Library Catalogue and Professor Greenough's Catalogue.

[36] I, 68 ff. Since dates of novels are always mentioned in the text, I omit them in footnotes unless the edition used is of another year. Likewise, footnotes mention the place of publication only when it is other than London, where the great part of all surviving novels appeared.

[37] II, 85 ff.

[38] *Monthly*, XXXVII (1767), 147; *Critical*, XXIV (1767), 34.

allegorical satire is Smollett's *Adventures of an Atom* (1769), attacking the English government in general, but Newcastle, Pitt, and George II in particular; about a hundred pages are devoted to a narrative of the Seven Years' War, of which the sole purpose is to ridicule the British administrations.[39]

Bancroft's *History of Charles Wentworth* (1770) came, as has been said, of personal experience; the hero spends most of his time in South America, where he easily gets rich, but where he generally stays in the background to let the author lecture on natural science.[40] Mrs. Brooke, in her *History of Emily Montague* (1769), spends part of her time in conveying information about Canada, part in describing beauty, and a great deal in telling the thoroughly conventional love-story of Colonel Rivers and Emily, most of the action in which was placed in Canada for no other reason than that the author happened to know about it.[41]

In this period, action and background are fused only in stories in the Noble Savage tradition, which broke into fiction as early as Mrs. Behn's *Oroonoko* and had appeared more recently in Shebbeare's *Lydia* (1755) and Edward Kimber's *History of the Life and Adventures of Mr. Anderson*[42] (1754). Within our period comes Arthur Young's *Adventures of Emmera* (1767), the action of which takes place almost entirely in America. The theme is the happy avoidance of the evils of the

[39] Tobias Smollett, *Works* (New York: Scribner, 1901), XII, 264 ff. A key leaves no doubt about the identity of the allegorical personages: Japan is England, Fatsis(s)io (both spellings appear) North America, and so on. Frank W. Chandler, *The Literature of Roguery* (Boston and New York: Houghton Mifflin, 1907), II, 319, describes the work as "an inane account of the buffooneries and imbecilities of an unreal Japan."

[40] Tompkins, *op. cit.*, pp. 27-28. I have not been able to examine this work.

[41] The *Monthly*, XLI (1769), 232, comments, ". . . the remoteness of the scene does not affect the characters, which are those of English officers and English ladies. . . ."

[42] For a summary of *Lydia* see Bissell, *The American Indian in English Literature*, pp. 89 ff., and George Saintsbury, *The English Novel* (New York: Dutton, 1913), pp. 139-140; of the *Life and Adventures of Mr. Anderson*, Bissell, pp. 87-88.

world by retiring to a rustic hideaway in unspoiled America. In the same year appeared *The Female American; or, the Extraordinary Adventures of Unca Eliza Winkfield*, which, unlike most novels dealing with America, goes back to the seventeenth century and even starts with a general history of the founding of the Virginia colony. A relatively small part of the action, which is not unlike the Pocahontas story, takes place in America;[43] the rest has to do with Robinson-Crusoe-like adventures on an unidentified island. The story is an obvious steal from Defoe, a charge which the author and "editor," that omnipresent intermediary, try to forestall by sheer brazenness.[44] *The Female American* suffered in turn, however, for it was even more unblushingly plagiarized by *The Life and Wonderful Adventures of Henry Lanson* (1800),[45] which has the same general outline and many identical details. The only bluff at originality is changing the chief character to a man, with consequent rearrangement of detail, and making the story contemporary; the island, the Indians, the conversion of them, and the ideal life among them are all the same. But more interesting than the resemblances is the fact that a story with an American background should have been considered salable enough to justify foisting it on the public a second time.

During the '70's the one novel in which America plays an important part, *Adventures of Alonso* (1775), was probably written by an American.[46] But, oddly shunning current events, he is devoted to Latin scenes; about half of the action takes place in South and Central America, where the hero has gone, partly to escape embarrassing circumstances in Europe, partly for a career, and where the author provides us with a good deal of not unentertaining melodrama.

Major use of the war was first made by an apostle of senti-

43 (Newburyport, n.d.), pp. 1-37.
44 Page 127.
45 Conjectural date in the B. M. Catalogue.
46 On the title page of the New York Public Library copy is a written note, "By Mr. Digges of Warburton, in Maryland."

ment, S. J. Pratt, and an apostle of liberty, Robert Bage, a duo who established patterns for many fictional outpourings. In 1780 the former turned out *Emma Corbett, or the Miseries of Civil War,* the title of which is a candid index; in 1781 the latter, *Mount Henneth,* in which the adventures "flow from a state of war, which he detests,"[47] and which moved the *Monthly* to remark on

the Author's sprightly manner of reasoning on a subject which graver politicians have not discussed with more solid argument, in long orations in the house, or in laboured productions from the press.[48]

The action of about one-half of Pratt's work takes place in America, a fact which the *Critical* ignores, while commenting on its "pathetic strain," "vivacity," and "natural flow of imagination."[49] Pratt wanted merely to excite *"the tear of Sensibility,"*[50] and that he succeeded is no doubt indicated by a reference to his work in another novel nineteen years later.[51] In Bage's tale the war is more a convenient background than an integral part of the plot; although one is always conscious of it, it exists more in conversation than in reality. Exposition rather than narrative also carries the war through *Reveries of the Heart; During a Tour through Part of England and France* (1781), which makes little of geography but is an almost continuous diatribe against North's government, especially the American measures. The author is violent against an army "notoriously made up of highway robbers, house-breakers, shop-lifters, swindlers, pick-pockets, thieves, and vagabonds."[52] The travel-note is likewise to be found in *Francis the Philanthropist* (1785), which, in thus introducing one part,

[47] Tompkins, *op. cit.,* p. 196.
[48] LXVI (1782), 130.
[49] XLIX (1780), 462.
[50] (4th ed., London and Bath, n.d.), I, v.
[51] Miss [A. A.] Hutchinson, *Exhibitions of the Heart* (1799), I, 147-148.
[52] I, 174.

In the spring of the year 1781 two English travellers, neither of the smellfungus, the mundungus, or the sentimental-*sans-sentiment*, tribe, set out from Paris,[53] surveys several important elements in the literary scene. Perhaps the more can therefore be made of the author's dependence on the American war in rather lengthy episodes. Here it plays host to the ancient love-and-honor motif, which is worked out in Captain Tom Edwin's conflict between his duty to England and his love for Anna Middleton, daughter of an American senator.[54]

Half of *The Liberal American* (1785) is taken up with two plot-elements involving America, which, however, never emerges distinctly but is only a nominal background for long-familiar actions. The title, therefore, is further evidence of the commercial value of *American*. The hero, Mr. Elliot, "the most accomplished man in America,"[55] is only another of the innumerable second-hand Grandisons. Approximately half of *The Fortunate Sisters* (1782) has to do with Virginia, where the hero, Oliver, has an estate which is highly important in his relations with various English characters. This property has the function of the *deus ex machina* which more usually descends from the Indies. In B. Walwyn's *Love in a Cottage* (1785) "the scene lies in America," and ". . . events . . . are few, but . . . interest the Reader. . . ."[56] In 1786 we jump back into the Noble Savage tradition with *The Cacique of Ontario*, presumably by Professor William Richardson of Glasgow, an example of the long-popular Indian-captivity story.[57]

The first novel with a strikingly original American character and with an unmistakable American background is *Adventures*

---

[53] (Dublin, 1786), p. 37.

[54] Pp. 212 ff.

[55] I, 170.

[56] *Monthly Review*, LXXIV (1786), 472. I have not been able to examine this book.

[57] The attribution is made by Professor Greenough's Catalogue. For an outline see the *Critical Review*, LXII (1786), 392. For a discussion of the dramatized form, see Bissell, *op. cit.*, pp. 142 ff.

of *Jonathan Corncob, Loyal American Refugee* (1787); it is remarkable that it should have such an air of reality, since what the author does, essentially, is to transfer to a new scene the main features of the very old picaresque genre. But he is at the beginning of a new tradition, too, when he makes apparently the first English literary use of *Jonathan* as a type name, which, by the way, appeared in the same year as Tyler's *Contrast*. Although it was the United States, which "by the end of the Revolution . . . had emerged as Brother Jonathan,"[58] our Jonathan is a Loyalist. The *Monthly* commented on the book:

Jonathan's burlesque representations of the manners of his country-folk, the fanatical New Englanders, form, we believe, on the whole, a tolerably good caricature resemblance of the lower classes in that country . . . he thought, perhaps, that his ridicule of *"the Jonathans"* would render his work the more acceptable in this country.[59]

At the start the author represents himself as travelling in an English stagecoach, telling a gentleman his story, and being assured that "it was *strange, 'twas passing strange;'twas pitiful, 'twas wondrous pitiful.'"[60] The gentleman suggests that he write it, an idea quite appealing to the impecunious Jonathan. After this introduction he goes into a tale of adventures which take place almost entirely in America, chiefly in New York and Boston, and also on the high seas between them and in the West Indies, and which show that the author was not ignorant of the scenes he was using. In these places occurs a typical picaresque history with a Loyalist as hero—amorous and military adventures, indifferent self-seeking with indifferent success, with no depth of conviction or emotion but with an occasional touch of feeling, many difficulties with extrication by shrewdness or accident, a nonchalant catch-as-catch-can existence, with humor more important than ethics, with skin to

[58] Constance Rourke, *American Humor* (New York: Harcourt Brace, 1931), p. 12. See also Jennette Tandy, *Crackerbox Philosophers in American Humor and Satire* (New York: Columbia University Press, 1925), pp. 1-19, for Jonathan's history in American literature.
[59] LXXVII (1787), 495-496.
[60] Page 4.

be saved rather than soul, but with a little too much maturity and cynicism to be completely happy-go-lucky. Jonathan is a New Englander who can take care of himself by hook or crook, who can take advantage of what the situation offers, who can see through people and circumstances. He is essentially a sophisticate; he knows the world; but he doesn't stick to business. So he doesn't get on. He is always poor. He is an itinerant rather than a true Yankee. He is too cosmopolitan. He has the Yankee mind, perhaps, but not the Yankee character. He is undependable, superficial; some basic stability is lacking. He is on the fence between the picaresque hero and the real Yankee.

The author has a gift for Smollettian scenes, a trained eye for the ridiculous and the farcical. But the story is not all muscle-comedy; there are touches of the Fielding irony that demolished Thwackum and Square. Everything is virile, and there is an unblushing earthiness that drew reproaches from the reviewers.[61]

As one would expect, there is no serious treatment of the war. It is a comic-opera war, too burly for Gilbert and Sullivan, but not real. There is not a great deal of it; it bobs in and out as Jonathan's worldly progress occasionally takes an unwelcome military turn. Neither he nor anyone else has a real interest in it. It is forgotten at will, and it is never accounted for. Guns resound—or fail to resound—for the comic purposes more generally served by amorous or bacchic episodes. Yet the story probably grew out of some real knowledge of the war.[62]

[61] *Monthly, loc. cit.; Critical,* LXV (1788), 150.

[62] The absence of a real emotional quality does not mean the absence of an occasional specificness suggesting actual experience. Besides, there is a rather provocative parallel between Jonathan and a Loyalist of the time, Benjamin Thompson, Count Rumford, as his story is told by Lewis Einstein, *Divided Loyalties: Americans in England during the War of Independence* (Boston and New York: Houghton Mifflin, 1933), pp. 114 ff. Einstein refers to Rumford as "this penniless and obscure Yankee refugee" (p. 115) and says of him, "Of patriotism he had none, of national feeling as little. . . . He cannot be called a traitor, though he fought against his country. Nor, properly speaking, was he a loyalist, for there was barely profession of loyalty in the service he gave to George the Third" (p. 114). All that would do admirably for Jonathan.

74

Two years later the war makes its next appearance—in H. M. Williams's *Julia* (1789), about half of which, the episodic narrative of Mr. F——, deals with America in 1776.[63] In 1790 there was a triple outburst of Americana—*Louisa Wharton*,[64] *Caroline* by Dennett Jaques,[65] and Mrs. Lennox's *Euphemia*. The first two are concerned almost wholly with the war, which in both cases is simply added to a typical love-story without any real fusion of elements, so that what the *Critical* says of *Caroline* is applicable to both:

> This lady has no great right to the name of heroine, for she remains quietly at New York, in peace from all attacks but those of love. Though the story is told in a plain easy manner, and amuses for the time, we cannot avoid styling it a trite, hackneyed tale, while reflection does not furnish one hint or character to induce us to make a single effort to rescue it from oblivion.[66]

Mrs. Lennox devoted about half of *Euphemia* to an account of America which is mainly informative, based, as it is, on personal experience; as for the plot, it could just as well be placed anywhere. Speaking of these novels about America, Miss Tompkins says:

> . . . we see little of the normal life of the country, and must not expect any great degree of accuracy in the pictures of its conditions. There is one pleasant exception; the popularity of American subjects stirred in Mrs. Charlotte Lennox, then an old woman, the memories of her youth, and in *Euphemia* (1790) she conducts that patient wife to New York, takes her up the Hudson to Albany with a Dutch skipper, shows her an Indian camp and the working of the Indian fur

---

There is a rough parallel of experiences: clerking in a New England store, interest in cod trade, moving to Boston, being attacked as a Tory, indifferent departure from family, naval experiences, and so on. Coincidence, of course, may be the explanation.

[63] (1790), I, 241 ff.

[64] This novelette is undated. Internal evidence suggests approximately 1790.

[65] On the flyleaf of Vol. I of the Harvard Library copy (London, 1830) there is a penciled note, "Written by Dennett Jaques of Chelsea—born Sep 11 1758/ Died 1835." The review in the *Critical* quoted above makes it clear that the surviving 1830 work is the same as that of 1790.

[66] LXX (1790), 97.

trade, and causes her to winter in Schenectady and Fort Hunter, where the service is read in Dutch and Indian in the Mohawk chapel. *Euphemia* blends instruction and entertainment according to the old recipe. . . .[67]

Mrs. Rowson's *History of Charlotte Temple*[68] (1791) places a typical seduction story in America, where there is no reason for its being except that the distance impedes rescue and thus facilitates Mrs. Rowson's reaching a lachrymose extreme. As in *Caroline* of the preceding year, the characters are almost all from England, the plot is from England, and except for the place-names the background is no more American than English. Even the tremendous doses of pathos seem insufficient to account for the novel's running to over one hundred and fifty editions. In her autobiographic *Fille de Chambre* (1792) Mrs. Rowson again used America, although only for about one-sixth of the book, which tells of Miss Abthorpe's leaving England to join her father in America, of their uneventful life there before the war, and of their distresses after the outbreak of hostilities.[69]

The year 1793 saw Mrs. Smith's *Old Manor House* and Gilbert Imlay's *Emigrants*.[70] In accordance with her constant love of America, Mrs. Smith places about half of her story across the ocean. Letters dated in 1776 set the time, but the war, which provides the starting point, is ultimately submerged by the stress of personal interests of which Orlando, the hero, is the center. All the action of *The Emigrants* takes place in America, with various interests and motives: the love-affair of Caroline and Capt. Arl—ton; the letters on divorce, rebuked by the reviewers;[71] accounts of American life, and "several

[67] *Op. cit.*, pp. 184-185.
[68] Though Mrs. Rowson is usually treated as belonging to American literature, her English birth, and the fact that she spent a good many years in England, justify her inclusion here.
[69] (Baltimore, 1795), pp. 154 ff.
[70] Imlay's case is the reverse of Mrs. Rowson's; born an American, he became somewhat a citizen of the world. His book was published in London in 1793.
[71] *Critical*, IX (New Arrangement, 1793), 155; *Monthly*, XI (Second Series, 1793), 469.

lively descriptions of American scenes."[72] Twice again Mrs. Smith uses American scenes—in *Wanderings of Warwick* (1794), which is concerned largely with the war and the West Indies, and in *The Young Philosopher* (1798), which mingles a war-story with an idealization of America according to a formula indicated by her quoting Crèvecoeur.[73]

The war really comes into its own in Mrs. Parsons' *Voluntary Exile* (1795), which devotes nearly all of its five volumes to events in America. The war is done in detail from beginning to end, and the narrative is interlarded with all sorts of side-episodes; the hero, Henry Biddulph, in addition to being in every battle of importance, spends some time in a Quaker retreat, meets and has long talks with a hermit (a pet fancy of the age), gets lost in the woods and thus makes possible the introduction of various irrelevant matters, meets and falls in love with Harriott Franklyn, in his affair with whom the conventional complications drag through three and a half volumes. The war, as already noted, has a remarkable run at the end of the century, figuring centrally in Mrs. Hervey's *History of Ned Evans*[74] (1796), George Walker's *Cinthelia*[75] (1797), The Officer's Tale and The Clergyman's Tale in the Lees' *Canterbury Tales* (1799), and the long story "The Soldiers" in *Tales of Truth* (1800).

Of the remaining works in the final decade, Mrs. Anna Maria Mackenzie's *Slavery* (1792) may be dismissed here with the remark that the title is sufficiently clear and the note that the action dashes back and forth between England and the West Indies, with a bit of the American Revolution and the French Revolution tossed in for good emotional measure; of *Idalia . . . Founded on Facts* (1800) it is only necessary to remark

[72] *Monthly, loc. cit.,* p. 468.
[73] III, 32. Mrs. Smith footnotes her source.
[74] See the *Monthly,* XXI (Second Series, 1796), 207. This work was not available for study.
[75] See the *Critical,* XXIII (New Arrangement, 1798), 352-353. I have not seen the book.

that it is obviously not founded on facts, that there is no reason for staging one-half of the action in Canada, whither, without effort at local color, publisher Lane's hack had merely transported a set of English characters in archetypal relations to one another.

Finally there is a group of five novels which may be treated as a unit because of their opposition or devotion to the Noble-Savage-Golden-Age-in-America ideal. Two of these are relatively well-known—Bage's *Man As He Is Not* (1796), which is the decalogue of primitive virtue, and Walker's *Vagabond* (1799) which belongs to the satirically reactionary school of the *Anti-Jacobin*. Three others, quite important, have been practically ignored: *Berkeley Hall* (1796), which prods the savage with one amusing dig after another; *Disobedience* (1797) by Eugenia De Acton and *Henry Willoughby* (1798), which plunge into a headlong glorification of the American backwoods. In this collection, the Age of Reason and Romanticism are talking simultaneously.

*Man As He Is Not* contrasts primitive virtue and civilized lack of virtue by throwing the Grandisonian and painfully priggish Hermsprong, supposedly an American Indian, into English scenes, where his excellence puts everyone else to shame, or at least attempts to. The lesson is reinforced with a long disquisition on the differences between European and savage society,[76] but, quite ironically, a time-worn happy-ending technique seriously damages the lesson by turning Hermsprong into an Englishman who had merely been brought up among the Indians.

Walker's *Vagabond* slashes at everything "liberal"—with chief cuts at Hume, Godwin, and Rousseau among persons; the French Revolution among events; and the noble savage, natural virtue, liberty, and equality among ideas. The chief characters are Professor Stupeo, Dr. Alogos (whose names are confessional), his niece Laura, who is the balance wheel, and her

[76] (3rd ed., 1809), II, 19 ff.

lover Frederick Fenton, a student boiling over with radical enthusiasms. The central part of the book is an excursion to found a backwoods Utopia in America, where squabbles, Indian scalpings, and mosquitoes effectually wreck illusions.[77]

*Berkeley Hall,* very long in a day of long novels, but amusing in a day of dull novels, is one of the few in which the action takes place almost exclusively in America. The starting-point is the home of a refugee nonjuror, Dr. Homily, in Elizabeth, New Jersey, where there occur various domestic incidents and love-stories, conventional enough in type, but told with unusual virility and humor and with delightful absence of sensibility. The time is vague, though references to fighting with the French and a passing proviso, "should they [the colonies and mother-country] ever be separated from each other,"[78] furnish a *terminus ad quem.* The most interesting section centers in an associate of Homily, one Dr. Sourby, a Scotch "philosopher" apparently modeled on Hume, not unlikable, but sharply satirized for his modern view of society and politics, which he imposes on his ward, Timothy Tickle, a hero mainly in the Tom Jones tradition. The satire takes the form of a hilarious experiment in utopianism, a communistic venture in Pennsylvania. This comes to the same end as the similar idealistic scheme in *The Vagabond,* with a good deal of farce, but with an underlying humor and geniality equaled in no other work of this school.

Finally we have *Henry Willoughby* (1798) and Eugenia De Acton's *Disobedience* (1797), which bring to a close the study of Romantic primitivism with portraits of ideal rustic communities of which the success is narrated with equal parts of humorlessness and ecstasy. The former tells of Anachoropolis, near the Falls of St. Anthony on the Mississippi, the latter of a prodigiously flourishing private venture in Kentucky.

This whole group of books provides an at times fascinating

[77] (1st American, from 4th English, ed., Boston, 1800), pp. 130 ff.
[78] III, 404.

illustration of the dependence of fiction on travel books; a study of sources shows clearly how some of the ideas about America got into novels. Some writers acknowledge their borrowings. Mrs. Smith, we have already noted, quotes Crève-coeur. The author of *Berkeley Hall* refers to a work which is still exasperatingly elusive:

The author of *The Book, or Continuation of the Moral World,* adver-tises for volunteers to go as a colony into some interior part of America; and the basis of his plan is, that there is to be no exclusive property in things and persons; all individual preferences to be resisted, and each mother is to suckle the child of another rather than her own.[79]

In *The Vagabond* George Walker refers sneeringly to Imlay's account,[80] which is mentioned more neutrally by the author of *Disobedience.*[81] Imlay, in fact, was a cornucopia; after getting out his guidebook to Kentucky in 1792, he incorporated a good deal of it in his *Emigrants*[82] of the next year; then the route of travel to the West which he describes—Philadelphia to Pitts-burgh overland, and then down the Ohio—is followed pretty closely by both *The Vagabond*[83] and *Disobedience,*[84] so that we have one travel-book and three novels with marked similarities in outline. Imlay even contributes to Mrs. Parsons' *Voluntary Exile.*[85] Finally, it is his *Emigrants,* I strongly suspect, which provides the locale of the American venture in *Henry Willough-by.* Henry joins a Quaker community at the Falls of St.

[79] II, 339 note.
[80] After giving a very colorful description of Kentucky scenery, Walker notes, "See Imley's [*sic*] *Romantic* account of Kentucky" (p. 166 note). Walker is probably satirizing Imlay in Citizen Common, who flamboyantly recounts the glories of Kentucky (pp. 165 ff.).
[81] A quotation on Kentucky scenery is considered amply identified merely by "Imlay" (IV, 204 note).
[82] I, 48 ff.
[83] Pp. 164 ff.
[84] IV, 94 ff.
[85] In *A Topographical Description of the Western Territory of North America* (3rd ed., 1797), p. 169, Imlay describes the "modulated buffoonery of the mocking bird." Mrs. Parsons says that the mockingbird "amuses him-self with imitating all other birds" (II, 118). But Imlay's exact words appear in *Disobedience* (IV, 203).

Anthony, of which I find no historical account.[86] But in *The Emigrants* Captain Arl—ton had visited this region and immediately afterward had gone into a description of the *"Illinois country"*[87] which, by a quick-reading plagiarist, might have been taken to refer to the St. Anthony region. At any rate, the novel contains several pages of scenic description strongly reminiscent of the Imlay rhapsody.[88] *Henry Willoughby* then makes a remarkable stab at literary honesty by using quotation marks around a long account of the life at the Quaker community of Anachoropolis,[89] but I have yet to discover either the passage or anything about an Anachoropolis. The novel account is especially long-winded in setting forth a modern educational system, the main thesis of which, self-government, was much "in the air" at the time. The division of people into five ages suggests Rousseau's, but Rousseau's groups have different characteristics.

The most complex compilation of sources, however, occurs in *Disobedience,* which makes one acknowledgment to Imlay, but which then goes on, with no further hint of indebtedness, to describe an American paradise in a rhapsodic welter of borrowings from Imlay's *Topographical Description,* Crève-coeur's *Letters from an American Farmer,* Filson's *Discovery, Settlement, and Present State of Kentucky,* a letter from Thomas Cooper on affairs in Pennsylvania, a letter from a resident of Muskingum, Ohio, and possibly a letter from Priestley, already settled in Pennsylvania. *Disobedience* was published by the notorious Lane of Leadenhall Street, who just the year before had issued a single-volume collection of a dozen works on America, including those by Filson and Cooper and headed by

[86] *Henry Willoughby,* II, 224 ff. Jonathan Carver's *Travels Through the Interior Parts of North-America, In the Years 1766, 1767, and 1768* (1778), pp. 70-71, describes the place favorably, but in much too little detail to provide a basis for the elaborate account in the novel.

[87] III, 36 ff.

[88] II, 227-230.

[89] II, 231 ff.

a "third edition" of Imlay. It is no great gamble to picture Lane setting a hack at work with a scissors on the firm's own compilation of Americana. The travel books had had a good sale; hence they were whipped together into a novel. What is more, the Lane people, or, specifically, Miss De Acton, exhibited the ingenuity of long experience in artistic thievery, for almost never were borrowings made in order of occurrence; instead, passages were taken from widely separated places and patched together in crazy-quilt fashion. Of such value was the Arcadian-American dream to one sector of the reading public.[90]

This note on thefts concludes a sketch of those novels between 1760 and 1800 in which American scenes and affairs played a leading or at least an important role. To these might be added a few others which contained major episodes across the Atlantic. Charles Johnstone's *Chrysal* (1760-1765) had a long section on life among the Indians,[91] which will immediately call to mind the adventures of Lismahago in *Humphry Clinker* (1771). In the longest single episode in *The Birmingham Counterfeit* (1772) the shilling-hero gets into the possession of Isabella, daughter of Lord Lenox, and learns her past history. Prisoner on a French ship, she was rescued from it by an English boat, the captain of which promptly informed her that he had to go to South Carolina. He fell in love with her and, about the time they arrived at "Charles-Town," two months later, secured from her a promise in writing.

He took genteel lodgings for Isabella in Charles-Town, and watched every opportunity to give her fresh marks of his delicate love and constant esteem.

Their stay at Charles-Town was only two months, which passed away swiftly in the eyes of Isabella. . . . The time being arrived for their

[90] I hope at some time to present a detailed study of the influence of travel-books on prose fiction in this period, since I already have on hand considerable evidence. The novels are not important enough to make their sources a matter of moment, but the revamping of factual accounts into fictitious *mélanges* shows not only the popularity of American subjects but also the devious means by which impressions of America were created.

[91] For a summary see Bissell, *op. cit.,* pp. 96 ff.

departure from Carolina, they set sail, and in two months arrived at the mouth of the British channel. . . .[92]

As there is no effort to recreate local background, one may assume that some touch of America was a conventional advantage.

Sometimes America merely serves as the starting-point for a novel, as in Mrs. Gibbes' *Friendship in a Nunnery* (1778), in which the heroine "is driven to board in the . . . convent by the American troubles."[93] For *The American Wanderer* (1783) America does nothing more than provide a title of presumptive sales-value for an author who might just as well style himself "an *English Recluse*."[94] References to America are generally after-thoughts, and the writer is so weak technically that he constantly gives himself away; such a phrase as "our gay neighbors,"[95] applied to the French, would hardly have come from an American in the days when America was months away.

The hero of *The Kentish Curate* (1786) is "carried to America," where he has dealings with Congress and goes through a military campaign.[96] In *The Fair Syrian* (1787) a philosophic Quaker makes an excursion to Philadelphia and discusses the war.[97] America joins another new contributor to the novel, Science, in *The Balloon* (1786), in which a young American, wrecked on an African island, makes a smoke balloon that is then taken charge of by a spirit, Amiel, as a means of introducing a satirical survey of politics.[98] The *Book of Oddities* (1791) by "Toby Broadgrin" contains a short story of which

[92] II, 149-150. The *Critical* quotes the "genteel-lodgings" paragraph and snorts, "Is not this exquisitely sentimental?" (XXXIII, 326).

[93] *Critical*, XLVI (1778), 300.

[94] *Critical*, LV (1783), 341. In 1792 an anonymous correspondent of the *Gentleman's*, criticizing Wesley's love affair in Georgia many years before, emits a sneer, in passing, at this novel: "Instead of *wandering* in the beaten paths of France, permit me to say a word or two to my *first wander* [*sic*] in the *then* unknown paths of America. . . ." (LXII[1], 23).

[95] (Dublin, 1783), p. viii. See also pp. 4, 8, 221.

[96] *Critical*, LXIII (1787), 77.

[97] *Monthly*, LXXVI (1787), 325-328.

[98] Tompkins, *op. cit.*, pp. 190-191.

the scene is Paraguay.[99] Reviewing *Memoirs of a Scots Heiress* (1791) the *Critical* took especial notice of the "American adventures," which,

with the death of Captain Dibart, are well executed, and we have seldom seen a scene of more interesting pathos, than the whole of the adventure on the sand-bank, concluding with the loss of the paddle.[100]

The last indication of the extent of fictional and popular interest in America lies in the number of editions of these novels. Of the two thousand novels written in the period, it is safe to say that seventy-five per cent never got beyond a first printing, while such important ones as *Humphry Clinker* were constantly reprinted. Two editions indicate considerable attention, three positive popularity. Hence it is interesting to find *Chrysal* going through twenty-one editions.[101] Pratt's *Emma Corbett*, Walker's *Vagabond*, and Bage's *Man As He is*, all greatly concerned with America, ran up six editions apiece, Mrs. Smith's *Old Manor House* and *Ethelinde* five each,[102] and Mrs. Brooke's *Emily Montague*, four. The following had three editions: *Female American, Caroline, Man As He Is Not, Mount Henneth, Friendship in a Nunnery, Francis the Philanthropist, Slavery,* and *Theodore Cyphon*, and the following, two: *Berkeley Hall, Adventures of Emmera, Liberal American, Henry Willoughby, Adventures of an Atom, History of Ned Evans,* and *Adventures of Alonso*. It is not impossible that the American elements in these novels had something to do with their popularity. At any rate, the public was served with many transatlantic scenes, and few subjects had a wider audience.

99 (3rd ed., Dublin, 1791), pp. 247 ff.

100 III (New Arrangement, 1791), 356.

101 All figures represent my own count in the author-file of Professor Greenough's Catalogue. They include both English and American editions, and two editions appearing at different places (usually London and Dublin) in the same year are counted separately.

102 Mrs. Smith was very popular, and, since all her novels introduced America is greater or lesser degree, it is interesting to observe that *Emmeline* achieved four editions, *Celestina* and *Desmond* three, and *The Banished Man, Solitary Wanderer,* and *Marchmont,* two.

That situation may be attributed in large part, either directly or indirectly, to the war. When the American Revolution halved the British Empire, it apparently served, not to decrease literary interest in the West, but to publicize America. Through its own dramatic appeal, and through the general interest aroused by the new political and economic situations which it produced, the war was influential in keeping English literary discussion of America at a higher level than that of the East and West Indies, despite their remaining British. Contradictory though it seem, it is also probable that the war strengthened English interest in the Indies by making it of necessity a more concentrated one. But most important, the Revolution stimulated an easily discernible increase in the literary interest in America; after 1780, many more novels than before dealt mainly with the Western Hemisphere.

The interest is demonstrated by the frequent use of *America* or *American* in titles, by the popularity of the books with American scenes, by the fact that about fifty per cent of all the novels examined included some use of America, whether in passing reference, in an episode, or throughout a major part of the plot. Furthermore, some three dozen novels used America as the whole background or as a very important part of it, and another dozen contained important American episodes. From these we can form some idea of what America meant to the reading public—distant scenes, the war, the Indian, and, toward the end of the century, an outburst of utopianism associated with the French Revolution and stimulated by travel-literature. Arguing the ideal pro and con, a whole coterie of novels refurbishes travel accounts for a second consumption; the arch-thief of them all is a veritable olio of Crèvecoeur, Imlay, Cooper, and Filson, singers of glorious America. America was in the imagination again as it had not been since the days of Raleigh. And the imagination was touched off by the war.

CHAPTER IV

## NARRATIVE TREATMENT OF THE REVOLUTION

i

In studying the influence of the war on the production of
novels in Chapter II, and on the extent of the fictional interest
in America in Chapter III, we have been dealing, in a measure,
with the conjectural; noting earlier and later conditions, and
from them deducing probabilities. Now, however, we come to
certainties—the influence of the war on the contents of novels.
The outmoded best sellers, saccharine or sensational, are open
before us, and it is to be seen what they said.

By way of prolegomenon we may recur to the infertility of
the periodical essay, which often bordered on fiction. In 1779
Mackenzie's *Mirror* printed a letter from a subscriber who
wished for "intelligence from America" but supposed the
omission "was in order to save the tax upon newspapers."[1] The
*Lounger* merely praised Strahan the printer for his early com-
prehension of the dispute and his anxiety that "a permanent
harmony [be] restored between the two countries."[2] Cumberland's *Observer* pictured a querulous Leontine raging at the
"fine pass" the world had come to, especially in its economic
derangements; he, of course, had supposed that that was "what
it would come to with your damned American War."[3] The
closest that Godwin's *Enquirer* came to that sad matter was a
long comment, psychologically penetrating, on Washington's

[1] *Ed. cit.,* I, 7.
[2] Henry Mackenzie, *The Lounger. A Periodical Paper, Published at Edinburgh
in the Years 1785 and 1786* (4th ed., 1788), I, 270.
[3] Richard Cumberland, *The Observer* (New ed., 1822), I, 112.

farewell.[4] And that was the story as told by the latter-day Spectators.

In the years 1766-1768, however, *The Batchelor*, "by J. Jephson, John Courtenay, etc.,"[5] had united the subjects of war and America, but here, of course, the reference was to the Seven Years' War,[6] which had its adherents among novelists for many years. The moralizing note creeps into both Mrs. Brooke's *Lady Julia Mandeville* (1763), in which Mr. Mandeville attacks

a war which has depopulated our country, and loaded us with a burden of debt from which nothing can extricate us but the noble spirit of public frugality;[7]

and into *Memoirs of a Coquet* (1765), in which Sir Simon Hubble-Bubble, "having squeezed a great many thousands out of a place under the government," defends the *status quo:*

Don't tell *me* . . . that the nation is in a bad way—all party, prejudice—'tis as plain as two and three make seven—Don't we go on without supplies?—What the devil would you have?—Have'nt we got a d--n-d large quantity of land yonder, there, in *America,* and a fine fleet of ships at home?—What the devil would you have?[8]

But most frequently the war gains entrée through the hero's going off to fight, and thus being off-stage for a while, or else coming back wounded or promoted. So Charles, the illegitimate son of a French general in Mrs. Griffith's *Delicate Distress* (1769), won a convenient captaincy,[9] but Bellozane, in Mrs. Smith's *Emmeline* (1788), was so pressed by social demands in France "that he had hardly time to modernize his appearance after his American campaigns."[10] Sometimes the war merely

[4] William Godwin, *The Enquirer* (1797), pp. 313-314.
[5] Penciled on verso of title-page of Harvard Library copy (Dublin, 1769).
[6] I, 84; II, 121, 152.
[7] E. Phillips Poole, ed. (London, 1930), p. 120.
[8] Pp. 135-136. For uniformity's sake blocked quotations of speeches are left without quotation marks, which in the originals are used not at all or very erratically. Other punctuation is preserved.
[9] (Dublin, 1787), I, 102, 115.
[10] (Philadelphia, etc., 1802), II, 253.

figures in a brief anecdote, particularly in such a potpourri of fact and fiction as *The Fashionable Tell-Tale* (1778) or as the *Book of Oddities* (1791) by "Toby Broadgrin." The former has an anecdote about the commander of an English ship stationed at Boston,[11] the latter about one "Americanus," who,

noble by birth, great in sentiment, genius, and valour . . . was . . . appointed commander in chief of an expedition that was glorious as it was arduous. He conquered an almost inaccessible enemy; and the success that crowned this enterprize could be surpassed by nothing but the courage, skill, and intrepidity of the leader.[12]

All this sounds like Wolfe, but from so promising a start the author goes off to a joyful depiction of the commander's scandalous wife. Wolfe and Quebec, however, had a mild run in romance. Mentoria, the Athene of Mrs. Rowson's *Mentoria* (1791), is the daughter of a "brave soldier" who was killed at Quebec.[13] Captain M——, in Ann Thomas' *Adolphus de Biron* (1794), entertains his company with a tale of his experiences at Quebec, "which was purchased with the Loss of that youthful Hero the brave and gallant Wolfe."[14] In Sophia Lee's Clergyman's Tale in the *Canterbury Tales* (1799), Henry Pembroke, unhappy in love—here is an example of a very frequent motivation of a transatlantic tour—goes to Canada, meets Wolfe, who quite approves of his "conscious integrity," and whose "marks of confidence" change Henry into " a military phaenomenon."[15] After Quebec, described in detail, Henry is threatened with "a consumption," a pet tear-jerking device of lady novelists, and hence returns home. In *The Sailor Boy* (1800) there is a young man who "longs to be a soldier, that he might go to America to fight the French."[16] The business of shipping young warriors to Canada hangs over into later years;

[11] (2nd ed., 1778), I, 36.
[12] (3rd ed., Dublin, 1791), p. 123.
[13] (Philadelphia, 1794), I, 15.
[14] (Plymouth, n.d.), II, 96.
[15] Harriet and Sophia Lee, *Canterbury Tales* (1797 ff.), III, 248 ff.
[16] II, 140.

in *Idalia* (1800), the action of which takes place in the '80's, Captain Brisbane is so dispatched, merely so that he can be rumored dead and later revived and happily brought to light.[17] The Seven Years' War, it is obvious, made no contribution to plots or technique.

ii

The American Revolution, in one way or another, figures in approximately seventy-five novels between 1776 and 1800; they are distributed as follows:

| Period | Number of Novels | Per- centage |
|---|---|---|
| 1776-1780...... | 6 | 15% |
| 1781-1785...... | 9 | 20% |
| 1786-1790...... | 25 | 32% |
| 1791-1795...... | 22 | 30% |
| 1796-1800...... | 15 | 15% |

The figures justify Miss Tompkins' remark that "it was ten years before it [the war] was at all freely handled"[18] by the novelists. The slow start seems explainable on the ground that time was needed for perspective and for some infiltration of knowledge through acquaintance with ex-soldiers and through histories of the war. Once the subject was established, fashion would keep it going for a time, and then there would naturally be a decline; the whole curve of the rise and fall of the subject is about what one would expect.

In discussing the novels here counted, it seems most convenient to proceed chronologically; to attempt a purely topical procedure would involve us in long-drawn-out and confusing division and subdivision. For the sake of a working classification, I shall group the novels by half-decades, and the advance

[17] I, 242; II, 249, 257.

[18] *Op. cit.,* p. 69. For the figures on which the percentages are based, see the table of Negative Results in Chapter III.

from period to period will give some evidence of what the war meant in fiction during the last quarter of the century. In each quinquennium it will be simplest first to dispose rapidly of those works which mentioned America most cursorily and then to outline those stories in which there is more elaboration.

While fighting was still in progress, it received only a brief glance from fiction. S. J. Pratt's *Pupil of Pleasure* (1776), primarily an anti-Chesterfield tract, talks about the war but makes no real dramatic use of it. Lieutenant Vernon writes that he can have the command of a company in America, which, he feels sure, will be economically advantageous. Then, being a model young man, he remembers himself: "Another point is, my own thirst for glory."[19] Still more incidental is the place given American affairs in a trio of novels in 1778. Miss Bingley, in Lady Mary Hamilton's *Munster Village,* while writing to Lady Eliza Finlay on the technique of husband-management, says she would adopt "the late example of the *Premier* with the Opposition" in agreeing with the hypothetical gentleman and in thus compelling him "to commence hostilities with himself if he meant to *continue* the dispute." She footnotes *Premier:* "In the conciliatory Measures proposed concerning America."[20] A similar sort of reference-value appears twice again. The satirical *Trip to Melasge* snaps at the impertinent person who

will trip across the room, and, with an air of intimacy and friendship, whisper in your ear what is universally known—a courier is arrived from Hanover—a messenger is hourly expected from America with particular dispatches, and, with shrugs and airs of importance, insinuate he is in the secret. . . .[21]

In another fantastic voyage, *The Travels of Hildebrand Bow-*

---

[19] (2nd ed., 1777), II, 51.

[20] (Dublin, 1779), II, 68. The reference is no doubt to the proposals of Lord North in February, 1778, to "a bewildered and dejected house" (see Trevelyan, *The American Revolution*, Part III, p. 356).

[21] I, 138-139.

*man* (1778), the traveler leaves Luxo-Volupto, that is, England, on February 1, 1776:

Our voyage was prosperous and agreeable during the whole month of February, and most part of that of March; no occurrence happened worth mentioning, except that we met, and spoke with several Armoserian [i.e., American] Privateers; who paid due honours to the Bonhommican [French?] flag, seeing us so well prepared for them; or what is more probable, having no design to make themselves any new enemies.[22]

With how little seriousness fiction could regard the war is shown in *The Relapse* (1779), in which Charles Sidley, tired of country life, had a sudden yearning for the military. "The fatal American War roused me from my inactivity, and called me to arms." Then he met Louisa Palmer, fell in love, married, and settled down easily. "Farewel [*sic*] to arms, to glory, to fame! Instead of being a conqueror, I became a willing slave. . . ."[23]

The decade was not to turn, however, without one real war-novel; four years had changed Pratt's idea of an American campaign as an easy means of increasing one's income, and in 1780 he got out *Emma Corbett,* the subtitle of which shows how thoroughly the war had become a reality—*The Miseries of Civil War.* Under such auspices, it is not surprising that Pratt should be an unremitting taskmaster in pouring pathos on the reader, in turning on tears with a fire-hose. The difficulties start in one plot involving the heroine's brother Edward, who, before going to America to fight, had secretly wed Louisa Hammond. He is reported dead; Louisa becomes a mother; and then Edward is again reported alive, but determined to keep on fighting for the colonies. Louisa goes insane, Edward is really killed, and then Louisa dies. Here is enough of the determinedly macabre, but there is still more in the other plot, that of Emma Corbett and Henry Hammond, who goes to

[22] Pp. 373-374.
[23] (1780), I, 40.

91

America to fight on the English side. Here is a fine setting for carnage. Emma's father is violently against the war, especially because of a bequest of £5000 to Emma "provided she *does not marry an officer, or any person concerned in promoting the contest*,"[24] which, deaf to parental persuasion, she refuses. Here the war is getting entangled in the popular bequest-romance, not to mention a variation of the love-and-honor theme. Henry writes that, as conciliation is in progress, he looks forward to

the joy when a truant child is restored to the protection of an offended parent. Great-Britain, all insulted as she is, ineffective as have been her affectionate advances, and scorned as have been her professed kindness [*sic*], shall receive with transport her America. The temporary estrangement shall only serve, like the quarrel of friends, to brighten the bonds of future amity.[25]

But the amorous metaphor does not stop the cannon, and Pratt perpetrates his next shock on the readers by having Henry reported killed. So Emma, in defiance of all the canons of conduct for young ladies, hies herself off to America on a solo quest for her lover, and "Oh, the pity of it" is the tune of her forlorn search. Pratt treats us to a good deal of this sort of thing:

We hear the shrieks of widows, and daughters, and fatherless children, as we move forward. Families are busied in burying their dead, rescued from the corruption of promiscuous carnage. Hearses and funerals pass thick along. The bell of death tolls out in every street; but Emma is still fixed in her design.[26]

The initial situation begins to fulfil its potentialities when Emma finds the body of her brother Edward and has to help bury it. Then Henry is reported 𝔇𝔈𝔄𝔇;[27] she finds him "with an arrow sticking in his bosom"[28] and sucks out the poison, saving him long enough for a death-bed marriage. But she has been

[24] II, 148.
[25] II, 170-171.
[26] III, 78.
[27] III, 98.
[28] III, 111. For another use of the poisoned-arrow motif, see *Elfrida* (1786), III, 159.

92

poisoned and **MUST DIE**; soon she is **DEAD**,[29] and Pratt has triumphantly finished his necrology. In this book America is adding new lines to old patterns, although, with the predetermined slaughter and the emotional wash, the result may seem a bizarre congeries of rattletrap romance and silly sensationalism. So it is, largely, and yet it is not without occasional power to move. Further, Pratt could make his characters a little more alive than most of his contemporaries, and if, by the standards of our times, he is ridiculous, still, by the standards of his times, he was unusually effective.

### iii

In the first half of the '80's the war not only gets into a few more novels but also captures more space and earns a slightly more varied treatment. It is a little less of a minor match on a side-court, and there is more action, either narrated or implied. An apparently unique treatment of a theme popularized by Defoe occurs in Helenus Scott's *Adventures of a Rupee* (1782), in which appears

one of those unfortunate females, who fall a prey to the passions of men, before they know the value of that virtue which they can never recal [*sic*]. She had been present at several engagements in the West Indies and America, where she had fought on board a ship of war, performing every office of a seaman with skill and courage. So well had she acquitted herself, that she received the proportion of a man, on a division of prize money.[30]

Nostalgia for the departed treasure was more frequent than Amazonian achievement. Nor was success always the note of the military incidents, which were rather on the bloody side. In a chapter of alleged autobiography in *Man in the Moon* (1783) William Thomson muses on childhood pleasures in his rural Scotch home, where he hopes to end his days "lamenting

[29] III, 181, 190.
[30] (A new ed., 1783), p. 115.

93

the hard fate of five faithful brothers untimely slain on the American shore."[31] Untimely demise is much less tearful in Theophilus Johnson's *Phantoms* (1783), in which Mr. Sandys, accused by his mistress of stinginess, snaps back,

pray what do you mean by ungenerous, Madam? Was it ungenerous to settle an hundred a year upon you for life? And pray, Madam, was it ungenerous to buy your brother a commission, which was all money thrown away; for in three months he was sent to America and was killed in the first skirmish. . . .[32]

But flippancy in the morgue is rare, and death usually plays a heavy dirge on the heartstrings, especially when it unravels the Plot of the Divided Family, established by Pratt. Mrs. Catherine Parry imitates this in *Eden Vale* (1784), throwing prospective brothers-in-law, Melville and Conway, into the war on opposite sides. Mrs. Parry's method is to hide her head and the heads of all her characters in the sand; thus she glibly, and with no indication of interest on her part or anybody else's part, reports Melville, in the British army, as "gone abroad somewhere." Then Edward Conway's family becomes aware that he also is in America, but

extremely zealous in the interest of the Bostonians. Totally ignorant of the world or its pursuits, we should never have concerned ourselves in ministerial affairs, had not our Edward's situation rendered everything that passed in America of the greatest consequence to us. I examined the news-papers with careful anxiety; the accounts from that part of the world filled me with the most alarming apprehensions. I wrote to beseech him to return home. . . . What could steel his heart against our ardent entreaties![33]

It is inevitable, the reader sees long in advance, that one of the combatants kill the other; Conway is the victim, but, for tragedy's sake, Melville must also die.

Besides these tales of reckless passion are others in which the

[31] I, 50.
[32] I, 140.
[33] I, 60-61.

young men are thoroughly delighted to avoid hostilities. In *The Ring* (1784) Captain Belleville not only shows an amazing ignorance of the possible going-abroad of his regiment, but thinks he will apply for an exchange, "as my mother and aunt both declare they can never survive my being sent to America."[34] This is less surprising than Captain Hillgrove's comment on the effected exchange—"at which I sincerely rejoice, as his own regiment is ordered to America."[35] There is other evidence that the book was written by a fluttering "young lady," in whose eyes, as always, the army was only a sort of tangent to the social whirl, amorous but proper. An interpolated narrative tells the story of the Marquis de Guzman, who was captured by an American privateer and taken to Boston, but who bought his liberty and got back to England without difficulty. Of a piece is *False Friends* (1785), in which Lord Weston and his brother Ned, harassed by gambling debts and unsuccessful love, look toward America, where, as the elder writes, "a friendly bullet may put an end to all my cares."[36] Lord Weston gets a captaincy, Ned a lieutenancy. Their friend Stanley tries to cheer them up with the news that a peace is in the offing; the Rt. Hon. Lord Wimbleton pities the "noble fellows";[37] Miss Eliza Watson turns "pale as ashes";[38] but fortunately for the health of everyone, "the generous Hervey" is soon able to write, "You will have no occasion to go to America, as a peace is nearly concluded."[39]

The remaining works in the period try to go beyond the frivolous. *Adventures of a Hackney Coach* (1781), an episodic tale, ranges from the satiric to the maudlin. At one point there is a eulogy of

[34] III, 48-49.
[35] III, 94.
[36] I, 121.
[37] I, 144.
[38] I, 230.
[39] II, 34-35.

. . . the offspring of the glorious Granby! Methinks I see thee, blissful Spirit! with a branch from thy palm of victory binding his youthful brows! hear thee tell him, when his country calls, to remember thy unshaken loyalty and victorious fame; the soldiers view him with paternal fondness, tracing delighted in his youthful countenance the lines of valor and humanity! Happy youth![40]

Then come several episodes which are the first hints at the Formula of the Old Soldier, long a favorite; the combination of the wooden leg and the kindly eye was irresistible, especially when a good dose of hard luck was thrown in. Here we have only a starting point. The hack goes to a funeral of an officer who had been in America, and one of whose praiseworthy characteristics is "the affection he bore his faithful nurse; whose husband was one of the unfortunate soldiers that fell at the battle of Bunkers-Hill."[41] Then there turns up a pickpocket who "was an officer in America, lost considerably at hazard, and was necessitated to sell his commission to discharge some pressing debts."[42] Finally there is the story of the country girl who came to London looking for work, not ineffective because of a rare note of sound psychology:

She said her sweetheart had listed for a soldier, and had gone to America; that she could not bear the country after him, for he used every evening, as duly as the sun went down, to meet her in the meadow where she was milking, and assist her going home. . . .[43]

The old soldier gets a good many pages in *Francis the Philanthropist* (1785), in which the charitable hero finds the veteran, on crutches, in debtor's court for forty shillings. Both he and his daughter had met rather hard times in America. Francis agreeably repairs the father's fortunes and falls in love with

[40] (3rd ed., 1781), p. 12. The reference is apparently to Granby's third son, who was made captain of the *Resolution*, went to America in 1780, and was fatally wounded at Dominica, April 12, 1782 (*D. N. B.*, article "Manners, Lord Robert").

[41] Page 14.

[42] Page 74.

[43] Page 77.

the daughter. Another major element in the book amplifies the love-and-honor plot for which the foundation had been laid in Pratt's *Emma Corbett*. Captain Tom Edwin of the English army had been detailed to capture a member of Congress, had lost the senator, but came up with the wife and daughter. Gallantry leads him not only to secure their freedom with the argument that "detention . . . would not only draw on us the increased aversion of our American enemies, but the contempt of that gallant, though faithless, nation,"[44] but also to deliver them personally to the senator. Since Tom has now fallen in love with the daughter, Senator Middleton, averse to her marrying an enemy, proposes that Tom change sides and get a higher rank in the American army:

and you will have the glorious satisfaction of contributing to the formation of an empire of freedom, where virtue, bravery, and abilities, can alone lead to honour, fortune, and command. But, if you are un-convinced by my arguments; if neither love, ambition, or the desire of honest fame, can prevail on you to exchange the banners of tyranny for the trophies of liberty; if you will still remain the purchased slave of monarchy, the mercenary hireling of oppressive despotism,—adieu—.[45]

The senatorial manner naturally sends Tom back to the banners of tyranny, and Anna gets into the power of her "old persecutor, the hated, detested, infamous, Major Singleton" of the American army.[46] But a happy-ending marriage is inevitable, and the expansive spirit is so irresistible that

the old gentleman and his son-in-law are now engaged in a friendly contest, whether the captain should dispose of his estate in England, or Mr. Middleton of his American property; that the father and daughter may be no more separated.[47]

The Alphonse-and-Gaston finale does not obscure the fact that the novel has more mature intentions than the average and

[44] Page 231.
[45] Page 234.
[46] Page 250.
[47] Pp. 286-287.

succeeds reasonably well in presenting a balanced interpretation of characters on opposing sides.

The old soldier receives extended treatment in what is thus far the best novel dealing with the war—Robert Bage's *Mount Henneth* (1781). The remarkable thing is the humor, in a theme where pathos was conventional, and in a form of literature as yet predominantly solemn. Lacking an arm and a leg, and about to be whipped for stealing turnips to appease the hunger of poverty, the veteran is heavy with sentimental appeal; yet Bage chooses to make him refreshingly ironic. He had joined the army and been shipped to America,

where a great deal of victuals being to be got for a little labour, I was quite transported. This easy state lasted but a short time, on account of the grumblings that arose about tea and taxation, a whole ship-load of which these moody devils tost into Boston harbour. So we were called from our cantonments to keep 'em quiet, and then they grew madder than ever. At last we came to blows, and then farewell peace and pudding. I had the honour to be one of the number that went to visit them at Bunker's Hill, where, I protest, they kept me in as pretty a sweat as that I had at the forest, and at last gave me a dose that kept me quiet till our winter's expedition to Halifax. . . . We found the air of several places, Trenton especially, not agreeable to our constitutions. . . . I was ordered for Quebec, and found myself one of that distinguished band who were destined to explore their way, like crocodiles, by land and water, through two or three hundred leagues of barren land. Though a cold country, I don't remember we were ever starved for want of work, or in any danger from repletion . . . skirmishes were almost as frequent as dinners. In one of these, where we had come to close quarters, I had the luck to be well pinked and slashed; and having retreated as long as I could run, at length I laid me down to die quietly like a hero . . . the surgeon dressed my wounds, and the next morning, to save time, sawed off my arm, and seared the stump. This was the most lively sensation I had ever experienced, but then it was glorious, and soldiers should be content.[48]

Two modern qualities are outstanding: the realistic attitude to war, and the easy, natural speech in a day when the Johnsonese

[48] (Vol. IX, Ballantyne's Novelist's Library, London, 1824), p. 191.

rather than the colloquial was the conversational mode. One's attention is seized in other ways by the main plot of the novel, which, taking place in 1778 and 1779, represents Americans, to a certain extent, as oppressed virtue; the hero is English, it is true, but the chief villain is also English. The former, Henry Cheslyn, first meets the American heroine, Camitha Melton, in a bawdy-house, where she had been sent by Captain Suthall of a British privateer after he had captured the American vessel on which she and her father had been traveling. Henry rescues her, installs her at Henneth Castle, and learns her family history:

> Mr Melton, it seems, had taken an active part in our ever-memorable quarrel with the colonies, at first when the troubles broke out; but having lost his two sons at Bunker's Hill, and thinking himself not well used by some of his own party, he had determined to leave the country and seek an asylum in France.[49]

Then her father, supposedly drowned, turns up, describing himself as

> one of those unhappy people whom your Parliament have voted rebels; an American, born in Rhode Island: more than this, I have been active in the cause of my country and should be obnoxious to your government if discovered . . . I detest treachery, and can never condescend to the office of a spy.[50]

He is accepted in Henneth Castle society, he is admired for his independence in trying circumstances, and he is allowed to lecture the English on the imminent downfall of their country. Talk finally gives way to action, and Camitha is kidnapped again by Suthall and taken on board his ship, which is appropriately captured by an American privateer. Ultimately all parties are happily reunited, and Suthall is killed by a Dutchman in a "dispute concerning Paul Jones."[51] If the bare outlines sound trite, the fact is that the characters are much more individualized than usual; Bage succeeds in sane treatment of characters

[49] Page 168.
[50] Page 193.
[51] Page 214.

99

on both sides, like the author of *Francis the Philanthropist* and Samuel Pratt, but he is more keen-witted than either, and less sensational than Pratt.

By 1785 types of war-stories were becoming quite varied, and they underwent still further development in the next half-decade. Here, where the war reaches its greatest power in fiction, we naturally find more plots in which the war plays a prominent part, but also many distinguished by brevity. In *Anthony Varnish* there is an amusing variant of the Formula of the Old Soldier; the hero

joins a begging soldier and his doxy. The former, with many oaths and digressions, tells how he fought at Bunker Hill and found his wife in Boston, as clever a girl as ever pillaged a battlefield. Among other tricks, he feigns the falling sickness with soap under his tongue.[52]

The Gambling Warrior, first noted in *Adventures of a Hackney Coach*, turns up fleetingly in Combe's *Devil upon Two Sticks* (1790), in which the impoverished officer, driven to France, feels it necessary to leave there in a hurry when the French are about to join the Americans. The same book tells how the financial burdens of the war have delayed improvements in the unworthy appearance of the royal palace. The Young Man Thirsting for Glory, Pratt's creation in *The Pupil of Pleasure*, appears again in Cumberland's *Arundel* (1789), the hero of which writes about his father's opposing his intention to enter the navy:

. . . and the full half of my life has been spent in regretting a dis-appointment which it is now too late to redeem, whilst I have the cutting mortification to see the whole world in arms against my country, and I remain an idle spectator of the glorious contest.[53]

Then we run into the Old Soldier again. Another variant is

---

[52] Chandler, *Literature of Roguery*, II, 334. See Tompkins, *op. cit.*, p. 48, for a résumé of the novel. See the *Monthly*, LXXIX (1788), 172, for mention of *The Half-Pay Officer*, which, "delineated by the pen of compassion," appears to be a more conventional treatment of the theme.

[53] I, 34.

the Unsuccessful Officer, played by Lieutenant Overbury in *Elfrida* (1786):

He had contended spiritedly against mortification or disappointment, in every possible shape, not finally despaired of victory, until, upon a peace taking place, he found himself leaving off, *where,* at the distance of many a laborious campaign [ , ] he had begun, with his little girl to participate in his obscurity and confined provision.[54]

In Mary Wollstonecraft's *Original Stories* (1788), a collection meant to edify the young, an old sailor on crutches tells about the shipwreck he was in during the war. The Grieving Relative is the theme of the interpolated story of Mrs. Shaughnessy in the undistinguished *Twin Sisters* (1788), but in Mrs. Shaughnessy there is a note of reality which makes her tale somewhat more than the repetition of an old device. After her husband's death, she says,

my sons, instead of going on with the farm, and dying honest men, as their father did before them, thought proper to rake and scrape all they could together, and go beyond seas, to America, to the wars, and die gentlemen for the king: though, as 'Squire Bullfinch told them, they would make the king richer by improving his lands at home, than by wasting his lands abroad. . . . And so, Sir, . . . my sons both died over the wide seas, in America, which they conquered, for their King, as long as they lived, and all for nothing, too.—God bless the Minister, for they say he was very generous—(he is my countryman, Sir)—and gave away what was lost, with both hands.[55]

Another type of story is that in which the war serves to explain some event or some part of an existing situation. Thus an autobiographic paragraph in Mrs. Rowson's *Inquisitor* (1788), of course involving the war, is part of the brief personal history of Mariana. Colonel Dorville, heir to a Welsh castle in *The Fair Cambrians* (1790), had been deterred from making planned improvements

by being engaged in the service of his country, to whose smallest interests he ever chearfully sacrificed his own. But, on his return from

[54] I, 2-3.
[55] II, 144-145.

America, at the conclusion of the war, he grew impatient to realize the scheme. . . .[56]

After his death his daughters are subjected to the unpleasant guardianship of a Miss Marshall, daughter of their father's best friend, who had been killed in the war. Then there is the Formula of the Missing Person, which throughout the war-novels did a rushing business. Already hinted at, it appears directly in an episode in Mrs. Elizabeth Hervey's *Louisa* (1790), in which Dame Allen's son bobs up surprisingly after he had long been thought dead. He had been impressed into the navy, sent to America, and experienced another very popular fate—Indian captivity.

The contribution of the war to the "short story" can be gauged in Harrison's *New Novelist's Magazine* (1786-1787), a collection of original and reprinted pieces, in which we find mostly well-established formulae. "The False Alarm" uses the war in the old Recognition Plot, the principals being a father and son, General Harcourt and Mr. Mandeville. Coincidence flourishes in "The Elder Sister and the Younger Sister," which unblushingly provides Lt. Cranstoun, after a jaunt to the war had led to his being jilted by Victorina St. Mar, with her younger sister, Adeline, whom he had picked up in America, as recompense. "The History of Captain Winterfield" first sends its hero, the sole support of his widowed mother and orphaned daughter, to Bunker Hill, "where so many British officers seemed cruelly selected for slaughter,"[57] and then subjects him to an Indian captivity, ancient of days. In "The History of Cecilia Webster" the heroine's brother Harry not only distinguishes himself in the navy but also "contracts an intimacy" with a young man who turns out to be his sister's husband. Coincidence strains itself hardest in "The Green Coat and the Brown Coat," in which the benevolent quixote, a very popular type, turns out to be the original seducer of a woman

[56] I, 3-4.
[57] (Vol. I, 1786 ,Vol. II, 1787), II, 4.

he has been befriending. She is an American matron, who, after her unfortunate experience with an English officer, had been forced to leave her husband, who died a suicide in battle, and had come to England. Another beneficiary of the hero was a woman who had been betrayed by an English officer en route to America. The conjunction of sex and the war, it is clear, produced nothing new, nor is it necessary to dilate on the super-annuation of other themes here noted.

Passing on to novels with longer war episodes, we find, in Anne Fuller's *Convent* (1786), the first example of the fairly frequent connection between America and France. The Comte de St. Pierre, in love with the fortuneless Hortensia De Aulay, had been encouraged by the latter's guardian, Madame des Estampes, to wed the girl in spite of opposition and then to seek a career in America. Details are not clearly worked out; we simply learn, ultimately, that the Comte had "served a campaign in America, and on the likelihood of the peace, returned home. . . ."[58] Much more interesting is a passage describing a channel-crossing. Aboard is a tutor, "an equal enemy of refinement, and the French nation," who bursts out:

Aye—aye! you're in a hurry to eat frogs and soup-maigre! go cram yourself with your filthy diet! plain roast beef is too gross for your nice stomach! 'twas such milksops lost us America; they were powder-ing their hair, when they should ha' been priming their musquets: for my part, I don't know no reason why we should maintain such drones in the hive![59]

Here America is tied into the long anti-French tradition with amusing forgetfulness that the frog-eating tribe also remembered to prime their muskets in the war. In *The Bastile* (1789) — a purely advertising title, for France and the Bastille receive little attention—the war in incidental to sex-comedy. A giant Irishman, a veteran, seizing the young man whom he errone-ously believes to have seduced his wife, roars,

[58] (n.d.), II, 164.
[59] II, 22-23.

103

. . . could you find nobody else to play your pranks upon but a
jantleman officer, who fought all the days of his life for his king and
his country?—Yes, neighbours, (said he, turning to the croud his noise
had collected from all parts of the house) this whipper snapper has
blasted my *lauriels* I brought from America, I who received no less
than six *martial* wounds in this very coat and hat you see on my back.[60]

If here the old soldier serves farce, another episode wrings all
possible pathos out of a war-death. The hero's aunt, daughter
of a very severe Mrs. Poplar, had eloped with a recruiting
sergeant.

Mrs. Poplar mortified and incensed that a child of hers should make
such a misalliance, refused her blessing and protection to the young
couple, who in consequence of her obduracy were obliged to partake
the fortunes of the regiment to which the serjeant belonged, in America,
where after fighting many campaigns, and experiencing a variety of
disagreeable vicissitudes, the poor hero was shot through the head;
and his wife with an infant in her arms, beg'd her way through the
enemy's country, till at length she was conveyed to England, by the
charitable subscription of some generous veterans, who commisserated
[*sic*] her forlorn condition.[61]

Fiction is replaced largely by fact in William Renwick's *Solicitudes of Absence* (1788), a personal narrative in which the war
serves only as a vague background for the expression of certain
of the author's ideas and feelings, concerned largely with the
need of bigger pensions for ex-naval-surgeons.

The Pratt and the Bage manners, more vivid in memory than
most, crop up again. The former is suggested by Mrs. Helen
Maria Williams's *Julia* (1789), enlivened by indiscriminate
carnage and an assemblage of horrors. A Captain F—— (still
the amazing passion for anonymity), we learn in a letter dated
"Long Island, 1776," "fell in the action of yesterday." He dies
in the approved manner, gazing at the profile of Sophia Herbert, although "his ruling passion, a thirst for military fame,

[60] I, 56-57.
[61] I, 42-43.

did not forsake him even in those last minutes. . . ."[62] Sophia was the daughter of a Virginia plantation-owner, whose eldest son is one of the "aid-du-camps" of George Washington, and whose youngest son is killed in a local attack by the British. Like Pratt's Emma, Sophia finds the corpse. Her falling in love with Captain F—— produces a family row. His death, already described, causes her to go through a mad-scene dating from Ophelia, but she recovers enough to die edifyingly. Bage's reappearance is fortunately in his own person, with *James Wallace* (1788). In *Mount Henneth* a veteran had been used for ironic reflections on the war; here, a young officer "fresh from America" most amusingly satirizes himself:

I am but a lieutenant, gentlemen; but, by G-d, the lieutenants bore the burden of command throughout the whole war, and the colonels ran away with the glory. It is not prudent, perhaps, in a young soldier, who expects, and damme I'll be bold to say deserves, preferment, to talk too much about his superiors; but by G-d, gentlemen, you see how the war has terminated! Damme, I would have eaten America, if I had had the command, before it should have terminated in this manner. I hate boasting, gentlemen, as I hate the devil and the Pretender; but I was sent out upon a secret expedition, and how do you think I conducted it? If I did not surprise the enemy's commanding-officer in the arms of his mistress, curse me. I delivered my gentleman to a corporal, and went to bed to the lady—a sweet girl, faith!—Another time, gentlemen, I was ordered to dislodge the enemy from a strong defile; a defile, gentlemen, is a hollow betwixt two impassable mountains. I had only one hundred men to perform this, and the devil a cannon would the general allow me, though he knew the enemy had six pieces at the mouth of the defile. Courage, gentlemen, is not the only thing required in a commander. What the devil would it signify to have led my hundred brave fellows to be blown to pieces? Damme, that would have been dash without spunk. Guess what I did. . . . Climbing perpendicular precipices thirty yards high, through briers and brambles, I got to the summit without the loss of a man. By the way, we caught four goats. You will wonder why, gentlemen; I'll tell you; I ordered dry gorse bushes to be tied to their tails—set them on fire— tumbled them headling into the defile, and a score of rocks after them—set up a

[62] (1790), I, 241-243.

military shout, and poured a volley of shot amongst them. Zounds, gentlemen, it was glorious—it was great—what confusion followed in the defile! By G-d, it was clear in twenty minutes![63]

Worn by synthetic horrors, hollowly elaborated, the reader is completely grateful for such authentic colloquial speech and for so beguiling a *miles gloriosus* and his walloping oaths and modesty. The aftermath is no less entertaining: a Scotch auditor suggests that the lieutenant lacks sense, the officer asks whether he has to stand for insults "by a lousy Scotchman" and demands a duel, the Scotchman throws snuff in the officer's eyes, grabs a poker, and threatens to "spleet" his skull.

The date or two which we noticed in *Julia* (1789) blossom into a whole calendar in *Argus* (1789), a fact which makes possible some slight investigation of historical accuracy. It is in 1781 that General Branlyffe is "raising a regiment, on his own account, for his majesty's service in America"[64] and Philip, a very typical hero, is offered a commission, which is

not disagreeable to his mother, however formidable a campaign in America may sound in her ears. The lad's thirst for military glory is so great, that it would be impossible to restrain him to the situation of a *peace*-soldier. . . . [He draws] a comparison between the situations of those who are now fighting, or perhaps falling, in support of their country's claims, and those who are here, lolling in the ease and inappetency of idleness. . . .[65]

So Philip goes, and there follows a most interesting treatment of history. He sails on June 1, 1781, and then we do not hear of him until November 30, 1783, when we learn that he "has seen hot service."[66] On January 5, 1784, Branlyffe makes a flying trip back with dispatches and gives a "glorious account" of Philip.[67] Then on September 2, 1784, Branlyffe is praised for sending Philip back on a mission and for "his strong recommen-

[63] (Vol. IX, Ballantyne's Novelist's Library), p. 399.
[64] I, 188.
[65] I, 190-191.
[66] I, 198, 205.
[67] I, 208.

dation of him to be removed to a regiment within the peace establishment."[68] It is quite obvious that through either ignorance or carelessness the author has continued hostilities for several years after the war was over.[69] Such use of fact is symptomatic of the realism of detail generally achieved by these novels. Indefiniteness characterizes Susanna H. Keir's *History of Miss Greville* (1787). When Harry Stanley has to embark for America, the news is called "disagreeable intelligence";[70] when Lord Cleveland's youngest son, Rivers, meets the same fate, Miss Greville becomes "pale as death."[71] After he is in America, the interception of letters by opposing relatives results in the break-up of the affair and the marriage of Miss Greville to Sir Charles Mortimer. When Rivers returns to Europe only to find his erstwhile fiancée the wife of Mortimer, he resolves to go back to the war to "seek relief in an honourable death."[72] This is the good old Formula of America-to-Forget. As soon as he had recrossed, he "eagerly solicited permission to conduct [a] . . . hazardous attempt"[73] and succeeded in suicide. Here the war merely trails personal griefs.

In the remaining half-dozen novels of this period, the war was a central plot-element, but summary can be brief because in most of them the war was entangled in matters to be discussed later. In *Fanny Vernon* (1788) the action all takes

[68] I, 210.

[69] If Philip had sailed on June 1, 1781, it is possible that he could have seen "hot service" at Yorktown, which capitulated October 19, 1781, but it would have been amazing for his family not to have heard about it until two years later. News of Yorktown actually reached England on November 25, 1781 (Trevelyan, *George the Third and Charles Fox*, II, 385). Hence one must conclude that the author thought fighting continued through 1783, although the Treaty of Paris was signed September 3, 1783. To top it off, the author has Philip coming to England with dispatches in 1784. Of course, he might have been transferred to the diplomatic service, but nothing is said about that. Nor does the author say anything which suggests that the war came to an end.

[70] (Edinburgh, 1787), I, 23.

[71] I, 104.

[72] III, 58.

[73] III, 205.

place at the time of the war and is conditioned by the war, and yet we see practically no fighting. Nor, indeed, need the action have taken place in America, except that the location apparently increased sales-value; geographical vagueness shows that the author had little idea what he was writing about. After Fanny Herbert decides rather hastily to marry Captain Vernon, she goes with him to America, where we follow her distressed pursuit of the army. Family pressure causes him to desert her, and the larger part of the book is devoted to her wanderings in the forest with her two children in an effort to reach a port from which she can embark for England. After various harrowing experiences with wolves and snakes, all three lose their lives. The war over, Vernon, remorseful, and ostracized by his fellow-officers, is taken off by "a consumption."[74] A similar geographical vagueness in *Louisa Wharton* (1790) suggests that the author had small idea what he was talking about, and again, although there is little contact with hostilities, the war conditions the action, partly by economic means, partly through the fact that Captain Francis Truman, Louisa's fiancé, is assigned to America, much to her grief, and that her brother George, who had been interested in saving the family property in Philadelphia, has joined the Loyalists there. Louisa laments, do not my misfortunes thicken on me? my father dead! my expectation lost! my brother engaged in the fatal quarrel! what prospect have I but misery?[75]

The customary disproportion of these sentimental pieces is exhibited when the Captain's father sends "express to the court of France to intercede with the Congress for his son's life."[76] Everybody has the fidgets.

. . . these cruel news-papers distracted me yesterday; one of them asserted he was positively dead, but one of to days [*sic*] has brought him to life again. . . .[77]

[74] (1789), pp. 126 ff.
[75] Page 30.
[76] Page 56.
[77] Page 59.

Of course the Captain shows up safe and sound at last, and the war is completely forgotten.

The exclamatory style continues in *The School for Fathers* (1788), which is in the Mackenzie lachrymose manner. With a war to separate two lovers who are patterns of sensibility, Edwina Bedford and Alfred Harley, one can imagine how damply the story comes out. The war enters mainly through the epistolary efforts of Edwina and Alfred to outdo each other in serving up doleful tales. Alfred opens the game with the story of the Dennisons at the settlement at Penobscot, the burning of which drove Mrs. Dennison and her three children into the icy woods for a series of sufferings in which the author manifestly delights, until a troupe of Noble Savages act as rescuers. Alfred apostrophizes:

Happy islanders! . . . Ye can never become the seat of desolation, or be witness to the dreadful scenes that rive the heart in the bare relation.[78]

Elfrida counters with the infinitely more harrowing tale of her brother-in-law and sister, Mr. and Mrs. Pleydell, who, determined Loyalists, are mistreated by Bostonians "inflamed with the spirit of independence";[79] Pleydell is jailed, and his wife and three children are ordered out of the city within twenty-four hours. Then follow forest horrors, with the children crying for food and one of them dying en route. Her husband escapes from jail and rejoins them; they find their way to relatives in Albany, but, because of the prices on their heads, feel insecure, proceed to New York, and sail for England. But they are captured by an American privateer, whose crew, seeing an English frigate approach, scuttle their prize and sail away. As the frigate pursues the Americans, the hounded English have to get into the long boat as best they can. There are more harrowing scenes as Mrs. Pleydell fights for the inclusion of her husband, who, believed fatally wounded, was to be left to

[78] I, 179.
[79] I, 214.

drown. At this point night and a storm approach simultaneously, and one of the children is "dashed to pieces before the
eyes of his distracted parents."[80] Ultimately they land in Scilly,
are helped by a fellow-mason, get back to England, and, undaunted, again leave for a "very good post in New York."[81]
One is amazed at this nonchalance in people in whose story the
war has been an *agent provocateur* of almost unprecedented
suffering.

Reference has been made to several novels which started off
with absorption in the war and then forgot all about it. Another
of these is H. Scott's *Helena: Or, The Vicissitudes of Military
Life*[82] (1790), in which the chief correspondents are Helena
Courtney, daughter of a British officer, and Lucinda Franklin,
daughter of a colonial officer. For a time Helena is a prisoner
and writes of a journey to Reading, Pennsylvania, where the
populace turned out to see the English captives, with sufficient
detail to suggest that the author was using some firsthand
account. The same note of authenticity creeps into Lucinda's
tales of the fear of Philadelphia as Howe approaches, and the
relief when he turns back to New York. In "Trent-town," New
Jersey, Helena is attracted by a colonial officer with "a majestic
deportment,—a commanding eye," who insists that prisoners

[80] II, 33. The *Monthly*, LXXVIII (1788), 252, probably has this hodge-podge of horrors in mind when it remarks, ". . . two or three hundred pages of such trifling and puerility . . . requires all the patience of a Reviewer. With respect to the historical *facts* which are here enumerated . . . we are unable to speak particularly of them: they are, however, of such a nature as to induce us to hope, *that they have not the smallest foundation in truth.* Were the charges exhibited in them *founded,* we think they would have made their way to us through some other medium than that of a novel."

[81] II, 39.

[82] It is presumably here that Scott is working off that interest in American ideals attributed to him in the preface to his *Adventures of a Rupee* (1782): "A passionate admiration of liberty and of great men struggling for its preserva-tion called his notice to America; and he formed the resolution of going to General Washington to make him an offer of his sword. But from this youthful sally, in which he consulted chiefly the vivacity of his temper, he was diverted by the prudence of his friends; and they were able to obtain for him the rank of cadet in the service of the East India Company" (p. iii).

receive good treatment, since Americans do not war on women and children.[83] She is horrified by the desolation of New Jersey, the unburied bodies "indiscriminately mingled together,"[84] but much cheered by the "amazing spirits" of some Loyalist troops[85] she meets. Finally, in New York, she is much concerned about an English soldier who has had his leg shot off; "poor young man, in the bloom of youth, to be cut off from all hopes of preferment."[86] After thus surprisingly showing her humanitarianism, Helena is off to England, and what additional tastes of war there are come in the rare letters of Lucinda. She gives details of the evacuation of Philadelphia, praises the humanity of Howe, and is "inexpressibly shocked" by the news that her Mr. Byron "by a fall over a cannon has broke his leg."[87] This restrained tragedy is followed shortly by a happy marriage.

*Caroline, Heroine of the Camp* (1790) is mainly a familiar social history in which the war is a decorative vignette. Having arrived at Boston shortly before the evacuation, Harry Courtney "behaved with the most undaunted resolution"[88] at the battle of New York. He turns author—a new touch—essaying a history of the war, which leads a fellow-officer to comment:

It will require no small share of genius to give a sufficiently descriptive account of the proceedings of the army so as to convince our countrymen at home that we have not been idle in the business we were sent out to accomplish.[89]

But that is dropped for society, and society for an appointment to assist Sir James Johnson in preserving his influence with the Indians, the appointment having been managed by a rival in love, Lord Bellandine, who wanted Courtney off the scene. So

[83] (Cork, 1790), I, 41-42.
[84] I, 43.
[85] I, 46 ff.
[86] I, 57.
[87] I, 223.
[88] I, 7.
[89] I, 103. Courtney had a big job. One has only to leaf through Vols. XVIII-XX of the *Parliamentary History* to realize how much dissatisfaction there was with "the conduct of affairs in America."

he is off to Quebec, where, when he is introduced to Governor Guy Carleton, "the justness of his ideas, and the humanity of his heart, was [sic] discovered and greatly applauded by him [Carleton]."[90] Courtney is successful among the "Outawas," joins Burgoyne, is present at Ticonderoga, and, in a subsequent skirmish, is in great danger because of the precipitancy of his Indian allies.[91] Thenceforth his wounds limit him to clerical duties, and ultimately he is sent to England with "private advices of the critical situation of Burgoyne's army."[92] This is the sum total of the war in this book, which is otherwise devoted to conventional amorous intrigues. In mentioning names and places, however, and mixing real characters with fictional, the author, like Scott in *Helena*, is making a new and a better effort to create a sense of reality.

Best in this period is *Jonathan Corncob*, the story of a picaresque hero whose unprincipled insouciance, liveliness of spirits, and unpretentious, devil-take-the-hindmost attitude to life, with now and then an undercurrent of real feeling, are a most refreshing change from cooked-up pathos and horrors, on the one hand, and sketchy unreality, on the other. As has been said, Jonathan's war is a comic-opera war which no one takes seriously; it bobs in and out in slapstick fashion, serving chiefly to get the hero into amusing situations or to satirize people he doesn't like. His first experience of it is on an American privateer:

After having been three days at sea, we fell in with an English vessel of nearly our own force, Cape Cod bearing W. N. W. 3/16 W. distant 25 leagues and a half. We kept our luff in hopes of gaining the wind, but not being able to fetch into the enemy's wake, we were

90 II, 2-3. Giving Carleton the role of the usual eighteenth-century humane hero happens to coincide with fact; see Trevelyan, *American Revolution*, Part II, I, 68-89.

91 II, 103 ff. Cf. Trevelyan: "More than one promising combination for surrounding and surprising the enemy was ruined by their [the Indians'] premature appearance on the scene of action. . . ." (*American Revolution*, Part III, p. 83).

92 II, 138.

obliged to pass under his lee, at three-fifths of a cable's length distance, and began the action at half past two P. M. . . . At four P. M. our captain turning round to me, had only time to say, "I *snort* now, brother Jonathan, they *blaaze away* like *daavils;*" when a cannon-ball broke his head, to my great astonishment. At this moment I believe we should have struck, if the English ship had not had a drum and fife upon deck playing yankee doodle: our indignation at the insult kept up our courage, and we continued the action till five P. M. when the enemy hauled his wind: we should have pursued him, but unfortunately our mizzen-top-gallant stay-sail bow-line, and smoke-sail haleyards were shot away, which it was necessary to knot and splice before we could renew the action. Our killed and wounded amounted to seven, including the captain in the number of the former, and among the latter our mizzen mast.[93]

Next day they meet a Dutch ship, with these results:

Our lieutenant . . . had been, before the war, a cod fisherman in these latitudes, and as he had never been accustomed to return to port without catching something, he hit upon the expedient of hoisting English colours and plundering the Hollander,

a stratagem which was "universally applauded by his countrymen."[94] In a short time Jonathan is in jail in Boston and in danger of being tarred and feathered by Bostonians to "divert their attention from their misfortunes"[95]—a defeat by the British. So Jonathan escapes and turns up aboard a British ship, where his efforts are directed chiefly toward satirizing a profane and vociferous officer very like the lieutenant in Bage's *James Wallace* of the next year. Their stupid captain is so slow in dealing with a fire that "we were in a fair way to be roasted, to the great satisfaction of the pious Bostonians."[96] Coming to New York, he devotes himself chiefly to amorous activities, although taking time out to note that the Hessians are never punished for marauding:

[93] Pp. 29-31.
[94] Pp. 32-33.
[95] Page 37.
[96] Page 41.

Whenever the troops of that nation saw any thing in an American house which suited them, they begged it in a civil way; though at the same time using an argument that was unanswerable—'If you vas one frynd to the Koning' said Lieut. *Hastendudenrot* of the *Trumbrick* regiment, 'you vas gif me your vatch; if you vas one repell, by Got I take it.'[97]

Then Jonathan's father Habakkuk tells of his and his family's difficulties as Loyalists. Ejected from Massachusetts, they went to Vermont.

. . . as soon as it was known that Corncob the tory was arrived, the whole neighbourhood assembled, and declared, that there was more pleasure in hunting a tory than in hunting a *skunk*.[98]

Habakkuk was made to run the gauntlet, and his collarbones and his skull were fractured; naturally the Corncobs fled, and by the "assistance of our brother tories and God's providence, we all came safe to New-York."[99] In exchange Jonathan tells his history, greatly embellished with heroic feats.

. . . even little Jeptha [his younger brother] was animated by it, and said he was *full of fight,* and longed to be *blazing away* at the rebels.[100]

After a long interlude in the West Indies, Jonathan is appointed purser on an English armed brig, which, on meeting the "Pica-roon American Privateer," surrenders without firing a shot. The American purser makes away with all of Jonathan's personal belongings. Jonathan next appears aboard a prison ship at Boston, where one of the prisoners prays thus:

O L--d our father, which art in heaven, of thy infinite goodness and mercy, look down, and d--n, c--se, bl-st, blow, burn, blind, sink, and utterly destroy the thirteen united states of America.[101]

In jail Jonathan has many unpleasant experiences, which are somewhat mitigated when Desire Slawbuck, to escape marrying

[97] Page 72.
[98] Page 108.
[99] Page 110.
[100] Page 111.
[101] Page 158.

whom he had fled his home long before, breaks into his cell from the neighboring one and says, "Kiss me, Jonathan." Various amorous adventures follow, and eventually Jonathan is again out of jail; then the ship on which he embarked for New York is wrecked off the coast of Rhode Island, and he is again prisoner. But he is sent to New York in exchange, and from then on, the war disappears. And at that we leave a novel that, if not great literature, is much more lively and real than most of its contemporaries, and more entertaining than any of them. It is ironic that the war should have produced some first-rate laughter at the period when literature was definitely turning its back on laughter.

As we finish the '80's, it is apparent that the fictional uses which the war served have become much wider and more numerous, extending from farce and humor at one extreme to melodrama, trying vainly to be tragedy, at the other. If *Jonathan Corncob* and Robert Bage use the war as a medium of satire, Pratt and his followers find in it a well of tears. Most of the novels are on the crying side, through divided families, missing relatives, and old soldiers. Or else there is old-fashioned romance, and then young men athirst for glory win promotions and come back to the bosoms of their fair ones. And in nearly every story there is less an individual than a type. At the end we must see what happens to these types after 1790.

### iv

In the '90's we leave the peak of the war-interest and trace the decline, apparent not only in the smaller number of novels but in the smaller parts assigned to the war. Uses of the war may vary a trifle, but quality hardly improves. The French connection appears again in Edward Sayer's *Lindor and Adelaide* (1791), in which the Marquis d'Antin, proprietor of a French estate, was "necessarily called" by "the war that took place in America" "to serve his king and country in the field."[102] Returning, he

[102] Page 5.

is disturbed by the new spirit of Revolution, the author's chief target. "Though still liable to pain from the nature of his wound,"[103] the Marquis shows at least Burke's consistency in a prompt tender of his services to the crown. In Mrs. Rowson's *Charlotte Temple* (1791) the war serves only to transfer an old sentimental tragedy to America. Seeing Charlotte as he is about to leave for the war, Montravile begins to "feel devilish odd about the heart."

"Pho," said Belcour, " a musket ball from our friends, the Americans, may in less than two weeks make you feel worse."[104]

Montravile cajoles Charlotte into taking the American trip with him by means of this sound psychological appeal:

. . . reflect, that when I leave my native land, perhaps a few short weeks may terminate my existence; the perils of the ocean—the dangers of war—.[105]

Then the war gives way completely to seduction and desertion. The Formula of America-to-Forget peers momentarily into Holcroft's *Anna St. Ives* (1792) when Frank Henley, the hero, believing his love affair to be hopeless, thinks of "sailing for America, where I may aid the struggles of liberty."[106] Like many others, he loses his liberal enthusiasm under the pressure of friends' opposition. The war receives merely verbal reference in Bage's *Man As He Is* (1792); Lord Aufchamp, suggesting moderation in managing Sir George Paradyne, moralizes, "I must confess, too peremptory a tone lost us America."[107] Fiction is now philosophical about a subject concerning which, indeed, it never had been very bitter. Military hard luck, already familiar, crops up again several times. Miss Conway and Mr. Fletcher, the charitable protagonists of *Frederica* (1792), are concerned about a woman whose husband has recently died.

103 Page 11.
104 (New York, 1814), I, 6-7.
105 I, 49.
106 (1800), IV, 50-51.
107 (2nd ed., 1796), I, 36.

I find this unfortunate man was a lieutenant in the army, and served in America last war, but being reduced to half-pay, which was insufficient to maintain them was obliged to sell it.[108]

In Mrs. Gunning's *Memoirs of Mary* (1793) Montague takes his wife, against the opposition of her parents, to America, and is killed there. The father thus disposed of, the novel leaps ahead some years to the story of the daughter, Mary. Here appears a new formula, obviously a product of the passing years, that of the War and Parents. Like Mary above is Miss Wilmot in Holcroft's *Adventures of Hugh Trevor* (1794), who tells how her father, disappointed in life, wanted to return to actual military service:

Early, however, in the American War, he obtained his wishes; unhappily obtained them, for, having been long unused to the baneful severity of camps, he and many more brave men were carried off, by the damps of the climate to which he was sent.[109]

But youthful fighters are not yet passé. Frances Moore in *Rosina* (1793) has an interstitial story about Captain Mortimer and Matilda, the daughter of General Selwyn, who had got the former a commission. "His regiment had been stationed for the last six years in America,"[110] and then he came back, and that is all. Imlay's *Emigrants* is almost as hurried; of Captain Arl——ton we are informed that in the war he had become a captain at sixteen and was "ever afterwards looked upon as one of the most heroic soldiers in the American army."[111] The Chaucerian fondness for nonpareils produces a plethora of heroes. Less usual are two other novels at this time. In Mrs. Smith's *Banished Man* (1794) Carlowitz, a Pole, speaks of the hopes the people of Poland had entertained of assistance from the English; and could not help remarking, how soon they had forgot the

[108] (Dublin, 1792), II, 112-113.
[109] (2nd ed., 1794), III, 53.
[110] I, 112.
[111] I, 87.

conduct of the Empress of Russia towards them in their war against America.[112]

Mrs. Hedgeland's *Madeline* (1794) thus attacks the heiress-wife of Captain Adolphus Glanville:

. . . [she] gave full play to dissipation, and an inordinate desire for admiration. By every tender remonstrance, her husband strove to reclaim her, but her nature was incorrigible, and when she followed him to America, blushed not to own, that his society was her least inducement.[113]

Usually, we notice, the Europeans who enter the American war, on whichever side, are admirable rather than otherwise, but in Henry James Pye's *Democrat* (1795), an attack on sans-culottism, a French adherent of the cause of American liberty, Jean Le Noir, is made an out-and-out rascal.[114] With political satire as his objective, Pye is very restrained in his use of the war: "To give an account of all our hero's adventures through the course of the campaign would be superfluous."[115] Later a French refugee, the Count de Tournelles, holding a post-mortem on the war with friends in England, similarly specifies:

It is needless to enter into the details of a war . . . though it is impossible to avoid making a remark on the strong proof that event gave of the fallacy of conjecture on the future issue of human affairs.[116]

The Count tells how Le Noir was only a dishonest fellow whom he had hoped to correct by taking to America, but who,

[112] II, 56. Russia took the lead among neutrals by issuing a manifesto, March 8, 1780, against violation of naval rights of neutrals. The proclamation was aimed at Britain and produced a "terrible and ever-increasing peril" (Trevelyan, *George the Third and Charles Fox*, II, 72-73).

[113] I, 92-93.

[114] A striking fact, in view of the American interest in the book signified by the appearance of an American edition in the same year as the English. The American publisher may have gambled on the title. In his "Preface to the American Edition" he makes what looks like a desperate play for interest by treating the book as a lesson against being deceived by French agents communicating "with all the 'grumblers' in the United States" (I, vi).

[115] I, 6-7.

[116] I, 65.

on receiving necessary reproofs, had deserted the army. Thus does Pye dispose of liberalism. In Edward Davies' *Elisa Powell* (1795) we return to the old soldier, happily of the ironic variety originated by Bage. Found playing his harp, the veteran is induced to tell his story, which started with his going to London to make his fortune:

He soon found it, in one of those traps which are baited for raw countrymen. For three guineas, a royal bounty! he disposed of the boasted privileges of an Englishman. Tricked off in the livery of his sovereign master, he was conducted over the Atlantic, and, at Bunker's hill, received the reward of his valour. . . . "Owing to some informality in my application, and a mistake in my surname, it was thought proper my courage should be entitled to no other reward than the pound of American hobnails and bullets, which had been already discharged. I was, consequently, induced to become a pensioner on the good-humour and generosity of my simple countrymen."[117]

The War-and-Parents theme appears again in *Jemima* (1795). Major Davison had proudly refused a commission in order to go "independent in a marching regiment";[118] his wife went along for a five-year stay, and then the Major's being wounded sent them home. It is the son whom they had had in the meantime in whom the heroine is interested. War, love, and hardship mingle familiarly in *Matilda* (179-),[119] which starts off with the fact that Captain Berkeley had "distinguished himself by his valour and humanity"[120] in America and then returned to Scotland to marry Matilda V—— over her father's opposition. Their consequent material difficulties face solution when

Berkeley recollected that Edwin, a Welchman, whose life he had saved in battle, and who afterwards had served him with grateful fidelity, now lived in his native principality on his paternal farm.[121]

[117] I, 186-189.
[118] I, 15.
[119] (n.d.). Internal evidence suggests the early '90's as the approximate date of the novel.
[120] Page 3.
[121] Pp.4-5.

Edwin, thus introduced by a mnemonic spasm even more remarkable than those inspired by the most callous authors bent on salvation, does the Good Samaritan in the style proper to novels.

Among the longer war-stories in the early '90's, we first come across the rather popular incest or potential-incest plot,[122] and America takes its part again in familiar scenes. In Mrs. Smith's *Celestina* (1791) the war is the means of a necessary discovery of identities. Lady Horatia Howard finds that the title-heroine is very like her brother who had "lost his life in America, in that war which tore it from the British empire."[123] Willoughby, in love with Celestina but thinking that she is his sister, travels about the continent looking for evidence and conveniently comes across the Count de Bellegarde, who has all the information. Celestina is really the daughter of a Captain Ormond (Lady Horatia's brother), who had secretely married Bellegarde's sister years before and had been separated from her by the opposition of her father—always an agent of tragedy, or romance, or intrigue. Ormond's regiment had been ordered to America, as had Bellegarde's. Bellegarde had found Ormond among the Indians and taken care of him until he died of his wounds.[124] Willoughby is now free to follow up the affair with Celestina.

Mrs. Mackenzie's *Slavery* (1782), topical in its appeal, not only makes the most of the title-subject, but, with the catholicity of the tearful school, drags in everything that might appeal to sensibilitarians—conditions in England, the American war, and the French Revolution. It is a good instance of that interweaving, already pointed out, of American matters with the leading trends of thought at the time, in exposition or narration. Here, the war enters through Miss St. Leger's writing Miss Hamilton, in the most stilted style that any of these novels can

---

122 See Tompkins, *op. cit.*, pp. 62-66; Baker, *op. cit.*, V, 93, 107-108, 128.
123 (2nd ed.,), II, 11, 280.
124 IV, 275 ff.

show, about her father, General St. Leger, who had lived at Boston on his estate until the war led him to send his wife and daughter away from "those scenes of distraction" to safety in Jamaica.[125] Silence leads them to think that the General, "to avoid the loyalists, has fled to the back settlements."[126] Here is a good instance of Mrs. Mackenzie's novelistic ineptitude: she wanted a general because most novels dealt with the "higher classes," but it never occurred to her to make him act like a general, or, indeed, any other sort of warrior. Reported dead to his anguished family, who suffer various difficulties, the most distressing of which are monetary, the General finally turns up, posing, for safety, as a Mr. Vincent. He has a very sad tale:

Ruined by your late broils in America, he was upon the point of losing his life with his property; but, after various misfortunes, obtained that protection in an enemy's domains which his own country denied. . . .[127]

Just why, as a pro-colonial, he lost his property and had to seek protection in English territory, is utterly confusing, unless it be that the colonials were disgusted by his indefatigable running away. But, like any heroine's father, he is treated as completely admirable, even when he throws away his insignia and roams the woods incognito until finally, a "noble fugitive," he is cared for by natives in the Blue Mountains. The author is no more conscious of the burlesque than she is of misinterpretation of the backwoods spirit as consisting exclusively of the flattering servility to rank inevitable in popular novels. The reader's mystification increases when the General decides to

sail for Jamaica, to settle those affairs which he feared his defection from his king might have endangered; but he was accused of holding treasonable correspondence, and a long and tedious imprisonment followed. . . .[128]

[125] (Dublin, 1793), p. 84.
[126] Page 85.
[127] Page 218.
[128] Page 224.

A traitor to the king, he cherishes the remarkable hope of salvaging English property; and a friend to the rebellion— though hardly a helpful one—he is jailed by the colonists! The explanation of such a muddled tale, of course, lies in the author's determination, at whatever cost to fact or probability, to use all the old misfortunes conducive to tears in sentimental readers. The maudlin reaches a climax when we learn that after being freed he

for some time subsisted upon the bounty of those generous Americans who knew him only as an unfortunate sufferer, emancipated from confinement by their humane intercessions. The brilliancy of his talents, at sudden but not frequent periods, breaking through the gloom of a disturbed mind, induced these valuable friends to propose a voyage to Guadaloupe. . . .[129]

When an author set out to exhibit nobility in distress and the heart-catching generosity of sentimental humanitarianism, she could blandly ignore every probability, every result of a state of war. It is so bad that it is difficult even to laugh. Along with the principal incredibilities there is the minor one of the history of Mr. Abrams, the villain of the piece. When the General's wife and daughter first hear that the General is dead, Abrams turns up with a forged will making him executor. How Abrams, who had been the General's secretary and then a grafting petty agent in the army, had created this document and then palmed it off as genuine is never clear. So Mrs. Mackenzie is consistent in inconsistency.

The time of Mrs. Smith's *Old Manor House* (1793) is the war, but generally the military is subservient to the amorous and domestic interests surrounding the love affairs of Orlando Somerive and Monimia Lennard, and of Captain Warwick and Isabella Somerive. If not too successfully, the book at least makes an attempt at interpreting the war in relation to the individuals concerned. General Tracy, Warwick's uncle, also has his eyes on Isabella and is supposed to have had his nephew

[129] Page 225.

assigned to an American regiment to get him out of the way. Orlando is afraid the fight will be over before he reaches America (the Young Man Thirsting for Glory), but we at last find him with a small troop who are to force their way through enemy country to open communications with Burgoyne, whose courage Mrs. Smith praises at length. Orlando grieves about "all the horrors and devastations of war,"[130] and he is worried about the children of his friend Fleming, who had been killed, but even more about Monimia's being "liable to the insults of Sir John Belgrave."[131] The British make a disastrous retreat:

Fatigue and famine, great as those evils were, seemed less terrible to the minds of the English, than the certainty that they must very soon surrender to an enemy whom they at once abhorred and contemned.[132]

Orlando's final war-experience is the perennial Indian captivity, from which he escapes only to be captured by the French. He gains freedom through a promise no longer to participate in the war, a promise easily adhered to, since it brings him back to England and the pursuit of Monimia. With that he is "too much occupied," when given a newspaper,

to be able to attend to public occurrences, interesting as they were at that period to every Englishman, and particularly to one who had seen what Orlando had seen, of the war then raging with new violence in America.[133]

Thus does Mrs. Smith unshackle herself from the military affairs of which, although she presents them with more integrity than her colleagues, she has become tired. Still there remains Orlando's brother-in-law to be accounted for, and so *The Wanderings of Warwick* (1794) has something of the war, although it no longer stimulates Mrs. Smith's best endeavor. Since she had talked herself out in the preceding novel, here we have little more than a sketchy following of campaigns, though not

[130] (2nd ed.), III, 268 ff.
[131] III, 319.
[132] III, 288-289.
[133] IV, 153.

with the complete superficiality and inaccuracy of many other novels. Warwick, missing his regiment because of his marriage with Isabella, sets out for America in a boat of his own, which is captured by an American privateer, the *Rattlesnake*. Recapture by an English frigate, and an interlude in the West Indies, precede his arrival in New York, where he stays "without suffering any other than the common inconveniencies which must ever be felt in the seat of war."[134] Domestic notes follow until Warwick is ordered to direct the transfer of some troops from Philadelphia to New York, is wounded in a skirmish, sent to help defend Stony Point, and made prisoner by General "Waine."[135] Another wound gains him a discharge, and the family goes to the West Indies, practically finished with the war. Returning to England they are attacked by a French ship among the crew of which "more than a third were Americans,"[136] and, back in England, Warwick turns his affairs over to an old member of his regiment who "had been wounded in America, and returned with his health much impaired" and who did the business

perfectly to my satisfaction; though I had unavoidably contracted so many debts in America, that I received not above a third of my arrears.[137]

A sketchier but more lurid summary of military activities occupies about forty pages of Mrs. Rowson's *Fille de Chambre*, (1792) in which an account of family hardships is introduced with this premonitory purple:

But when fell discord spread her sable pinions and shook her curling snakes, how soon this blissful prospect was reversed; frighted at the horrid din of arms, hospitality fled her once favourite abode, mutual confidence was no more. . . .[138]

134 Page 29.
135 Page 36.
136 Page 73.
137 Pp. 259-260.
138 Page 149.

The embellishments scarcely improve the history of the imprisonments of a family head trying to remain neutral, the gloomy sequence of which, making no particular contribution to our survey, can be omitted.

Reviewing Lemoine's *Kentish Curate* (1786), the *Critical* remarked, "As this novel is of a new kind, we shall draw from it a receipt to make a similar one." The writer should collect great names, search magazines for the life and also adventures for the hero, spell names incorrectly, and pay no attention to anachronisms; finally,

Your hero may change his residence; and, if he can be fortunately carried to America, the petition of congress, with different proclamations, and the events of a campaign, taken from the authentic records of an old newspaper, will, with ease, fill a volume.[139]

Lane the publisher must have handed this "receipt" to Mrs. Eliza Parsons for *The Voluntary Exile* (1795). But she did not stop with a campaign and a volume: she took all the campaigns and filled five volumes. Mercilessly dissecting a history of the war, she extracted practically every battle and did it over, producing an utterly uninspired and unimaginative outline of history, magnificent in its dull and tireless completeness. The only concession to artistry is the alternation of war-scenes with the conventional ones of the social novel. Ultimately the latter become predominant, and the war, squeezed dry, does a customary fade-out. There is no real integration of diverse elements, and the military chronicle, in addition to the mere conveying of facts, serves chiefly as a basis for humanitarian outbursts. By the end of Volume II our hero Biddulph has gone through the campaigns in New York and New Jersey and the fighting around Philadelphia; Volume III touches on Valley Forge,[140] some campaigns in New Jersey, and, briefly,

[139] LXIII (1787), 77.

[140] Mrs. Parsons outdoes Mrs. Mackenzie in transferring the drawing-room spirit to the camp and thus finds American virtue consisting in a profound respect for English upper classes. When Biddulph was taken prisoner, "the

125

Burgoyne's predicament; Volume IV makes a retrospective reference to "Bunkers-Hill" and covers Burgoyne with limitless detail, including the McRae incident; Volume V brings in the French, and then Mrs. Parsons, suddenly but not disappointingly weary, gives up her rivalry with the encyclopedias. This epos is interlarded with episodes which constitute a definitive assemblage of all motives and plot-types known to minor fiction of the day; as the reader meets character after character who without the slightest invitation or excuse stops to tell "his history," he wonders that the indefatigable Parsons did not kill forever any interest that anybody might have felt in war-fiction.

Yet, in spite of its ridiculousness, the novel is not without its importance: it is the first historical novel about the American Revolution. Mrs. Parsons does not deal with young people of the time of writing and introduce the war as related to their elders, but throws her whole story back fifteen years and deals with characters who were then at the appropriate age for heroes and heroines. Fifteen years was a short time; still, she had to reconstruct a time that was really thrust into the past by more recent spectacular events, and to divest herself of a present in which America had taken on a set of much wider meanings and associations. She was at the beginning of a long tradition in the novel.

This is the last extensive treatment of the war; in the last five years of the century, the plots are usually shorter, and the novels, of course, fewer. Twice again we have to deal with Mrs. Smith. The hero of *Marchmont* (1796) is seized in France during the French Revolution and receives help from an old invalid who

---

commanding officer of the party . . . learning that Mr. Biddulph was a young man of family and fortune . . . ordered him every accommodation their situation would admit of" (III, 129). Thus the woman-novelist's conception of the life military.

had been a prisoner to the English in the American War; had been cured of a wound he received in the action; well treated, and exchanged as soon as he was able to move.[141]

But *The Young Philosopher* (1798) goes back to war-time to stage a raid, suggested by the ventures of Paul Jones,[142] on the coastal palace of the Glenmorrises. After Glenmorris, taken prisoner, is absent for a long time, Major Killbrodie, who has been in America for some years with his regiment, turns up with a gruesome tale about prisoners of the Americans. Seeking to get possession of the estate, the Major introduces the first "atrocity" stories on record—

of some who had been hanged, or suffered to die in dungeons in the most squalid wretchedness and want; then, as if the picture was not sufficiently terrific, he added that others, particularly those who had been seized by privateers, and who were not therefore considered as being in the slightest degree protected, by the laws of nations had been given up to the natives of the country, to be tormented by every hideous invention of cruelty, till fainting nature could endure no more.[143]

But Glenmorris comes back reporting that his captivity had not been intolerable, although he was really in the hands of "bucaniers" who held out for exorbitant ransom. Apparently we have here a representation of the popular idea of the first American naval hero, although references to privateers already cited no doubt reflected the Jones legend. Getting back to the story, we find Glenmorris taken by his "ferocious captor" to Boston, where Glenmorris's approval of colonial ideas wins him popularity and assistance in raising funds to meet "the unjust demand" of the captain.[144] Here ends Mrs. Smith's long connection with the war, a subject to which she was more consistently devoted than any other author. Another farewell to arms is that of Robert Bage, who also came back to the war periodically. In *Man As He Is Not* (1796) Hermspong, telling

[141] IV, 89-90.
[142] Mrs. Smith acknowledges the source of the idea in a footnote (II, 89).
[143] II, 118.
[144] II, 242-243.

his life-story, records that his father had planned to lecture on philosophy or conduct an academy in America,

> But these schemes, and similar to these, could not now be thought of, and were not indeed promising from another cause—the quarrels then arising between America and her mother country.[145]

Later, after they had spent some years among the Indians, his father's plan to return to Philadelphia was also upset "by the war that gained England the loss of her colonies."[146] Here, I think, is our only stab at paradox.

Brydges' *Arthur Fitz-Albini* (1798) again uses the war to help dispose of a parent—a more interesting one than usual:

> . . . his volatile temper was ill-calculated to manage a large rental, which gave him the appearance of a noble income, without really affording him any thing to spend. He shrunk from the Herculean labour, became a prey to the rascally impositions of attorneys and agents, and, in the fever of anxiety and disappointment, fell into a consumption, which, however, did not close his sorrows before it became necessary to endure the aggravation of parting with all his estates during the dreadful distress of the American war; after which he lingered but a few months. . . .[147]

Here is our first contact with economic disasters contributed to by the war, a subject to be treated more fully later. The rare spectacle of two fighting generations enlivens Mrs. Gomersall's *Disappointed Heir* (1796), in which the two families of Ormond and Thornby are brought together for companionship and consolation during Lord Thornby's absence in the war. Thornby retires from service after Rodney's victory, but his son goes back for more. In the meantime another gentleman, Westby, has lost a son in the war, since we need some grief without too much discommoding the main families. The Misses Purbeck, in *Matilda and Elizabeth* (1796), make the frequent confusion between authorship and the management of a missing

[145] III, 14.
[146] III, 28.
[147] II, 104-105.

persons' bureau. The mislaid lover is Huntley, who, like all of his ilk, is painful in absence, dramatic in reappearance, and loquacious in explanation. He goes into considerable detail about the battle of Saratoga, chiefly to utter another eulogy of Burgoyne. The defeat,

. . . however mistaken or misrepresented, was entirely owing to an unfortunate combination of circumstances, and not to any defect in the courage or conduct of the General, whose bravery, humanity, excellence of understanding, and still superior excellence of heart, will be acknowledged by every unprejudiced officer who has the happiness of being under his command, and by every person who has had the honour of his acquaintance. . . .[148]

Then follows the almost inevitable Indian captivity; this leads up to a distinctly new element—capture by Spaniards, transportation to New Spain, and amorous attack, by a Señora, who, balked in her intentions, causes Huntley no end of difficulties, including a trumped-up arrest, before he finally gets back to England. Another kind of exotic appeal appears in the Rev. Thomas Stabback's *Maria* (1796)—in the form of one Sigismund Sobieski,[149] who talks a great deal about Polish liberty, but who surprises the reader by having been in the English army during the war. America takes a part in the father-finding subdivision of the Recognition Plot[150] when it transpires, in the course of a conversation between Sobieski and young Stanley, that the latter is the son who had been born to Sobieski's wife after he had had the usual experience of being wounded at Bunker Hill. Sobieski stayed in America for the rest of the war, but the only incident to be noted is his having been compelled to leave the army by the contempt of his messmates after he had refused, through principle, to engage in a duel made imminent

[148] (Dublin, 1796), II, 177.

[149] For another Pole see Mrs. Smith's *Banished Man*, II, 56. In 1797 there appeared in Philadelphia a translation of Louvet de Couvrai's *Love and Patriotism*, the last few pages of which deal with the experiences of "Pulauski" in America. London got the book two years later.

[150] Cf. Mrs. Smith's *Celestina*, IV, 278; Harrison's *New Novelist's Magazine*, I, 275-278.

by his resenting "some illiberal expressions that were maliciously thrown out against" Major André by a fellow-officer.[151] Minor war episodes, now schoolboy knowledge, gradually seeping into prose-fiction.

Our next novels take us back once more to the tried and true pathos of parental demise. In *Elizabeth* (1797) the heroine's father is Major William Spencer, who had advanced in the army

not by any exertions of his family or friends, but by an almost unexampled uniformity of integrity and valour; and had received a wound in his breast, in the late war with America, which, from having been unskillfully managed, was at times very painful, and threatened a premature dissolution.[152]

It was the wound, it appears, which was "unskillfully managed," for the Major succumbs, and Elizabeth is off to a satisfyingly lugubrious start in the world. In Helena Wells' *Step-mother*[153] (1798) the relict is not a daughter, as the title suggests, but a wife. Major Wentworth, who "idolized his king," had an "unalterable" resolution to fight,[154] and, being a naval officer, he provides us with one of the few stories that deal exclusively with the war at sea. Nothing is important until "the gallant Rodney's victory on the 12th of April [1782]," when Wentworth had the honor of seeing Rodney in danger and of bearing down

with such impetuosity to his aid, as at once to break the line of the enemy. . . . While thus performing his duty, his arm was shattered by a cannon-ball. . . .[155]

He survived the participle but got drowned on the way back to

151 I, 238-239.
152 I, 1-2.
153 (2nd ed., 1799). The title-page says, "By Helena Wells, of Charles Town, South-Carolina," evidently meant to have advertising value. The dating of the preface, "London, February 6, 1799," suggests that Miss Wells may have been only a visitor at Charleston, if indeed she was there at all. One episode, however, describes how English officers at St. Augustine raised funds for the aid of Loyalist refugees from Charleston (II, 59).
154 I, 209-211.
155 I, 233-234.

England. There is more of the navy in *Henry Willoughby* (1798), which the *Critical* suggests depended upon Smollett.[156] Henry's ship, "the hell afloat," once visited the "Chesapeak,"[157] and at another time had a slight engagement with the French, but these events are only minor parts of a sharp satire on methods of naval discipline. Use of the war satirically also appears in Francis Lathom's *Men and Manners* (1799), which attacks noblemen's sons who raise regiments for purely selfish reasons. Widow Bridges tells how General Danby's son, to obtain a captaincy, had to raise a certain number of recruits, and how he secured her two sons by threatening the family with eviction, with the result that the father died of shock and the two sons were killed in battle.[158] Later another son of the General tries similarly to impress Mrs. Bridges's son-in-law; his refusal leads to eviction, to Isaac's begging, conviction on a charge of poaching, and ultimate death in jail. Finally the war is responsible for the death of Miss Orgale, orphan of an ensign in the navy.

America-to-Forget makes its last appearance in "William Cavendish" in the *Canterbury Tales* (1799), the hero of which, after a setback in love, is off to America to "risque a life apparently so little valued."[159] In the first battle he falls to the Indians, and Captivity stalks in to seize another slice of fiction. Our history closes with "The Soldiers" in E. H.'s *Tales of Truth* (1800), a most misleading title. In this long-drawn-out record of the experiences of Rodolpho and Horatio in America, a martial fate raffles off mistresses in a not unfamiliar fashion. E. H. finally marries the heroes to a couple of eligible American girls and ships the foursome back to Europe.[160] In the meantime

[156] XXIII (New Arrangement, 1798), 472.
[157] I, 161-171.
[158] (New ed., 1800), IV, 169-171.
[159] III, 32.
[160] IV, 154. On a flyleaf, detached from one of the volumes of the Harvard Library copy of the book, is written, "J. R. Lowell from Saml. Gore one of those, who, dressed as Mohawks threw over the tea"—a virile history for such a collection of insipidities.

there has been much straining for the tear of humanity and much adaptation of the old-line American possibilities, including the loss of Rodolpho and a whole company in the woods.[161]

## V

As one surveys this history of the war in the novel, he is bound to admit that the contributions are hardly of distinguished quality. They are plentiful, but they do not refresh, or vivify, or add stature to the novel. If the war is ever used in any mildly memorable way, what one perceives is the skill of the writer, which is just as apparent in the handling of other material. The failure of the war in narrative is shown most clearly in its falling into well-worn patterns, in its subservience to time-honored themes, in its reduction to easily phrased formulae. There is nearly always the mustiness of types, and type-actions usually mean type-characters. Convention speaks, and the beginning predicts and commands the outcome. One almost automatically baptizes the plots and counts them. The melodramatic, sensational plot occurs eight times—the congeries of humdrum frights and horrors long since relegated to the pulps. The Formula of the Old Soldier is found nine times, half of these, fortunately, in humorous or ironic manner. War and Parents—usually fathers who, by being killed or unsuccessful or unfortunate, affect the lives of the young folks—is a theme that gloomily overtakes us ten times, especially toward century-end, when it has a kind of chronological probability. The Grieving Relative, the situation in which the emotion is provided by a death in the war, pursues us six times with empty periods; a related type is the longing for a soldier away in the war, twice used. Some of the best possibilities lie in the Divided Family, which appears twice; Pratt originated this, a sound conception, but he couldn't achieve reality, and the

[161] III, 31. E. H. was probably borrowing from one of various novels like *The Voluntary Exile*, in which the hero is continually losing himself, but it is an interesting coincidence that in 1800 was also published *Singular Sufferings of Two Friends Lost in an American Forest.*

substitute is an exhausting din of death-cries. The Divided Family naturally suggests the Love and Honor situation, which occurs twice. Five times we suffer an Indian Captivity, four we are amazed by the Recognition Plot, twice we wait for the Missing Person to reappear, and six times we see used, in one way or other, the historic association between France and America. When we face the question of getting young men to America, we find various possibilities; four times it is a matter of economic or professional advance; three times we bow to the young man Thirsting for Glory; twice we contemn officers who are diverted from American duty by social activities. In many ways the war is only a side-issue of love affairs. America-to-Forget has four devotees, with lost love as the driving force. Once it is gaming debts, and that brings us to the two instances of the Gambling Warrior. Three times sea-voyages are interrupted by Privateers, and twice Paul Jones is mentioned by name.

Like Paul Jones, other war-time figures achieved some place in fiction—Burgoyne, Rodney, Howe, André, Wayne, Sir James Johnson, Governor Guy Carleton. Despite the characteristic vagueness of stories, there is considerable mention of dates, places, and battles, sometimes very inaccurate. And there are many verbal references to the war, often in quite other connections. Such writers as Bage and Mrs. Smith come back to the subject again and again.

These latter facts lead to our chief conclusion: that the war was important in the novel quantitatively; in prose fiction it appears to have received more attention than in any other genre. The circulating-library clientele was greatly interested in America and in the battles that took place there. Those events may not have produced art, but they were not neglected; in the nineteen years after Yorktown the pen followed the sword assiduously. Many of the narratives were episodic, but there were some nearly full-length treatments. Pratt conceived a good situation; Bage did some neat satire; Mrs. Smith tried to reduce

133

mere events to terms of character and real emotions; Mrs. Parsons created an elaborate historical novel. And one unknown writer combined the war and the picaresque tradition to produce the best of all the works, *Jonathan Corncob,* more than readable today in its uniquely consistent farce and humor. It appeared when fictional interest in the war was at its height—in the late '80's. In following years the stream of war novels continued, but they were relatively less numerous as other subjects were born out of current events and new literary fashions.

CHAPTER V

## CRITICISM OF THE REVOLUTION

i

The immediately preceding discussion of the influence of the American Revolution on novels dealt only with narratives. But besides mere stories, authors wrote down opinions; they criticized the scenes and the actors. These comments, whether formal arguments or *obiter dicta,* are now to be examined.

What we have seen of the novel so far hardly suggests critical acumen or philosophical bent. The minor eighteenth-century novelist had not yet learned to round out character and give it significance, to embody abstractions in corporal beings, to express his ideas dramatically. Too frequently his men and women were paper cut-outs, blown hither and yon as he wished, and leaving the reader indifferent. Often this result was due to lack of artistic integrity; authors aimed less at a "work of art" than at a large public, which, as today, meant reduction to a common denominator, exclusion of the individual, and inclusion of every old plot-trick that habit had made familiar.

But often the shortcoming, the superficiality, was due not to faulty intention but to technical incompetence. A number of the writers were quite intelligent, sensitive people; they viewed the events of which they wrote critically and even philosophically, and they understood their implications. They grasped the essential quality of war as clearly as does a Remarque or a Hemingway. But the books they made of it are dead. They had not yet learned to express their perceptions in a vitally dramatic form.

Yet the perceptions are there, and they are to be discussed in this chapter. Since they are so seldom a real part of the

135

story, it has been possible thus far to summarize plots without saying much about their significance and about the authors' attitudes. The attitudes become clear enough, however. When the novelist wanted to be sure that the reader grasped his intention, his meaning, he took time out and devoted himself to undisguised exposition, either through a mouthpiece or *in propria persona.* The habit was possibly a function of the "Age of Prose" or the "Age of Reason." Homily was traditional; the imaginative form, besides being unlearned, was not generally expected. Even when the "message" did become consistently dramatic, the drama was often only camouflage. In the novels of Miss Burney, for instance, whose characters had much more reality than most of their contemporaries, moral conduct was not enough; it had to be fortified by speech "sownynge in moral vertu." Her footnotes, if not existent in fact, were no less real than those of Erasmus Darwin. And more so with the minors. They had opinions and ideas, and, in a broad sense, their art did perform the office of social criticism. The criticism, however, appeared most often in expository interludes, in carefully steered conversations, in artificial dialogue.

The American Revolution was the subject of a vast amount of criticism by novelists: they commented on it directly, they interpreted it as a civil war, they discussed it on humanitarian grounds, they made an effort to evaluate the opponents. Although they sometimes gave their words to a character and strove for dramatic propriety, it was they, one may safely assume, who were talking.

ii

What the leading men of the time thought—the Burkes, Pitts, Johnsons, Wesleys, Humes, Adam Smiths—is general knowledge; less is known about the opinions lurking on less articulate levels. The Toryism of high office must have found many popular echoes; a probably indicative point of view is that which an essay of Richard Graves, the novelist, attributes to an old soldier:

Why, Sir, for that very reason I call them rebels; if they were our fellow-subjects, why should they not pay *taxes* as well as the rest of the king's subjects?[1]

George Parker, the theatrical man, describes the playright, Francis Gentleman, very ragged and rather drunk, haranguing an inn audience "on the *equity, justice,* and *policy* of the American war."[2] On the other hand, pro-colonialism was common. In 1779 Smollett's friend, Dr. John Moore, traveling on the continent, reports a long conversation on America with Frederick the Great, who concludes superciliously:

Enfin, Messieurs, je ne comprends pas ces choses là; je n'ai point de colonie:-j'espère que vous tirerez bien d'affaire, mais elle me paroit un peu épineuse.[3]

Then Moore proceeds to discuss at some length, and with considerable pain, the general European hope for the success of the colonies.[4] A student of Boswell remarks that, in view of his ideas about "subordination," "it is much to Boswell's credit that he espoused the cause of the American colonies against Johnson. . . ."[5] As late as 1795, when reaction was strong, Whiggism could find violent outlet in Charles Piggott's *Political Dictionary,* where there are many definitions such as these:

*America,*—a bright and immortal example to all colonies groaning under a foreign yoke, proving the invincible energy and virtue of Freedom, and enjoying a state of prosperity, since she has thrown off her dependence on Great Britain, hitherto unknown in the nations of Europe.[6]

[1] *Lucubrations* (London, 1786), pp. 91-92.
[2] *A View of Society and Manners in High and Low Life; Being the Adventures in England, Ireland, Scotland, Wales, and France, &c. of Mr. G. Parker. In Which Is Comprised a History of the Stage Itinerant* (1781), I, 70-71.
[3] *A View of Society and Manners in France, Switzerland, and Germany* (Boston, 1792), p. 335.
[4] Pp. 424-429.
[5] Margery Bailey, ed., *The Hypochondriack,* I, 247 note.
[6] Page 3.

137

*Nero,*—a king. During the American War, there was published a caricature print of a reigning Tyrant, in the habit of a Sultan. Behold the man![7]

*Sword,*—a weapon of offence and defence, put into the hands of mercenary troops, to deal destruction to all within their infernal reach. . . . A similar event, it has been reported, took place, a few years since, at Lexington, in America. . . .[8]

*Thirteen,*—United States of America; which bravely threw off the English yoke, and like all good Republicans, renounced the bug-bear of royalty.[9]

In view of the length of time for which such matters remained "in the air," it is not surprising to find the following distribution of novels which devoted either paragraphs or pages to comment on the war:

| Period | Number of Novels | Per-centage |
|--------|--------|--------|
| 1776-1780...... | 7 | 18% |
| 1781-1785...... | 9 | 20% |
| 1786-1790...... | 12 | 15% |
| 1791-1795...... | 11 | 15% |
| 1796-1800...... | 6 | 6% |

As one would expect, critical treatment of the war enters the novel more rapidly than narrative treatment, reaches a high point sooner, and declines sooner. It is easier to have an opinion on events than to utilize them imaginatively, and the nearer the events, the more active and widespread the expression of opinion. Once the war is over and the subject closed, there is less to argue about, while on the other hand the elapse of time, providing both perspective and the growth of legend, is necessary before storytelling comes into its own. Criticism, before 1795, declines less slowly than one would expect, a phenome-

[7] Page 86.
[8] Page 140.
[9] Page 148.

non due, as can be demonstrated from the novels themselves, to a revival of the American issue by the events in France.

S. J. Pratt, the first man to write a story about the war, was also the first novelist to express an opinion on it—in the same book, *Pupil of Pleasure* (1776). Since Lieutenant Vernon, the speaker, is the hero, we can assume that his point of view coincides, at the time being, with that of his creator. Vernon is the first of the honest soldiers whom we meet periodically:

I am one of those who side with that party which considers the dignity of Britain insulted by America. I was bred a soldier, and taught even from my cradle (for my father had won his laurels) to feel all the delicacies of martial majesty. In my opinion, Sir, the Sovereign of these realms is injured: his injuries are mine: it is enough for a soldier to believe his cause is just.[10]

Lady Mary Walker Hamilton does not bother to take sides; she feels that her era is making history, and in expressing her opinion, in *Memoirs of the Marchioness De Louvoi* (1777), she makes penetrating comment and prophecy:

We have but indifferent news from America: the situation of our affairs there will cover posterity with astonishment, though the present age regards it with indifference and tranquility. This justifies Cardinal de Retz's remark, that the events of our own times, however extraordinary, affect us faintly, and require time to give them their just weight and magnitude, which are lost by too near a view.[11]

We decline from philosophy in *Friendship in a Nunnery* (1778), in which Miss Smith, the American heroine, talks politics in a "style and language . . . of a superior order" and explains that all the Americans wanted to do was to show the king that his ministers were deceiving him.[12] A different interpretation of the American is made by Sir Herbert Croft in his suggested epitaph for Cornwallis,

[10] II, 52.
[11] I, 19-20.
[12] *Critical Review*, XLVI (1778), 301.

Who, by the Wisdom of his Counsels, and the Intrepidity of
his Designs, baffled the impotent Malevolence of base
Confederacy, and assisted in reducing a considerable
Part of the Western Globe to their original
Dependence on Great Britain. . . .
The Colonists, who knew his Virtue and admired his Valor,
revered him as their Conqueror, and caressed him
as their Friend.[13]

In turning Cornwallis into the faithful soldier, Croft shows the
usual Tory attitude.

The first five-year period closes with three rather lengthy
discussions of the war. *The Travels of Hildebrand Bowman*
(1778) summarizes the arguments on both sides and turns the
subject into a jeer at political insincerity. One group of disput-
ants talks of the "monstrous ingratitude of the Armoserians"
(i.e., Americans), who had been nursed and protected at great
expense; so easy was their life that emigration might have
depopulated the mother-country. Part of the trouble lay with
the original charters of the colonies, which

made them imagine they did not depend on the Cortesinas, but only
on the King. The posterity of a set of determined rupublicans [*sic*],
said he, should have been held in with a tighter rein. . . .[14]

Here we first enter the realm of political preconceptions. The
other side argues that the Armoserians "were the most oppressed and ill-used people under the sun." The traveler is at
a loss to understand this diversity of opinion until he is told,

It needs no other [explanation] . . . than that the one is out of place
and the other is in . . . for if they were to change situations (which
may possibly soon be the case), they would immediately change their
opinions and manner of speaking, both in public and in private.[15]

13 *The Abbey of Kilkhampton* (1780), pp. 129-130. Croft wrote before
Cornwallis's later reverses. A Tory, he had a pension of £200 for answering
two of Burke's publications during the war (*D. N. B.*). For the accuracy of
his portrayal of American feelings, see Trevelyan, *The American Revolution*,
Part III, p. 277.
14 Pp. 292-293.
15 Pp. 293, 295.

Lady Mary Hamilton comes back to the subject in *Munster Village* (1778), making Lord L——n and Lord C——d (obviously Chesterfield) the mouthpieces for a discussion that tapers off into a criticism of society. The latter says that he has little interest in women; he wants instead to know what is going on in America,

. . . being apprehensive of the consequences of the measures formerly adopted. Whoever would deprive men of their natural rights, is an enemy to the race of men. . . .[16]

Lord L——n agrees:

It is not enough, my Lord, that the English are a *miserable,* they render themselves a *ridiculous* people: And, after all the noise the brawlers make in the lower house, they only fight the battles, aid the wishes of the Americans, and exalt the triumph of the French![17]

Compared with what comes later, this is sober and detached analysis.

Criticism becomes violently emotional in Pratt's *Emma Corbett* (1780). Perfunctorily pro-British in his *Pupil of Pleasure* (1776), Pratt has now advanced artistically to attempting a dramatic representation of conflicting feelings. Charles Corbett, whose son has died fighting for the Americans, is fanatically pro-colonial, and hence he is bitterly opposed to the love of Henry Hammond, a British soldier, for his daughter Emma. Ultimately all the young people are killed, and the father is left alone, a bitter old man. Henry Hammond is mild in defense of his position; he echoes the words of Pratt's earlier hero, "It is sufficient to a soldier that he believes his quarrel to be just."[18] Between Henry's and Corbett's positions, for the sake of contrast, is that of the latter's friend, Robert Raymond, who remains neutral in his practice of general loving-kindness. The frenetic Corbett is unsurpassed in his advocacy of the

[16] II, 124. Cf. Chesterfield's *Letters,* ed. John Bradshaw (1892), III, 1332, 1335, 1336.

[17] II, 125-126.

[18] I, 10. Cf. *Pupil of Pleasure,* II, 52.

American cause; he vents such verbal thunderbolts as "the cause of liberty and heaven," "tyranny . . . [forging] chains for freedom," "this *assassination of America,*" "this fallacious plot against the rights of nature and mankind," "action so peculiarly base, so peculiarly barbarous."[19] Later he indulges in several breath-taking outbursts, of which the following is typical:

. . . those cruel *spoilers,* who have gone sword in hand into the bowels of a country, where my dear son has fallen a victim—a country which is most barbarously butchered, and to whose welfare I am bound by ties the most tender and interesting. I would reject *you* [his friend Raymond], I would reject an EMPEROR that should pretend to the hand of Emma, and yet sacrilegiously polute his *own* hand, in the life-blood of AMERICA. Oh, thou hapless land! thou art precious to me beyond the breath that I am now drawing!—beyond every hope I can form on this side Heaven!—beyond my daughter—yes, even beyond Emma, because thou art equally the object of my love, and more of my *pity*! The rapacious HENRY is gone to plunge another poignard in thy bosom!—the bosom of my country—the tomb of Emma's brother, and the vault of every generous affection. Nature herself lies bleeding on thy shore, and *there* the inhuman mother has plunged the dagger (with her own barbarous hand) into the bowels of her child!—

But oh the deep and tremendous restitutions are at hand; I see them, with a prophetic eye, this moment before me. Horrors shall be repaid with *accumulation* of horror. The wounds in America shall be succeeded by deep-mouthed gashes in the heart of Britain. The chain of solemn consequences advances. Yet, yet, my friend, a little while, and the poor forlorn one who has fought and fallen at the gate of her proper habitation, for freedom—for the common privileges of life—for all the sweet and binding principles in humanity—for father, son, brother—for the cradled infant, the wailing widow, and the weeping maid—yet, yet a little while, and she will find an avenger. Indignant nations shall arm in her defence.—Thrones and dominions shall make *her* cause their own, and the fountains of blood which have run from *her* exhausted veins, shall be answered by a yet fuller measure of horrible effusion. Blood for blood, and desolation for desolation! my poor Edward!—my buried property!—my massacred America![20]

19 I, 4-8 *passim.*
20 I, 160-163. Cf. also I, 175; II, 184-191.

If this wonderful mélange of Milton, Jeremiah, Shylock, Christmas books, and political oratory shows the author handier at invective than restrained passion, and produces emotional results of a kind hardly expected by the creator, still it demonstrates the popular division of feeling, the amazing heights which pro-Americanism could reach, and a freedom of the press today unknown.

In the first half of the '80's, there is the usual number of brief comments. The flippancy of Theophilus Johnson's *Phantoms* (1783) extends into one quick aside on America. The narrator, a gold-headed cane, is so certain of an opinion that "I will venture to lay my gold-head against any wooden-head in the universe," and he specifies, "Nor I don't mean the head of the American Congress."[21] A shade more serious is the comment of the title-character of *The American Wanderer* (1783) that he is very poor, "the great men of his country having borrowed his fortune, with out interest, to amuse themselves by waging war against their king."[22] The mother of Edward Conway in *Eden Vale* (1784) resents the war that has taken her son away:

How could he . . . abandon us for the false calls of an imaginary phantom! What reward can glory, can honour bestow, to dry the tear from the furrowed cheek of an aged mother, or to comfort the widow's unutterable woe![23]

Grief dwindles into personal discomfort as a cause of opposition to the war in *False Friends* (1785). The Rt. Hon. Lord Henry Wimbleton, tired of two months of camp life, writes from London to a friend in the country:

They talk of peace here. What say they in your part of the world? It is said it cannot be an honourable one; I for my part care not a jot whether it is honourable or not, provided there is one; for I am heartily sick of our summer encampments; and had much rather be with the gallant Rodney in the West Indies. . . .[24]

[21] I, 152-153.
[22] Page 133.
[23] I, 61-62.
[24] I, 21.

In *Francis the Philanthropist* (1785) we have a more principled expression of feelings, here again more dramatic than is usual. Senator Middleton, an American, objecting to his daughter's marrying an English soldier, proposes that the latter join the American army, but Edwin is again the faithful redcoat, though making a point rather of his consistency than of his convictions. He declares

that tenacity of principle was the first characteristic of honour and integrity, and that he whose opinions, either in religion or in politics, sat loose on him, was always deemed a bad, and generally a weak, man.[25]

The frequency of the dutiful warrior must have irritated the author of *Reveries of the Heart* (1781), who condemns that paragon by praising the opposite type, in whom

the duties of humanity could not be abrogated by a military oath . . . [and who] rather than be in a passion, because his prince is so, and commands him to go three thousand miles, and assist in scalping, tomahawking, and slaughtering man, woman, and child, . . . will not firmly believe that he and his counselors, alias place-men and dependants are infallible, and have a right to pick their pockets, or put them to death, just as to them, in their great wisdom, shall seem meet; who rather than perform so reasonable and religious a command, has thrown up the emoluments of his commission; aye, and even his share of American plunder, which at a time that all is dedicated to legal plunder is, let me tell you, no inconsiderable object.[26]

The anonymous writer, who obviously shares the spirit of Pratt, has also borrowed irony from a more virile source. He jabs the fashionable ladies of York:

They have no occasion to import dressed dolls to shew them the fashions, as was formerly done from Paris to London, and more recently from the latter to America, whither we now export only red coated ones six feet high, with just as much brains as the former.[27]

Another Smollettian sentence is worth quoting:

[25] Page 235.
[26] I, 26-27.
[27] I, 59.

I began indeed to suspect something was the matter ever since we went to war with the Americans; and, to support our honour and humanity, cut their throats; to shew our policy, threw them into the arms of the French; and to manifest our excellent Scotch economy, spent fifty-millions to raise a three-penny duty upon tea.[28]

The war was still in progress when this, one of the most succinct, pointed attacks we have come across, appeared.

In two novels Robert Bage talks a good deal about the war. Cheslyn, the hero of *Mount Henneth* (1781), refers to "this plague and pestilence of Britain; this jest of the surrounding nations—this American war!"[29] A unique point of view is that of a young Hessian modeled on Grandisonian lines, albeit possessing a hint of irony:

If, says he, you can make the Americans cut their own throats, you may succeed in retaining your sovereignty; for as to yourselves, and we Germans to help you, you really cut so few *per annum*, that you must call in the assistance of the next generation. The misfortune is, they breed as fast as you.

To be serious, says he, although I have been engaged in it, and am, besides, the subject of a despotic prince, I like neither the principle, nor the general conduct: above all, I detest the sordid part we have taken in it—[30]

Presumably Bage considered this the most effective way of lecturing the government for their use of mercenaries. In *Barham Downs* (1784) he says,

. . . since the world began, there have been but two general ways to govern mankind, by kissing, and by kicking. And it is astonishing, after such a world of experience, statesmen have not yet fully determined which is the best. It is owing to this I suppose, that the ministry of this enlightened age, kiss their own countrymen upon one cheek, their beloved Irish upon both, and kick America with all their might.[31]

[28] I, 110.
[29] Page 133.
[30] Page 236. Cf. *Jonathan Corncob*, p. 72.
[31] (Vol. IX, Ballantyne's Novelist's Library, London, 1824), p. 267.

And a member of an association for parliamentary reform lists, in a series of complaints, the fact

That as we never saw the least prospect of benefit from engaging in the American war, we see as little from its continuance.[32]

Political satire appears at its best in *A Fragment of the History of . . . John Bull* (1785), by "Sir Humphry Polesworth," in the tradition of the Arbuthnot pamphlets of 1712. George III appears as John Bull's nurse, who

was become extremely insolent, imperious and so obstinate withal, that you might well see she had a good portion of the *German* blood in her veins.

From this arrogance and pride, she had first engaged *John* in that fatal lawsuit, with his tenants in the *west country,* her cursed obstinacy was the cause of its being carried on, and her damned passion for choosing every person in *John's* service, was the reason she also took upon her to name *John's* lawyers and attorneys, and so furnished him with as compleat a set of rogues and petty-foggers, as ever any poor litigious man was ever blessed with.

Never was there a plainer or clearer case, than that of *John's,* and if it was necessary to go to law, which many sensible men thought neither necessary nor prudent; yet certainly the action being once brought, and the suit commenced, every one must acknowledge *John* was confoundedly ill used by his counsel, who run [*sic*] him to immoderate expence, without having genius or capacity, and without even inclination to take one decisive step that might bring this affair to a fortunate issue.

However all those rare gentry were the choice of the nurse, and therefore tho' *John* growled, he was determined to see it to an end, but Mrs. *Bull* [i.e., Parliament], being at length heartily tired, and complaining most grievously of the immoderate expence, she was fully determined to bring matters to a speedy conclusion—and the nurse seeing she could not help herself, employed *Malagrida* to compromise the affair, which he did, in so scandalous and bungling a manner, as both to disgust Mr. and Mrs. *Bull,* which occasioned his disgrace and dismission from his service.[33]

[32] Page 294.
[33] Pp. 18-19. The final reference is to Shelburne; see *Parliamentary History,* XXIII, 151, 498 ff., 571, 658.

Later George is represented as trying to throw the "war-guilt" on *Boreas,* obviously North, who, George says, "declared he had seen his error, respecting the conduct of the *West Country Lawsuit.*"[34] Pitt is then alleged, in time of danger, always to have saved his own skin by reminding the country of Boreas' West-Country lawsuit and Fox's plans for East India reform.[35]

Thus several satirical flings at the war finish this period in which criticism was proportionately at its greatest. Ironic comments on English administration make the best reading, although humanitarianism motivates some amazing violent attitudes. Besides the loyal military, there are few to approve the English measures.

As the period of decline begins, we run into frequent short notes, fewer extended critiques. Mrs. A. M. Bennet's *Juvenile Indiscretions* (1786) refers to the war as "the troubles which occasioned the mournful dismemberment of the British empire. . . ."[36] Anne Fuller's *Convent* (1786) introduces the first comment from a French point of view; Madame des Estampes, urging the lover of her ward to get married and then follow a military career in America, thus phrases her point of view:

Immediately after the union you shall seek glory in defending the cause of freedom. The present war gives most favourable opportunities for great actions. You are a natural enemy to tyranny, added she smiling, and in assisting the Americans, you will think of your father.[37]

In the person of a Quaker, Bage returns to a discussion of the war in *The Fair Syrian*[38] (1787). Short stories took little time out to discuss or characterize the war; when a young American lady in a tale in Harrison's *New Novelist's Magazine* (1787)

[34] Page 41.

[35] Pp. 114-115. Cf. a similar satire, Sir W—— L——'s *Young Hocus* (1789), in which much is made of England's inability to understand the coalition of Fox and North (pp. 58 ff.).

[36] (2nd ed., 1805), I, 38.

[37] I, 158.

[38] *Monthly Review,* LXXVI (1787), 325-328.

says of conditions in America, "Without, all was anarchy, distress, and war; but within our walls, all was elegance, and taste, and pleasure,"[39] she makes as much of a departure from skeletonized narrative as one ever finds here. Mrs. Bonhote's *Parental Monitor* (1788) turns the war to the advantage of the moralist in rather a politician's fashion:

Within the last few years we have known almost the whole world engaged in the sad tragedy of war. How the piece would conclude, happily none could tell; and although every act was replete with misery, many of its scenes exhibited such proofs of public spirit, virtue, and heroic fortitude as will ever reflect immortal honour on British valour, and strike terror to the souls of our united enemies. How often was private happiness sacrificed to public good; the most tender ties severed and torn asunder, to give place to the love of glory and the good of our country.[40]

This is one of the rather infrequent tributes to British spirit.

Indifference is the chief attitude to the war manifested in such a rollicking work as *Jonathan Corncob*, and, since the war served largely as a cornucopia of lively incidents, the expression of a point of view is subservient to comic effect. Once the drunken hero trips over a

sleeping sentinel, who finding himself waked in so rude a manner, thought it high time to call out *"who goes there?"* In the mean time, I was again on my legs, still repeating as I went along, "the rebel, the sad rebel!" The sentinel, provoked at receiving no answer but rebel, and not knowing whether I was one myself, or whether I meant to call him so, supposed in either case he was justified in shooting me, cocked his piece, and fired it without farther ceremony.[41]

Jonathan falls down and plays dead; the sentinel goes back to sleep. Thus national ardor in the picaresque. On another occasion some comments on the war serve merely to satirize Captain Furnace—his contradictory spirit, dogmatic manner, and synonym-laden style; a remark about Burgoyne leads him

[39] II, 258.
[40] II, 183.
[41] Pp. 64-65.

to explain all about Burgoyne, and another about Howe inspires him to explain that Howe "had no business to take" Philadelphia.[42] This pococurantism contrasts sharply with the dire Spenglerian outlook of Susanna Keir's *History of Miss Greville* (1787):

It is generally thought that on the present important crisis depends the fate of the British empire. After a progress so rapid, in luxury and refinement, we are taught, by the fate of other nations, to expect that it will have a quick decline. Whilst we deplore our licentious principles, and dissolute manners, as a nation, be it our care, as individuals, to stop the torrent of vice and folly, by cultivating every noble and generous sentiment, and displaying a virtuous and exemplary conduct.[43]

The homiletic spirit can arise on any occasion.

*The School for Fathers* (1788) is almost unique in making the favorably characterized persons strongly pro-British. Tearful Alfred Harley is kept out of the war by his mother, but he blushes not to fight when

every young man seemed particularly called upon to draw his sword against the combined foes of his country; France at this time having just begun her treacherous alliance with the deluded and rebellious Americans. . . .[44]

In Boston the Loyalist Pleydel "rejected the offer of friendship and protection from men, whom he looked on as movers of sedition, and instigators of rebellion."[45] Tried for treason, he says to the court, "your self-assumed authority," and "Ye seek to dismember yourselves from your mother country; and anarchy, with all its consequent evils, will sooner or later overtake you"; his family "may rejoice in the prospect of death, which will remove them from the habitation of evil and tyranny"; if his wife could "forget she was born a Briton," his hand "should now dash her from me" and "plunge a dagger in her bosom."[46]

[42] Pp. 81-83.
[43] III, 164-165.
[44] I, 98.
[45] II, 3.
[46] II, 4-8.

Such rabid fidelity to George III was rare; on the other side was the *History of John Bull,* and with it stands Philip Withers' *History of the Royal Malady* (1789). In one scene the primate of York is represented as reading to him of Canterbury a letter "from some *damned Methodist,* as I suppose, or *Presbyterian Fanatic,*" which complains,

> For whom does our gracious Monarch suffer? For the sins of his *transatlantic* Subjects, who revolted from their Allegiance, or for the sins of the People of Britain who endeavoured to reduce them to obedience?
>
> Will your Grace have the goodness to inform me when the measure of our Iniquities was full? Did they call for Divine Vengeance at the time we unsheathed the sword against our Brethren in America? To this cause are we to ascribe a dismembered Empire, defeated Fleets, captured Armies, and a ruined Commerce? Your Grace cannot be ignorant, that, on this supposition, it would have been happy if our crimes had provoked the Deity to afflict the Prince with Madness, and his Minister with Blindness, I mean *corporal Blindness,* twenty Years ago.[47]

The liberty assumed by publishers is well exemplified in this disgusted summary of English misfortunes. Efforts at palliation sometimes came out rather ridiculously, as in William Renwick's pleas for pensions for naval surgeons in *Solicitudes of Absence* (1788). He assures his ruler:

> Our quondam colonies, beyond the Atlantic, thought themselves aggrieved when they formed the desperate resolution of seceding; but it is more than probable that they now wish they had never seceded.[48]

Once on a tender subject, Renwick can't get off it. He speaks of "our happy situation (once the lot of the Western Continent)"[49] and prays,

> May the conviction of these truths, *which once gave happiness to the Western world,* have a favorable influence in the future conduct of the misguided part of your Majesty's people. . . .[50]

[47] Page 66.
[48] Page 229.
[49] Page 233.
[50] Page 239.

Seldom does a cause suffer from so glaring a *mésalliance* of bastard tact and pious patriotism.

*The Ramble of Philo* (1788) makes a plea for moderation in political thought by ridiculing a hot-headed opinion about America:

> . . . a very furious young man began to talk politics, and to swagger immoderately against the whole affairs of the nation. He swore, that if he were king of this country, he would see his subjects at the devil, but he would keep them in order, and make them know what it was to set him and the laws of the constitution at defiance, as they had done in the most shameful way imaginable.

Lest the reader miss the point, the author footnotes: "Alluding to the disputes in England on the revolt of America."[51] A similar tendency toward deliberateness is evident in *Louisa Wharton* (1790), which is interesting because there is hesitancy in the minds of the characters taking part in the war. Even the trusty soldier has doubts, though they soon be quelled:

> I wish that government may not find themselves wrong in their politicks in regard to its severity over the colonists, but this is not my province, my duty is to draw the sword in the defence of my king and country, to preserve if possible its legal territories.[52]

Likewise George Wharton, a Philadelphia Loyalist:

> I declared myself a friend to government, and consequently a foe to the Americans, as they deemed me; though God knows my heart, I wished for nothing so much as the establishment of that peace and tranquility which but lately united them to the mother country.[53]

Here is nothing profound, but there must be a mite of praise for an author who could make his characters occasionally reflect instead of whoop.

Perhaps the fullest discussion of the American war in the latter '80's is that in William Thomson's *Mammuth* (1789), an account of a Swiftian voyage, with Sternian details, appeal-

[51] (Dublin, 1789), p. 125.
[52] Page 22.
[53] Page 29.

ing to the love of the fantastic, and performing the ancient function of satirizing the native heath. Among the Mammuthians, African aborigines, the traveler has as cicerone and protector a "good-natured hierophant" with whom he discusses many things, among them America. The traveler fears that the loss of America will cause an eclipse of his Majesty's glory, a word which the hierophant cannot understand:

Then . . . your hierophant is a gainer by the severation you mention; for his name would never have been so much talked of had he not lost America.[54]

The traveler defends the king by blaming his advisers—no novel procedure:

. . . the ideas of the hierophant himself appeared to be natural and judicious. No sooner did he learn, for he had been kept long in the dark, that the Americans were resolutely bent on emancipation from our government, than he sent commissioners of peace with offers of reconciliation, and redress of grievances. These being rejected, he determined to push the war with vigour; and he would have done it, had he been properly served.[55]

As consolation, the native offers the flattering reminder that a new star has been named after George, but the traveler argues that George cannot rule the stars.

Neither, said he [the Mammuthian], was he able . . . to govern America. . . . Besides, is not his constellation, his *Georgium Sidus,* which now bears his name instead of that Columbia you mention, as well governed as if he governed it himself?[56]

Criticism continues in the first half of the '90's, more frequently than one might expect, because of the connection between the American and the French Revolution. Of the eleven novels which contain relevant comments, six introduce French

[54] I, 245.

[55] I, 245-246.

[56] I, 247-248. The reference is to Herschel's discovery of Uranus in 1781 and his unsuccessful effort to name it "Georgium Sidus"; see James Sime, *William Herschel and His Work* (New York: Scribner, 1900), pp. 69-74.

people or matters. In his *Lindor and Adelaide* (1791) Edward Sayer makes the Marquis d'Antin voice his own opinions. In duty to his king, the Marquis went into

a distant and perilous war, which his own private opinion censured as unprovoked, and which from its nature and situation could not but be peculiarly disagreeable to a nobleman of France.[57]

The hero of Mrs. Smith's *Desmond* (1792) finds a defense for the bloodiness of the French Revolution:

. . . when all the ill that has yet happened (allowing even the most exaggerated account of it to be as true) is compared with the calamities of only one campaign in America, for a point which at last we did not carry, and ought not to have attempted; I own I am astonished at the effrontery of our ministerial declaimers, who having supported the one, have dared to execrate the other.[58]

John Trusler's *Life* (1793) contains a unique expression of opinion—by two Italians seated in an English coffee-house in Paris during the French Revolution. The relevant parts of the dialogue proceed thus:

*1st. Ital.* "The English quarrelled with America, blocked up her ports and sent an army into the country, to cut the throats of their fellow subjects!"

*2d. Ital.* "They did—but the offence given was of that nature, that called for all their spirit and resentment. Perhaps you are ignorant of the cause, it was no less than" . . . *here he whispered as if unwilling to mention it publickly.* . . .

. . .

*1st. Ital. goes on.* "They have not only exhausted their treasury, and run themselves 250 millions in debt, but have sacrificed a million of lives, and for what?"

*2nd. Ital.* "I'll tell you—England could do no less—her honour was

[57] Page 5. Cf. Sayer's pamphlet, *Observations on Dr. Price's Revolution Sermon* (1790), in which he says that the French and American Revolutions are only "bungling imitations" of the English. As for the Americans, "their misfortunes are their punishment" (p. 14). Cf. Renwick, *Solicitudes of Absence*, pp. 229, 233, 239; *Berkeley Hall*, I, 304.

[58] III, 90-91.

at stake. I will admit that in the contest she lost America, but what did she get?"[59]

From this relatively calm discussion we plunge into a diatribe against Thomas Paine in Ann Thomas' *Adolphus de Biron* (1794):

Foremost in this daring Attempt [the French Revolution] is Thomas Paine, who began his political Career by publishing *Common Sense,* a Book which was as much a Libel on the Title it assumes, as his *Rights of Man* is on the Constitution of his Country. It was this seditious and inflammatory Book, which incited our Fellow-subjects in America to shake off their constitutional Dependence on the Parent State, and to dismember the British Empire.[60]

We might expect something of the same sort in Pye's *Democrat* (1795), which is an attack on the principles of the French Revolution and which introduces several Frenchmen in American scenes. But the only direct comment on the war is made in an English stagecoach by an American Quaker, who, strangely, discusses tactics:

Though I have not made military matters at all my study, indeed both my profession and my religious opinions have been contrary to such an engagement; yet I think I can pretty accurately state the causes of the defeats we experienced during that unfortunate war.[61]

An interruption forestalls a military disquisition. Finally, in Mrs. Parsons' *Voluntary Exile* (1795) a French hermit, Routier, who has found his haven in New Jersey, tells the hero, Biddulph, his point of view at considerable length:

I think them an oppressed people, whose equal claims to the general rights of mankind, Liberty and Free-will, are oppressively infringed by the English, and consequently that every generous nation ought to support the one, and oppose the other. . . . Power may be stretched too far, your nation *lorded* it over America, she was at least roused to a sense of feeling the heavy rod, yet remonstrated only, and *implored*

[59] III, 35-36.
[60] II, 66. The blast against Paine is much longer (II, 66-79).
[61] II, 38-39. The Quaker was a popular type in novels.

more indulgence; her supplications were treated with scorn and in-dignity, an army was sent to reduce them to "unconditional obedience," in other words, to make them slaves; they revolted against the tyranny, and the consequence is an effusion of blood, a determined hatred, and an universal combination against the English power.

The Englishman Biddulph replies:

I have no enmity to the Americans; but I think it the duty of an English subject to support the measures of the King and Country, at least till he is convinced they go too far. This war has never met my decided approbation, and, I hope, a very short time will convince these people, their natural friends must be the English. I hope I shall see peace established on the firm basis of love and confidence.[62]

Another obedient soldier, although, like Truman in *Louisa Wharton,* less of a fire-eater than a doubter.

Leaving the field of French associations, we find in Sadler's *Wanley Penson* (1791) a hero (his name doubly suggests his character) who bewails his susceptibility to social pressure:

Thou knowest how from the beginning, in my heart, I condemned the principles of the American war; how I trembled, how I still tremble for its consequences; how persuaded I was that my ideas of it were politic, rational, and just, and easily to be defended on either of these grounds: I say *thou* knowest this; yet when in G——, where the people would be for Lord N——, though Lord N—— were for the devil, I feel myself abashed even at the idea of being suspected to entertain notions, however just, that may turn against me the common cry.[63]

The common-cry was less against him than Wanley perceived; still he has much more psychological perception than the aver-age hero. Greater courage of convictions appears in Rebecca in Mrs. Rowson's *Fille de Chambre* (1792), to whom Mrs. Sackville, a possible employer, says,

[62] II, 144-147. The hermit was as popular in fiction as the Quaker, if not more so.
[63] II, 100-101.

". . . Well, I dare say they are all in fine confusion there; but let their distress be ever so great, it is no more than they deserve, a parcel of *rebels.*"

"They may have been misled," cried Rebecca, an enthusiastic ardour animating her expressive countenance; "but they are in general a brave, benevolent set of people."[64]

One passage in Imlay's *Emigrants* (1793) is in the tradition of violent denunciation:

. . . the depravations of that wicked and inhuman war. Would GOD its history could be expunged from the records of my country! for I would gladly cast a veil over events so inglorious; . . . and I would gladly believe the ministry is not so incorrigible, but were they to be rightly informed of the effects of such inhuman murders, they would not encourage them in future.[65]

There is a rare situation in Mrs. Gunning's *Memoirs of Mary* (1793), in which Lord Auberry, very unfavorably character-ized—hot-tempered, cruel, unfaithful to his wife—is made the exponent of freedom, demanding of Colonel Montague how he can ever justify

. . . carrying arms against your brethren and fellow subjects in America, with whom we wage war unjustly? The regiment to which you belong, I am well informed, is in the number of those appointed by the Administration, to execute the savage massacre of their savage contemplation. . . .[66]

In the first half of the '90's the fullest discussion of the war comes in Mrs. Smith's *Old Manor House* (1793), and, as might be expected, in Mrs. Parsons' interminable *Voluntary Exile* (1795). Although Mrs. Smith presents both sides, her un-mistakable Americanism appears in her converting the hero, Orlando Somerive, from a faithful British soldier to a theoretic supporter of the opposition. While his fellow-soldiers consider the Americans

[64] Page 193.
[65] II, 84.
[66] I, 49.

as men of an inferior species, whose resistance to the measures, whatever those might be, of the mother country, deserved every punishment that the most ferocious mode of warfare could inflict,[67]

Orlando begins to marvel that the war "was not only pursued at a ruinous expence, but in absolute contradiction to the wishes of the people who were taxed to support it."[68] An American prisoner's story

served only to excite his pity for them, and a pity not unmixed with respect; while his astonishment increased as he considered the infatuation of the British Cabinet, or rather the easy acquiescence of the British People.[69]

After he is out of it, Mrs. Smith talks of the Americans'

. . . fighting in defence of their liberties (of all those *rights* which his campaign as a British officer had not made him forget were the most sacred to an *Englishman*).[70]

Before Orlando had actually got into the war, the question had been what his rich aunt, Mrs. Rayland, would think of his participation; Orlando's father supposes that since she considers Americans

descendants of the Regicides, against whom her ancestors drew their swords, it is not, I think, very unlikely that she might approve of her young favourite's making his first essay in arms against those whom she terms the Rebels of America.[71]

Or, as it is put later, since she considered

Americans as rebels and round-heads, to conquer them seemed to her to be not only a national cause, but one in which her family were particularly bound to engage.[72]

Mrs. Smith does not like Mrs. Rayland, nor General Tracy, who thinks

[67] III, 272.
[68] III, 274.
[69] III, 276-277.
[70] IV, 153.
[71] II, 48.
[72] III, 203.

that those wretched, ragged fellows, without discipline, money, clothes, or arms, will be unable longer to struggle for their chimerical liberty;

nor does she have much fondness for Orlando's mother, who

now believed that the Americans were a set of rebellious exiles, who refused, on false pretences, "the tribute to Caesar," which she had been taught by scriptural authority ought to be paid;[73]

nor, we suspect, for a comic-strip uncle, who drinks

Confusion to the Yankies [sic], and that there may soon be not a drop of American blood in their rebellious hearts.[74]

Despite the majority vote, Mrs. Smith's position is plain. Like her, Mrs. Parsons records the opinions of practically everyone in her book. Biddulph we have already seen on the fence; it is impossible to track down all the other proponents and opponents, most of whom repeat what has already been said, but the best of whom—best, in the author's intention—lean toward the colonies. When Biddulph first plans to go to America, he is opposed by his friend Barrow,

who looked with horror on a war which must cause such an effusion of blood . . . [and who] sought every argument, judgment, justice and humanity, could suggest, to divert him from his purpose. . . .[75]

Strangely, it is a fellow-officer who talks to him of their "wrong conception of the Americans."[76] An American Quakeress addresses him as "one of the oppressors of this country . . . cruel oppressors and assassins!"[77] But the English army is

extremely discontented at the news of a conciliatory bill being brought into parliament . . . [and] bitterly complained of their inactive life, and a situation so replete with mortification, as being possibly obliged to relinquish all their projected schemes of glory, and retire disgracefully from America.[78]

[73] III, 3-4.
[74] III, 120.
[75] II, 27.
[76] II, 62.
[77] III, 78-79.
[78] III, 177-178; IV, 8.

CRITICISM OF THE REVOLUTION

A half-dozen comments in the last five years complete the record for the century. Miss De Acton's *Disobedience* (1797) offers a final long passionate apostrophe to America by Mr. Eddows, whose investments had been ruined by the war:

And bleeding as thou art at thy yet unbound-up wounds, and still stretched on the ground, where thy proud oppressors, though they could throw thee, could not bind thee. Stript as thou art of every ornament that peace and affluence could bestow, still art thou more lovely, more desirable in my eyes, than all that tawdry Europe, tricked out with the glittering bawbles of a splendid poverty can offer to my acceptance. . . . Thou wilt rise more vigorous from the contest: thy oppressor, even while she carries her head so high, and marches forward with so proud a step, only hastens to that ruin which she refuses to see. . . . I turn, with disgust and contempt, from a country, which, not having magnanimity enough to allow the just claims of a part of its citizens, has wanted the skill and power to inforce its in-justice. . . .[79]

Pratt and the Old Testament seem to have contributed equally to this outburst. In *Henry Willoughby* (1798) there is a rare case of neutrality resulting from loyalty to England plus sympa-thy for the colonies. Morthermer, having deserted the bondage of the British navy, gets to New York only to learn

that war still continued to desolate that fertile country; for though the cause of liberty was at that period very successful; nevertheless, the rulers of England blindly sought to crush, with hordes of German mercenaries, the budding liberties of North America. I had a strong inclination to engage in the defence of the cause of freedom. I was convinced of its justice; yet twelve months spent in incessant toil and cruel bondage, had not been sufficient to remove the prejudices I had imbibed in my youth. I still retained a filial affection for the land that gave me life, and thought it a crime to wage war against her offspring. I therefore resolved to remain neuter. . . .[80]

Mrs. Smith's *Young Philosopher* (1798) once again unites the two Revolutions in a portrait of the liberal Armitage, who is disliked by the coarse and gossipy Mrs. Crewkherne.

[79] IV, 60-63.
[80] II, 221-222.

She could not speak with patience of a man who had parted with his own wife, though it was her own wish. She hated a man who affected to revere, and had written in favour of the Americans; nay, who had aided and abetted, as far as in him lay, the atrocious French Revolution. . . .[81]

This is an interesting picture of the three chief vices that conservatism could impute to a liberal. Anti-liberalism is the attribute not of an unpleasant character but of the author himself in George Walker's *Vagabond* (1799). Here we find an enthusiastic young radical who believes in "the glorious dawn of liberty that is breaking from the shores of America"; a merchant, Ketchup, who has little doubt "but we shall be able to reduce the Americans to obedience"; and his opponent Adams, who gives greater credit to French assistance but breaks up the discussion through the hilarity caused by his vile geography, chiefly exemplified in his contention that the French should march overland to aid the Americans.[82] Walker satirizes philosophy as mere opposition to the multitude or to the *status quo:*

Peace was about this time established with America, and the whole country rang with exultation.—During the war, no one had more execrated the system than the Doctor [Stupeo, radical theorist], and every lecture concluded with an apostrophe to peace. He now mounted the pulpit in the Hall of Science [the name of the lecture barn], and to prove that he was a very great philosopher could find fault with every thing, and was staunch at all times and all seasons against government. He declared that the peace was the most disgraceful that could possibly be made; that it would not continue a twelvemonth before we should be driven from Canada. He declared, that, like Milton's devils, mankind were only born for rebellion and revolution, that all their joy was to riot in destruction, murder, and violation.[83]

Likewise reactionary, Pye's *Aristocrat* (1799) touches the war only in another inserted story of a hermit, who has the attitude

[81] I, 175.
[82] Pp. 47-48.
[83] Pp. 148-149.

of Henry Willoughby. Member of an "illustrious family" of Scotland, he had joined the French army to support himself and had been sent to America.

As a Briton, my heart revolted at the idea of serving against my king and country. My father had drawn his sword against what he thought was a foreign usurpation, in the cause of one he esteemed his lawful sovereign. But the claims of the house of Stuart were now over. . . .

With some difficulty I got leave to change my regiment for one in the East-Indies, where, at least, I was more likely to be engaged against oriental auxiliaries than my own countrymen.[84]

To close the century, we have, in Helena Wells's *Constantia Neville* (1800), a final gallant and loyal soldier, de Eresby, who is killed in a duel which

had originated from the one party praising the Americans for their resistance, and speaking in terms highly disrespectful of Great Britain, for her attempt to subjugate them. De Eresby had with more justice than prudence declared, that all men who thought so were poltroons, if they remained in a settlement receiving protection from a government, whose ministers they vilified, &c.[85]

Though outside our proper field, Thomas Erskine's Whig *Armata* (1817), as a continuation of the critical tradition, is interesting enough to note briefly. The tenor of this political romance is illustrated by the early paragraphs on the American situation:

Unhappily for Armata [England], the lust of dominion, or rather of revenue, beyond the usefulness or even the capacity of enjoyment, ensnared her into a contest with a great and growing people, to obtain by force what duty and affection had spontaneously held out to her.

. . . The inhabitants of Hesperia were her own children, worshipping with the same rites the God of their common fathers, speaking the same language, following in the track of the same laws and customs which fashion and characterize a people.

[84] I, 144-145.
[85] (2nd ed., 1800), I, 70.

As he warms up to the subject, he lets fly with such phrases as *"this monstrous claim"* and "this insane project."[86] On France's part he makes the most sensible comment of the time:

. . . when Capetia [France] saw this domestic quarrel she should seize the opportunity of turning it to her own advantage.—In the cause of it she could take no other interest than mischief, as the colonies of Armata were contending for their liberties; whereas the Capetians had been for ages the devoted subjects of a monarchy nearly despotic, and seemed to glory in their degredation.[87]

Erskine is generally closer to fact and less flamboyant than most of the mourners for the "desolation of America."

As one gazes back over this collection of comments and criticisms, either watery with emotionality or tough in realism, he sees immediately another of the influences we are seeking: the war, besides providing some seventy-five novels with plots and episodes and allusions, furnished another forty-five with material for discussion, not with stories, but with something to talk about. "Timely topics" included American affairs for a generation; metempsychosis was frequent, and, where labored a novelist, up sprang a journalist. And, as we see, he editorialized voluminously. Without the war, obviously, he would have had to find other faults and figures to prick with his quill. Without the war, many a howl of anguish and many a leer of contempt would have gone in search of a political godmother. Without the war, many a sentimental young thing and many a repressed apprentice, nerves on edge at the circulating library, would not

[86] (2nd ed., New York, 1817), pp. 51-53.
[87] Page 72. In a note at the end of the book Erskine adds, ". . . I am no friend to republics, *and would shed the last drop of my blood for a monarchy like ours.* . . . This declaration has no application whatever to the United States of America, the formation of which I have always considered to be the most auspicious aera in the history of the world, and vindicated by the principles of our own revolution. I intended only to express my total dissent from those *amongst ourselves* who publish republican doctrines applying them to the disparagement of the British constitution, and for the same reason were I an American citizen I should say to the disaffected that I was no friend to Monarchies" (p. 211).

have had their breath quickened and their critical sense flattered by jibes and homilies which applied to half a world. Novelists looked at the war, saw its potentialities as well as they could see anything, and made the most of it.

What they made of it, when the oracular trance was upon them, took different forms. Three of them merely cried for peace at any price. Eight merely lectured on history, or saw both sides, or served up neutrally minded dramatis personae. Five times we find commendation for faithful soldiers, jealous of the honor of George, but two of these the writer, with an extra heartbeat for the colonies, improves with a dash of skepticism; two others are attacked for indiscriminate obedience to the command, "Fire!" Colonels should be subject to referenda, thought the tender. Eight saw legality with North, and two of these were rather emphatic about it, one even touchy; two tossed off the colonies with laughter or flippancy. But more impressive is the reckoning on the other side of the ledger; a heavy demand was running American stock higher than even a twentieth-century chauvinist might expect. Eight saw legality against North, who, in the realm of mere opinion, gets an even break. But besides these, we find five strong votes—six, counting Erskine's *Armata*—against the English stand, votes accompanied by explanations that range from angry protest to vociferous denunciation, to the hysterical tantrums of *Emma Corbett* and *Henry Willoughby,* whose gnashing of teeth and beating of breasts must have embarrassed America, if America knew. Pleas for America merge with attacks on destructive Britain. Nine authors and characters take up this offensive warfare, most of them humorous or quippish or ironic, many of them premier-baiters and throne-twisters by temperament, a few, heavy-handed calamity-howlers. The American chorus all but drowned out the Loyalist literati.

Here is the impressive aspect of this material. The quantity of the criticism is significant, but that consideration is submerged by the predominant pro-Americanism. It appears that popular acceptance of the American point of view was large, much larger than is generally supposed, even in historical treatises which speak regularly of a divided England. If there were only a minority opinion in favor of the colonies, it is hardly possible that literature, especially this popular literature, would show much sympathy for the rebels and transmogrify them into victims of tyranny. But the bias is unmistakable. And it may safely be said, therefore, that these novels, once alive but now only thinly surviving on the serenest of library shelves, shed some light on a small corner of political history.

One could debate whether writers, frantically tearing their hair or smartly cutting at government, were playing to the grandstand or spreading a gospel with unshakable conviction. A few individualists such as Pratt, Bage, and Mrs. Smith were undoubtedly exhibiting that post-Popean virtue, lauded crescendo as the century grew—"speaking from the heart." As for the rest, it doesn't matter. We know practically nothing of them, anyway. What we are interested in is that they had an audience, from whichever direction stimulus sped. Here, economics is more important than ethics, and many novelists estimated correctly a popular addiction to rebelliousness (chronic case or acute attack), a delight in tripping up the old order, the deep joy of kicking the ins in the shins, or "the sympathies of the human heart." So they embraced the Americans and kicked the English, and business must have been good.

The bosom-beating brethren may seem either ridiculous extremists or keen-eyed profiteers. Despite their mediocrity, one can see in them some faint "criticism of life." For all the fury and the frenzied invective, they are, in a way, detached. They are, for instance, not the "patriots" one might expect; the wartime tense union against outer foes does not stimulate mere propaganda. There is no modern "war psychology." Literature, if neither scientific nor philosophical, is still somewhat the observer and commentator. And it has courage, too; jeremiads and philippics are not all products of reckless abandon. Criticism, even if highly emotional, persists at a time when all emotions might be supposed to be running together in one direction. Here we have, perhaps, some slight evidence on the problem of art and its subservience or superiority to contemporary social and political influences.

Finally, one cannot leave the subject without repeating a reference to the freedom of the press, a remarkable freedom to have made possible the publication of some of the invectives here quoted. Whether the large school of American supporters had something to do with it, or whatever the cause, a really amazing latitude was allowed to expression of opinion.[88] Translated into modern terms, many of these novels could not be printed, under parallel circumstances, in the twentieth century.

### iii

Another aspect of criticism of the war was the interpretative. Understanding of the basic character of the war went hand-in-hand with sympathy for the Americans. They were warriors in the same cause for which many Englishmen at home were fighting—preservation of constitutional liberties. There were two factions in both England and America. The American Loyalists joined hands, either physically or spiritually, with the forces of government; the rebels were supported by the "radicals," who "declared that it was not only expedient but right for Great Britain to grant what the colonists demanded."[89] The war was a civil war.

Modern use of the term is beginning to lose its original air of novelty. As Thompson remarks,

[88] "Although the papers were much fettered in reporting parliamentary proceedings, apparently they were little hindered in printing opinion concerning American affairs; and even after hostilities had begun they showed few traces of such repression. . . . It is doubtful if any present-day government would permit papers to print so much in favor of its enemies as did the English papers after Lexington and Bunker Hill" (Hinkhouse, *Preliminaries of the American Revolution*, p. 31).

[89] Clark, *British Opinion of the American Revolution*, p. 180.

Burke saw what British historians are just realizing—the American historians with some reluctance—that the American War of Independence was a civil war. . . .[90]

*The Cambridge History of the British Empire* discusses it as such.[91] An article in the *Dictionary of National Biography* remarks, as a matter of course, "The American war, like all civil wars, had made the soldiery more ferocious and less easy of control. . . ."[92]

A modern novelist attributes the idea of a civil war to Charles James Fox.[93] Trevelyan states that after Burgoyne's defeat the conflict "was no longer regarded as a civil war, but as a war of conquest."[94] There is ample evidence of the former interpretation. In 1775 and 1776 appeared in London a periodical entitled *The Crisis . . . to be Continued Weekly during the Present Bloody Civil War in America.* The *Critical Review* of 1778 says, apropos of Phoebe Gibbes's *Friendship in a Nunnery*, "The civil fever never presumes to approach the parties concerned in this novel."[95] As early as 1780 appeared *The History of the Civil War in America.*[96] In the same year came forth the *Emma Corbett* of Pratt with this sub-title: *Or the Miseries of Civil War.*

Pratt was not the only novelist to recognize the fundamental nature of the struggle; other novelists did it, and, what is more, almost as a matter of course. They lamented the state of affairs passionately, but they claimed for themselves no especial powers of perception. Some they must have had, however, thus to sense "what British historians are just realizing." It is not unpleasant to concede some understanding to writers of whose overwhelm-

[90] *A Scottish Man of Feeling*, p. 251.

[91] J. Holland Rose, A. P. Newton, and E. A. Benians, edd., *The Cambridge History of the British Empire* (1929-1933), I, 761-763.

[92] Under article "Abercromby, Sir Ralph."

[93] James Boyd, *Drums* (New York: Scribners, 1926), pp. 361-362.

[94] *American Revolution*, Part III, pp. 394-395.

[95] XLVI, 300.

[96] *Critical Review*, L, 440-445.

ing mediocrity one is ever conscious. For them one can at least salvage some tittle of credit as historians.

Between 1776 and 1785 three novels enter our ken—Pratt's *Emma Corbett* (1780), the anonymous *Reveries of the Heart* (1781), and Mrs. Parry's *Eden Vale* (1784). The first-named, with the more than candid sub-title already noted, is of course squeezing the last droplet of sorrow from civil war. Praiseworthily, Pratt attempts to expound his thesis in dramatic terms: Charles Corbett's son dies fighting on the American side, his son-in-law, Henry Hammond, on the English, and, with the latter, Emma Corbett. Of the triple slaughter Pratt makes the tearful most, with a din of outcries about the family struggle in the larger sense. Charles Corbett tells Henry Hammond,

The vigour with which you have sought to obtain an authority to go forth *amongst* your countrymen, *against* your countrymen, bears in it something shocking to my nature,[97]

and to his daughter he laments,

—That accursed war!—that dire *American* contention!—that civil fury which hath separated the same interests of the same people![98]

The children are no less capable of grief and righteous anger. Emma speaks of

a large and once *loving* family divided against itself. Whom are *we*, Louisa, to consider then as enemy, and whom as friend? WE suffer, alas! bitterly, from the contest on either side.

Oh, God of tranquility! heal up the *mutual* wound, and suffer not that which is terrible between different people, even in *hostile* nations, to become more intolerably so by allowing it to rage amongst *brethren!*[99]

Henry makes a passionate invocation to peace, which is implored to return to

*that earth* from whence the mistakes of altercating relations have so long affrighted thee! Melt the hearts of contending countrymen . . .

[97] I, 7.
[98] II, 83.
[99] II, 141-142.

let the countenance of offended Majesty share the tenderness of a
father. . . . Expand thy snowy wing over the same people—replace
brother in the embraces of brother, and friend in the foldings of friend.
Let a soldier in *this* instance supplicate thee to sheathe the sword.
Reserve his arm for the *natural* enemies of his country, and make it not
a duty to go forth against a *civil* foe.[100]

Finally, after all the children are killed, Charles Corbett is left
solitary, pointing a moral: "I am childless, Sir Robert. . . .
Behold what CIVIL WAR has done for me."[101]

*Reveries of the Heart* continues the plaint, though with less
predetermined anguish. The narrator writes to a friend:

Alas! dear Will, how woulds't thou now be afflicted to see thy fellow
soldiers employed to kill their countrymen in a region where all thy
corps received formerly such extraordinary instances of kindness, and
more than Hibernian hospitality?[102]

Then he turns to irony, making Lord North plead thus:

You entrusted this empire to my care, when at peace, and united in
all its parts; I have effected a total separation of a large portion of it,
and brought you into a most disastrously dangerous civil war; therefore,
be unanimous in supporting me; who alone am able to bring about
peace, the true end of all war.[103]

This approach is more palatable and more effective than the
usual pathos, to which we return in Mrs. Parry's *Eden Vale*.
Deliberately or not, Mrs. Parry borrows Pratt's scheme of the
family divided against itself, but she carries it unhesitatingly to
the logical extreme: Melville, the hero, making a charge, kills
an opposing officer, who turns out to be his prospective brother-
in-law, Conway; Melville calls himself "a wretched fratricide,"
wishes for death, and meets it in the next battle.[104] An aunt
makes a rather modern attack on "the real authors" of the
trouble:

[100] II, 171-172.
[101] III, 192.
[102] I, 29.
[103] I, 115.
[104] I, 65-69.

Would to Heaven . . . that the sad story of my woes could soften
their obdurate hearts, and lead them to sheath the sword they draw
against their fellow-subjects. . . . Surely your gracious Monarch is
kept in ignorance of this scene of desolation and distress, or, attentive
as he is to the religious and moral duties of life, he would not be
unmindful of his subjects, who have an equal claim on his love, if
melting beyond the torrid zone, or freezing amidst Canadian snows.[105]

The parenthesis on royal virtue does not obscure the main point.

Five novels between 1786 and 1790 achieve excitement in
touching on the civil war. *Elfrida* (1786) introduces the theme
in an outcry against all war:

The carnage of war . . . seems to be the convulsion of nature—To
behold beings, not only of the same form, but of the same religion,
climate, family, slaughtering each other, to gratify the wild passions of
ambition, anger, and pride, is an absolute alienation of both benevolence and reason—to see what devastation the rude hand of death is
permitted to make in the peace of mankind, by rending asunder every
soft, gentle, and endearing tie, and leaving widows, orphans, and childless parents, to people the world, and to deluge it with tears. . . .[106]

In a discussion of the American war, the traveler in *Mammuth*
(1789) stresses the split at home, explaining to the native
that the dismemberment of America naturally sprung out of our free
government; that the temporising policy of administration on one hand,
and the factious clamours of opposition on the other, had equally promoted the revolt. . . .[107]

*The School for Fathers* (1788) lunges at the war, and especially
the Americans, with all the spirit of a drunken crusader:

Fatal contest! unhappy, unnatural war! How much have they to answer
for who were the first instigators of it! . . .

How long will this fatal delusion continue, that thus divides families,
and plunges nations in endless ruin? This unnatural war, carried on by
prejudice and faction, how will it read in the annals of history? A
child resisting and flying in the face of its parent. A parent perhaps too
rigorous in asserting its claims to obedience.[108]

[105] I, 71-73.
[106] III, 149.
[107] I, 245.
[108] II, 44-45.

The last sentence is the sole concession in a work strongly pro-English. But it keeps emphasizing the fact of the civil war. Elwina writes Harley about her sister in Philadelphia who "has experienced all the rigours of civil war,"[109] and, mercilessly relating the story *in extenso,* she entitles it "The Calamities of Civil War."[110] The heroine of Helenus Scott's *Helena* (1790) writes,

—the calamities I daily hear and see, inspire me with compassion for the unfortunate sufferers, and ardent wishes for the termination of this unnatural contest between sister countries. . . .[111]

The distinction between an "unnatural war" and a "natural war," frequently made, indicates that the former term is tantamount to "civil war." Such an idea was in the mind of the heroine of *Louisa Wharton* (1790) when she bandied these words about: "an unnatural war in America," "the consequences of this unnatural war," "such a war as this . . . which sets father against it [*sic*] son."[112]

Again in the first half of the '90's five more novels in one way or another make the same interpretation. Mrs. Smith's *Old Manor House* (1793) refers to "the present war, carried on against a part of their own body."[113] Imlay's *Emigrants* (1793) talks about "an indelible stain, upon the authors of that unnatural war, which no time could remove."[114] Mrs. Rowson's *Fille de Chambre* (1792) is again livid with rhetoric:

. . . fraternal love gave place to jealousy, dissension, and blind party zeal. The son raised his unhallowed arm against his parent, brothers drenched their weapons in each other's blood, and all was horror and confusion.[115]

[109] I, 162.
[110] I, 205. Harley approves the title (II, 50).
[111] I, 27.
[112] Pp. 6, 24, 25, respectively.
[113] III, 274.
[114] II, 83.
[115] Page 149.

In *Desmond* (1792) Mrs. Smith aims, as usual, at sense. Of his experiences in America, Montfleuri says:

I saw there such scenes as have left an indelible impression on my mind, and an utter abhorrence for all who, to gratify their own wild ambition, or from even worse motives, can deliberately animate the human race to become butchers of each other.—Above all, it has given me a detestation of civil war, for the fiercest animosity with which the French and English armies have met in the field, was mildness and friendship in comparison of the ferocity felt by the English and Americans, men speaking the same language, and originally of the same country, in their encounters with each other.[116]

But it was Mrs. Parsons' *Voluntary Exile* (1795), which, surpassing practically all other books in the treatment of all phases of the war, makes the most of the idea of a civil war, even leading the *Critical* to comment that the "calamities of war, especially of civil dissension, are well depicted."[117] The hero, Biddulph, first considers entering the fight; his friend

Mr. Barrow, who looked with horror on a war which must cause such an effusion of blood, destroy our own countrymen, and plunge so many thousands in misery from the opposition of principles subsisting in almost every family on both sides of the water.[118]

In America Biddulph, oozing humanity, comes upon various distress-cases, one that of an old man whose two sons had died fighting on opposite sides, "perhaps . . . by each other's hands," and who himself dies, with this benediction:

I die in charity with all the world, I forgive our cruel persecutors, and I pray Heaven soon to end this unnatural and destructive war![119]

Biddulph's newly acquired Quaker friends

often reprobated the unnatural war, which had turned kindred against kindred, and laid the foundation for bitter animosities among families and friends, never, perhaps, to be extinguished.[120]

[116] I, 153.
[117] XIV (New Arrangement, 1795), 352.
[118] II, 27. The predicates often get lost in the horrors.
[119] II, 106.
[120] II, 116.

Mrs. Nesbitt develops the same point of view: "Ah, sir, the horrours of a civil war never can be repaired, never can be forgotten."[121] On one occasion Biddulph, inspired by a beautiful scene along the Delaware, rhapsodizes, approaching the Prattesque:

Happy country! . . . how fertile thy vallies, how beautiful thy hills, how magnificent thy rivers! ah! why should that monster, party rage, devour thy fair prospects, and let desolation loose in a country like this; a country formed to diffuse its blessings to the utmost extent of empires! O that I could see America return, like a misguided child, to her parent, Britain, and that parent, with open arms, receive the penitents with unbounded generosity. But alas! bitter remembrance of past injuries; the widowed wife; the childless parent; the wretched orphan; whole families plundered and destroyed by that dreadful scourge, a civil war; all these, smarting with injuries, sinking under accumulated wretchedness, raise their voices against peace and harmony, cry aloud for revenge, and urge a continuance of those horrors under which they groan![122]

Biddulph, given to the unrestrained emotionalism with which woman-authors usually graced their heroes, disburdens himself of another long lamentation on the horrors of war, which

in all places, and among all nations, must produce equal calamities in those countries that were the seat of the war; yet still in America it was aggravated by the remembrance, that its inhabitants were descended from Englishmen, who were once all brothers, under the same government, and partakers of the mutual benefits which flowed from each country. He sighed at the reflection, and heartily wished those unnatural disputes might have a speedy termination to their general advantage.[123]

More hard-bitten is another officer who thinks that

matters have been carried too far for a reciprocal agreement to take place. Like family feuds, the near connexion between them heightens every injury, whether supposed or real, and the bond of affinity once broken can never be firmly knit again.[124]

[121] IV, 167.
[122] IV, 76-77.
[123] IV, 198.
[124] III, 174.

The century ends with four more relevant passages. T. S. Surr's *Barnwell* (1798), a novelization and modernization of Lillo's play, with the evil influences on Barnwell now taking the form of the new free-thinking, brings in the past history of one Mental, Barnwell's adviser. He had just been getting established in America "when those civil broils of which the world has heard so much broke out," and since he preferred not to fight, and "the progress of the civil war rendered my abode in America dangerous and disgusting," he returned home, eager to "bury in oblivion my country's shame."[125] Mrs. Smith's *Young Philosopher* (1798) talks about "the inveterate hatred generated by the unnatural war."[126] The heroine of *The Stepmother* (1798) thus introduces the main action of the story:

From the peaceful serenity which we enjoyed we were awakened by the rumour of war. The civil commotions in America brought me to my recollection how short lived all human enjoyments were.[127]

And she says of her husband, after he has entered the war,

. . . the sorrow which pervaded his bosom at witnessing the calamities of civil war, where brother was opposed to brother, and the father armed against the child whom he expected to be the prop of his old age, was of itself sufficient to render his present situation truly comfortless.[128]

Very like this is a speech in *Tales of Truth* (1800):

Mrs. Marshall had felt much for the distracted state of her country, in which every natural tie had been snapped asunder, in unnatural contest.—Father fighting against son, and son against father; brother against brother.—Merciful heaven! Nature bled at every pore!— humanity shrinks even at the recollection.[129]

The exclamatory style carries us back to the beginning of our

[125] (4th ed., 1807), I, 175-177.
[126] II, 241.
[127] I, 209.
[128] I, 213.
[129] II, 157-158.

history. Still more reminiscent is the episode of an English soldier who has just killed a young Englishman:

. . . as he viewed the livid countenance of the youth, his lips trembled, his eyes had the broad gaze of horror.—Nature bled!—He gave a scream of anguish, and fell on the body of *his son* whom he had *murdered*.[180]

So at the end we have the ultimate worst made of the situation first introduced by Pratt and Mrs. Parry. And there are the same typographic aids to emotion, which few authors, indeed, have disdained.

Enough novels to demand attention, decrying civil war, made an interpretation which a century and a half later is accepted as the final truth. Not that they were consciously analytical; it is even possible that they had merely got hold of a speech tag which they counted on to stir emotions. Thus they may have been gratifying the trade rather than expressing a conviction or a perception. I am inclined to think, however, that they really grasped the fundamental issue, if for no other reason than that the inartistic violence of the emotion, however it may induce irritation or indifference, indicates a considerable measure of sincerity. Not all the abhorrence of civil war could have been a pose. There was a real sense of a catastrophic division within one political family.

Once again we cannot leave a subject without a note on the freedom of the press. Here the direct or implied condemnation of the government shows even more unrestraint than in the preceding section and is whipped up into a kind of frenzy which has few modern parallels. So, in tracing the idea of the civil war, we have a further glimpse of what fiction could do very early in its adolescence.

iv

By now it is more than apparent that the authors writing about the American Revolution were fondly devoted to pictur-

[180] IV, 109.

ing the horrors of war, to making the cup of misery run over, to wringing from every situation showers of emotional effect. Sometimes we find mere rant, sometimes artistic bungling argues insincerity and results in the ridiculous, sometimes insight into character and a modicum of deftness create an evocative scene. Often we are dealing with hacks and charlatans, equally often with writers of honest intentions. These latter represent an increasing sociological sensitivity; they are primarily not tear-jerkers, but reformers, and they exemplify the growing sympathy for human ills and suffering that was to change the old order and lead, at long last, to the social renovations of the nineteenth century. Reform bills date ultimately from the "new humanitarianism" of the eighteenth century. And that, like other strands in the whole fabric of the times, is to be traced in the novel.

Human sympathies went out in various directions. At least three books attacked that old custom of the country, impressment.[131] Slavery evoked a growing chorus, a leader in which was Mrs. Mackenzie's *Slavery* (1792). *The Batchelor* (1766-1768) pleaded for the Irish[132] and inveighed against English cruelty in conquest,[133] a theme seized upon by various novels. *The Female American* (1767) expressed pity for the Indians and fear of divine wrath, "for our God is just, and will weigh our actions in a just scale."[134] The philosophical Shechem, in Walker's *Theodore Cyphon* (1796), asked,

Where . . . was Providence, when Alexander slaughtered his thousands? Where, when the gold-thirsting Spaniards put the knife to the throats of millions of Mexicans and Peruvians?[135]

In *Henry Somerville* (1798) there was further interrogation:

[131] George Parker, *op. cit.*, II, 120 ff.; Mrs. Mackenzie, *Slavery*, pp. 38-39; George Walker, *Theodore Cyphon* (Alexandria, 1803), II, 48.
[132] I, 100.
[133] II, 120-131.
[134] Page 9.
[135] II, 267.

What tribes among mankind, either east or west, have we rendered happy by visiting them? It appears to me that we have disturbed their tranquility, deluged their shades with blood, set up ruin and horror in the place of peace, and with the name of religion burned their altars, and disgraced our own by intolerant persecution: India, America, Africa, islands, deserts, all have felt the contagion of European injustice, wherever Europe has extended her flag! I pitied the fate of Captain Cook as sincerely as any man: but had I been a native of Owyhee, I should have assisted in his death.[136]

*Sentimental Memoirs* (1785) raised an early voice in behalf of the East Indian. Captured and mistreated in India, Captain Erskine remarkably says,

. . . it was no more than every *Englishman* deserved from a Race of Men, who had been long treated in a Style which was not only a Dishonor to *Christianity,* but to *Humanity* itself.[137]

Such words, reminiscent of Burke, occur twice later in other novels.[138]

Humanitarianism, with so many ramifications, included an attitude to war, with which we are especially concerned, and at which we may be surprised. Pacifism is rather given to usurping the crown of modernity, whereas, in fact, the movement against war began at least as early as the eighteenth century. By a good many people, even in pre-Napoleonic years, the glories of battle were considered as much an *ignis fatuus* as they are by present-day anti-militarists. Richard Price, economist and radical, speaks of a federation of states as the first move toward *"universal peace."*[139] William Godwin, philosopher extraordinary, has a long argument against war, contending that defense "is the only legitimate cause."[140] Thinkers might not count in an esti-

---

[136] (Dublin, 1798), p. 180.

[137] II, 255-256.

[138] Clara Reeve, *Destination* (Dublin, 1799), I, 179-180; Walker, *Theodore Cyphon,* II, 52.

[139] *Observations on the Importance of the American Revolution, and the Means of Making it a Benefit to the World* (Dublin, 1785), p. 15.

[140] *Enquiry Concerning Political Justice* (1st American, from 2nd London, ed., Philadelphia, 1796), II, 111. For the whole discussion, see pp. 104 ff.

mate of popular opinion, but second-rate story-tellers do. It is significant when Watson's "Sassoonan," in the *New Novelist's Magazine* (1786), takes time out for this discourse:

Indeed, the wars to which avarice has prompted the Europeans, will ever remain, in the annals of the world, as a blot on human kind. We are taught to dishonour the ravages committed by Caesar, Alexander, and the Tartarian conquerors; but we return to them with some complacency, after viewing the cruelties committed by Europeans on nations too rude and unskilful in war to afford them any honour from their conquests. The wars that have arisen among the Europeans themselves from objects of gain, if they be less execrable, they from thence enable us to regard them with the contempt and ridicule that is due to the meanness of their quarrel.[141]

Against all the opponents of war I find only one—Lady Mary Walker Hamilton—who thinks it futile to hope. She says, in the *Memoirs of the Marchioness De Louvoi,*

A perpetual peace is not in the decrees of Providence, which, if such a thing had been intended, would have given men a different character. War seems to me a necessary evil: if we were designed for absolute uniformity, we would never have been afflicted with plagues and earthquakes.[142]

And that, also, is modern.

Richard Price expressed his hopes for peace in a pamphlet on the American war. In fiction, there is a somewhat similar union of ideas in such a title as *Fanny Vernon, or the Forlorn Hope; A Tale of Woe; Containing Scenes of Horror and Distress that happened during the War in America,* and here we are back with the sorrows and afflictions that have claimed a great deal of attention. The point is that many of the novels of pain and suffering used their material not only for its own sake but also to serve an idea—the ugliness and futility of war. In so doing they manifested the awakening humanitarianism of the era. They not only described war scenes in America, but

[141] I, 170.
[142] I, 20.

from these went on to denounce war. Thus America played a part on the broad stage of social history; it was influential in the opposition to militarism. The novels record and make the most of that influence. Without fighting in America, there would have been less immediate stimulation of the fight against warfare, and the novels would have been without excellent material for giving voice to and advancing the cause. There are not many of them, on the whole, but they appear with regularity, even maintaining their vogue at the end of the century, when most American subjects were yielding ground rapidly.

Between 1776 and 1785 there are five of them, two by the ever-present Pratt. He introduces the subject in *Shenstone Green* (1779), describing, in a passage reaching a climax of modern enough tone, the foundation of an ideal village on a "barren heath," the condition of which

arises not from the desolation of conquest. The heaps of rubbish which impede our passage *here,* are not created by the ruins of some fair city, which hath fallen the victim of a military fury, who magnifies murther into patriotism.[143]

He reaches his best heights, however, in various outbursts in *Emma Corbett,* which is ever with us. Once Emma addresses the "spirit of contention" as

thou, who ragest most unnaturally in the human bosom, (where all the graces and affections should inhabit) and settest man against man. . . . Oh, mischievous WAR! armed at all points against the happiness and humanity of the species—how various and how dreadful are thy horrors![144]

Later she describes war—

this dire *daemon* of *battle* . . . who, with giant footsteps, tramples upon the best and most beautiful affections of the soul—who delights to hear the wail of the wounded, and the groans of the expiring— whose vessels sail upon a sea of tears, and are wafted by sighs which

143 I, 63-64.
144 I, 46-47.

are extorted from the tender bosom. I see, I see the sanguinary power. He shoots athwart the realms of affrighted fancy, in a robe of crimson ten times died in the blood of his votaries. The soft verdure of the spring withers as he advances. The streams of plenty, which fertilized a happy world, stand checked in their progress, or roll onward a bed of troubled waters. Behold where the ruthless monarch approaches. The bounties and the beauties of nature fall before him.—Territories are torn up by the roots, and empires mingle in the common ravage.[145]

After being magnified by this thunderous personification, war is reduced, ironically, to *"glory-crowned murder,"* and his works are recounted with a few physical details which, if not altogether redolent of an actual battlefield, at least do better than the "promiscuous carnage" on which the pen-struck misses, brought up on the *Rambler,* were likely to depend in their assaults on delicate sensibilities:

See—see, into that wretch's quivering side, the ball has just entered!— Here lies a head severed from the body.—There are the mangled reliques of an arm torn from the shoulder; and there the wounded horses are trampling upon their wounded masters![146]

These attacks on war—and they are by no means all that he has to say on the subject—all stem from his American material.

*Reveries of the Heart* (1781) interlards discussion of the Revolution with similar onslaughts. The author is incredulous of an officer who has boasted of performing executions:

Would you think it possible that any one could be so hardened in the trade of war, as to boast of having put to death a number of persons unarmed, unresisting, and even on their knees begging for mercy.[147]

Elsewhere the writer falls little short of the ravings of Pratt, as in commenting on the veteran officer, "modest, courteous, humane":

Pity that his trade should be fighting; and that in the execution of what is called his duty, or in a battle, he has as few reflections on the

[145] II, 6-7.
[146] II, 131-132.
[147] I, 31.

miseries, enormity, and viciousness of war, as any of those execrable machines called common soldiers; whom we construct with musquets, red coats, fierce cocked hats, and high sounding words; wind up with wine or spiritous liquors; and set a-going down the great direct infernal high road, with drums, trumpets, and artillery.[148]

But this is really a level above Pratt, who had no irony.

I said I acquiesced in their being the most gallant, brave, and humane army that ever marched to burn peaceful villages, plunder equally friend and enemy, and tomohawk, scalp, or bayonet promiscuously man, woman, and child.[149]

And he is keen in sneering at the waste of time in

reading Archbishops of Yorks sermons in defence of war; which a pacific person, like you, may think needs few encomiums to English-men, who, for above a thousand years, have been steeped to the very lips in blood, without almost a single interval of peace. But all our wars, like those of the Romans, Tartars, and other heroic wolves, have been just, whilst the peaceful sheep have ever been in the wrong.[150]

The wail of a bereaved aunt in Catherine Parry's *Eden Vale* (1784) returns us to the literal:

How many hearts are with me this moment weeping tears of blood!—How many widows, mothers, and orphans, are now deploring their irretrievable losses!—Can *they* look up to that throne for mercy, from which all power is delegated, whilst hapless wretches are every day slaughtered by the obstinate and cruel perseverance of bloody-minded men?[151]

There is a rare note of the mock-heroic in *The American Wanderer* (1783), in which the traveler says that his letters to America will probably not arrive.

It is true that war, that plague of human kind!——War, the vicious hobby-horse which my beloved countrymen are now riding through thick and thin, will prevent my transmitting them——[152]

[148] I, 33.
[149] I, 174.
[150] II, 72-73.
[151] I, 71-72.
[152] Page 150.

But comic relief is rare and denunciation continues through the late '80's, usually the outpouring of a bereaved relative or of a sympathetic observer. Aspersions on government, no new thing by now, flicker through the philippics. Ellison, in *Elfrida* (1786), having been through the war, sums up,

. . . such are the miseries which the annals of blood and desolation record—such are the agonizing woes, by which our best victories are purchased—and such events are what supply our public prints with those articles of intelligence that light up the politician's face with smiles of exultation, and give gladness to what is called the loyal heart—and yet we bestow the pompous epithets of good and great upon our actions, which thus leave an indelible stain upon our humanity.[153]

The vocabulary is set. The verbal conventions hold even in the interpolated verse which adorns most of the prose works of the period. Although they are derivative to the last syllable, Renwick still believes that his couplets in *Solicitudes of Absence* (1788) are heroic and powerful:

> From war's malignant reign what evils flow;
> Eventful parent of each tragic woe!—
> How many fathers grieve for children slain!
> How many sons lament their sires in vain!
> How many widows fruitlessly deplore
> The husbands fated to return no more!
> Commerce and arts the hostile aera mourn,
> And towns and cities undistinguished burn.
> Hence antient lore from Eastern empires fled,
> And dreadful ruin o'er each region spread;
> Regions no more with envied bulwarks crown'd,
> Nor o'er the world triumphantly renown'd.[154]

Sometimes a single line is explicit enough, as in Mrs. Smith's *Ethelinde* (1789), which tells how in America Colonel Chesterville had "beheld with firmness the savage scenes of slaughter from which humanity recoils."[155] Helen Maria Williams is a trifle more expansive in her comment on the war-death of Sophia in *Julia* (1789):

[153] III, 149-150.
[154] Page 194.
[155] (2nd ed., 1790), III, 29.

She is at rest, and this cruel war had made her happiness impossible. Alas, how dreadful are the effects of war! Every form of evil and misery is in its train: the groans of despair are mingled with the song of triumph, and the laurels of victory are nourished with the tears of humanity.[156]

But *Louisa Wharton* (1790), as is proper in a story devoted largely to the war, brings us back to the protracted chant:

O! the pride of princes, the thirst for dominion, the ambition of the great! what ravages does it make! alas! they feel not the woes of a bleeding country, they hear not the cries of the innocent, and all the ills which attend upon murdering war; but such a war as this in particular, which . . . dissolves the ties of friendship, clips the wings of commerce, and tinges the earth and sea with crimson; well might the poet exclaim,

"Ye Gods, what havock does ambition make among your works!" The drums beat, the trumpets sound, the cannons roar, the pride of nature falls without distinction; the leaden death invades my Truman's heart, my brother bleeds, my father,—oh! my dear Fidelia, the idea is too horrible to support. Eternal Providence, avert this direful scene, mitigate the horrors in view, and soon restore that harmony and concord we once so happily enjoyed.[157]

Of the five novels in the first half of the '90's which make sorties against military diplomacy, one of the more pertinacious is Mrs. Smith's *Old Manor House* (1793), which goes into page after page of invective. There is more than indignation *in vacuo*, however, as Mrs. Smith's effects always depend upon descriptive details that show either a good imagination or the aid of a good reporter. Attention is centered on two events— the passage in the transport, and Burgoyne's campaign. As the boat prepares to depart, the "distracting hurry," "the quarrels and blasphemy," the "rage of commanders and the murmurs of the commanded," the "unfeeling avarice" of buyers and sellers are new to Orlando Somerive, who hears,

[156] I, 263.
[157] Page 25.

with a mixture of wonder and disgust, the human tempest roar in which he was now engaged, and for the first time enquired of himself what all this was for?[158]

Then he finds himself

in a little crowded vessel, where nothing could equal the inconvenience to which his soldiers were subjected, but that which the miserable negroes endure in their passage to slavery.[159]

A cornet, scion of a rich family, is in very bad condition:

And now sick and desponding, this unhappy child of foolish affluence wanted a nurse much more than a broad sword—No puling girl just out of the nursery was ever more helpless. . . .[160]

Heat, disease, calms, and finally a terrific storm contribute to taking all the glory out of war; Orlando is shedding illusions.

and when he considered a number of men thus packed together in a little vessel, perishing by disease; such of them as survived going to another hemisphere to avenge on a branch of their own nation a quarrel, of the justice of which they knew little, and were never suffered to enquire; he felt disposed to wonder at the folly of mankind, and to enquire again *what all this was for?*

In due time his rhetorical question becomes more passionate:

Merciful God! can it be thy will that mankind should thus tear each other to pieces with more ferocity than the beasts of the wilderness? Can it be thy dispensation that kings are entrusted with power only to deform thy works—and in learning politics to forget humanity?[161]

Again the fling at government. Mrs. Smith is less original when she reaches her second big talking-point, the Burgoyne campaign, and a single quotation will show her substance and manner here:

Even from these wretched temporary abodes they [the Americans] were often driven, to make way for the English soldiers; and their women

[158] III, 241.
[159] III, 243.
[160] III, 245.
[161] III, 248 ff.

183

and children exposed to the tempest of the night, or, what was infinitely more dreadful, to the brutality of the military. In a war so protracted, and carried on with such various success, these scenes of devastation had occurred so often, that the country appeared almost depopulated, or the few stragglers, who yet lingered round the places most eagerly contended for, had been habituated to suffer till they had almost lost the semblance of humanity.[162]

Here is a good example of simultaneous hatred of war and sympathy for America. To these is added contempt for politicians in a final ironic soliloquy of Orlando, who sees a wounded veteran:

yet perhaps [he] has been disabled from acquiring them [the necessaries of life] by having lost his limb in the service of what is called his country, that is, in fighting the battles of its politicians; and having been deprived of his leg to preserve the balance of Europe, has not found in the usual asylum a place of rest, to make him such amends as can be made for such a misfortune! All the horrors of which he had been a witness in America now returned to his recollection; and the madness and folly of mankind, which occasioned these horrors, struck him more forcibly now than when his spirits were heated by having been a party in them.[163]

Some of Mrs. Smith's paragraphs sound shopworn, of course, but it is clear that she far surpasses most of her contemporaries in intellectual control of her material and in effort to impart reality to such frequent abstractions as "sufferings" and "horrors."

Mrs. Mackenzie's *Slavery* (1792), devoted to another kind of humanitarianism, speaks of "the war, which will ever be remembered with horror by surviving sufferers."[164] Imlay's *Emigrants* (1793) is entirely conventional:

When the ruthless hand of barbarous war has in many places desolated the fairest country upon the face of the globe. . . . Who can help feeling an indignation against such gothic practices?[165]

[162] III, 269.
[163] IV, 181-182.
[164] Page 84.
[165] III, 126-127.

The old-soldier episode in Davies' *Elisa Powell* (1795), with a few realistic details in the Smith manner, strives for peace rather than pathos. The soldier tells how at Bunker Hill he

received the reward of his valour. This consisted in the contents of a canister, which, exclusive of half a dozen hits of less consequence, eased him of an eye and a foot, and, without taking away the power of playing a tolerable strum on his favourite instrument, new modelled his hand into the shape of an Ourang Outang's paw. . . . "As much of me as fell at the head of our lines was, indeed, allowed to have fallen gallantly; but I confess that the fragments I still carry about are much in love with peace. . . ."[166]

Mrs. Parsons outdoes herself in shrieking, of course, and her *Voluntary Exile* belongs largely to the less effective manner of generalization and declamation. For the sake of making war ultra-horrible Mrs. Parsons concocts an atrocity story of twentieth-century stamp: a couple of Hessians rape two American girls in the presence of their father and brother, as a result of which one of the girls commits suicide and the other is "suddenly seized with a violent convulsion, attended with hickups, that in a few minutes put an end to her existence."[167] The rather simple expiation of lost "virtue" by hiccoughs relieves one of too profound a sense of moral catastrophe. Nor is one too upset by infinite paragraphs of rant by Biddulph, although their existence is very significant as far as the anti-war theme is concerned. In one of his reflective jaunts into the woods (he does not get lost this time, a fact which shows that his creatrix occasionally resisted temptation),

he was overwhelmed by a profound melancholy, the horrid effusion of blood he had witnessed, and even partook in, seemed, on sober reflection, when not animated by the example and ardour of others, to revolt equally against humanity and Christianity. . . .[168]

Here he runs into another episode involving Hessian improprie-

166 I, 187-189.
167 II, 202-204.
168 II, 91-92.

ties, and begins "to shrink at the horror and devastation of war."[169] Wounded, he is saved by Quakers, who tell him,

The trade of blood, in which thou, young man, art engaged, is equally repugnant to Christ's precepts, and to humanity.[170]

Christian and humane injunctions are again and again called to the attention of the erring. After a dying American has given him a token to take to his fiancée, Biddulph exclaims,

Great God! . . . what scenes are these! Why, did I ever join in an undertaking so wounding to every feeling of humanity! Unhappy man! thou art cut off from expected happiness perhaps, and the original of this copy (untying the picture and looking on the representation of a very beautiful young woman) this amiable young creature is doomed to hopeless anguish and heartfelt sorrow.[171]

"Shocked and disgusted" by further military experiences, he quits the army. His epilogue on war states the theme which all the quotations in this chapter illustrate:

[He] deprecated the horrors of war, which in its extension, was productive of so much misery to individuals, and very rarely benefited the community at large. War, in all places, and among all nations, must produce equal calamities in those countries that were the seat of war. . . .[172]

Mrs. Parsons is often too easily made fun of. Doing what a modern review would call "tracing the influence on a sensitive young man of the bitter actualities of war," she accomplishes what in her day must have been a not ineffective job of campaigning.

In the last five years of the century, when one might expect interest in the subject to have lapsed, both because there was decreasing attention to the American war and because events in France were encouraging new military efforts in England, there are seven novels with an anti-war bias. In *Ned Evans*

169 II, 108.
170 II, 117.
171 II, 162.
172 IV, 197-198.

(1796), Mrs. Hervey showed an acquaintance with American scenes which the *Monthly* thought not quite

compatible with the detestation of war, and the regard to the rights of mankind, which are warmly expressed in various parts of the work.[173]

Mr. Eddows in *Disobedience* (1797) talks of his losses in

this iniquitous struggle between power and right: but I make little of that. My individual sufferings are nothing in the scale of that aggregate of misery and loss, which has been designed and executed by those who never heard the cry of war, or abated one atom of their refined luxury, to soften the evils they imposed.[174]

G. Thompson's Sternian *Sentimental Tour* (1798), naturally enough, contains an outburst against war.[175] The Misses Lee, guessing at the nature of a battlefield which they had never seen, tell us that

the bloody hand of man had strewed carnage and desolation . . . the ghastly countenances of his fellow-sufferers, as they lay motionless and bleeding, induced him to close his eyes in silent and nameless agony.[176]

One is reminded of modern munitions inquiries by a passage in George Walker's *Theodore Cyphon* (1796):

Theodore had been adjusting an account of gunpowder and bullets, privately sold in Canada to some Indian chiefs, and lamenting the savage state of our nature, the horrors of war, and the attending train of human calamity, till his mind overflowed with pity at our delusions, and with grief, that those delusions must continue till man is no longer man.[177]

Here again is one of the rare signs of an author's mind actually working. But emotions alone dominate several relevant passages in the *Tales of Truth* (1800) of E. H.:

. . . war was raging with all its sanguinary horrors in America, that favored and hospitable land. . . .

[173] XXI (Second Series, 1796), 207.
[174] IV, 63.
[175] (Penrith), pp. 57-58.
[176] *Canterbury Tales* (1799), III, 34.
[177] I, 34.

She was one of war's victims . . . the day arrived when they [her sons] were *obliged* to take a part; they must fight, or suffer imprisonment. *Compulsion* was the order of the day—strange contradiction!

The American soldier, whose musquet killed the youth, prepared to strip him.—Savage custom, and sanctioned by civilized beings![178]

Last to be considered is *Henry Willoughby* (1798) with its satire, probably inspired by *Roderick Random,* of conditions on a battleship. The evils are made most emphatic by the fact that both the title-hero and his best friend, Morthermer, although neither is pacifistic or picaresquely frivolous, independently desert the navy in the middle of the American war, with the complete approbation of the author. In view of all the patriotic soldiers we have come across who stuck even to unpalatable duty, we may assume that the provocation was serious, although the satirical intention leads to *bizarrerie*. Attack is centered on the commander typified by one Neptune Namur, bastard of an admiral and "one of the nymphs of Gosport," who combined the "excessive pride and ambition" of his father with the "brute ignorance and depravity of morals" of his mother.[179] He opens his reign with the announcement that any infringement of discipline will be greeted by four dozen lashes. Henry comments:

I must do captain Namur the justice to say, I never knew him in any instance ever to have relaxed from this declaration.[180]

Then follows a very vivid detailed description of the hell into which the West Indies heat and the general living conditions had turned the boat.[181] Another ship was literally referred to as "the hell afloat," with its hard work and inadequate food and drink; the confusion resulting from a storm causes about half the crew to be beaten up, and a battle with the French leads to a continuation of the epidemic of punishment and

178 II, 85, IV, 103-104, and IV, 109, respectively.
179 I, 179-180.
180 I, 181.
181 I, 182 ff.

court-martialing. If this is overdone, it is at least a relief from the sentimental talk of the lady-novelists about "the gallant Rodney."

The material in this section, though brief, is important. Here the influence of the American war is not so much to give novelists something else to talk about as it is to provide them with substance to which they can attach certain feelings and convictions which are a part of the Romantic renascence. Thus in a small way, though unmistakably, the Revolution adds further impetus to the major movement of the period. The incipient humanitarianism, though not always distinguishable from professional sentimentalism eying the cash-register, generally gives an impression, if not of good judgment, at least of sincerity. Of the two approaches taken by the peace-lovers, the less felicitous, to us, is that of the rampant abstractions dear to the Age of Reason, bounding off into fantastic grandiloquence. At that, the quickening conscience affects us less adversely than an older staple, second-hand morality; rant goes down better than cant. But what can not merely demand tolerance but almost elicit admiration is the second approach, as seen in Mrs. Smith—the effort at realistic details which dramatize the fearfulness of war. On this we bestow our brightest laurel, *modern*. Here is the first intimation of the deromanticizing of battle in the post-1918 manner. A part of it is the slaps at cabinets and congresses, the office-men who declare war in their own muddlement and vanity. The amount of anger directed at them, and the unfettered utterance of it, are further signs of that extraordinary freedom of the press which many books have now attested to.

The painfulness and loathsomeness of the American war, real or imagined, sharpened up a humanitarianism which began to pierce all illusions about war. The novel mirrors the new growth of human sympathies, or at least shows how much more vocal they were becoming; here is the beginning of the humanitarian novel.

V

In view of the pro-American bent in novelists who criticized the war, of the realization that the war was a civil war and the consequent sympathy for fellow-strugglers in a common cause, and of the humanitarianism arising out of the war and especially out of the sufferings of the Americans, it is altogether natural that novelists should have expressed admiration for the stubbornness and independence of the out-numbered, hard-pressed, often half-starved colonists. What we may call American spirit did receive considerable approval, to be summarized in this concluding section of the chapter.

Interpretations of the American temper are not entirely consistent but fall roughly into two groups, each paced by an English colonel. It was as early as March 6, 1765, that Colonel Barré praised to the Commons the American endurance of hardship, love of liberty, and persistence in the face of English neglect. Answering complacent English arguments, he eulogized and prophesied:

They protected by your arms! they have nobly taken up arms in your defence, have exerted their valour amidst their constant and laborious industry . . . and the same spirit which actuated that people at first, will continue with them still. . . .[182]

The colonel of another mind was Gage, who spread abroad the idea that

Americans were unwarlike as a community, and pusillanimous as individuals. That agreeable and convenient idea had been eagerly caught up by the noisiest members of the Government, and had been employed by them in public as an argument against those who condemned their policy as hazardous.[183]

The swashbucklers found some adherents in fiction, but few in comparison with those who were convinced of American perseverance, courage, and independence.

[182] *Parliamentary History,* XVI, 38-40.
[183] Trevelyan, *The American Revolution,* Part I, p. 284.

190

CRITICISM OF THE REVOLUTION

*The Adventure of a Bale of Goods from America* (1766),
a rather feeble political satire, is first to pay tribute to colonial
spirit. After the Stamp Act, Isaac Roderiguez, a merchant,
found Bostonians "so enraged against every thing English"[184]
that he hopelessly returned to England, reporting thus to an
ex-minister:

. . . all is Vengeance yonder—the Colonies breathe the Spirit of
Liberty, they will have no Stamp—they know what is unconstitutional;
they meet—they confer—they begin to understand each other—Force
will be in vain—their Multitudes will baffle it—and their Insanity is
so great that they refuse the most charming Things if English. . . .[185]

If this broadside was actuated merely by economic anxiety,
politics alone animates the heroine of Mrs. Gibbes's *Friendship
in a Nunnery* (1778), quoted by the *Critical:*

Hear these truths, said the little Niobe—hear my wrongs, cried she,
bursting into tears, now that her rage had spent itself—and learn to
revere a nation that will teach you, though sorely against their wishes—
no human power shall oppress them with *impunity.*

The reviewer admits that this would be all right in a "republican print," but,

. . . from a young lady who is "turned of fourteen." What may not
be expected from the old men and sages of that happy continent, when
its maidens, its babes and sucklings talk, and write, and reason thus![186]

The first unfavorable interpretation of the colonial mind occurs
in the inevitable *Emma Corbett* (1780) of Pratt. Henry Hammond, the loyal British soldier, says of offers of conciliation:

They are formed, methinks, to suit the ambitious and grasping spirit
even of an American, and they must, I think, be accepted.[187]

But the book as a whole leans sharply in the other direction.
Even the neutral Raymond thus describes the Americans: "On
every brow is defiance. In every eye flashes the bloody de-

[184] Page 10.
[185] Page 15.
[186] XLVI (1778), 301.
[187] II, 169.

termination."[188] Edward Corbett is pro-American to the last exclamation:

The English persist to call those cowards whom they prove to be men, and feel to be heroes. To-morrow I shall once more fix the bayonet, and shoulder the musquet. *Every* man fights in this country; we arm not for pay but for property, not for the wages of war, but for liberty and life.[189]

The next faithful soldier lurks in *Francis the Philanthropist* (1785); though in love with an American girl, he can still characterize her countrymen as "that gallant, though faithless, nation."[190] While bravery is the virtue most frequently accorded the Americans, *Reveries of the Heart* (1781) makes a point of their humanity. After a good deal has been said about the brutality of the British army, there is an ironic summary: since military success depends upon "strength of body, and obstinate brutality of mind," the Americans were bound to lose, "their army consisting of citizens, who had a portion of human nature in their composition."[191] In *The American Wanderer* (1783), however, the Welshman Rubijo returns to the older theme; after a lecture on various antiquities, he

finished with panegyrics upon the Congress; upon the sacred fire of Roman virtue, which well nigh extinguished by the Goths, was re-kindling with redoubled blaze, in the hearts of the americans![192]

Francis Truman, the faithful soldier in *Louisa Wharton* (1790), is less scornful than convention demands, expecting an indefinite continuance of the war after learning

that the Americans are well armed, well disciplined, and above all resolute to a man to secure their freedom.[193]

[188] III, 78.
[189] III, 43.
[190] Page 231.
[191] I, 178.
[192] Pp. 199-200.
[193] Page 22.

The matter of discipline is probably reported with more accuracy by Montfleuri in Mrs. Smith's *Desmond* (1792):

I saw, amidst the almost undisciplined Americans, many instances of that enthusiastic courage which animates men who contend for all that is dear to them, against the iron hand of injustice; and, I saw these exertions made too often vain, against the disciplined mercenaries of despotism; who, in learning to call them rebels, seemed too often to have forgotten that they were men.[194]

Mrs. Smith again takes up the cry in her *Old Manor House* (1793):

Elate with national pride, they [the English] had learned by the successes of the preceding war to look with contempt on the inhabitants of every other part of the globe; and even on their colonists, men of their own country—little imagining that, from their spirited resistance,
"The child would rue that was unborn
"The *taxing* of that day."[195]

After returning to England, Orlando Somerive is strongly affected by an account of how the Americans,

fighting in defence of their liberties . . . had marked their route with the blood which flowed from their naked feet in walking over frozen ground. . . .[196]

Nonpareil disciple of documentation that she is, Mrs. Smith points the moral with a footnote:

The perusal of the history of the American Revolution, of Ramsay, is humbly recommended to those Englishmen who doubt whether, in defence of their freedom, any other nation but their own will fight, or conquer.[197]

In her *Young Philosopher* (1798) she notes astonishing corollaries to American idealism. Glenmorris, taken to Boston for ransom by a piratical privateer, says of the New Englanders:

. . . they were determined to be *free,* and were now making the

[194] I, 153-154.
[195] III, 4-5.
[196] IV, 153-154.
[197] IV, 154 note.

noblest exertions to resist what they deemed oppression. I found that with a few of them the inveterate hatred generated by the unnatural war they had been driven into, extended to me, merely because I was an Englishman . . . but in others the noble flame of liberty seemed to have purified their minds from every narrow and unmanly prejudice. . . .[198]

Superior to her colleagues in quantity if in no other way, Mrs. Parsons reiterates everything said about American spirit. In her *Voluntary Exile* (1795), Biddulph, en route to America, is told by his friend Osborne,

I much fear, we shall gain little glory, and lose much blood in our endeavours to subdue a people so numerous, so desperate, and fighting for liberty and independence.[199]

This is hindsight, of course. Although the battle of Brandywine was a defeat, it "greatly increased the reputation" of the Americans,

from the firm and undaunted courage they had displayed during the engagement. Animated by the presence of a General, whom they loved and revered, they fought to distinguish themselves under the eye of a Washington, and to deserve his approbation, they fought like lions with the greatest intrepidity. . . .[200]

Fortunately without the Aristotelian simile and interpretative phrase, the Washington theme continues. At Valley Forge:

The wonderful resolution, patience, perseverance, the attachment to their General, which pervaded throughout the whole American camp, evinced such unshaken determination to bear with every inconvenience, and struggle through every difficulty under his command, whom they looked up to as a father and a preserver, that every thinking, sensible mind was convinced, the war would not be of a short duration, should England persist in her demands, and prosecute the war until America was tired, or entirely subdued.[201]

Even Quakers and women join the chorus of will to victory.

[198] II, 241.
[199] II, 62.
[200] II, 163.
[201] III, 127-128.

194

Taken captive, Biddulph is in charge of a Colonel Mifflin, who had been a Quaker; but inspired by military ardour, and a desire of serving his country, he had quitted his household gods, and . . . his sect, and repaired to the Jerseys, that he might have the glory to command under General Washington.[202]

And a Mrs. Nesbitt mixes rhetoric and patriotism:

. . . we may lose our dearest friends; we are not Stoic's, to see our husbands, brothers, children, cut off for ever; our property destroyed, even our personal safety endangered every moment; we do not see all this with apathy, or a false heroism—no, we feel, keenly feel, our misfortunes; but the necessity, the duty that called them forth to venture all in defence of their country and their freedom, supercedes all selfish considerations; and though our tears will flow from tenderness, they are unaccompanied by any regret. We glory that our sons, our brothers, have performed their duty, though we are the sufferers.[203]

It is Mrs. Humberston of Eugenia De Acton's *Disobedience* (1797), however, who not only has courage but is a sort of embodiment of the democratic principle, the spirit of homespun; she comes close to being the first frontier heroine.

Descended from ancestors who fought, in the wilds and forests of America, [for] that freedom of thought and action which was denied them in Europe, she had imbibed with her mother's milk the purest principles of republicanism; and she preferred, with the utmost sincerity of mind, the coarsest russet stuff, when worn in the land of freedom, to the most gorgeous garment that could be bestowed by the hand of a monarch. She had seen, therefore, the diminution of their property rather with exultation than repining; and now that it was almost wholly gone, she appeared more proud of her poverty than the most ostentatious person could have been of their riches. Notwithstanding this decided and vigorous turn of mind, her manners were gentle and feminine; her heart soft and yielding; and her temper sweet and obliging.[204]

Thus a potential Maid Marian Americana still remains an

[202] III, 129-130; cf. IV, 166.
[203] IV, 167.
[204] IV, 86-87.

acceptable eighteenth-century heroine, loving liberty, of course, but still properly flattering to the male. Her husband, it will be gathered, cheerfully lost all of his property "in the prosecution of a dispute which he thought justified by every law, moral and divine."[205] An author who fancied panegyric as much as the present one was bound to place another verbal flurry in the mouth of Mr. Eddows, the malcontent Briton:

> . . . I hail, with joy and gratulation, that equitable and truly heroic land, where we have seen the hero quit the trowel for the truncheon; the printer rise to the legislator; and the man of peace and modesty become the defender and saviour of his country. . . . Could you know the instances of heroic self-denial and suffering, of patience and courage, of exertion and forbearance, that have been manifested by people of all ranks, ages, and sexes, in that oppressed, and now triumphant country, you would not wonder at the warmth of approbation which marks my opinions and my sentiments, nor at my resolution to make one of its citizens.[206]

American spirit received the almost unanimous admiration of the novelists who commented on it. Once or twice Americans appear as pusillanimous or grasping or perverse, but such views were largely dramatic, attributed to soldiers who could not very well think differently. Yet one or two of them were permitted to concede some virtues to their opponents. Almost without exception the characters of whom their creators especially approved made it a point to be impressed by colonial fortitude and pertinacity. It may be that here the function of the American war was to provide a vent for a latent urge to hero-worship that, except for Wolfe and Cumberland, had found little outlet for many decades. Certainly the material was conducive to the emotionality characteristic of most of these novels. In all its uses the war made an appeal to love of pathos, to admiration, enthusiasm, sympathy, scorn, hatred, employed all devices to stir up, and to satisfy a wrought-up, reader.

205 IV, 84.
206 IV, 63-64.

This corner of prose fiction, however, keeps forcing itself on one's attention as a footnote to history. A few writers had principles, and they were for America. Most writers merely wanted money, and they were for America. Publishers, no mean estimators of public fancy, must have discerned a wide sympathy for the colonies. Novels, conventional in technique, characters, and morality, espoused a cause that was an especial favorite of the radicals—paradoxical enough, since radicalism rarely adopts the anonymity of our fraternity of scriveners. More paradoxical, the cause of the radicals was popular; else these dozens of novels here discussed could never have been written. Demos was having a fling, a new kind of holiday. Let it be called Romanticism, if there must be a label, but let there be added a codicil: that for once a "movement" was not merely a stir in the higher intellectual atmosphere.

On the lower levels, where there was density of population, sizable crowds were cheering American valor when they might have been expected to raise their voices in hosannas for British exploits. They were damning the war as foolish, impracticable, and unjust when they might have been expected to show "patriotism" as it is usually thought of in war-time, to chant the old *dulce-et-decorum-est* litany. They were sympathizing with the woes and afflictions of Americans, puncturing the romantic illusions about war, resenting their own losses and sorrows, when they might have been expected, on the one hand, to let the Americans down with a "serves them right for their impudence," and, on the other, to relish their own immolation to the tune of "die for dear old empire." They were abominating the "murder" of kinsmen, an "unnatural war," a "civil war," when they might have been expected to hear a throne and ministry which shouted "Treason!" and to call the Americans rebels who deserved the worst fate. In interpreting the war as a civil war they were ahead of their times, and they were probably establishing their whole viewpoint. On that basis they could criticize, sympathize, and eulogize as they did, not attack as rough retrospection might assume. They could express themselves with an abandon that makes modern "freedom of the press" look puny. The novels certainly show a divided England. It stood, but it was remodeled. Here we see, informally, what made the remodeling possible.

# Chapter VI

## TREATMENT OF ECONOMIC PROBLEMS

### i

The Revolution itself, whether in narrative or discussion, was not the only aspect of British-American relations that inspired comment by English novelists between 1760 and 1800. There were also the preliminaries—taxation and cognate economic issues. The novel, we have seen, seldom lacked opinions on anything, and, when taxes were the moot question, again fiction cast a vote. It was the Stamp Act which first achieved publicity for the colonies, giving them an important position in the press;[1] so it is not surprising that fiction, often unblushingly journalistic, debated stamps as did the periodicals. During the war, the group of people who sustained the greatest material disadvantage were the commercial class,[2] and their prominence naturally led to the expression of their viewpoint in novels. After the war, the new relationship brought marked economic advantages for England, and again the influence of dollars and cents became perceptible in literature.

Economic matters, as they enter the catholic domain of the story-teller, fall into four divisions. We have, in the first place, some discussion of colonies and colonization; in the second, of taxation in principle and practice; in the third, of the commercial influences of the war; in the fourth, of war in its relation to private property. Only the last finds its way consistently into the narrative proper; otherwise we are dealing largely with undiluted exposition.

[1] See Hinkhouse, *op. cit.*, pp. 58 ff.
[2] See Clark, *op. cit.*, pp. 51 ff.

ii

Oliver Goldsmith was worried about the problem of colonies before anxiety became official. *The Citizen of the World* (1760-1761) expresses a very definite, positive point of view:

The best English politicians, however, are sensible, that to keep their present conquests, would be rather a burthen than an advantage to them, rather a diminution of their strength than an encrease of power. It is in the politic as in the human constitution; if the limbs grow too large for the body, their size, instead of improving, will diminish the vigour of the whole. The colonies should always bear an exact proportion to the mother country; when they grow populous, they grow powerful, and by becoming powerful, they become independent also; thus subordination is destroyed, and a country swallowed up in the extent of it's own dominions. . . .[3]

But Goldsmith was playing Cassandra. Doubtless a more attentive ear received Mrs. Brooke's *History of Emily Montague* (1769), a Baedeker *qua* fiction:

It is not only our interest to have colonies; they are not only necessary to our commerce, and our greatest and surest sources of wealth, but our very being as a powerful commercial nation depends on them: it is therefore an object of all others most worthy of our attention, that they should be as flourishing and populous as possible.[4]

That is the other extreme. Smollett was less convinced, apparently, although his comment in *Humphry Clinker* (1771) does not commit him irretrievably:

Our people have a strange itch to colonize America, when the uncultivated parts of our own island might be settled to greater advantage.[5]

Charles Johnstone sided with Goldsmith. His *History of Arsaces* (1774) describes an Oriental people, the Byrsans, who planted colonies which "drained their own country of its most useful inhabitants." It seems clear that his allegory refers to America:

[3] (3rd ed., 1774), I, 56-57.
[4] II, 228-229.
[5] *Works, ed. cit.*, IV, 132.

Time shewed the consequences of this conduct. These colonies, en-creasing in numbers, in proportion to the depopulation of their mother country, by such emigrations; and flourishing in all the arts carried from thence, at length felt their own strength; and scorning a depend-ance no longer supported by sufficient power, took the first plausible occasion to shake it off; and ever after carried themselves like states allied upon equal terms, rather than subjects.[6]

Rare, indeed—a minor novelist having a prophetic vision. A similar, though less foreseeing, allegory is that of *Hildebrand Bowman* (1778), which points out that a country of limited resources, and with high taxation, was likely to be ruined by emigration to colonies where life was infinitely easier and op-portunities correspondingly greater.[7] Then the work goes on to contend that colonial troubles lay

even in the very original Charters of the Colonies, which by giving them a constitution similar to that of the mother country, made them imagine they did not depend on the Cortesinas [Parliament], but only on the King.[8]

The depopulation-argument had made another appearance in *Adventures of Alonso* (1775), the hero of which, when he wonders why England has not seized the Spanish colonies in America, is told by the governor of Guadalajara,

the English have too much sense to envy us possessions that have been the ruin of our country;—besides, they receive more advantage by their being in our hands, than if they were in their own.[9]

That is, England not only avoids depopulation but receives all the Spanish treasure in payment for her manufactures, a state of affairs which puts Spain in the position of Midas.[10] It is

[6] I, 139-140.

[7] Page 291. This was more than post-1776 consolation, for fears of emigra-tion continued after the war. Crèvecoeur's *Letters* led to at least one determined expression of opposition, Samuel Ayscough's *Remarks on the Letters of an American Farmer; or a Detection of the Errors of Mr. St. John* (1783).

[8] Page 292.

[9] II, 60.

[10] II, 60-63. Perhaps the author had been reading Lyly, whose *Midas* (1592) had a similar idea.

doubtful, however, that the author had real convictions, for earlier Alonso had been made to rhapsodize:

> Besides, consider the present state of America;—the English colonies alone, on that continent, afford a prospect of rivalling the greatest empires of antiquity . . . [with] a more extensive philanthropy and an easier commerce among mankind than ever was known.[11]

Three brief comments after the war complete the record. Colonies must have remained a sensitive subject, judging by a footnote which the author of *Twin Brothers* (1787) appended to the first piece in the book, a couplet poem, "A New Colony Proposed and Considered," suggesting the establishment of a retreat for all varieties of liberals:

> A New Colony! I am afraid any proposal about a new colony will go ill at present.—*Colonies,* said the planner of a political dictionary, the rock on which Britain split. But the projector may say, If we have lost colonies, it is the more necessary that we find or erect new ones. Mine, he adds, is not likely to prove so troublesome as some others have been. A colony without religion, is at least free from the jealousy and murmuring respecting modes of worship, which, it has been asserted, contributed to the revolt of our colonies.[12]

*Berkeley Hall* (1796) regrets "a spirit of *conquest and colonizing,* which has generally impoverished and depopulated the parent states."[13] How thoroughly this attitude became established appears in an incident in Bage's *Man As He Is Not* (1796), in which Lord Grondale vamps up a charge against Hermsprong, the hero,

> that Hermsprong had endeavoured to entice Wigley to America; which, though not directly penal, might, in the present temper of the times, be made something of.[14]

The subject is brief, but there is enough of it to show America once again receiving some attention from novelists who were

---

[11] I, 138-139.
[12] (Edinburgh, 1787), p. 16 note. I have not been able to discover the source of the definition.
[13] III, 408.
[14] III, 124.

not minding their proper business, or else had not learned it. Here, however, we leave the accustomed emotional atmosphere and are in the calm of practical considerations. We are getting into the economic field which, in all its ramifications, drew rather copious comment from novelists.

### iii

Taxation, mundane as it is, had a fairly heavy run in fiction, starting with the Stamp Act controversy, which got all kinds of attention from press and parliament,[15] and was therefore much in the public eye. Novelists joined the crowd, often discussing taxes and their effects, but more often trotting off merrily on the tangent of political satire, always popular in English literature.

A pretense at fiction marks the first two treatments of taxation—*The Adventure of a Bale of Goods from America, In Consequence of the Stamp Act* (1766) and *The Ants* (1767). The former is not the adventure of a bale of goods at all; it is a stringing-together of a few conversations of the owner of the bale, Isaac Roderiguez, who, in January, 1766, that is, just before the repeal of the Stamp Act, has come back to England from America with an unsold shipload of goods. To his lamenting spouse he explains that he has been sent for by "a certain Minister lately in Office,"[16] who he hopes may purchase the stuff, since "the whole of that Ministry would be glad enough to have the Impression of all the Goods returned from America taken off." Here enters satire, for the Minister goes into a long incoherent explanation that does not explain:

I cannot look into your Bale, I am tied up—as are all our Party, from purchasing any Thing English—we have better and cheaper from France, rebought, when seized at the Custom-house.—The Weavers

[15] See the *Monthly Review*, XXXIV (February, 1766), 155 ff., for consecutive reviews of fifteen works bearing on the Stamp Act. See the *Parliamentary History*, XVI, 135-136, for a long list of petitions by English merchants' associations complaining of the adverse effects on trade of the Stamp Act.

[16] Page 11. The reference is probably to Grenville, in office April 10, 1763, to July 10, 1765. Isaac later refers to a "glorious two Years administration" (p. 21).

used those ill who supported me, and whom therefore I support—but that is over—we have English Spirits, and will bring certain Goods on again.—Yours, Mr RODERIGUEZ, and those others returned from America—shall shut out the newer Manufactories of the Weavers—The Americans, voted Rebels—your Goods, by them rejected, it will be patriotic to buy—We will unite for this Purpose, and abstracting from this, your Talents, Mr RODERIGUEZ, shall make you considerable— Your Fortune is my Care! But let me recommend to you, in talking about this Subject, to abstain from the Word Liberty—it ferments the English Mind—A little Liberty is a generous Cordial—but taken in too great Quantity, it renders some men Furious—the English are besotted with Liberty—the very Sound inebriates! . . . Again we will con- fer—at present the Party expects me—I must go abroad upon some Business.[17]

No wonder that Isaac was "not very well pleased."

*The Ants* pretends to give "the history of the stamp act in America, from its first imposition to its repeal"[18] in a formic allegory already explained. The narrator gets rapidly through the story of the passage of the act by the aid of the "junto," which assured the king that there was

no more effectual way of preventing these western subjects of his from ever revolting, . . . than by obliging them gradually to part with all their shining sand [gold] . . .;

through the resultant "confusion, tumult, and dismay," until finally

the cries of an injured people were heard, the prayers of the colony prevailed, and the mild, beneficent, and gracious sovereign of the hillock . . . [declared] his assent to the abolition of this most in- tolerable burden. . . .[19]

Almost all the rest of the story is an account of the Repeal Parliament, in which the legislators, designated by names taken

[17] Pp. 16-17. For an account of government difficulties with the weavers, who claimed that they suffered from "the encouragement of French silks," see *Parliamentary History*, XVI, 58.

[18] *Critical Review*, XXIV (1767), 34.

[19] II, 11-14.

from the *Batrachomyomachia*,[20] are so uniformly vicious as to be scarcely distinguishable—Meridarpax, Troxartes, Hypsiboas, Seutlaeus, Aeichenor, Troglodytes.[21] Only Lychopinax receives a favorable characterization. The fact that the characters are types, and the comment of the *Critical*, "the several speeches *supposed* [italics mine] to be made," lead one to believe that the author knew very little about the actual meeting of Parliament, the characters of the leaders, or what they said, but merely translated his violent antagonism to the whole business into furious speeches loosely distributed among legislators who seem equally to be "politically mad."[22] Hence identification, except of the group as a whole, seems impossible.

The first speaker is Meridarpax, of the "North Country,"[23] who delivers himself in this style:

shall a vile race of vagabonds, the off-scourings of the colony, wretches whom the humanity of our laws alone have [*sic*] exempted from a most shameful and ignominious death; shall such as these dare fly in the face of their allegiance to the best of sovereigns, and their duty and obedience to the prerogatives of his dignity, to which they owe their safety and protection? Shall they dare to set at defiance the legislative power of their mother-country, and trample under foot, with

[20] The author ironically denies the borrowing, asserting that he knows no Greek. This might be suspected from his use of *Aeichenor* for Λειχ η νο ρ. The regularity of the usage precludes the possibility of typographical error. In a search motivated by curiosity I have not found a manuscript, edition, or translation from which he might have borrowed the exchange of alpha for lambda. The odd alpha is still truant.

[21] I, xxxii ff.

[22] *Monthly Review*, XXXVII (1767), 147.

[23] I, xxxii. This suggests Bute. Unfortunately, the parts, points of view, and proposals of any one ant-legislator in no case correspond entirely with those of a historical legislator. A tentative identification is always upset by later evidence. Thus, what Meridarpax says also suggests the speeches of Grenville, Bedford, and Mansfield; and their attitudes and words, plus those of Northington, are suggested in other ant speeches. The only safe expedient is to identify the characters in the novel, as a group, with the defenders of the Stamp Act, as a group. Those in the novel are always much more vehement and uncompromising.

impunity, her most sacred laws and sanctions? Wretches without principle, religion, or truth![24]

After this has gone on for several more pages with cumulative violence, he moves

to appoint such a proportionable share of the expences of the government as shall appear to the wisdom of this assembly fitting and proper to be laid upon such disobedient subjects . . . that such proportionable share of such expences . . . be levied by martial law . . . and that it shall be deemed and declared high treason, for any of his majesty's subjects at the west end of the colony, upon any pretext, to contradict or oppose the execution of any of those orders which his majesty or his council shall enforce by martial law.[25]

Next comes the "sprightly" Troxartes, who, less violent, goes into a long legalistic discussion of the need for imposing restrictions on colonial trade, and concludes, therefore, that the proposed measure is "the wisest, the noblest, and most equitable" for "protecting and preserving the grandeur, majesty, and safety of the state."[26] Next is Hypsiboas, who asks whether they shall defer action

until these insolent, obstinate youngsters shall please to signify what sugar-plum, or what sweet thing, will best restore their tempers, and bless their mother-country with their returning smiles and good humour?

No, he thunders; "let the righteous vengeance of the nation they have insulted, be let loose upon them."[27] The floor passes to Seutlaeus, letter-writer and "director of his master's secret correspondence in all the various parts of the emmet world,"[28] who has made his way by flattering his royal master. He progresses from an initial Belial-like suavity to a demand that

[24] II, 24-25.
[25] II, 29-30.
[26] II, 39.
[27] II, 42-43.
[28] II, 21. Conway and Grafton were secretaries July 12, 1765, to May 23, 1766; see Robert Beatson, *A Political Index to the Histories of Great Britain and Ireland* (3rd ed., 1806), I, 404.

England enforce her power by "military weight, authority, and influence."[29] Thus he harangues on the advantage of using the army against the colonies:

. . . they may be gently soothed thereby to a stronger and warmer sense of their duty, and be gradually brought to a full and firm persuasion, that such gentle necessary chastisements and corrections, though for a time they may seem not joyous, but grievous, are entirely calculated with a mother's tenderness and love for their ultimate welfare, prosperity, and happiness.[30]

Irony gives way to fierce political satire in the description of two brothers, Aeichenor and Troglodytes, who are "diverting themselves with some of the little dirty concerns" of the hill and "are esteemed rising emmets . . . in the pursuits of ambition, guile, fawning, flattery, and dissimulation."[31] Aeichenor devotes himself to a long medical metaphor, urging a

course of purging physic, to carry off the remaining parts of the distempered humours, occasionally using caustics, blistering, or sticking plaisters, according to the nature of the symptoms, the degree of numbness and torpitude, and the various malignity which hath manifested itself in any of the extreme parts.[32]

He concludes with emphasis upon a "large and copious phlebotomy." Troglodytes takes the same tack, urging alternate courses of friction and flagellation.

The unlocking of the word-hoards comes to an end with a long oration by Lychopinax, the ideal legislator, who offsets what has already been said by censuring self-interest, false pride, superficial remedies, and unconstitutional procedure. Going into a long history of the constitution and its ideal functioning,

[29] II, 47.

[30] II, 48-49. Divested of the irony, the speech is not unlike the letters of Conway; see *Parliamentary History*, XVI, 113-120.

[31] II, 22-23. Two brothers prominent in government at the time being were George Grenville and Richard Grenville, Earl Temple; see *Parliamentary History*, XVI, 230 note.

[32] II, 56.

he regrets the low motives which now govern conduct, and he demands,

Let us with the utmost detestation and abhorrence, avoid the horrid practice of stripping our dependents and our vassals, and the labouring emmets, of every sort of all their superfluities, and plundering their granaries from time to time, for the only purpose of encreasing our hoards, or gratifying our extravagant, luxurious, and licentious humours, and supporting and maintaining the most egregious follies.[33]

The novel then evolves into a plea for governmental reform, failing to chronicle the actual repeal of the Stamp Act. Thus the taxation of America not only becomes the basis for one complete fictional work, but also, in that work, illustrates the close relationship between American matters and the attack on politics which became stronger in the next two decades.

The same point of view appears in Smollett's *Adventures of an Atom* (1769), less extensively, but just as vigorously. Smollett begins with the work of Charles Townshend, who was responsible for reviving taxation of the colonies, or, as Smollett puts it,

had in his great wisdom planned, procured, and promulgated a law saddling the Fatsisians [Americans] with a grievous tax to answer the occasions of the Japonese [English] government; an imposition which struck at the very vitals of their constitution, by which they were exempt from all burdens but such as they fitted for their own shoulders. They raised a mighty clamour at this innovation in which they were joined by Legion [the people], at that time under the influence of Taycho [Pitt], who, in the assembly of the people, bitterly inveighed against the authors and abettors of such an arbitrary and tyrannical measure.[34]

---

[33] II, 89-90. Lychopinax is of course an ideal, but, if drawn from life, might be considered a composite of Pitt and Camden. For their comments on taxation, suggesting those of Lychopinax, see *Parliamentary History*, XVI, 99, 103 ff., 168-170.

[34] *Works*, XII, 430-431. Because of his unpopular regime in Ireland, Townshend provided a link between Irish and American grievances; see *Baratariana* (essays, chiefly by Flood and Grattan, on Irish conditions under Townshend) (3rd ed., Dublin, 1777), pp. 67, 76, 92, 105.

After further acrimonious remarks meant chiefly to defend Bute, who had headed the cabinet from 1761 to 1763, Smollett records that the measure was withdrawn, "to the no small disgrace and contempt of the law-givers." He again goes off into political satire, returning to English plans to force American compliance:

> The Fatsisians, far from acquiescing in the proceedings, resolved to defend to the last extremity those liberties which they had hitherto preserved; and, as a proof of their independence, agreed among themselves to renounce all the superfluities with which they had so long been furnished, at a vast expense, from the manufactures of Japan, since that nation had begun to act toward them with all the cruelty of a step-mother.[35]

The story ends before we receive further details.

After these fumings we come across several efforts at balanced discussions. In her *History of Emily Montague* (1769) Mrs. Brooke tries to perch on a fence between expediency and prerogative. She believes American opposition to the Stamp Act to have been due to irritation at restraints placed on colonial trade with French and Spanish settlements, and she exhorts England to remember the advantages accruing to her from colonial trade.

> Taxing them immediately after their trade is restrained, seems like drying up the source, and expecting the stream to flow.
> Yet too much care cannot be taken to support the majesty of government, and assert the dominion of the parent country.[36]

Charles Johnstone's *Pilgrim* (1770), an imitation of Goldsmith's *Citizen of the World,* has an extended discussion of taxation between a worried moderate and an enthusiast. The former is prophetic in his anxiety:

> In this delicate situation, what is to be done? To support our authority may too probably plung [*sic*] us into all the horrors of a civil

[35] XII, 431-432.
[36] III, 39. In the same year there is another discussion of the subject in *The Private Letters from an American in England,* according to Mr. J. M. Clapp's note in Professor Greenough's Catalogue.

war! To give it up, will be to cut off our right, by giving up an empire, to establish which we have exhausted ourselves. The alternative is dreadful; nor dare I look forward to the consequence, whatever side we take.[37]

The splenetic defender of the colonies insists that unconstitutional taxation is thievery, and concludes, "They are not represented, and therefore they have given no consent."[38] The response is the *reductio ad absurdum,* now familiar enough:

If no person ought to pay taxes to the government who is not represented, I apprehend that much the greater part of the people of this kingdom have the same plea. Is any person represented, who has not even a right to choose his own representative? and how few! comparatively, how very few, among us, have that right? The consequence is obvious.[39]

Then comes a distinction between "external government and internal taxation," after which the argument is little above the yes-no-yes-no level.

Dr. Thomas Cogan's *John Buncle, Jr.* (1776) treats of current events in a highly metaphysical fashion, describing *The Planetarium Politicum, or Political Project,* a "Scheme to pay off the National Debt" caused largely by "our unbounded Liberality in fighting the battles of others."[40] He suggests that a recent invention be used for trips to the planets, the proceeds to go toward the debt. Should the inhabitants of other planets object, they

may be considered either as *Emigrants,* who have quitted our world without leave, and who therefore merit, not only this slight intrusion, but also the infliction of heavy fines, for their contempt of its laws and government; or they may be viewed in the milder light of *Colonies,* established from this their mother country, and of consequence subject to whatever laws we may think wise and proper to ordain. . . . With

[37] (1775), I, 216.
[38] I, 211. The first reference to taxation without representation which I have found is in an essay in *The Batchelor* (1766-1768), I, 65.
[39] I, 212.
[40] II, 263-264.

the *Moon* we may use yet greater freedoms. I would insist upon laying very severe imposts upon her, as every astronomer can prove her entire dependance upon our globe; nor could she, without the closest alliance with us, maintain her station in the universe for four and twenty hours together, but would inevitably be swallowed up by some superior power. The light she enjoys from this Orb, ought most undoubtedly to become the subject of parliamentary enquiry: it being proved to a demonstration, that she receives in a tenfold proportion to what she communicates to us. I humbly propose therefore that a due estimate be taken, that we tax the difference, and pass a vote of an eternal eclipse in case of an obstinate refusal.[41]

This is assuredly weak, and one wonders why, in view of the unbounded frankness of previous writers, there should be such a cumbersome allegory.

Several more novels offer discussions. *The Travels of Hilae-brand Bowman* (1778) is relatively calm on both sides. The pro-tax party argues:

. . . the nation had incurred an additional debt of about sixty millions; how unreasonable it was to expect, that the mother country should continue to bear all the burden, when they were become so able to take a share of it . . . Another Nomra rejoined, that if a certain tax which was laid on, had not been repealed by a former administration . . . it would have executed itself, and we should have had no rebellion. But the Armoserians by that weakness were spirited up to oppose every tax that should be laid on them; thinking that non-importation would make such a clamour among the Merchants, as to frighten the Ministry.[42]

The other side is more emphatic, reiterating the taxation-without-representation argument:

. . . was ever any thing heard of so unconstitutional? What signifies your having nursed, and defended them, at the expence of sixty millions of gorgerines, till they are grown powerful enough to go to war with you; if you will now take their money from them without their con-

[41] II, 269-270.
[42] Pp. 290-292.

sent? Surely the mother country gets enough by her exclusive trade with them . . . without thinking of taxing her own children.[43]

It is an interesting comment on the British public that taxation can be rehashed again and again, in very thin disguise, and with very familiar arguments, without voluble protest. Even when the war was practically over, so relatively individualistic a writer as Bage could go on with the old subject in the old method, inserting in *Mount Henneth* (1781) a dialogue between Carthage and her colonies in the Hesperides, which she has decided to tax. The Hesperideans want to impose their own tax, which Carthage refuses to hear of.

*H.* Honestly, now, did you do this for our sakes, or your own? But be it for ours, we are making your people a large return, by working for them with all our might. The greatest part of the whole profit of our industry has been always yours, permit it to continue so. Turn all our trade into your own harbours, as you are wont. Tax in your own country the commodities which you make us buy. But let us be favoured with the privilege your people so justly boast of, as their greatest safeguard. Let us give and grant our own money.

*C.* As a benefit of your trade, it may be something to our people in general; but what is it to the necessities of government? We want a benefit flowing full and fast into the exchequer; we don't understand your roundabout way of sending it through the body of the people.

. . .

*H.* We cannot consent to it.
*C.* Then by G-d we will dragoon you, till you do.

. . .

So Carthage sent out fleets and armies, and spent as much of her money in five years, as she expected to get out of her colonies in one hundred.[44]

Bage's long-observed preference for the American cause made him no great originator. A novel detail occurs in *Letters Written by an American Spy* (1786), in which, according to the *Critical,* the "spy," who is really only an American Quaker, says that Grenville has told him that he would be glad to accept

[43] Pp. 293-294.
[44] Page 126.

any other tax that America might propose, and to consider this a prologue to a regular consultation with the Americans. The reader joins the reviewer in surprise: "We do not recollect this circumstance. . . ."[45]

Like *The Ants,* Sir W—— L——'s *Young Hocus* (1789) uses taxation as a starting-point for broader political satire. In many ways, also, the work is like *A Fragment of the History of . . . John Bull* (1785), already summarized in respect to its treatment of the war. Again there is a sneer at the "virtue" of Pitt,[46] who appears as Young Hocus, but who naturally has no part in the scenes which here concern us. Too, England, represented by John Bull, is characterized as sensible and just, while the onus of misdoings is laid upon Mrs. Bull, that is, Parliament.

> You know that the late Mrs. Bull was a woman of very changeable temper; for some time she was for murdering all John's tenants who resided on the other side of his herring-pond, because they would not quietly submit to be rack-rented by Mrs. Bull and her steward [George III] at pleasure; as for John he was, in this business, very much hoodwinked and cajoled by both.
>
> Mrs. Bull one day said to him, "For shame husband, how can you have any bowels for those tenants of yours in the West, who live at no expence, and pay you a mere trifle of rent? . . . Rack them, rack them, John. . . ."[47]

John shows no disposition to be deceived by this approach:

> You talk like a downright credulous, vain, avaricious, unthinking woman; you are imposed upon by the steward, who is himself imposed upon by his cormorant clerks; I say, remember the fable of the hen with the golden eggs. My tenants in the West are not so rich as you would lead me to imagine. . . . Supposing besides that the Ohio was claret, and the Mississippi Madeira, the St. Lawrence red-port, and

[45] LXII (1786), 155-156.
[46] (Vol. I ["No more published"—H. C. L. Catalogue], n.d.), p. 137. The subject is allegorized as Young Hocus's relations with Mrs. Bull. Cf. *A Fragment of the History,* in which Pitt is referred to as Pam, obviously from Pamela (p. 23). The general outline and attitude of the satires are quite similar.
[47] Pp. 5-7.

every other river there, champagne and burgundy . . . still I say it would be wrong to raise their rents, and particularly in the manner you two want them raised. The maxim of John Bull is, live and let live. . . . I am sure that for every ten per cent. profit they have from me they in return give me twenty, therefore I say that to rack-rent them more would be following the fable of the hen and the golden eggs, and d—n me if I do it knowingly.[48]

Unfortunately this tribute to the spirit of England had to be followed by the admission that Mrs. Bull had her way for many years, until the ultimate outcome

came like a thunderbolt upon Mrs. Bull; and John's determined perseverance threw her into a consumption. With the utmost reluctance she gave up the point; and she afterwards grew so dangerously ill, that the steward, by John's desire, was obliged to call in the assistance of Dr. Rectitude, whose prescription soon brought her about again: but the D'rs. death unfortunately happening, she was left in a very disagreeable state.[49]

Here the subject of taxation is presented with some novelty and vividness, and the political satire gains in effectiveness through the effort at urbanity.

*Jonathan Corncob* (1787) makes an excellent comic episode of American reactions to taxation. In Boston Jonathan finds a tarring and feathering in progress,

in consequence of the culprit's having fished in Boston harbour with a drag net, and caught a chest of tea. The tea had been thrown over-board from an English ship, by the pious Bostonians some years before, but as the double cover of wood and lead had preserved it from injury, the offender had sold it to his neighbors, contrary to law. He asserted in his defence, that he had not exacted the duty of three-pence per pound, but this excuse would not do, as it was six weeks since the Bostonians had tarred and feathered any body.

Accompanied by the hooting populace he was driven out of town. . . .[50]

[48] Pp. 8-11.
[49] Pp. 19-20. Rectitude is Rockingham (p. 20 note). On the beneficent results of his ministry in the summer of 1782 see George Macaulay Trevelyan, *History of England* (New York: Longmans Green, 1926), p. 557.
[50] Page 28.

Three times in the last decade of the century is there mention of this earliest phase of the dispute. In *The Old Manor House* (1793) Mrs. Smith remarks in passing that the English

saw not the impossibility of enforcing in another country the very imposts to which, unrepresented, they would not themselves have submitted.[51]

The *Tales of Truth* (1800) of E. H. has, in a passage overflowing with sensibility, a mournful reference to the time "before *avarice* had lit the flame of discord in that happy land."[52] Finally in *Berkeley Hall* (1796) there is another adaptation of taxes to narrative use, and, as in *Jonathan Corncob,* a rather hilarious one. England, however, appears only subordinately to local disputes, intriguing in their variations from actual history. The occasion is a meeting of the inhabitants of a Pennsylvania settlement caused by the disputed jurisdiction of Pennsylvania and New Hampshire in that section, the account of which muddles, but understandably muddles, historical events. The sheriff is on hand for the collection of levies for a Canadian expedition, the discussion of which is facilitated by general bibulousness:

The hum, bustle, and confusion, resembled those of the fair of St. Bartholomew, or Stourbridge. The general cry was against paying any taxes, either imposed by New Hampshire, Pennsylvania, or Great Britain, for waging the Canadian war. . . .[53]

[51] III, 4.

[52] II, 123.

[53] II, 381-382. The scene appears to be in northeastern Pennsylvania. In view of the satire of an ideal community, the author may have had in mind the Cooper and Priestley plans for the banks of the Susquehanna. He may also have been thinking of the Wyoming settlement, the history of which provided the basis for Campbell's *Gertrude of Wyoming.* The Wyoming settlement was made by emigrants from Connecticut, and there were Pennsylvania-Connecticut disputes about boundaries; see Henry H. Hoyt, *Brief of a Title in the Seventeen Townships in the County of Luzerne: A Syllabus of the Controversy between Connecticut and Pennsylvania* (Harrisburg: Historical Society of Pennsylvania, 1879). I can find no record whatever of disputes between Pennsylvania and New Hampshire. Other material in the novel suggests that the author may have been using, as a source, *A General History of Connecticut* [by Samuel

There is a general outburst of oratory on all sides, climaxed by a speech the ending of which clearly suggests that, although the action of the novel appears to be taking place back in the years of French-English imperial conflicts, the author had anachronistically utilized the facts of the Whiskey Rebellion, which took place several years before he published his work (1796):

Liberty and property for ever, and no taxes, no duty on whisky, no exciseman, sheriff, or bailiff! Huzza! Huzza![54]

The meeting ends in a free-for-all.

As long as fifty years after the Stamp Act, when there were many more exciting events to argue about, Thomas Erskine's *Armata* (1817) could once again damn English mismanagement; Armata, he says,

insisted that an useful, affectionate, and distant people should pay for the support of wars she had foolishly involved in at the other extremity of our planet?—Can the human imagination extend farther to the belief, that even *this monstrous claim* was acceded to?—the children of a misguided parent desired only to know what she demanded, that they might have the grace of rendering it as a spontaneous grant, to be bestowed under the same forms of government and under the sanction of the very magistrates which she herself had created for the purpose.—Must I lastly trespass upon, or rather insult, your credulity, by telling you that even *this* offer was refused? Though revenue was the object, the unlimited grant was rejected, and the revenue after all given up to enforce a nominal demand.—Many eloquent and solemn protests of

---

Peters] (2nd ed., London, 1782), which records so many different interstate disputes (pp. 75 ff.) that the novelist may easily have got his parties confused. It is interesting, by the way, that two novels satirizing American Utopias also make fun of land controversies; George Walker's *Vagabond* (1799) brings in Pennsylvania-Virginia disputes (p. 170).

[54] II, 385. The author, who appears to be well read, might easily have used any one of several publications on the Whiskey Rebellion: *The Proceedings of the Executive of the United States, Respecting the Insurgents* (Philadelphia, 1794); Hugh H. Brackenridge, *Incidents of the Insurrection in the Western Parts of Pennsylvania* . . . (Philadelphia, 1795); William Findley, *History of the Insurrection in the Four Western Counties of Pennsylvania* . . . (Philadelphia, 1796).

our most illustrious men of that time were opposed in vain to the insane project. The whole strength of Armata was put forth. . . .[55]

The author, though famous as a Whig, is little harsher than many of his predecessors, and, like most of them, he is chiefly interested in the wider problem of good government.

Between the first pamphlet fiction against the Stamp Act and this final extended allegory attacking English principles of taxation, there is a steady stream of opposition to the manner of dealing with the colonies. At no time is there an outright, flatfooted defense of English method and attitude. Some novelists discuss the matter from both points of view, usually with a more emphatic exposition of the American stand. But of all these discussions of taxation, a wide majority condemn the English heartily, either for unconstitutionality or for plain bad judgment. Once again in this third-rate, but quite significant literature, do we find that "patriotism" means something other than a mere huzza for the actions of the home-government, whatever they may be. The tenseness of a period of conflict, which produces what we call war-psychology, does not force all opinions into a single pigeonhole.

Behind the support for American resistance lies less of the emotionalism, less of the sympathy that characterized the attacks on the war, than of a fairly rational concern with the rightness of English governmental processes. While nothing profound, there is still an effort at genuine political criticism. It is possibly this concern with fundamental principles that accounts for the large number of allegories which we have seen. It might have been dangerous to venture forthright attacks on governmental exercise of powers; there was little sympathy for frank exponents of "first principles," as is seen in the treatment of Priestley. Hence there was safety in imaginary ant-worlds, Japans, Carthages, and Armatas. Disguises, however, were as transparent as they were intended to be; a thin veil of illusion does not conceal further strong evidence of the freedom of the

[55] Pp. 52-53.

press. On the other hand, it was safe enough to rage with open fury about the war on humanitarian grounds; to call a governor inhumane is not to suggest that his conduct is illegal.

iv

In tracing taxation through prose fiction, we have naturally come across various references to the economic value of the colonies to England. The relation of America to commerce, to business and finance in England, was the subject of a good deal of discussion, which the present section will examine briefly.

There were always doubters, critics who considered that an empire cost more than it produced. Among them was Goldsmith:

And what are the commodities which this colony, when established, are to produce in return? Why raw silk, hemp, and tobacco. England, therefore, must make an exchange of her best and bravest subjects for raw silk, hemp, and tobacco; her hardy veterans and honest tradesmen, must be trucked for a box of snuff or a silk petticoat. Strange absurdity![56]

In *The History of Emily Montague* (1769) Mrs. Brooke, at times empire-minded, once admits that England cannot spare the number of colonists she should have. She even confesses that the English, because of their love for their native land and their maladaptation to hardships, are not good colonists at best.[57] In *Humphry Clinker* Smollett makes a realistic note on the alleged advantages of commerce:

The only solid commercial advantage reaped from that measure [Scotland's union with England], was the privilege of trading to the British plantations; yet, excepting Glasgow and Dumfries, I don't know any other Scottish town concerned in that traffick.[58]

Edward Davies' *Elisa Powell* (1795) is more general and more emphatic:

[56] *Citizen of the World*, I, 57. Cf. *The Traveller*, 397 ff., and *The Deserted Village*, 51 ff., 283 ff., 341 ff. For a criticism of this gloomy view, see *Gentleman's Magazine*, XL (1770), 271.

[57] II, 229-230.

[58] *Works*, IV, 168.

. . . it seems evident, that, from our extraordinary exertions in this way, we have not received all those brilliant advantages which Englishmen generally suppose. Could we calculate the expences of forming, defending, and, at last, attempting to subdue our commercial colonies in America, together with the expences of those formidable arguments and bloody wars which we have undertaken almost solely for the protection of our commerce and dependencies, and could we deduct the whole from the national wealth, as it now stands, we should be more competent judges of what we have really gained by the bargain.[59]

Finally, in *Henry Somerville* (1798), there is an inquiry whether any voyages of discovery do anybody any good, whether, for instance, advantageous trade has been established with Hawaii. The answer is:

In some of the islands we have established good factories, which carry on extensive trade, and produce great influx of property and revenue at home.[60]

The party of the second part expresses an opinion widely held in novel-writing circles. The early Mrs. Brooke, it appears from *Lady Julia Mandeville* (1763), felt strongly about the advantages of Canada, if the inhabitants were satisfied by mild laws, liberty of conscience, and constitutional freedom, and taught the beauties of Anglicanism. Further,

. . . if population is encouraged; the waste lands settled; and a whale fishery set on foot, we shall find it, considered in every light, an acquisition beyond our most sanguine hopes.[61]

The whole point of *The Adventure of a Bale of Goods* (1766) is that trade has been good and the Stamp Act has ruined it. *The Ants* (1767), though primarily concerned with political satire, says much about English economic hopes of America, nurtured as a place to which they could ship

all their own superfluities, and the various produce of their industry at the east end, and exchange them there for those necessaries which were

[59] I, 130-131.
[60] Page 181.
[61] Pp. 156-157.

to be found in abundance in the western parts, in such a vast profusion and variety as should enable them to supply all the various hillocks in the emmet world with whatever they had to spare, at their own option and their own prices, so as to aggrandize and enrich themselves according to their own pleasure, industry, or abilities, consistent with the general welfare of trade and commerce.[62]

After attacking the Stamp Act, Lychopinax expresses the hope that all the ants will unite

to open, extend, and encourage every track of communication with the different parts of the hillock, by the most upright, faithful, and honourable dealings; to establish commerce upon its true foundation, a mutual attention to the various, real, or artificial wants of one another, without cozening, over-reaching, biting, and nipping. . . .[63]

One aspect of colonial trade is mentioned only once; the hero of *Adventures of Alonso* (1775) at one time casts his lot with an English sea-captain who points out "the great advantage that was to be reaped by carrying on a contraband trade with the Spanish settlements."[64] *The Travels of Hildebrand Bowman* (1778) represents the pro-colonial English as arguing,

Surely the mother country gets enough by her exclusive trade with them . . . without thinking of taxing her own children.[65]

After the war, of course, commerce became active and mutually profitable, a fact probably responsible for the cheerful picture of commercial success in several stories. In Combe's *Devil upon Two Sticks* (1790) there is a Scotchman,

recommended by his master as a fit person to be entrusted with the care of a considerable cargo, which was to be sent as a venture to one of the British Colonies in *North America*. He made the voyage with so much success, that he was requested to conduct a second.

[62] I, 69-70.
[63] II, 108-109.
[64] II, 25. Later pages chronicle great success. Earlier parts of the novel have a great deal to say about Portuguese trade with Latin America, possibly intended to have especial significance for the English; see I, 71, 85, 101 ff.
[65] Page 294.

The Horatio Alger vein continues when he sets up business himself:

In short, he was the first trader who cut a yard of cloth for sale in that part of the world.—This spirited commercial novelty, was productive of such universal benefit, as to attach the whole custom of the colony to him; and he took care to preserve it:—so that, in a few years, he left *America* not only with a considerable fortune, but with the general regard and confidence of the people among whom he had lived, and returned to pass the rest of his days in his native country.[66]

Another Scotch merchant turns up in Mrs. Smith's *Celestina* (1791); he "was engaged in the American trade, by which he was making a respectable provision for his family."[67] But in her *Letters of a Solitary Wanderer* (1800) Mr. Holwyn, finding his business in bad condition,

had gone to America, to Lisbon, Barcelona, and afterwards to France, in hopes of saving the house by collecting many of its debts before its distresses were known.[68]

Later it is reported that, having run away with another man's wife, he

had gone to America, on one of those commercial speculations in which he was still engaged.[69]

Here we run into an element in the concept of America to be discussed later: the belief in America as an infallible source of easy money or rapid wealth. Finally the valedictory in *Berkeley Hall* (1796), written as if early in the century, predicts great prosperity for England

if the legislature free as much as possible from restrictions, and en-courage by bounties, its manufactures and commerce; if it promote the fisheries on its own, and these coasts. . . .[70]

[66] (3rd ed., Dublin, 1790-1791), I, 187-188.
[67] II, 249.
[68] II, 201.
[69] II, 217-218.
[70] III, 407.

So we close with a reiteration of the faith in fisheries which introduced the series of comments on the commercial importance of America.

We are dealing more directly with the influence of the war when we come to those novels which refer to the bad effect of the war on trade and finance. Recognition by novels of the relation between the new world and the markets of the old world was shown as early as 1755 in *The Devil upon Crutches in England,* in which financiers plot to

sink the Stocks, that they may purchase the cheaper. *New England* is to be swallowed up by an Earthquake.[71]

When tremors of a sort did begin to shake New England, the effects in England were first noticed, as far as we are concerned, by Bage's *Mount Henneth* (1781). Henry Cheslyn, the hero, "entered into partnership with a large American house." Then, as a friend of his puts it,

Every one knows to his sorrow . . . the wound given this country, by its breach with the colonies. Mr Henry's house struggled with its adverse situation near three years, but was obliged to stop payment in January last, and became bankrupt in March.[72]

Henry himself writes quite interestingly about the London market:

It is now near the time of the rescontres, and the angry bulls go bellowing up and down, damning the ministry, because the times are lowering like themselves [August, 1778]. Martinico taken, or Count d'Estaing, with his ships and men, conveniently deposited at the bottom of the sea, might enable these gentlemen to sell to advantage the stock they have contracted to buy. Now these are honest fellows, and heartily wish success to the arms of their country.

Not so the bears. . . .

71 (4th ed., 1759), p. 96. There is a similar incident in "Memoirs of a Sad Dog," attributed to Chatterton by the publisher Harrison and reprinted by him in the *New Novelist's Magazine* (I, 209).

72 Page 116.

The loss of Jamaica, or the defeat of Sir Harry Clinton, or any event which would give a temporary tumble to the stocks, would be propitious to these worthy gentlemen. . . .[73]

Charles Corbett, in Pratt's *Emma Corbett* (1780), had suffered:

Those fortunes which have been destroyed, those debts which have impoverished me, as well as those ample streams of commerce which rolled unobstructed from shore to shore, were all dedicated to injured America.[74]

*Reveries of the Heart* (1781) has several ironic comments on the economic aspect of the war: one, how the English, "to manifest our excellent Scotch economy, spent fifty-millions to raise a three-penny duty on tea,"[75] and another, put into the mouth of Lord North, "I have expended fifty millions of your treasure, to filch a thousand a year from the Americans."[76] There is, however, one scholarly note:

The wars . . . have given the north-west parts of the kingdom vast advantages in their commerce with America, their navigation to the rising empire being almost free from danger.[77]

The attack on North is paralleled by that of William Thomson upon Fox in *Man in the Moon* (1783), in which it is alleged that the thoughts of Demosthenes concerning Fox would include this inquiry:

Where is that substantial connexion with America, which you promised so confidently to establish? That advantageous connexion of commerce, such as subsists between Great-Britain and Portugal?[78]

The effect of war on money is dealt with by *Jonathan Corncob* in anything but a worried fashion. In Boston Jonathan sees a man handling his colonial money with extreme care,

[73] Page 128.
[74] II, 185.
[75] I, 110.
[76] I, 116.
[77] II, 70-71.
[78] II, 73. Cf. *The Speeches of the Right Honourable Charles James Fox in the House of Commons* (1815), II, 124.

although the "money of the congress had at this time lost three-fourths of its original value." The old gentleman sees Jonathan handle his own money with relative carelessness:

"I swear now," said the old gentleman, "but you seem to make very light of that money." "Why indeed," answered I, tossing the bills up in the air, and catching them again in my hand, "it must be confessed that this money is not very heavy." "I guess now," replied the old gentleman, "that you be a tory rogue, and it is such villains as you that depreciate the money of the state."[79]

Whereupon Jonathan is arrested for treason and spends two months in jail before making his customary escape.

Philip Withers' *History of the Royal Malady* (1789) compactly summarizes the war: "a dismembered Empire, defeated Fleets, captured Armies, and a ruined Commerce."[80] The plot of *Louisa Wharton* (1790) hinges partly upon the fact that the heroine's father "had been many years a very successful merchant" in Philadelphia;[81] hence a later tirade against the war includes the charge that it "clips the wings of commerce."[82]

The business sense manifested in this last series of quotations gives way to righteous indignation in several attacks on profiteering, very modern in their sound. Even *Jonathan Corncob* momentarily adopts an ethical point of view, though clothed in an apparently light-hearted irony. Jonathan attends the hanging of a Scotch soldier "for stealing, on a march, two cabbages and three beet-roots, marauding being a capital crime in the military code," and remarks to a fellow-observer that he

heard an officer declare . . . that two army commissioners, and a navy agent victualler, had each robbed government of 100,000 l. "Oh!" said the gentleman, "that was the officer's way of expressing himself, for these supposed robberies consist only in what was formerly called peculation and malversation; but is now expressed by the term perquisite, or as the French call it, *tour de bâton.*"

79 Pp. 35-36.
80 Page 66.
81 Page 3.
82 Page 25.

He goes on to explain account-juggling and other such familiar practices, and concludes,

You see that this is so far from being a robbery *vi et armis,* as in the case of the cabbages and beet-roots, that every thing is carried on in the most regular manner possible. . . .[83]

Mrs. Smith has no delicacy of touch; on the same theme, she hits out with all her usual spirit:

And that the ministry should, in thus purchasing glory, put a little more than was requisite into the pockets of contractors, and destroy as many men by sickness as by the sword, made but little difference in an object so infinitely important; especially when it was known . . . that messieurs the contractors were for the most part members of parliament, who under other names enjoyed the profits of a war, which, disregarding the voices of the people in general, or even of their constituents, they voted for pursuing.[84]

Here is another of Mrs. Smith's often startling anticipations of a later century. Touching the same subject briefly in *Desmond* (1792) she is a bit lighter. The hero is describing the uncle of Mr. Bethel:

It is not her youth or her beauty, that recommended his present favourite housekeeper; but the skill she had acquired in studying under a French cook, at the house of a great man, who acquired an immense fortune in the American war, by obtaining the contract for potatoes and sour crout.[85]

After all the gloomy accounts of the economic effects of the war, there are a few bright anticipations of the subsequent improvement. As early as 1781 a novel looks forward to post-war mercantile possibilities. In Bage's *Mount Henneth* Mr. Melton proposes

that Harry [Cheslyn, the hero] and I should associate in the mercantile way, and, making Cardigan our port, stretch our canvass over the Atlantic; that is to say, when ministers will permit. One of my occu-

[83] Pp. 67-70.
[84] *Old Manor House* (1793), III, 250-251.
[85] III, 174.

pations in Rhode Island was that of building ships. There is a little cove within four hundred yards of Camitha's lawn, which a little money might change into a dock. Let that also be assigned to Harry and myself. Your timber will find the most profitable market; and, in two years, the business, in all its branches, may give employment to about one hundred of your people.[86]

The point of view generally held by economists, that England was better off without the colonies, is expressed in Pye's *Democrat* (1795), in which the Count de Tournelles, a French refugee, thus speaks to an English friend:

The termination of the war appeared in the eyes of all Europe most glorious to us, most humiliating to Great-Britain; and every nation augured an elevation of our national prosperity, and a depression of yours, as the inevitable consequence. But how different has the consequence really been?—The loss of your colonies does not seem to have had the smallest effect on your commerce or your power. . . .[87]

Mrs. Parsons, of course, had the benefit of *ex post facto* knowledge to aid her when she made the hero of *The Voluntary Exile* (1795) predict,

Surely their mutual interest, their commercial connexions, will soon convince both, that to destroy each other must weaken both states, and throw all the advantages of trade into the hands of . . . other powers . . .,[88]

and say,

I think peace between England and America to be the most desirable event for the future prosperity of both.[89]

To complete the record, *Henry Willoughby* (1798) describes the post-war situation from the viewpoint of America:

We found the freedom of the Thirteen United States established by the valour of their citizens, and their independence acknowledged by

[86] Page 238.
[87] I, 65.
[88] II, 147.
[89] III, 174.

226

all the powers of Europe. Commerce was restored to the merchant, and the farmer again reaped his corn in safety.[90]

The whole subject of colonial relations, as discussed by and presented in novels, has now been dealt with—theories of colonization, problems of taxation, and commerce, all of them, considering that they are hardly at home in fiction, introduced by novelists with remarkable frequency. Thus tracking down another aspect of American matters in the novel, we learn more about both the novel and the times. Insofar as the popular novel accurately measures opinion, we see that, with regard to the economic, and especially the commercial, value of colonies, there was some division of opinion: most people assumed the advantages, but a few emphatically attacked that idea. As for the effect of the war, it was an almost unanimous opinion that England was killing the goose that laid the golden egg. But after the war, things surprisingly began to pick up again, and novels hinted the hope of a new prosperity. All these opinions are presented largely in expository fashion, though occasionally the idea is embodied in a plot. These plots, of course, are infinitely rarer than those based on the war itself.

v

There remains the subject of war and private property, which restores the novel to its long-absent proper function—story-telling. As we have seen, merchants and investors lost during the war; likewise real-estate owners suffered. Here were not abstractions but persons taking part in action or at least experiencing some emotion. The alien property-owner, for instance, was a rather popular type in fiction. It became more or less conventional for the American Loyalist to be denuded of estates and possessions, an outcome which, when it ignored the historical fact of post-war restoration of property, fed successfully the lust for pathos. Confiscation, in fact, became so popular that an author occasionally rushed in to snatch money

[90] II, 278.

and belongings from a pet character without bothering to be logical about it. Mrs. Mackenzie's *Slavery* (1792) has an English general of French descent fighting for the colonies, being deprived of his property, whether by the English or the Americans is not quite clear, and rushing off for safety, first to the American backwoods and then to the West Indies, incomprehensible asylums from equally incomprehensible despoliations. Clarity, however, has nothing to do with tears.

There are about seventeen plots or episodes involving lost property, several of them by the pens of old standbys. Bage makes two contributions, one in *Mount Henneth* (1781), the other in *Barham Downs* (1784); two characters' similar reactions to loss and to love would today be listed in a column of "Peculiar Coincidences." In the former novel Cheslyn writes to his brother:

Thou knowest with how stoical an apathy I bore the loss of my property, by this plague and pestilence of Britain; this jest of the surrounding nations—this American war! But the sufferings of the all-accomplished Miss Melton, of the girl I love, or fear I love, raises the storm of passion too high for restraint.[91]

In the latter novel, Davis complains of the loss of the love of Lucy Strode:

To whom can I fly for consolation under the common evils of life, if my Lucy refuses to be my comforter? The last ships from Carolina have brought me no remittances, nor hopes of any. A sugar vessel, freighted for me, has been taken by the enemy, and by a mistake of my broker's, not more than half the cargo insured. But what are these and a thousand evils more of the like kind, compared with the loss of your smiles, my Lucy?[92]

Going back to Cheslyn, we find him commenting on the property of Mr. Melton, who left America during the war:

[91] Page 133.
[92] Page 248.

. . . the Americans will confiscate, because he deserted their cause; and the English, because he did not.[93]

So rare a phenomenon as antithesis is worthy of note. It is very different from the exclamatory, hypertypographical manner in which Pratt has Charles Corbett announce what the war has done to his finances:

The *decisive* blow came yesterday upon me. I had, ere this, in reserve, one rich casket—but it is gone: the last capture has deprived us of it. It would have been enough for *my* age and for *your* youth, but the post of yesterday—.[94]

Here the loss is an important plot-element, since it gives Corbett additional reason for trying to marry his daughter to the moneyed Robert Raymond and thus increases the tenseness of the situation. In *The American Wanderer* (1783) the loss is largely incidental; the hero is fortunate enough, in his travels on the continent, to meet a French physician who refuses fees because the patient's "resources from America were cut off" and who offers to play host until he can get the income of his estate in America remitted to him.[95] There are no further complications.

Sometimes there is a new twist in that the war acts as a cloak for the roguery which victimizes a character. In Mrs. Bennet's *Juvenile Indiscretions* (1786), Clara Elton's father had

married Sir Henry Dellmore's daughter, an American merchant, in extensive and flourishing circumstances: he received with his lady a fortune of twelve thousand pounds.[96]

Then, unhappily, the war came on.

Mr. Elton's property, to a large amount, happened unfortunately to be in the hands of the persons whose principles were at any rate to obtain riches; who had the sagacity to foresee that the public ruin

[93] Page 198.
[94] *Emma Corbett*, II, 84.
[95] Page 286.
[96] I, 35. An "American merchant" was not an American who sold things, but an Englishman who traded with Americans.

would be their private benefit, and rebellion a sponge that would rub out all accounts with their correspondents on this side the Atlantic. Nor need we add how well those plans succeeded. . . .[97]

In *The Voluntary Exile* (1795) Mrs. Parsons subjects the Newtons to the same hard luck. They had lived in great prosperity,

> but when the quarrel begun between the English and the Colonies, a very wicked man, who had possession of a good part of Mr. Newton's fortune, being his partner, run'd away, and joined the English, carrying all he could with him, and leaving all the debts upon poor Mr. Newton.[98]

After all the mournful tales of financial reverses, Jonathan Corncob's jaunty acceptance of pillage as a means of livelihood is thoroughly delightful:

> As soon as I was landed at New-York, I associated myself with a party of loyalists, who having been driven from their estates, plundered with great propriety all those in the vicinity: their incursions were frequent in the Jerseys and Connecticut, and they seldom returned without bringing with them some few head of cattle prisoners. My employment among them consisted in keeping an account of the sale of the booty, as well as of the distribution of its produce, and I was scarcely ever engaged in any of their expeditions.[99]

Otherwise we have little more than the hard-worn story of sequestration, with little pretense of originality. A short story in Harrison's collection tells of a Loyalist young lady who was taken to England by a friend:

> Her husband was a Loyalist; mine had been so, and the rebels made this a pretext to rob me of all my possessions—too light a punishment for crimes so deep.[100]

The device occurs several times in *The School for Fathers* (1788). The Dennisons lost most of their fortune, and "all

[97] I, 38-39.
[98] IV, 195.
[99] *Adventures of Jonathan Corncob*, pp. 44-45.
[100] *New Novelist's Magazine*, II, 259.

their landed property was seized on by the Congress."[101] Likewise the Pleydels; the officer assigned to eject the wife and
children from Boston stripped them "of every shilling, and
hardly left them clothing to shelter them from the inclemency
of the weather."[102] These untoward events are succeeded by
the multitude of sufferings demanded by popular taste. The
author records, finally, that when the Americans captured a
ship, their chief activity was "to pillage her of everything
valuable."[103]

*Louisa Wharton* (1790) entwines love, war, and economics
in a presumably irresistible pattern. Louisa's father was a
merchant; "the principal of our fortune was at Philadelphia";
and she was "supposed to be a match equal in point of money
to many in this kingdom." Then came the war.

. . . every one who had property in that country were alarmed; my
father's whole was there, the consequence might be fatal. . . .[104]

Mr. Wharton and his son George fly to Philadelphia to guard
their interests, and Louisa's prospective father-in-law, Sir James
Truman, becomes very cool at news of her potential poverty.
Then all is lost, Sir James becomes positively icy, and Louisa is
reduced to needlework. But the *deus ex machina* is inevitable—
a rich uncle; and, to pile profit on prosperity,

. . . we have hopes of a restoration of at least part of our property
at Philadelphia, when the peace takes place.

By way of climax, Louisa demonstrates the heroine's Pamelian
excess of third-rate morality, and deficiency of all logic, truth,
and modesty, by thus haranguing the reader:

. . . we may moralize on the wonderful work of Providence, which,
after such a variety of hardships, has at length rewarded all my suffering with love, wealth and honour; and thus we may see that persever-

[101] I, 172-173.
[102] I, 215.
[103] II, 28.
[104] Pp. 3-6.

ance, industry, and virtue, will at last conquer and triumph over every opponant.[105]

Mrs. Rowson several times calls her family difficulties to the reader's attention. In *The Inquisitor* (1788) she says,

My father refusing to join the Americans, his property was confiscated, and he returned with his family to England in a distressed situation.[106]

There is a little more detail in *Fille de Chambre* (1792), in which Colonel Abthorpe is at first unwilling to join the British army for fear of loss of property. The Americans, however, confiscate his property anyway, later promising restoration if he will accept a commission in their army.[107] Imlay's *Emigrants* (1793) offers the sufferings of one P. P——, who, after fighting under Wolfe, found the Revolution a great obstacle to establishing his farm and homestead.[108] Mrs. Smith, original though she often is, picked up whatever she could find in the world of fiction. *Celestina* (1791) has the story of a Mr. Elphinstone, who, at the time of the war, had property in America "which was thought recoverable." Finally he goes in search of it,

. . . and though that country was no longer under the government of Britain, and his expectations of success greatly diminished, he contrived to persuade those persons who were interested, to furnish him with a small supply of money. . . .[109]

But, like other ventures of his, this also ended in failure, and Mrs. Smith gratifyingly spares us the happy monetary ending.

At the very end of the century two more books appropriate the loss-of-property motif. In *Disobedience* (1797) this kind of economic setback contributes three times to the settlement of the American West that the author plagiarizes Imlay to advertise. There is first Mr. Eddows, who had

[105] Page 64.
[106] (2nd American ed., Philadelphia, 1794), p. 139.
[107] Pp. 149, 157, 160.
[108] II, 81 ff.
[109] II, 308.

some mercantile concerns, in which, before the American war, he had been sufficiently successful. The events that happened in the progress of that inglorious dispute, had proved fatal to this part of his property;— and he now saw himself, at the close of it, reduced to the moderate income that he could draw from his few paternal acres.[110]

Although far from starvation, he is in a rage against England and a fever for emigration, to which he entices the hero and heroine. In Philadelphia:

The consequences of the war had reduced many families to indigence; and emigration was the universal topic of conversation.[111]

Then there is Colonel Humberston of Virginia, who had lost everything in the cause of colonial liberty:

And from this indifference to his personal interest, it had happened, that the struggles which secured independance to America deprived Colonel Humbertson of nearly all that he could call his own, his courage and his honour excepted.[112]

He and his family join Eddows and his proteges in the Kentucky venture which is a major part of the story. The last of the characters to suffer economically from the war are found in *Tales of Truth* (1800), both in minor roles. One is "a widowed mother, an American, who adhered to the royal cause" and whose "fortune was diminished" accordingly;[113] the other is a hermit whose love for his woodland retreat is strengthened by the fact that "the decrees of the Congress have sequestered my landed property, as an emigrant."[114]

Here ends the tale of the contributions made to the novel by American relations in their economic aspect—colonies, taxation, commerce, and private property as affected by the war. Once again we can point out that, for subjects that sit but awkwardly in fiction at best, they fill many pages, which, under other

[110] IV, 55.
[111] IV, 77.
[112] IV, 85.
[113] IV, 72-73.
[114] III, 106.

circumstances, would have had to find their burden elsewhere. This is influence on the simplest level—the statistical. What perhaps commands greater attention, though it lead us from matters of immediate literary import, is the picture of the times emerging from this troupe of synthetic romances, feather in cap, but very down at the heels. We have a fairly good insight into the middle-class mind from 1760 to 1800, its collection of wise saws, quips, theories, and platitudes, with which it could reach rapid and easy conclusions on nearly all colonial issues. These all grew out of the war or the events and conditions which produced the war. Prose fiction discussed them, occasionally made stories of them, for its clientele.

These American matters alone do a pretty good portrait of the novel. You may not teach an old dog new tricks, but you may get a puppy to vary his repertoire a bit. The popular novel was both puppy and old dog. It grew old before it grew up; without reaching maturity, it had a firm set of habits and customs and conventions. Essentially, the war taught it nothing, for all the old rules had a mighty grip. But the ancient tricks underwent some variation. To flirt a moment longer with the canine metaphor: where before the dog had stood on its hind legs in the parlor, it now stood on its hind legs on the front porch. It is the old act in a new setting. So American subjects fitted into old patterns, but made them look a bit different. The lasting impression, however, is that of unquenchable perseverance in iteration. In the war-plots proper, in the civil-war plots, in the humanitarian stories, in tales of economic woe, the same line-up of characters, the same sequence of incidents, the same half-maudlin tone—all parade, without embarrassment, again and again. It is needless, however, to push the artistic indictment of the minor novel; its sins are accepted *a priori*. What continues to surprise is that there could be so much repetition without killing the trade. When the tireless rehearsal is that of the American show, one can conclude how much interest there must have been.

# CHAPTER VII

# AMERICA IN SATIRE AND CRITICISM OF ENGLAND

Still the tale of heresy is not complete, and the inquisition finds greater depths to display. Even the most warm-blooded of comforters, binding the wounds of desolate America, and the sharpest of snipers, relentlessly picking off hard-hearted ministers, were actuated only by the war. Their indictments were specific. In none did we find such general, such inclusive, castigations as some of the following. One P. P——, in Imlay's *Emigrants* (1793), makes this exclamatory protest in reference to his departure from England:

. . . how impolitic are those institutions, that drive men of spirit to look for hospitality and more humanity in foreign states. . . .[1]

And a Mrs. F——, on a visit to London, writes her sister Caroline in America,

. . . when I contrast the simple and sincere manners of the people of your hemisphere, with the studied ceremony of European customs, I not only lament that I am not with you enjoying the charms of those Arcadian regions, but I assure you, my dear sister, I envy you that felicity which flows from the genuine sentiments of nature.[2]

Mrs. Il——ray's comparison is still sharper:

Every species of luxury has followed, and in the sumptuous banquets of the times, the flow of sentiment and the zest of reason, have been succeeded by sallies of false wit, and the harmonious sounds of soft music. Effeminacy has triumphed, and while the sofa has been the pleasurable seat of the lover, the toilet has been the place where his manliness was displayed.[3]

[1] II, 80.
[2] II, 121.
[3] III, 137-138.

Helena Wells's *Constantia Neville* (1800) argues on economic and humanitarian grounds:

But where poverty is scarcely known, and a white person reduced to a state of servitude is a phenomenon, the squalid wretchedness which daily presents itself to the eyes of Americans or West Indians on their arrival in Europe, must have a powerful effect.[4]

Finally, Eugenia De Acton's *Disobedience* (1797) makes a rather heavy-handed contrast of Mary Challoner, English by birth but an enthusiastic pioneer in America, and Agatha Humberston, labeled a New Yorker, but actually an English heroine, fond only of city life and the ballroom. En route to Kentucky, she mourns her crowd of lovers, and she resents being

separated nearly two hundred miles from every civilized country, by high and rugged mountains, and wilds almost impassable. . . .[5]

Her daintiness and silliness are disparaged through praise of Mary's enthusiasm for the new life and its honest virtues, so different from the artificialities of a conventional existence.

Thus from praise of America comes unfavorable criticism of English custom and character, a conjunction to be observed further in *Emmera, The Female American,* and *Henry Willoughby,* and other novels depicting romantic utopias in America.[6] The contrast, says the *Critical* of *Emmera,* is "dull, immoral, and improbable"[7]—a verdict applicable enough to novels professionally crying up an American Arcadia and therefore bound to cry down Europe. In such books, however, the attack on Europe will be seen to be really incidental to the main issue, which is the praise of America. In the present chapter we are devoting ourselves to another type of story, in which the attack on England (or Europe), or on some aspect of its life, is first in the author's intentions, and in which, consequently,

[4] I, 129.
[5] IV, 88.
[6] See Chapter IX.
[7] XXIII (1767), 274.

the praise of America is only incidental. The relation between this material and that in the preceding chapter is that in both there is hostility to the things close to home—to the attitude, spirit, or life. We have already seen the subjects of colonization, taxation, and war developing into satires of much greater scope than the immediate issue suggests. Now we shall follow through the satires which have their roots in American subjects but which extend into a quite different atmosphere.

I have said that here "the praise of America is only incidental." That praise may be implied rather than stated, and, indeed, it may not exist at all. In the war-stories which execrated the English, the sympathetic bath tapped for the Americans seldom implied a grand, sweeping whitewash of everything American at all times. It meant merely an emotional laving at the moment, under the given circumstances; America was not a perennial Galahad, evoking successive waves of admiration and awe. However bitterly they may excoriate the old world, writers who regularly mention America do not necessarily point with pride. Rather than a shining example, she may be merely an innocent bystander, whether casualty or only observer. The author may find in America, or in something American, a quite remote starting-point, or a scarcely audible suggestion, for a satirical train of thought. But, in justification of this chapter, it must be emphasized that America does some service in a critical or satirical process, whether she is neutral or is in a clearly established position among the combatants.

These satires and criticisms, which at the least mention America and at the most depend heavily on her, represent mainly another influence of the war, which, either directly or through the antecedent events, is the springboard from which they leap into the fray. Sometimes, however, America makes ingress in other ways. Several novels, for instance, fall into the long anti-Catholic tradition in English literature. Johnstone's *Chrysal* tells the story of a confessor who extorts, by threats of the Inquisition, every possible bit of gold from a Peruvian who confesses that he has cursed a Jesuit whom he had found in the "act of carnality" with his wife. Actuated by love of gold, the same father casuistically excuses a general who has raped his brother's wife and then killed her; later, when the general flees to the monastery for sanctuary, he is forced to join the order or be turned over to the pursuing brother.[8] Cullen's *Castle of Inchvally* (1796) puts slightly less strain on the imagination:

Look to South America—see a *holy father of the church,* armed with a cross in one hand, and the less devouring sword in the other, followed by a clan of christian bloodhounds stalking with desolation in his train through a nation of the most unoffending and amiable of existing beings, and letting loose havoc among them![9]

Similar is an ironic passage in *A Trip to Melasge* (1778):

Was not the petulance of those millions of Mexicans deservedly punished, who uncivily [*sic*] obstructed Cortes's curiosity to visit their capital, and rejected the blessing of an intercourse with Europeans? Was there not refined policy in throwing Motezuma [*sic*] into chains?[10]

A much more prolific source of satire was the colonization of America, with the struggles between England and France. Goldsmith began it in *The Citizen of the World* (1760-1761), in which Lien Chi pokes fun at the rivalry evoked by mere vanity. Canada, he says, had been undisturbed for centuries until the English learned that

those countries produced furs in great abundance. From that moment the country became an object of desire; it was found that furs were things very much wanted in England; the ladies edged some of their cloaths with furs, and muffs were worn by both gentlemen and ladies. In short, furs were found indispensably necessary for the happiness of the state. . . .[11]

France had a similar experience.

[8] (4th ed., 1764-1765), I, 36 ff. Cf. *Adventures of Alonso,* I, 90 ff.
[9] III, 96-97.
[10] I, 24. Cf. II, 174.
[11] I, 55.

Wherever the French landed, they called the country their own; and the English took possession whenever they came upon the same equitable pretensions. The harmless savages made no opposition; and could the intruders have agreed together, they might peaceably have shared this desolate country between them. But they quarreled about the boundaries to their settlements, about grounds and rivers to which neither side could shew any other right than that of power, and which neither could occupy but by usurparion [*sic*]. Such is the contest, that no honest man can heartily wish success to either party.[12]

A like attitude appears in Frances Brooke's *Lady Julia Mandeville* (1763), which says that

After so long, so extensive and bloody a war, a war which has depopulated our country, and loaded us with a burden of debt from which nothing can extricate us but the noble spirit of public frugality,

only those object to peace "who gain by the continuance of war" and whose "clamors . . . are inconceivable, clamors which can be founded only in private interest."[13] Lady Mandeville

forgives the cits for their opposition to peace, because they get more money by war, the criterion by which they judge every thing: but is amazed that the nobles, born guardians of the just rights of the throne, the fountain of all their honors, should join those interested 'Change-alley politicians, and endeavor, from private pique, to weaken the hands of their sovereign. . . .[14]

Mrs. Brooke is still more emphatic in *The History of Emily Montague* (1769):

It is impossible to behold a scene like this without lamenting the madness of mankind, who, more merciless than the fierce inhabitants of the howling wilderness, destroy millions of their own species in the wild contention for a little portion of that earth, the far greater part of which remains yet unpossesst, and courts the hand of labour for cultivation.[15]

[12] I, 56.
[13] Page 120.
[14] Page 156.
[15] I, 8.

*The Ants* (1767), hysterical in lambasting the Stamp Act, is almost Goldsmithian in laughing at Anglo-French quarrels:

> . . . a neighboring colony of white emmets [French], having taken it into their heads that hats were a much better and more profitable wear, both for the male and female emmets, than either woollen, worsted, or leather caps could possibly be; . . .

decided to restrict the red emmets (English),[16] hiring Indians to scalp them, and taking advantage of "some grievous political blunders" of the English who, bent on speed,

> endeavoured to plant the various parts of this west end of the colony with a confused collection of all sorts of emmets, from any hillock, wherever they could find any of the inhabitants disposed to migrate; so that this part of the settlement was a strange motley mass of all colours, sizes, and sorts, without distinction; by which means the settlement was deprived of that political noose which ties other emmet communities together so effectively. . . .
>
> Hence sprung the following mischief, that each set, sect and party, would only mind their own concerns and granaries, without respecting the public weal; and so becoming a confused, disorderly, disjointed rabble.[17]

The French were further aided by the English system of granting

> to any court emmet who was skilled in the mysterious arts of intriguing, such or such a portion, known and unknown, of the west end of the hillock . . . without paying the least regard to any ants who might already be in possession. . . .[18]

Once the French point of view receives favorable treatment—in Johnstone's *Reverie* (1762):

> As for the present war in particular, it took its rise solely from their [the English] presumption and injustice. Under pretense of our having forcibly possessed ourselves of some spots of land which belonged to them in the boundless deserts of America, they fell upon our defence-

[16] I, 70-71.
[17] I, 73.
[18] I, 76-77.

less merchants without any previous declaration of war, and took numbers of them in a cowardly pyratical manner.[19]

In *Chrysal,* however, Johnstone just as easily takes the other side:

The insatiable ambition of the *French* had prompted them to strive for the enlargement of their territorities in *America,* where they already possessed a hundred times more than they were able to make any use of. The possessions of the *English* . . . were also uselessly extensive. . . .[20]

England, of course, was bound in honor to defend even a bloated territory, and her ineptitude in the ensuing war, won though it was, draws sharp fire from Johnstone, who condemns "shameful inactivity," "unnecessary preparations for improbable occasions," demoralizing delays, prolongation of the war for profit, and "brutal rashness . . . so fatal to others."[21] George Augustus, third Viscount Home, is "so sick of the whole scene" that he asks for a detached company with which to show that the English really can "conquer more formidable foes, than naked savages, led by a few wretched *Frenchmen."*[22]

Smollett's *Adventures of an Atom* (1769) sails into the war with greatest fury. Braddock, Smollett says, was appointed

not that he [Cumberland] supposed him possessed of superior merit, but because no leader of distinction cared to engage in such a disagreeable expedition. . . .[23]

After the slaughter of Braddock's army, "like sheep in the shambles," the King

consoled himself by observing, that his troops made a very soldierly appearance as they lay on the field in their new clothing, smart caps, and clean buskins; and that the enemy allowed they had never seen beards and whiskers in better order.[24]

[19] (1763), II, 82.
[20] II, 213.
[21] II, 104.
[22] III, 132.
[23] Smollett, *Works,* XII, 265-266.
[24] XII, 267-268.

When the charge is made that Braddock might have done something besides standing still, Cumberland defends him:

I hope . . . that the troops of Japan [England] will always stand without flinching. I should have been mortified beyond measure, had they retreated without seeing the face of the enemy . . . and as for advancing, the ground would not permit any manoeuvre of that nature. . . . It was the fortune of war, and they bore it like men:— we shall be more fortunate on another occasion.[25]

Satire falls heavily on Pitt, especially for his alleged ignorance of the terrain at Quebec and of the military principles involved in the attack. He is represented as counting on mere luck to overcome the tremendous theoretical disadvantages of the English.

He reflected that the demon of folly was capricious, and that as it had so long possessed the rulers and generals of Japan, it was high time it would shift its quarters, and occupy the brains of the enemy; in which case they would quit their advantageous posts, and commit some blunder that would lay them at the mercy of the Japonese. With respect to the destruction of Quib-quab [Quebec], he had heard, indeed, that the besiegers ought to be ten times the number of the garrison besieged; but as every Japonese was equivalent to ten subjects of China, he thought the match was pretty equal. He reflected, that even if this expedition should not succceed, it would be of little conse-quence to his reputation, as he could plead at home, that he neither conceived the original plan, nor appointed any of the officers concerned in the execution.[26]

The news of Quebec Pitt turns to his utmost personal advantage, and the public begins to lick his "sweaty socks," forgetting that the "real conqueror" of Quebec "was no more."[27]

In *Humphry Clinker* (1771) Smollett is much milder, paying his respects to the inadequate compensation and the unfair

<hr/>

25 XII, 268.
26 XII, 346-347. Smollett was much amused by the now-famous story about Newcastle's not knowing that Cape Breton Island was an Island; he refers to it in *Adventures of an Atom* (p. 264) and in *Humphry Clinker* (*Works*, III, 180).
27 XII, 363.

treatment given to war-veterans such as Lismahago, Colonel Cockril, and Balderick.[28] The same theme arouses the ire of Mrs. Bonhote in *Rambles of Mr. Frankly* (1772)[29] and of Bage in *Mount Henneth*.[30] Here, however, we are getting into the school of pathos which the old soldier was usually forced to attend dead or alive. This institution, indeed, became a literary nuisance, and, when Jane Austen was in her 'teens, she was moved to laughter by the tearful tales of American casualties, whether maimings or death. A young lady's letter explaining why she is called "Miss" is an excellent epitome of a popular sentimental plot:

> I married, my Sophia without the consent or knowledge of my father the late Admiral Annesley. It was therefore necessary to keep the secret from him and from everyone, till some fortunate opportunity might offer of revealing it.— Such an opportunity alas! was but too soon given in the death of my dear Capt. Dashwood—Pardon these tears, continued Miss Jane wiping her Eyes, I owe them to my Husband's memory. He fell my Sophia, while fighting for his Country in America after a most happy Union of seven years—[31]

Almost as prolific a source of satire as the Seven Years' War was the subsequent attempt of the English to pay for it by taxing the colonies. What novelists said about taxation we have already seen; it remains to be pointed out how this subject led on to criticism of the government. *The Adventure of a Bale of Goods* (1766), primarily a warning about the adverse effects of the Stamp Act on commerce, ventures a few axioms on government; Grenville, through a set of incoherent remarks attributed to him, is represented as wishy-washy and hedging. The merchant Isaac Roderiguez tells his wife of

the genuine Perplexity of a Man of ordinary Genius—who finds himself in an Exigence he did not foresee, and cannot manage! . . . Our

[28] See III, 85-88, IV, 17 ff.
[29] (Dublin, 1773), II, 92.
[30] Pp. 206-207.
[31] *Love and Freindship* [*sic*] *and Other Early Works Now First Published from the Original MS.* (New York: Stokes, 1922), p. 133.

Colonies require a new Scale—Some may perhaps reckon themselves all potent with the old— or may not be Masters of any at all—But let that be as it will—the whole of their Scrape came from want of Seeing! yon Minister is, in my Mind, an honest Man, that is, with the Designation a little modified: For Honesty in the Complex leads to Candour, and Candour never can lead to Injustice—To the Colonies he has been Unjust.[32]

Having the same initial impetus as the preceding book, *The Ants* (1767) likewise veers away from its major subject and comes to an end with a plea for governmental reform. Lychopinax, the ideal senator, after attacking the measures advanced for subduing America, proposes the curbing of avarice, which has brought "bribery, venality, faithlessness, fraud, overreaching, deceit, lying, railing, backbiting, nipping, scratching." He urges that legislators begin "with a radical and effectual process, to root out all the seeds of distemper and disorder" and especially the "selfish disposition which hath so greatly tainted the minds and the practice of all ranks."[33] Particularly, they must cut down expenses. Such an unheard-of suggestion produces an uproar that leads to the dissolution of the assembly.[34]

In *The Travels of Hildebrand Bowman* (1778) taxation is a starting point for satirical comments on lack of conviction and on ineptitude in politicians.

Good God! cried another; can men have the impudence to act in such a barefaced manner? Very easily, returned Bonaris, we see it every day; they find out subterfuges and equivocations; and at the worst, if one has been in an error, is he always to persist in it? . . .

In this affair of the Armoserians [Americans], continued he, I own the opposition carried things a little too far; for by their speeches in the Cortesinas, printed pamphlets, and writings in the news-papers (there being some great names amongst them), the rebels were spirited up, by thinking they had their approbation, and expecting a diversion made at home in their favour. By this means they have probably been

[32] Page 19.
[33] II, 83 ff.
[34] II, 95-96.

led by degrees to carry things farther than they at first intended, and at last to the greatest extremities. . . . Thought I to myself, a little of Queen Tudorina's [Elizabeth] government would do this Nation no harm, no more than Old England.[35]

This is the lone case in which criticism of the existing regime produces nostalgia for the "good old days."

Taxation produces two more satires of government, each of which vindicates England as a nation at the expense of her ministers and politicians. *The History of . . . John Bull* (1785) especially attacks Parliament:

From this arrogance and pride, she had just engaged *John* in that fatal lawsuit, with his tenants in the *west country,* her cursed obstinacy was the cause of its being carried on, and her damned passion for choosing every person in *John's* service, was the reason why she also took upon her to name *John's* lawyers and attorneys, and so furnished him with as compleat a set of rogues and petty-foggers, as any litigious man was ever blessed with.

. . . *John* was confoundedly ill used by his counsel, who run him to immoderate expence, without having genius or capacity, and without even inclination to take one decisive step that might bring this affair to a fortunate issue.[36]

Again, *Young Hocus* (1789) represents John as being "hood-winked and cajoled" by Parliament and the King. But when they urge "rack-renting" the colonies for his financial advantage, he replies with hearty honesty, expressing a point of view like that of Lychopinax in *The Ants*:

As for my debts, let them be rubbed off by your own frugality, and by my steward's not going to law with the stewards of the neighbouring estates. You insinuate that my Western extortions would enable me to keep more servants. John Bull, madam Gossip, has too many servants already by half; for do not one half take all the labour, and the other half take all the pay? Respecting those laces and embroidery you say we would acquire by the rack-rent, know that John has lace enough,

---

[35] Pp. 295-298. Probably similar matters are to be found in *Revolutions of an Island: An Oriental Fragment* of the same year, in which Britain is satirized as Niatirb (*Critical Review,* XLV, 394).

[36] Pp. 18-19.

while he has one laced hat remaining to cudgel for at a revel. And as to embroidery, I know no use you have for it; strip off the tinsel of your tongue, Mrs. Chatterbox, and do not pull it out by the hundred yards, one after another, like a ribbon-conjurer, swearing that your glittering tin foil, from Cornwall, is the real silver of ancient Greece and Rome.[37]

Of course Parliament persists until war results. The contention of the satirist remains the same as that in *The Ants:* honesty and frugality will solve all difficulties.

History moves on, and, once the war is afoot, it also is fertile in satire of the English government. In contrast with the criticism of the British attitude to America which we have already seen, the passages with which we have to deal here aim at mismanagement, mistaken policy, short-sightedness, and such errors. Thus Mr. Melton in Bage's *Mount Henneth* (1781) sees the whole conduct of England at the time of the war leading to disintegration:

Your country, says he, is ruined. To say nothing of the war, or suppose it successful, you are verging to destruction by the silent operation of finance: your public virtue is gone, or resident in an inconsiderable part of the middle ranks; the head and tail of the fish—stink horribly. As a friend, the best political wish I can bestow upon you is, that you may be undone with all convenient expedition: a lingering death is terrible. When the struggle is over, you may again be happy; for you *will* be poor, and *may* be wise.[38]

The year 1781 was plentiful in reminders of administrative slips. Bage barely provides an introduction to the terrific tirade loosed by the author of *Reveries of the Heart,* who devotes himself particularly to a verbal destruction of Lord North. North harangues on his accomplishments: a civil war, loss of half the empire, expenditure of fifty millions to "filch a thousand a year from the Americans."

---

[37] Pp. 11-13.
[38] Page 197. The point of view had already been expressed in *Private Letters from an American in England* (1769).

I have appointed Gage and Burgoyne, whom I now revile; and Howe, whose character I am endeavouring darkly to assassinate, to conduct the war, and having afterwards endeavoured, by every hidden and open means to shew they were totally unfit for the purpose; therefore allow me now to go on appointing such others as my clear intellects may persuade me to be proper. . . . I have mistimed every succour, every expedition. . . .[39]

The public seems to prefer demagogues and charlatans:

. . . in short, the quack in every art and profession, is the only one who is employed. This folly has lost us America; and will, if not corrected, lose us our lands, properties, and liberties at home.[40]

English officials are ignorant, the King acts on the theory of "set a rogue to catch a rogue," and every American Loyalist

loudly proclaims by oaths and addresses, what he will do in England, where in reality he cannot be of service; and leaves his native country, where by his own account four-fifths of the inhabitants were ready to second his valiant efforts, had not fifty cowardly rascals, called a congress, discomfited two millions of them. . . . I likewise firmly believed with the valorous Germaine, that their troops were a set of the most cowardly rascally ragamuffins that ever disgraced a field of battle, except the French at Minden; and that therefore it was much better to run away from such scarecrows than to stain or rust with their plebeian blood our bright swords, and so render them unfit for a royal review or levee.[41]

As for the ministers' utter ignorance of "nature or her works":

They justly reprobate all history, except the seven champions of Christendom, and the manufactured tales of M'Pherson and Dalrymple, with other romances, from whence they borrow their own notions of war and government.[42]

Occasionally the satirist mentions the Irish, who, he says,

seemed to me very like those wicked varlets the Americans, who, forgetting that some hundred years ago our ancestors had begotten their

[39] I, 116-117; see also I, 158.
[40] I, 124.
[41] I, 170-174.
[42] II, 16-17.

ancestors, had now the impudence to deny the plenitude of our fatherly power, to chastise or confine them as we thought proper. . . . This doctrine, although might seem so reasonable that few would venture to oppose it openly, yet was completely overthrown by a trifling reserve that every good Englishman perpetually kept in his own breast; which was, that he was the only complete judge of this time arriving.[43]

Statesmen are completely undependable:

Year after year has disseminated from the throne promises of the speedy subjugation of America and the French nation: yet, when we hoped to reap the wished-for harvest, disappointment as to the past, accompanied with equally fallacious expectations as to the future, are all that we are able to glean, in return for thirty millions expended, and the loss of thirty thousand men.[44]

Yet the public eagerly believes lying propaganda:

Were I to enumerate all the untruths that have been spread during that time of the wishes of the Americans to become subject to us; their quarrels among themselves, and with the French, a volume would be insufficient for the purpose; yet at this present moment are these swallowed as greedily as ever, and will be so, I doubt not, throughout the present contest.[45]

In all these passages, obviously, the writer is not expressing an attitude to the war as such; he is not fundamentally sympathetic with the Americans. What he is distressed and angered by is the follies of governors and governed, the maladministration and the credulity, the ignorance and blindness and deceit that replace a rational understanding of and sensible conduct of events. America is the point of departure in a satire that, if not so inclusive as that of *Gulliver's Travels,* yet extends far beyond the immediate situation.

*Ways and Means* (1782), which suggests selling the House of Lords as a means of political reform, has a syntactically confused prolegomenon on revolutions as betraying "a dangerous Influence, secretly inherent in, and fraudulently undermining

[43] II, 96-97; see also II, 124.
[44] II, 115.
[45] II, 120-121.

the Constitution."[46] An immediate reference is not even clearly implied, though it must be part of the intention. There is a contrasting explicitness in Thomson's *Man in the Moon* (1783), the author of which, like the writer of *Reveries of the Heart,* is badly upset by the conduct of ministers, especially Fox. He is severely criticized for

the inconsistencies and bare-faced assertions which have so often disgraced your public conduct. How, in the name of truth and modesty, could you affirm in the English house of commons, that you had a peace in your pocket? You offered to treat with the Americans for a peace as a *commis* or messenger, and affirmed, that there were persons, not far distant, who were empowered by the colonists to negotiate with England a separate pacification. By and bye you hold yourself the reigns of government, and not all your entreaties and unbounded concessions can prevail either with America or Holland to negotiate separately from the king of France. And how, indeed, could you expect, that the enemies of your country would treat for a peace on equitable terms, when you declared your resolution to withdraw the troops from America? when you affirmed, that you could not discover so much as a pretext for a rupture with Holland? and asserted that the state of the nation was so inconceivably wretched, that you was afraid to mention it?[47]

Fox is utterly imperturbable, and everyone else is utterly surprised, as he answers:

Lord Shelburne, I can easily discover, intends to patch up a peace, to establish himself in power. Whatever the terms of that peace shall be, I am resolved to arraign them, and to prove from the state of that bulwark of Britain the navy, that the nation is in a condition to dictate the conditions of pacification, not to receive them. . . . from repeated experience I am perfectly satisfied that the good people of England will swallow any thing.[48]

Again the satirist, like his predecessors, is disgusted by what he believes to be not only errors of policy but unblushing deception.

[46] Page i.
[47] II, 71-73. See Fox's *Speeches,* I, 285-286; II, 83; John Drinkwater, *Charles James Fox* (New York: Cosmopolitan, 1928), p. 224.
[48] II, 74-75.

A half dozen years before this flock of satires in the '80's, Pratt's *Pupil of Pleasure* (1776) had drawn an unusual lesson from the war. Lieutenant Vernon had gone bravely abroad to fight for his country, and his dutiful conduct led Thornton to write Sedley:

> Are they [Vernon's letters] not indications of a mind busied in schemes superior to thine? While Mr. VERNON is anxious to serve his country, thou art exerting thyself to disgrace it: while he is desirous to obtain the consent of a beloved and beautiful wife, to suffer his absence in consideration of his glory, thou are CHESTERFIELDING it how thou mayst dishonour beauty, without admitting the very ideas of love.[49]

The essential unifying element in all these passages that relate to the war is that they are not primarily concerned with the war as such or with whether it is right or wrong, but rather with the mistakes, at one extreme, or the vices, at the other extreme, which it brings to light in English government and society. America is just a starting-point or else a neutral background. As such, she contributes to the inception of the political novel.

Most of the novels in which America introduces satire, or provides material for it, appeared between the '60's and '80's, the type after that disappearing almost completely. No doubt the eclipse was due mainly to the passing into history of the events conducive to that sort of treatment. It is also possible, however, that the very successful consummation of the war, for America, may, by eliminating sympathy for the underdog, have diminished the benevolence previously lavished on America. A new, strong, triumphant nation could not figure too appropriately as an innocent bystander wounded by the ricochet of European shots in the dark, for even a vagrant sympathy hardly falls upon the manifestly capable. Nor, perhaps, is a winner permitted even the most tenuous implications of flattery which, however faintly, are imbedded in the self-criticism of a loser who is reflecting on a late misfortune and the agency thereof.

[49] II, 64.

In other words, it may be that, in the decline of such satires, seldom lauding America outright, but often tacitly granting her the equivalent of at least mild approbation, there are some faint flushes of evidence of the realistic attitude to America which we see subsequently developed.

For a while, at any rate, American scenes and American history were very suggestive to the minds of satirists. The erring ways of friars and holy fathers, the cruelty of conquerors, the follies of colonial enterprise which gobbled up indigestibly huge masses of land—all drew literary acrimony. Critics were sharper and more numerous when they considered the English scene between the Seven Years' War and the Revolution: the incompetence, miscalculation, and even knavery displayed in fighting the French, taxing the Americans, and then fighting the Americans. The diatribes were an indirect result of the American troubles, without which novelists would have to find other access to the false gods whom they wanted to dethrone.

CHAPTER VIII

SUMMARY AND TRANSITION

i

Since chapter summaries have indicated fully enough the significance of the material thus far presented, I do not plan additional forays in deduction. Rather, at the risk of displaying an unprincipled abandonment to recapitulation, I wish to draw together in one place the conclusions reached separately.

It requires no verbal prestidigitation to lump together Chapters II to VII as a unit embodying the quantitative aspect of this study: the question has been, To what extent has the war influenced certain literary phenomena or appeared in literature? and the method has been statistical.

In the first place, there appears to be fairly strong ground for believing that the war was responsible for a very sharp decline in the production of novels from 1775 to 1785. It is difficult to believe that that decline, coextensive with the war, was entirely coincidental. Nor is it to be solemnly attributed to a sudden increase in high seriousness. What appears probable is that a welter of pamphlet literature evoked by all phases of the American dispute, as didactic and as exciting as fiction, may have partially diverted the attention and the energy of readers into other channels. The probability—and I do not claim that we have more than that—is strengthened by the decline during the war, or the rise after the war, or both, of other literary types such as the historical novel, the Gothic novel, the Oriental tale, and works showing an interest in Scandinavian literature, Celtic literature, and antiquarianism. Viewing the statistics, one sees as at least possible the conclusion that the end of the war released energy for the revival of old or the creation of new literary forms.

In the second place, the war seems unmistakably to have increased the total use which the novel made of America. Partly the American disputes culminating in the war, with the attendant parliamentary and journalistic furore, acted as an advertising agent for America; partly the war was responsible for a new social and governmental experiment that was the object of intense interest in an era of political renovation; partly it introduced economic problems, and ultimately brought about commercial advantages, that directed further attention to the West. Through this combination of circumstances, the habitués of the circulating library read more about America after 1783 than before. Too, they read more about America than about the remaining poles of their empire—the East and the West Indies. But literary interest in the latter was increasing. America in flight appears not only to have attracted more attention to itself, but to have made England's chief remaining possession of greater moment and imaginative appeal.

In the third place, and least debatably, the influence of the war appears in the unexpectedly large quantity of novels in which either the main plot or major or minor episodes had to do with the Revolution. Seventy-five of these attest to a popular interest which, as far as their works show, was not shared by the writers who to us are the major literary figures of the period. The discrepancy between literary levels is not unusual.

In the fourth place, the war was almost equally influential in providing many pages of critical comment on current events, discussion of policy, evaluation, and interpretation. Here we see the novel as Expositor; characters talked instead of acting, and authors had no hesitancy in stepping upon the stage. Such commentaries tended to move in several specific directions—to attack the British attitude rather than to defend it, to emphasize the fact that the war was a civil war, to use it as a rostrum for humanitarian appeals, to laud the spirit of the American compatriots.

Finally, the whole background out of which the war grew

contributed subjects for both discussion and narrative. Colonial policy, the value of imperial expansion, the question of emigration, the theory of taxation—all had to face the verdict of the storytellers. There was especial devotion to commerce, before, during, and after the war, and to the fate of property and investments in war-time. Further, the feeling that relationships had been mismanaged in many fields led on to criticisms and satires of government that got far away from the American event or scene which was the point of departure.

These are the direct influences of the war. Had history taken a different course, many books, such as *Jonathan Corncob* among the most entertaining, *The Voluntary Exile* among the longest, *Emma Corbett* among the most emotional, and *Mount Henneth* among the most thoughtful, could not have been written, the effect of many episodes would have had to be achieved differently, and many homilies would have gone in search of a subject.

The last four types of influence have, in this summary, been passed over rapidly. As we trace the war in the content of novels, however, two additional conclusions automatically suggest themselves. The first has to do with the character and quality of the novels themselves, the second with the times in which they were written, with public opinion on current events. In reviewing each of them, we make, perhaps, some slight contribution to knowledge.

What our ancestors read about the American Revolution provides a fairly trustworthy clue to what they read about other subjects that broke into fiction. In war-plots we see a thoroughly conventional design, a cautious sticking to old narrative routes. We see many typical characters, but few realized individuals. We see a jejune phraseology of academic abstractions, rarely the concrete word. We see a hackneyed pattern of relationships, a predictable sequence of melodramatic or polite experiences, scorning plausibility, and deferring as long as possible their inevitable consummation in a tried-and-true denouement. We

254

see characters, such as they are, developed verbally rather than dramatically. We see homily on one hand and exaggerated pathos on the other as the chief winds that waft these machine-made galleys over a painfully circuitous route to a final comfortable haven sheltered from the rough seas of reality by love, wealth, and propriety. Only an occasional shipwreck, without benefit of life-boats, adds zest to the custom-bound experience. But all this is nothing new. We could arrive at the same conclusions through other media than the war-stories. They fitted into the parvenu society of fiction with only a slight altering of conventionalities.

Finally, what our ancestors read about the American Revolution gives some clue to their ideas on contemporary history, to the frame of mind in which they viewed current events. This great anonymous expanse of fiction is the best canvas on which to find painted the opinions of the man in the street; the authors seldom, in any real sense, touch the picture, and the clientele dictates the show. That clientele must have thought much more about American matters, been much less apathetic about the war, than is supposed. What is more, it must have thought very differently from what one might expect. It seems thoroughly logical to anticipate a consistent animosity against the "rebels," as in *The School for Fathers,* but that book belongs to a woefully weak minority. Antipathy to Americans is negligible in comparison with sympathy and even admiration for Americans, whose misery and whose heroism are important in plot after plot. More impressive than the action is the exposition, in which characters and authors hold forth tirelessly on the stupidity, the futility, and the madness of the war; the injustice and cruelty of arming against a part of one's own nation, of conducting, that is, a civil war; the brutality and barbarity of settling a political dispute by "persecution" and "murder." There is no restraint upon invective, no limit to damnation.

Whatever kind of art is here, we have at least a minor social document, which bears out the historical fact, increasingly evident, that the war was minority politics, not a national crusade. Nor could that minority, powerful as it was, dictate opinion. As a result a literature which is full of patriotism—love of England, of the English constitution, of English freedom—shows anything but war-time patriotism as conventionally understood. No propagandist slogans regimented emotions behind a westward-borne flag. The large world of the novel—characters, authors, readers—was relatively independent, and, given to stereotyped inanities and trivialities though it was, it was less often comatose than perspicacious. Its arguments were better than its inventions. If stories were soporific, irritating, or nauseating, opinions and interpretations were often much to the point. Insight into ministerial skullduggery on one hand, and understanding of a civil war on the other, were not the products of chauvinism and incompetence and stupidity.

His Majesty's loyal opposition, in literature, was remarkably insistent and stubborn both during and after the war; it was as unsparing as government organs were fulsome. Here, as I have said frequently enough, is evidence of an unusually healthy freedom of the press. Beyond that, greater importance lies in literature's retaining so much freedom from politics, from the immediate ends sought by a transitory point of view, from the hypnotism of objectives striven for by temporarily dominant power; that is, from merely contemporary facts that becloud greater issues, distort insight, and shackle whatever perception one has. Not that our novelists were prophets or soothsayers. Take the most individual of the group—Pratt, Bage, Mrs. Smith; none of them is a seer blest. They had their share of astigmatism, prejudice, and illusion. But, in a very modest way, they were artists, not entirely without integrity. They were trying to be critics of life. What they stood for may be dated, sentimental, or visionary, but in some things they saw a bit further than leading ministers and Tory squires. Even professed liberals did not go so far, or speak so strongly, as these unknown story-writers who laboriously manufactured volume upon volume that today is entombed, without memorial—deservedly, to be sure—in peaceful stacks. Yet if one were to write a treatise on some such subject as "War and Its Effect on Literature," he would find a few relevant matters here.

## ii

Such are the direct influences of the war and their implications. America, however, gained access to the novel in other ways; in fact, she had a number of functions and positions in literature which had little or nothing to do with the war and which had existed long before Grenville's schemes of taxation began to cause unexpected reverberations. The meaning of America, as we have seen, began to find literary expression almost as soon as the new world emerged from Chaos.

With statistics and history of facts, so to speak, out of the way, we can get on to the history of ideas about America, the growth in the concept of America. The Renaissance carried all its buoyancy and freshness and bloom into its picture of the new world. Naturally we expect some dimming of lustre as education by time produced new facts, or as, paradoxically, the vague splendid outlines of dawn grew into the fixed, definite shapes of daylight. No doubt high noon, with perfect lighting, has not yet been reached. But, from the early nineteenth century on, we can see the English attitude to America dominated mainly by the desire for fact and analysis.

The search for truth must have begun long before, since roseate hopefulness does not in a day subside into the temper of a fact-finding commission. Critical severity was barely hinted at by 1700; by 1800 it was almost established. The eighteenth century, then, becomes the fulcrum for a single, momentous swing of the see-saw of opinion. Within the century, the disturbed last forty years, the period of transition, innovation, and upheaval, are inevitably the time of revaluations. The spirit of these decades, with their changes in social, political, and literary standards, creates a strong antecedent supposition that the

concept of America, bound up with various contemporary movements, will have assumed a different content.

Specific circumstances support the hypothesis—America's leaving home and starting out in the world for itself. The year
1783 marks the end of the second period of England's relations
with the western hemisphere. The first period was from the
discovery to the Spanish collapse, during which English interest,
as Rastell lamented, was sluggish. The Tudors and the church
and the theatre and Latin and Italian literature came first. Then
the Armada ran afoul of Aeolus, and from 1588 to 1783 there
was the second period, in which England was actively interested
in America for colonization and empire, for its wealth, for
social and political experimentation, for a dozen potentialities.
During those two centuries there was no single event, no sharp
break, no fundamental disillusionment to cause a marked re-
vulsion of feeling.

Then came the war. America walked out of the firm and set
up business for itself. No longer could England view the new
world as an agency and expression of its own greatness; no
longer could it entertain the same hopes of unbounded profit
from natural resources; no longer could it enjoy the stimulating
sensations of paterfamilias to a flattering dependency. It got the
first real knowledge of its sons who had left home; it suffered
painful opposition, lost money, struggled in wildernesses. One
can hardly expect that its concept of America would remain
the same.

So we come to the second possible influence of the American Revolution—the influence on English thought concerning
America as that thought is reflected in prose fiction. This is an
indirect influence. Often the war has nothing to do with the
novels, except as it antedated or postdated them. Sometimes,
of course, war-stories are important. And, as in studying the
direct effects of the war, we find evidence not only in narrative
but also in expository passages.

The concept of America has been spoken of as if it were a

single, precisely definable idea, subject to changes which can be described exactly. Unhappily for classification, it is always a series of ideas, and the best that one can hope to do is to find running through them some dominant attitude or principle of interpretation. In the Renaissance, that appears to be a broad hopefulness, an optimistic anticipation; in the nineteenth and twentieth centuries, criticalness, realism, often colored by a preference for the less savory. Here are the dominating moods long before and long after the war; in examining the period 1760-1800, we shall see what was the tendency of thought just before and just after the war. The question is whether the development within this smaller compass parallels and dove-tails with the larger one from Columbus to the present time. If it does, the war will certainly appear to be influential in the change.

The material to be set forth will answer the second of the two major questions posed at the outset. The first introduced a quantitative examination: How much was written about the American Revolution? The second problem is qualitative: Of what kind are the ideas about America? The two categories, however, are not mutually exclusive. In recording the extent of fictional treatment of the war, we have already seen something of English attitudes. And, in examining the latter directly, we are bound to introduce statistics, for the ideas which occur more frequently are obviously of greater importance, and the frequency of occurrence before and after the war leads to the heart of the whole study—the influence of the war.

The type of ideas likely to occur is hinted at by the Renaissance picture of America. What, for instance, happens to the original gold-fever? Is America still thought of in terms of its material potentialities? Does the romantic idealization of a new, clean, unspoiled land continue? Can America still be used as a basis for comparisons unfavorable to Europe? Is it still a refuge for the weary and the heavy-laden? Is it still a convenient jumping-off place for undesirables? What of the character of

Americans? Do they as a whole manifest the admirable qualities apparent in colonists fighting for liberty? And just what
did those colonists achieve? What are the virtues and evils of
the new politic? How can the land of liberty reconcile itself
to slavery? What can be said for its management of religious
problems?

The answers which novels make to these questions should
provide the interpretation of America in the late eighteenth
century and show the difference between it and the concepts
which held sway before and after that transitional era.

# CHAPTER IX

## EVOLUTION OF THE GOLDEN AGE

### i

America's kinship with the manifold evolution of Romanticism was sketched in Chapter I. The link is clearest in the history of "romantic primitivism," the reaction against institutionalism, society, and "civilization" which appeared most spectacularly in the glorification of the forest primeval and the asseveration of its conduciveness to the good life. Pantisocracy is the pre-eminent exemplar. Other Susquehannas and their ideal communities appear in our novels.

The seekers of an innocuous environment fled vitiating institutions and a debilitating society; from a virginal nature they mined strength, honesty, goodness, tenderness, and depth of thought. Such fertility not only made the Noble Savage what he was but could infuse worn humanity with new virtue. Unspoiled woods not only restored the physical and spiritual weaklings that civilization made of men, but repelled evil and barred man-made vice. Hence the effort to find a better life, to recreate an actual Golden Age in the primitive surroundings which fostered the unalloyed happiness and excellence of Indians, Africans, South Sea Islanders, and other rather distant natives not handicapped by literacy and law.

The reasons for envisaging America as the site of a new Golden Age are clear enough. The ideal life which was imagined had a varied genesis, springing in some cases merely from a personal desire to escape the immediate present and to enjoy the chimerical advantages which are always the chief lure of the unknown, in others from the more positive intention of reconstructing society on a new set of better principles. What-

261

ever the details, improvement was the announced aim, and flight the essence. The objective was asylum or utopia, and the anticipated amelioration was political, social, psychological, or spiritual.

The other end of the rainbow was the goal of a triple quest, for the adventurers, if we rank them by their aims, were aristocrats, middle class, or proletariat. The most pretentious or the most sensitive of them sought a Golden Age proper; the next group, more crass, expected neither balm for the stricken deer nor a salve for society, but merely professional or economic betterment. Such prospective emigrants thought solidly about lower taxes, higher incomes, better markets, safer positions, and other material advantages. They foresaw a Land of Promise, a comfortable Canaan; they anticipated permanence. They were not "taking a flier" but making an investment, and they would join, help build, and grow up with the new community. In the great society of westward-looking hopefuls they were the middle class.

The third class of pilgrims, the proletariat, expected some immediate material gain, generally monetary, but perhaps professional; they were the "get-rich-quick" group. They appreciated the resources and potentialities of the new land, from which they hoped to gain as much as possible as rapidly as possible. They were not exclusively transients, and they might have foreseen permanence, but they often planned to return to Europe, and always their emphasis was upon immediate improvement. They were shallow, having neither the ideals of the Golden-Age group nor the stability of the Land-of-Promise group.

Our problem is to see how much of an impress each of these groups made on fiction and how reasonable and tenable their points of view were considered, and in our findings there should reside a dependable outline of the current ideas about America. If the relation among them is constant, and if American pilgrimages appear with marked consistency during a forty-year period, then there is obviously little change in the concept. But if any of these themes grows or declines in number, or if we find ventures turning out unsuccessfully, or if we find satire turned upon the picture of a materially or spiritually beneficent America, we may conclude that there has been a serious change in the original hopefulness about America. And the time of the change must be noted.

ii

Our days
Wiser are they, or nobler? The age of gold
Shines in the past, not now.

So versifies Alexander Grosart, with regretful finality, in a momentary digression from editing.[1] "The past" probably does not refer to the Elizabethan age, which itself had applied the "Elisium motif" to America.[2] Chapman and Drayton had actually used the term *Golden Age* with reference to America. They were really followers of Sir Thomas More, for, with the discovery of America, "utopia, as a fresh conception of the good life, becomes a throbbing possibility."[3] The same stimulus must probably be conceded coauthorship of Bacon's *New Atlantis* and Cowley's plan for an ideal university. Cowley[4] and Davenant, as we have already seen, actually planned trips to an American ivory tower, and as unlike figures as Marvell and Waller idealized life in the Bermudas. An applied idealism was responsible for the founding of New England, Pennsylvania, and Maryland.

The Hesperides continued to draw wistful glances in the

[1] Prefatory sonnet to *The Complete Works in Prose and Verse of Francis Quarles* (Edinburgh University Press, 1880).

[2] Foster Y. St. Clair, *The Myth of the Golden Age from Spenser to Milton* (Thesis, Harvard University, 1931), pp. 305-306.

[3] Mumford, *The Story of Utopias*, p. 61.

[4] Discussing Boswell and the Noble Savage, Miss Bailey makes a discerning comment on Cowley, who "shows the difference between the seventeenth and eighteenth centuries; he required still the pleasures of a civilized life, and idealized nothing but solitude and peace. Those who followed him sought the ideal in the life of the savage himself" (*Hypochondriack*, I, 84 note).

263

eighteenth century. Like Herbert, Berkeley "looked to the New [World] to save humanity and preserve a Christian civilization" and hence

conceived his grand imperial project of founding a university at Bermuda, which was to form the centre of a Christian civilization.[5]

An equal hopefulness, though of different tone, was actually reduced to practice in various French settlements in America, conceived in

that mood of dreamy idealism which was a common French attitude of mind where the New World was concerned.[6]

An English attempt to realize an ideal was Priber's venture among the Cherokees of South Carolina in 1733.[7] In August, 1772, a resident of New Orleans wrote to the *Gentleman's* recommending settlement west of the Allegheny and north of the Ohio, where, he says, "will be the Paradise of America."[8] Two decades later there was a real outburst of enthusiasm of this sort. Imlay was an energetic advertiser, and he and Mary Wollstonecraft planned to put his precepts into practice.[9] Thomas Cooper, no less fervid, described an ideal location in north-central Pennsylvania,[10] where, also, the Priestleys planned a Utopia, and two poets, Pantisocracy. When the elder Priestley left England, the Society of United Irishmen of Dublin assured him, ". . . you are going to a happier world—the world of

---

[5] *Cambridge History of the British Empire*, I, 626.

[6] H. M. Jones, *America and French Culture*, p. 149. Two of the best known were Gallipolis, Ohio (pp. 147-149), and Le Champ d'Asile, Texas (p. 156). Other idealistic ventures that might be mentioned here were Asylum and Economy, Pennsylvania, which Professor J. L. Lowes has called to my attention.

[7] See Verner W. Crane, "A Lost Utopia of the First American Frontier," *Sewanee Review*, XXVII (1919), 48-61.

[8] XLII (1772), 355. This, it might be noted, is just north of Imlay's country.

[9] Ralph L. Rusk, *The Adventures of Gilbert Imlay* (Indiana University Studies, Vol. X, No. 57, Bloomington, 1923), p. 21. The same passage also describes Brissot de Warville's plan to emigrate.

[10] In a letter added to Imlay's *Topographical Description* (3rd ed., 1797), p. 197 note.

Washington and Franklin."[11] Two years later he wrote from Northumberland, Pennsylvania:

The advantages we enjoy in this country are indeed very great. We have no poor; we never see a beggar, nor is there a family in want. We have no church establishment, and hardly any taxes. This particular State pays all its officers from a treasure in the public funds. There are very few crimes committed and we travel without the least apprehension of danger. The press is perfectly free, and I hope we shall always keep out of war.[12]

All the evidence here presented is effectively summed up by Crane Brinton:

It [the Golden Age] was not, however, sufficiently real; the natural goodness of man had, if possible, to be placed in a contemporary setting. Ignorance could still happily find that setting in America. Washington became the perfect copy of virtue, an example of the way a man developed away from civilization. The fair tale of the golden age had come true in the United States.

> There social order first began
> And man was reverenc'd as man.
> All were obedient, all were free,
> And God's own law—equality—
> Dispensed its blessings with a lib'ral hand,
> And banished vile oppression from the land.

Or again, this perfect state could safely be placed in the future. . . . The natural goodness of man thus strengthened by projection into the historic past, the New World, and the future, is next to be brought into actual politics.[13]

By way of completing the picture, we may note briefly the dreams of the Romantic poets. Blake's flattering symbolization of America has already been mentioned;

. . . in the later writings, although his faith in a return of the Golden

---

[11] Edgar F. Smith, *Priestley in America 1794-1804* (Philadelphia: Blakiston, 1902), p. 14.

[12] *Ibid.*, p. 92.

[13] *The Political Ideas of the English Romanticists* (Oxford, 1926), pp. 26-27. The quotation, Brinton notes, is from J. Samson's *Oppression, or the Power of Abuse* (1795), p. 14.

Age is no less assured, he thinks of the means by which man is to attain it as a process divinely ordained and of some duration.[14]

Campbell, whose family background connected him with America, who for a time was considered by Americans to be the poetic mouthpiece of liberty, and who in both 1797 and 1817 thought of seeking an American haven from the ills of Europe,[15] wrote *Gertrude of Wyoming,* "an interesting example of the survival into the nineteenth century of the notion of an American Arcadia,"[16] which produced praise and an essay on Anglo-American relations by Washington Irving,[17] and from an American who knew the scene, a gentle criticism of the discrepancy between the literary and the actual[18]—a very illuminating reaction to the dreams of absentee idealists. In Byron there is a last flicker of the Kentucky illusion fashioned by Imlay: Quite late in life he can write of Daniel Boone and the Kentucky pioneers:

> Motion was their days, Rest in their slumbers,
>   And Cheerfulness the handmaid of their toil;
> Nor yet too many nor too few their numbers;
>   Corruption could not make their hearts her soil;
> The lust which stings, the splendour which encumbers,
>   With the free foresters divide no spoil:
> Serene, not sullen, were the solitudes
>   Of this unsighing people of the woods.

This idyllic Kentucky is the 'dark and bloody ground' of American pioneer tradition.[19]

And of "A land beyond the Oceans of the West" Shelley says,

14 Sloss and Wallis, *op. cit.,* II, 83.

15 For the relationship between Campbell and America, see Thompson, *A Scottish Man of Feeling,* pp. 335 ff., 394.

16 Brinton, *op. cit.,* p. 196.

17 Fittingly enough, it is prefixed to W. L. Stone's *The Poetry and History of Wyoming* (New York, 1844).

18 Rev. John Todd, *The Lost Sister of Wyoming* (Northampton, 1842), pp. 57-58.

19 Brinton, *op. cit.,* p. 150.

That land is like an Eagle, whose young gaze
Feeds on the noontide beam, whose golden plume
Floats moveless on the storm, and in the blaze
Of sunrise gleams when earth is wrapped in gloom.[20]

We have gone somewhat afield in recording all the enthusiasm and anticipation which America evoked in emigrants, planners, prophets, and poets; praising a republic is not quite the same as seeking solace in a wilderness. Still, in all these citations there is the same underlying spirit—utopianism, the hope for a Golden Age, focusing on America. And when we see the earlier intoxication leaving a final hang-over even in the nineteenth century, we can judge how strong and extensive the idea was. Now we come down specifically to the novels. They, interestingly enough, were not nearly so receptive to the idealizing tendency as its popularity elsewhere leads one to expect.

Once or twice there is an unlocalized yearning for the Golden Age, as in *Adeline* (1790), which reflects sadly on the present-day improbability of achieving "the peace and harmony of the golden age."[21] Henry Man's *The History of Sir Geoffry Restless* (1791), satirizing the devotion of its hero, a denatured Sir Roger de Coverley, to Price-Priestley liberalism, comes closer to home. Sir Geoffry lectures a county court on the desirability of civil liberty, and from that suggestion of America proceeds to link, in enthusiastic paean, the Golden Age, Sir Thomas More's Utopia, and the perfect unfettered life in Arcadia.[22]

The perfect unfettered life in American Arcadias appears first in Arthur Young's *Adventures of Emmera* (1767). Since this book has been amply summarized by both Bissell[23] and Fairchild,[24] it is not necessary to go again into the details of how Emmera's father fled from an evil civilization to form a

[20] *The Revolt of Islam*, Canto XI, Stanzas 22 ff. For comment, see Brinton, p. 172.
[21] I, 16.
[22] I, 111 ff.
[23] Pp. 98-99.
[24] Page 94.

happy wilderness community "in which men can live according
to the dictates of nature"; how Emmera and her lover Chetwyn
visit England, only to find the life there intolerable; and how
finally they

return to America, there to dwell happily and innocently in the wilds,
with only the good Indians for company.[25]

The story is one of the most effective proponents of primitivism,
since the major characters do practice their professions; since
they live the rustic life without attempting to change it fundamentally, as do other pilgrims, by superimposing Christianity;
and since the author escapes the unconscious inconsistencies
which often make his type of evangelist absurd.

*The Female American* (1767) is much less convincing in its
advocacy of the backwoods. With two separate stories in which
to embody the ideal, the author constantly slips into realistic
touches or Anglican missionary work that unintentionally ruins
his effect. In the first episode in Virginia, William Winkfield,
an Englishman, is saved by the squaw Unca, a literary descend-
ant of Pocahontas, and led into a bower

composed of the most pleasing greens delightfully variegated with the
most beautiful flowers; a shady defence from the sun, which then shone
with uncommon heat.[26]

The Imlayesque profusion of superlatives clearly foreshadows
William and Unca in a perfect Adam-and-Eve existence, spoiled
only by the peculiarly un-Arcadian activities of the jealous
Alluca, who forgets native nobility sufficiently to indulge, in
seeking homicidal consolation for her unrequited love, a pro-
clivity for poisoning. Nature, however, comes to the rescue of
the poisoned hero, for, as he walked with Unca, they gathered
some flowers,

the smell of which quickly dispelled the fumes, and fortified the brain

25 Fairchild, *loc. cit.*
26 Page 12.

so powerfully, that he was soon perfectly recovered, and his strength and understanding both entirely restored.[27]

Even with this, William is not satisfied but must needs convert Unca. The second story is that of their daughter, Eliza, who finds a similar idyl among Indians on an island, unidentified but presumably American. Eliza also Christianizes the Indians, thus introducing an institution which her type is supposed to hate, but this inconsistency never bothers her. In fact, she and her cousin William decide to spend a lifetime enjoying insular excellence, and a Captain Shore is also smitten with the idea. He says,

Since what has befallen me, I shall not like to reside in England, nor any more to be concerned in worldly affairs; therefore if you think me a true convert, let me join in your society.[28]

First, however, they returned to England not only to get rid of Winkfield's needless fortune but also to "bring over such books and things as might be useful to us in our retirement." Like Cowley, they preferred the woods plus philosophy, and thus true primitivism goes a-glimmering. Still, they believed they had found a latter-day Golden Age—and in America.

With the exception of Edward Bancroft's primitive paradise among the Indians of South America,[29] already referred to, one has to leap over two decades to the period of the French Revolution before finding another novel picturing a contemporary Golden Age.[30] Then comes the outburst at the center of which were the inspirational letters of Crèvecoeur and the travel works of Imlay, Cooper, and Filson. Following these picturesque salesmen, and drawn by savannas, magnolias, and mockingbirds, the imagination usually turned south, though sometimes

[27] Page 21.

[28] Page 212.

[29] For Bancroft's *History of Charles Wentworth* (1770), see Miss Tompkins, pp. 29-30; *Critical Review*, XXIX (1770), 358-364; *Monthly Review*, XLIII (1770), 67; *Gentleman's Magazine*, XXXIX (1769), 145-149.

[30] *Feelings of the Heart* (1772) sets up pastoral perfection in India, describing "this terrestrial paradise," "the new Arcadia" (II, 149-150).

this ideal equipment was set up, with no attention to geography or climate, along the St. Lawrence. Mrs. Rowson, however, was content with the North as it was, thus eulogizing New England in *Fille de Chambre* (1792):

> Ere this [the war], the inhabitants of New England, by their hospitality and primitive simplicity of manners, revived in the mind of our heroine the golden age, so celebrated by poets. Here were no locks or bolts required, for each one, content with his own cot, coveted not the possessions of his neighbour; here should a stranger make his appearance in their little village, though unknown by all, every one was eager to show him the most civility, inviting him to their houses, and treating him with every delicacy the simplicity of their manner of living afforded.[31]

This paragraph is unique in a series of descriptions calumniating dour Puritanism. The perfect scene shifts from New England to Pennsylvania in *The Voluntary Exile* (1795) of Mrs. Parsons, in many ways a panegyrist. Her hero Biddulph finds his ideal among a retired colony of Quakers who live "entertained by the mocking bird" "in a sequestered vale" where "was a beautiful lake that run [*sic*] through the trees."[32] ". . . enchanted with the beauty of the scene, and the various warblings of the melodious little creature," bursts forth:

> Happy, happy beings! . . . favourites of Heaven, like the patriarchs of old, you enjoy every blessing of nature uncorrupted; here peace and happiness dwells [*sic*], undisturbed by the commotions of a selfish world![33]

Yet despite all the blandishments, Biddulph, like most of the enchanted Englishmen in these novels, finally goes back to England.

Two of George Walker's novels illustrate the conflict between progress and primitivism of which Miss Whitney writes.[34]

[31] Page 149.
[32] II, 118-119.
[33] II, 119-120.
[34] Lois Whitney, *Primitivism and the Idea of Progress in English Popular Literature of the Eighteenth Century* (Baltimore: Johns Hopkins University

While *The Vagabond* (1799) attacks the idealizing of the primitive, *Theodore Cyphon* (1796) shows at least some hospitality to a retreat from European evils to the American wilds. The title-hero has had many misfortunes:

Wearied and disgusted with what I had suffered in England, and seeing no end to the vindictiveness of my father, or the nefarious practices of my uncle, I adopted the design of attending Mr. Hanson to America, and settling in some impenetrable forest, where the labour of our hands might supply our exigencies, and the surplus provide against the intrusions of weather, and, perhaps, in time afford us some of those superfluities which are like fruits on the road across a parched land.

. . . I pleased myself with the patriarchal prospect till I had lost myself in the wilderness. . . .[35]

Actually, however, Theodore found refuge in Holland.

Always a friend of America, Mrs. Smith paints it rather idyllically in *The Young Philosopher* (1798), which is under the influence of Crèvecoeur. One actual quotation from him[36] and such phrases as "his [Glenmorris's] metamorphose [*sic*] from a Scottish chieftain to an American farmer"[37] and "the great book of nature is open before me"[38] make her inspiration clear. When Mrs. Glenmorris has difficulties in England, her daughter Medora, in whom is embodied "perhaps the most striking of the portraits of natural goodness,"[39] remarks,

We never had these hateful perplexities in America. . . . Oh! that we had never left America. . . . I never recollect a moment's uneasiness till I came to England. . . . Oh! my dear Delmont, if ever I should belong to you, take me, take me to America![40]

The voice of wisdom continues to reside in Medora, who urges

---

Press, 1934), pp. 222-223. ". . . there is no attempt to reconcile these conflicting points of view." Later she speaks of "the universal fact of intellectual inconsistency" (p. 327).

[35] I, 253.

[36] III, 32. In this instance she footnotes her source.

[37] II, 255.

[38] IV, 392.

[39] Whitney, *op. cit.*, p. 263.

[40] II, 261-263.

her mother to give up a futile property-hunt in England and return to America, "where we had always enough for our wishes"[41]—again an echo of Crèvecoeur. Glenmorris, visiting England, is shocked by

the toil and fatigue which were incurred to make a splendid appearance at such an immense expence as would have supported in America fifty families in more real comfort and plenty.[42]

He summarizes all his hopes:

To cultivate the earth of another continent, to carry the arts of civil life, without its misery and its vices, to the wild regions of the globe, had in it a degree of sublimity, which, in Glenmorris's opinion, sunk the petty politics and false views so eagerly pursued in Europe, into something more despicable than childish imbecility . . . he rejoiced that he had made his election where human life was in progressive improvement, and where he had not occasion to turn with disgust, from the exercise of abject meanness to obtain the advantages of affluence, or with pity from fruitless efforts to escape from the humiliations of poverty.[43]

The book continues with expression of hope for the time which will make possible the project in America, with its philosophic confusion upon which Miss Whitney comments.[44]

The spirit of escape and reconstruction also appears in Imlay's *Emigrants* (1793), written in praise of American life, with its political and economic advantages framed in Arcadian trimmings. Imlay refers to

the fairest country upon the face of the globe,—a country [of] which Voltaire said, "if ever the golden age existed, it was in the middle provinces of America."[45]

Miss W—— thus invites Mrs. R—— to America:

[41] III, 111.
[42] IV, 199.
[43] IV, 201-202.
[44] *Op. cit.,* p. 264.
[45] III, 126.

Come to these Arcadian regions where there is room for millions, and where the stings of outrageous fortune cannot reach you. . . .[46]

On a site on the Ohio Captain Arl—ton plans to put into operation

a system conformable to reason and humanity, and thereby extend the blessings of civilization to all orders of men . . . to form in epitome the model of a society which I conceive ought to form part of the polity of every civilized commonwealth.[47]

Reason and humanity, it seems, will be served by a tract sixteen miles square, the total divided into parcels each of which is to be possessed by a war veteran in fee simple; unrestricted eligibility for election to a house of representatives of twenty members, meeting every Sunday; universal manhood suffrage; unrestricted freedom of speech in the house. These are the basic rules and regulations of a society which the author avers already exists. The captain's wife adds numerous descriptive details about the "delightful spot," "altogether enchanting," with its "stupendous cataract."[48] In the evening they "walk into the sugar groves" where neighbors dance "to the rude music of the country."[49] They rarely dine at home, so great is hospitality. This Golden Age, of which only leading characteristics have been mentioned, obviously borrows too much civilization to be more than conventionally idyllic. Whatever the objective, however, America would do.

Eugenia De Acton's *Disobedience* (1797), a mélange of unacknowledged borrowings from Crèvecoeur, Filson, Cooper, and especially Imlay, tells about the departure from England of Mr. Eddows—a fatherly leader and exhorter, but a violent opponent of everything English—and William Challoner and Mary Hastings, his young converts, to seek a freer, happier, and less troubled life in America. The latter two are the quintes-

[46] I, 92.
[47] III, 128-129. Other details are given in the following pages.
[48] III, 162. Her rhapsody goes on for four pages.
[49] III, 167-168.

sence of devotion and applied enthusiasm, and, needless to say, their venture is exuberantly successful. The actual trip is preceded by a quantity of rhetoric from Eddows, partly denunciation of England, mostly praise of American liberty, equality, and fraternity, and entirely inspired by the *Letters of an American Farmer*. Few virtues there are that are not conceded to America. The travelers arrive in Philadelphia, decide to go to Kentucky, join forces with the Humberstons of Virginia, make the Imlay trip across Pennsylvania by wagon and down the Ohio by boat; here we are provided by rhapsodic descriptions of natural beauty which are purloined from Imlay. Arrival and settlement in Kentucky cause no abatement of ecstasy, but unrestrained enthusiasm for the beauty, the abundance, the fertility, and the conduciveness to every form of joy and satisfaction waltzes on in a delirium of superlatives. Their tract

united in itself every advantage that a settler could desire—Wood, water, cane, fruitful plains, and luxuriant vallies, were offered to his choice; while the country, spreading out into the most beautiful undulations, or rising into gentle hills, from which flowed a thousand streams, formed a region enchanting beyond description.[50]

There is a moment's relaxation of emphasis on the material:

The happiness of this knot of friends now seemed beyond the possibility of increase; but, when they considered that this happiness depended not upon the opinions nor the caprices of others; that it rested neither on rank nor wealth; the smiles of monarchs, nor the favours of their ministers, but that it was the genuine offspring of pure virtue, of honest industry, and ardent affection—neither did they fear its diminution.[51]

Mr. Eddows was especially happy "in the convinction [*sic*] that he now breathed the true air of freedom."[52] There followed detailed description of the produce of grains, vegetables, fruits, and trees, and an account of the easy, free, generous, good-humored, and utterly happy mode of life.

[50] IV, 143.
[51] IV, 148.
[52] IV, 149.

The scheme varies and propaganda *viget mobilitate* when Mary is sent back to London to aid her distressed mother, an objectionable harridan who is now to have coals of fire heaped on her head by amiable youth. Thus the author can both contrast American virtue with English vice and also convert a nasty reactionary to the advantages and joys of the new life. The contrast is accomplished by Mary's spurning the advances of the married Lord St. Albans. Winning over a recalcitrant mother is not so simple; in fact, it takes Mary into tireless dissertations, conglomerates of Imlay and Crèvecoeur. The first text is: "What is the true dignity of man but usefulness?" Mary's contentions essay modesty:

> To say that disappointment or misfortune are banished from the fruitful and flowery plains of Kentucky . . . would be to say what never can be true of the habitations of man; but I may safely aver, that there is less of both in these happy regions than in any other part of the earth with which I am acquainted. A sufficiency of the necessaries of life may be acquired by any one who can, in the least, endure trouble or fatigue. The fear of hunger and nakedness need not assail any one who has the use of his limbs: every one works for himself, and all work is sure of its due recompence. . . .
> . . . cleanliness, health, plenty, and cheerfulness, are the offspring of industry. . . .[53]

The argument proceeds to demonstrate the advantages of religious tolerance in America and of the absence of savages—a peculiarly civilized note!—in Kentucky, "that earthly paradise."[54] Mary's mother yields and migrates, and the story ends with further apostrophes to the beauty and progress of America.

Here is primitivism of the inconsistent variety that Miss Whitney has often noticed in eighteenth-century works: our idealists are retreating from civilization, and yet they are taking civilization along with them—minus certain aspects of it that they

[53] IV, 204-205.
[54] IV, 223.

do not like. Nevertheless, whatever the confusion of principle, optimism depends on America, where promise makes perfect.

In *Henry Willoughby* (1798) a disgust with life is again the genesis of a sally into American wilds. Morthermer is very out of sorts because of his experiences in the British navy, and he has no inclination to join the American army. In this frame of mind when he reaches New York, he appropriately falls in with some Quakers, frequent in novels. He is employed by a Friend who "was going to remove to the back settlements until the war was over,"[55] the objective being the falls of St. Anthony (Minneapolis):

A few quaker families had established a settlement at that sequestered spot; where, apart from the busy intrigues of a vicious world, they pursued, unmolested, the noblest and fittest occupations of man—the shepherd and husbandman.[56]

This new pastoral idyl shows an author not only weak in history[57] but also muddled in his conception of Quakerism, for his colony enjoys "the utmost latitude of skepticism."[58] He has evidently mistaken religious tolerance for the intellectual ideal on which the Age of Reason flattered itself—another instance of the "intellectual confusion" of which Miss Whitney speaks.

The physical advantages of the colony, named Anachoropolis, if a degree less radiantly bountiful than those of the Kentucky resorts, still are conducive to "Arcadian felicity."[59] The author is more interested in abstract matters, especially education, which he describes at tiresome length, very oddly using quo-

55 II, 223. For the Quaker attitude to the war, see Rufus M. Jones, *The Quakers in the American Colonies* (London: Macmillan, 1911), Book V, Chapter 9, "The Friends in the Revolution." Nothing is said here about actual migrations to avoid warfare.

56 II, 224-225.

57 By 1784 the most westerly Quaker settlement was in Tennessee; see Rufus M. Jones, *The Later Periods of Quakerism* (London: Macmillan, 1921), I, 399. Chapter XI, "The Great Migration," records no movement which could have been the basis of the novel.

58 II, 239.

59 II, 229.

tation marks but not deigning to indicate his source. Whomever he quoted, or pretended to quote, his propositions are consistent with the new educational liberalism and are roughly similar to Rousseau's. The method is as follows:

"Man," they say, "ought to be provided within himself, with every possible precaution for his own preservation, and not to trust to accident or chance for relief in the hour of danger." They also assert, "that for want of proper cultivation and improvement, the organs of sensation are far from being so useful as they might be made. . . ."

Hence they practice the use of one sense at a time, so that they can learn to read a printed book thirty or forty yards away.[60] Before learning more about education, we are told that the Anachoropolitans practice religious toleration and communism, with one hour of work per day sufficient to satisfy all their wants.

As the infantine state of Anachoropolis renders sumptuary laws unnecessary, and its want of commerce prevents the influx of superfluous commodities, their legislator has devised no expedients against luxury and voluptuousness, assigning for his reason, that as most of his endeavors had been directed to the improvement of the mind, it would be ridiculous in him to enact regulations, which were only necessary for nations in a state of decline, or just emerging from barbarism.[61]

The implied perfectionism of the last phrase once more gives us the usual blend of discordant philosophies.

Education is divided into five periods, the first extending through the second year, the second through the fifth year. Here the children learn science by observing the action of the Mississippi and philanthropy by the transference of their affections from families to the community at large; they develop

---

[60] II, 231-232. Cf. *Emilius; Or, A Treatise of Education. Translated from the French of J. J. Rousseau* (Edinburgh, 1773), I, 254 ff. Rousseau discusses the development of the senses but avoids the Leatherstocking extreme here exhibited.

[61] II, 242-243.

physically through stress on sports.[62] In the third period, extending through the twelfth year, emphasis is on voluntary education, sought through a sense of "its necessity and importance,"[63] and adults teach in rotation for three-month periods.[64] Practical lessons cultivate individual interests, and "enquiry and doubt" are encouraged, for the youth "may one day become the Newton, or Boyle, of Anachoropolis."[65] Complete freedom marks the fourth period, from the thirteenth through the nineteenth year:

. . . the page of history shall convince them of the happiness of their condition, and forbid them to repine after the vices and luxuries of Europe.[66]

Having acquired supremacy of reason, they go into the fifth period, where, until death, experience is the only teacher.

Morthermer spends two happy years in the community. Upon his telling of the outside world (as an educator, he would probably have met the prescriptions of the totalitarian state),

The young would shudder at the vices of the civilized portion of the globe, and be thankful that fortune had placed them beyond the reach of their baneful influence. They were wont to execrate the land that assumed the proud title of their mother-country; but their parents would remind them, that England produced a Shakespeare and a Milton, a Newton and a Locke.[67]

Patriotism motivates a rare concession in utopia. A further surprise is their discovery of the need "of many of those conveniences, which custom has ranked among the necessaries of

[62] II, 250 ff. The divisions differ from Rousseau's. On the observational method, cf. *Emilius*, I, 296 ff.; on sports, I, 40-46, 203 ff. Rousseau cites four sources for the idea.

[63] II, 258-259. Cf. Godwin: "No creature in human form will be expected to learn any thing, but because he desires it and has some conception of its value; . . ." (*Political Justice*, II, 373).

[64] II, 260.

[65] II, 262-263, 265-266. Cf. *Emilius*, I, 367, 294.

[66] II, 268.

[67] II, 274.

life" and of the desire for property left behind them,[68] which one might think that their present competence and ease would make unnecessary. Happy though he is, Morthermer is glad to accept the commission, and that is convenient, since he has to be transported back to England for the contrast à la *Disobedience*. When he reaches the old country, his parents promptly die of joy, and he decides to return:

Europe presents no charms to detain me: her vices I detest, and her luxuries and arts I disdain. I long to visit my regretted savanna, or wander amongst the venerable oaks and pines, where peace and solitude hold undisturbed dominion. My heart has lost its relish for the gay scenes of the busy world.[69]

When Henry, the title hero, thinks of joining him, Morthermer glorifies the "peaceful retirement" of Anachoropolis thus:

In my beloved retreat . . . whilst you admire, you will be taught to venerate—whilst you love, you will be taught to esteem. There, my friend, the evening of our days may, like the evening of a summer's day, be pregnant with delight and happiness; and in the wane of life, not a cloud of sorrow shall obstruct the sunshine of our prosperity.[70]

Henry agrees, and Morthermer is full of anticipation:

Poverty and her heart-chilling train, are now banished from my presence, and the necessaries of life are no longer numbered among my wants. I bid adieu to distress and despair, and encourage the pleasing hope, that the remainder of my life may be spent in the enjoyment of ease and tranquillity.[71]

*Henry Willoughby* concludes the case for the Golden Age, for utopias, Edens, paradises, and Arcadias in America. Prairies and timberlands, for two centuries hailed as asylums and as nurseries of a better society, received a final accolade before *Martin Chuzzlewit*. As we look ahead of our novels, we see the end of the myth; in fact, the end is already in sight. All the

[68] II, 275.
[69] II, 282.
[70] II, 285-286.
[71] II, 286-287.

anticipation of a good life freed from poverty, distress, and despair might seem pleasantly naïve did it not give the impression of vast insincerity. When we see the wide influence of Imlay and consider his purely commercial intentions, a great hollowness sounds forth in the hyperboles. Readers, of course, may have accepted advertising brochures as major prophecies, for, as Miss Whitney remarks, "There were various ways in which fashion vitiated thought in the eighteenth century."[72] A two-century-old fashion dies slowly, and America had long had a romantic feather in its cap. But thought was gaining strength, as we shall see. The American war, though it produced a political novelty that for a time threatened to inherit the aureate garb of the preceptive plains, began to stimulate, if my hypothesis is correct, a serious reconsideration of American virtues.

### iii

*Martin Chuzzlewit* was not an initiator. In our period, the Golden Age met objections as soon as it raised its head—in Young's *The Adventures of Emmera* (1767). The *Critical* was doubtful:

His design is simple and commendable, that of contrasting the social with the sequestered state of life, and shewing how dangerous society may prove to virtue. His retir'd scenes are laid in America, and are infinitely preferable to those he has exhibited in Europe. . . .

The life which Sir Philip leads with Emmera may be relished by such readers as are enamoured with ideas of Platonic love and sylvan retirement.[73]

The *Monthly,* more likely to be hospitable to such a theme, was half-hearted:

If there is any thing exemplary in this very romantic performance, it must consist in the reader's imitation of the good people's love of retirement, and totally quitting society, on account of the bad people by whom it is infested.—This, however, is an effect that will

---

[72] *Op. cit.,* p. 329.
[73] XXIII (1767), 272-273.

seldom happen from the perusal of any book, especially a work of mere invention.[74]

It is doubtful, in fact, whether Arthur Young actually felt the sentiments implied in the creation of a perfect little society in the American woods. When the elder Chetwyn plans his retirement, he is not immediately greeted with the wild approval customary in such stories; in fact, he meets very reasonable opposition from the most sensible person in the book, Mr. Boyde:

A very just sentiment beyond all doubt; but can anyone suppose, that to put it in practice, it is necessary to bury one's self in woods and wilds! Nothing more ridiculous! Such a conduct consists in nothing more than flying from those enemies we have not the courage to encounter. How much superior is the life of him who lives in the midst of vice and temptation, uncontaminated by example—untainted by the sad influence of his age! . . . Can he have any inducement but indolence, to retire to a people who want him not? To quit a service of trouble and activity, for an idle life of contemplation, study, and wandering? . . . Surely you cannot be so infatuated with every thing wild and American as to suppose most hermit-like retirement may not be practiced in England?[75]

Here is convincing opposition, which, with its incisive ethical analysis, is a strong brake on the total effect of the novel. Young is not the only novelist who gulps at primitivism but fails to swallow it completely. Holcroft's *Anna St. Ives* (1792) contains a project for an ideal community among the American Indians, but lack of fervor in the projector, plus the united opposition of everyone else, results in a still-born idea. Holcroft did not gain enthusiasm, as Miss Whitney's summary indicates:

Frank Henley, despairing of winning Anna, looks around for a field in which the 'energies of mind might be most productive of good' and decides that the savages of America will offer him the best material for the founding of an ideal society. Anna moreover talks of 'her beloved golden age, her times of primitive simplicity.' Twelve years later, however, Holcroft pulls himself out of this sentimentality and repudi-

[74] XXXVI (1767), 239.
[75] I, 51-54.

ates both the fables of the golden age and the current idealizations of the Hottentots and Esquimaux.[76]

The leafy-bower philosophy of what I have called the Imlay circle faced constant attack. The *Critical* snaps at Miss De Acton's *Disobedience* that

it is in some places rendered tedious by the stale political allusions and rhapsodical declamations in favour of emigration to America.[77]

The *Monthly,* traditionally considered liberal, is much more heavy-handed in dealing with Imlay's *Topographical Description,* fertile in suggestion to bucolic novelists:

In attending to the American writers, . . . we constantly perceive them describing uncultivated nature, as the ancient poets described the golden age, and as poets of our own times delineate pastoral scenes, in which the nymphs and swains, with their way of life, appear the very contrast of every thing of the kind that comes under our knowledge . . . however romantic and beautiful, a country, fresh from the hand of Nature, may appear in such representations, to invite emigrants, we must read with cautious discrimination, as we well know that many situations are more delightful to visit than as residences. . . .[78]

By the time of *Henry Willoughby,* however, the *Monthly,* goaded by a fad, no longer restricted itself to cautioning, but subjected illusions to a knock-down-and-drag-out treatment. The characters, the review says,

are unnatural: they never did nor could exist; and his system, which he gradually developes, in regard to the renovation of society, is as impracticable as his representation of the present state of it is incorrect. There are many vices and evils to cure among us; yet not enough to make it necessary, in order to the enjoyment of happiness, that we should abandon our country for the deserts or savannahs of America.

Novels have lately been the vehicles of certain speculative principles, in which these are artfully exhibited as established truths, essential to the improvement and happiness of man; and human nature in her present state is blackened beyond reality, in order to give them effect.

[76] *Op. cit.,* pp. 254-255.
[77] XXV (New Arrangement, 1799), 233.
[78] VIII (Second Series, 1792), 390-391.

We protest against this as an unfair proceeding; and no system can be good that wants such aid.[79]

The prosecution here makes a masterly summation, which encourages one to believe in the essential sanity of the decade. One is encouraged still more by such novels as *Berkeley Hall* (1796) and Walker's *Vagabond* (1799), both of which turn hilarious laughter and withering scorn upon the Noble-Savage idea, and attack the imaginary ideal community in the American wilds with farce, humor, and irony.[80]

Dr. Sourby in *Berkeley Hall* is a thorough-going radical of the natural-good school, scorning Mr. Lumeire's contention that "though men in a savage state . . . are subject to fewer *apparent and express restrictions* of liberty, they are to more *real* ones."[81] Dissatisfied with a very comfortable domesticity in New Jersey, Sourby wants to try the life of nature, and he gets his chance when he is able to attribute the halting progress of Timothy Tickle's love-affair to "the destructive refinements of civilized life,"[82] and consequently to persuade the young man to join him in experiencing the salubrious influence of the forest. They head north from Bethlehem, Pennsylvania, passing through a great deal of romantic scenery, and finally arriving in northern Pennsylvania in what might be either the country of the Priestleys or the Wyoming settlement glorified by Campbell.[83] The Doctor exclaims:

Here nature reigns in true sublimity and lovely simplicity. Here we shall meet men in their original innocence and independence, untram-

[79] XXVII (Second Series, 1798), 233.

[80] For a discussion of the significance of these books with reference to the philosophical trends of the day, see Whitney, *op. cit.*, pp. 271 ff., 310 ff.

[81] I, 297.

[82] II, 338.

[83] Interesting as it would be to find a specific satire of the Priestleys, who represented the liberalism which the author opposed, Northumberland is farther to the west, and the journey there would have been longer than the novel indicates. Of course, few novelists were even mediocre geographers. The presence of the New Englanders suggests the Wyoming settlement; on the other hand, the book satirizes New Englanders on various occasions.

melled by forms, or the yokes of ancient institutions. Here the heads of men will not be deluded by prejudices and falsehoods, nor their hearts corrupted by flattery, envy, pride, and ambition. Here we shall find the true nature and life of man.[84]

Then the author proceeds diabolically to demonstrate "the true nature and life of man." The pilgrims arrive at a blockhouse, a sort of inn, where Sourby's holding forth on his theories leads to his introduction to Mr. Phineas Chauncey, "a very respectable settler from New England." Phineas falls in exactly with the Doctor's point of view:

Here indeed, Sir, you will find men entirely estranged from the follies, crimes, and artifice of civilized cities. Internal rectitude serves in place of law, and of bolts and locks for security.[85]

Phineas had been graduated from Yale and had studied law, but "sick of the chicanery of the practice, and the villany of the world" he and some others had fled to this idyllic spot to spend the rest of their days doing good and recovering from the vices contracted from the world.[86] The result is that he sells the place to Sourby, who finds its rather limited supplies and deficient agricultural development compensated for by its beauty. Then Phineas departs, "leaving our travellers to commence the golden age, and their lives of primæval innocence and simplicity,"[87] and to perform the rather arduous task of cleaning out the dirt and repairing the furniture. The next step is for Sourby to take the kitchen wench, Polly Macguggerty, as his wife, untrammeled, however, by any ceremony; her rank makes no difference except that it will enable him to restore the subjection of the sex intended by nature and so ruinously disregarded by polite society.[88]

The Golden Age begins with terrific summer heat, with the

[84] II, 341.
[85] II, 342.
[86] II, 343.
[87] II, 348.
[88] II, 352-353.

appearance of mosquitoes and flies which are like "one of the plagues of Egypt," with the complete insubordination of Polly Macguggerty, with the discoveries that there is no market from which they can secure supplies, that roads are wretched and communication difficult, and that the neighbors are not only low and ignorant but given to making depredations on the Doctor's land. He

began to find that the spirit of pride and self-interest, the love of power, wealth, and distinction, prevail as much in wilds and cottages as in cities and courts.[89]

Satire is cleverly pointed through the author's having the situation described by the negro servant Sancho—a type of savage often idealized and made the mouthpiece of criticisms of society—in a letter to his lady-love in New Jersey. He finds the place "almost out of creation" and says, ". . . it seems very *unnatural* to me for gentlemen to live like *savages* or *beasts.*" The chief difference between this and home is that here there are more dirt and vermin, no conveniences, harder work, high expenses, company more ignorant than the lowest at home, and fare worse than in the kitchen at Berkeley Hall.

Or if they like to imitate the beasts, they should burn the books, throoaway hammers, spades, and plows, strip off to the buff, and *dig with their nails, and tear the raw meat with their teeth, catch what they can, and the weakest go to the wall, and club law* prevail. . . .

They have, he says, no more liberty than at Berkeley Hall "except *liberty of playing the fools by ourselves,*" bad roads, poor food, dangerous animals, savage Indians, bad drinks, and no company. He is shocked by the Doctor's connection with a "coarse and vulgar" woman, and he concludes with a reference to "this life of a Turk, a savage, or a dog."[90] All this is the antithesis of what the dreamers usually imputed to the negro by way of belief and attitude toward life.

[89] II, 356.
[90] II, 357 ff.

Illusions are further shaken when another pious New Englander, a Mr. Truby, appears with an introductory note from the departed Phineas Chauncey and leads to the discovery of some gold bars supposedly buried by Captain Kidd; he refuses to share in the find, which is joyfully hailed by even the proponents of primitivism, but does accept one hundred pounds to distribute to the poor. After he leaves, the gold bars turn out to be copper covered by gold foil.[91] Sourby begins to be suspicious, and the author comments,

In truth, these *veteran rogues* had thought our adventurers very proper game, and, having profited sufficiently of the follies of *Independent Hall,* had retired into New Hampshire to enjoy the fruits of their villany.[92]

Next, "Mrs. Sourby's" relatives begin to flock to the hall for entertainment; Polly faints, the Doctor rages, and cousin Dennis, threatening him for his villainy, gets $10. On this Dennis and his followers get drunk, attack the hall, plunder the barn, and retire. Seeking legal redress, the Doctor goes to a community meeting, but this turns into a free-for-all over taxation, the Doctor's only achievement being a shot in the leg.[93] Returning, he finds that Polly and her male relatives have disappeared, having stolen everything they could lay hands on, and he concludes,

Well, if I recover, my honest fellows! we'll off, as soon as I can sell this fatal spot, to human society again, and the joys of Berkeley Hall.[94]

The completeness with which they have been plundered, plus snow four or five feet deep, leaves them nothing to live on but some game they secure with great difficulty. Sancho learns that Polly was a prostitute, that Dennis was her "bully," and that the troupe has fled to the settlement of the Blue Mountain

[91] II, 364 ff.
[92] II, 373.
[93] II, 381 ff.
[94] II, 391.

Boys. The Doctor finds himself diseased, and hopes that persevering treatment will save some fragments of his face "as a sad memento of the effects of *marriage by the law of nature*."[95] Their troubles come to a climactic finale when they are taken into custody by "a gang of free-booters" who resent the fact that their title to the land is from Pennsylvania instead of New Hampshire, as it should be.[96]

Thus ends the vision. Sourby's madness is malignant, however; and it takes an Indian captivity, in which Noble Savages turn out to be a lustful and bloodthirsty tribe of barbarians, to bring him completely about to a proper sense of the values of civilization. It is unfortunate that a sketch of this sort deprives the story of the rich humor and intellectual vigor which the author, who often suggests Fielding, possesses, for this tale alone is evidence of the superior competence—greater plausibility, more real characters, better narrative gifts—of the satirists of the Golden Age in America. They are realistic and sane; the proponents, maudlin and flighty.

The irony of *Berkeley Hall* is fundamentally genial, good-humored. When we come to the satire in Walker's *Vagabond*, we find much sharper tones, often sardonic, because the author, employing a different technique, lets injuries fall on both just and unjust. While, in a number of ways, it coincides with *Berkeley Hall*, it goes much further, satirizing not only the rustic life but also the exaggerated claims made for the new democracy. In various details it provides both a running commentary on the flamboyant dreams set forth in *Disobedience* and a spirited attack on Imlay. It seems less a work of sheer invention, suggesting often that the writer had at least talked with people who had had actual experiences in America.

When Frederick, the young enthusiast in the story, is haranguing an English country mob on the radical principles he has learned from the theorist Stupeo, a country gentleman

[95] II, 396.
[96] II, 397.

interrupts him with a query whether the new system does not merely pander to the popular desire

to live without labour, to plunder the rich, and pay no regard to those laws which were made purposely to restrain the passions? And because this is easy to be done, you call it truth and liberty, and patriotism,

and he concludes the expression of his point of view, most familiar in the twentieth century, with the remark that such people would find it "very easy to establish themselves in America."[97] This possibility leads Frederick into rhapsody:

. . . there beneath the vine trees of our own planting, we should sit and talk of love: beneath the date tree and the olive we should sing hymns of peace, and in the sylvan shades should we be united in harmony and celestial affections.[98]

These Wallerian echoes excite in Dr. Alogos, another radical, a craving for immediate emigration, but his niece Laura, always the voice of common sense, objects to the scheme

as a wild-goose chase after happiness; and the arguments she used almost convinced the Doctor that all pleasure was ideal, for, as to dates and olives, not a single tree grows in all North America, which obliged Frederick to own he meant only *figurative* expression.[99]

This rare note of botanical realism sinks into silence when Alogos has experiences which cause him to complain,

. . . I am become quite sick of society, and all human nature together. I will go and bury myself in the wilderness of America, where no mob will burn my house and destroy my library[100]

—obviously a reflection of the experiences of Priestley at Birmingham. He immediately begins collecting information on

that delectable country, where poor people live better than the rich; where provisions are so plentiful, you may have to take them away, where more is paid to the mechanics for their labour than the articles

[97] Page 95.
[98] Page 130.
[99] Page 131.
[100] Page 153.

sell for; where there are no taxes, and where the travellers *bundle* with the daughters of the family.[101]

The sociological observation, occasionally appearing, serves to suggest ulterior motives. The party decides on Philadelphia, where they will

begin to breathe on the broad basis of truth and reason; there all the puerile distinction of religion and country are unknown, and man is respected for his good qualities.

Laura objects, and the maid won't go without being married to Alogos, who has plans like those of Sourby in *Berkeley Hall*. They are en route:

A pleasant gale wafted these adventurers from the detestable island, where every thing was conducted in the worse manner possible, and where law and religion influenced the majority of men. . . .[102]

Their praise of the city of Washington leads the Captain to tell them that it is all on paper, that "the chief advantage attending this city is, that it is contiguous to the estate of the President," that he is "amused with the golden dreams of emigrants," that the glorification of America is chiefly the work of real-estate agents (the first shot at Imlay, and perhaps, also, Cooper), and that people

might be certain, if America was that happy land held out to them by designing men, all the vagabonds in Europe would not be invited to its bowers.[103]

They find Philadelphia disappointingly small; on the streets they are "hooted at by the children, and called vagabond English, with other opprobrious names," to the surprise of Frederick, who "thought the Americans made no distinction of country."

They procured lodgings at an extravagant rate, and calling for re-freshment, received some very coarse cakes, wretched butter, and salt

[101] Page 154.
[102] Page 155.
[103] Page 156.

289

meat, for in summer no *fresh* meat will keep a day; and for this they paid more than the best articles would have cost in London.[104]

Then comes their first experience with the new democracy. When they protest feebly against food and prices, the waiter angrily demands whether they "mean to stigmatize Congress"; and when Dr. Alogos tells the waiter that he would like to talk to his master about baggage, he is answered thus:

My master! I don't know such a man. Do you think I am a slave?— I am a republican, a free-born American. But who are you? some lousy, beggarly emigré, come here to cut wood and hew stone for us.[105]

The heat is almost suffocating, and the mosquitoes are a plague; the travelers discover that although laborers' wages are relatively good, costs are so high that they can hardly live, and one "half of them soon die of fevers and agues"; when Frederick suggests to the innkeeper's daughter that she bundle with him, she says, "If you insult me, our Matthew shall bundle you into the Delaware."[106] At night they are disturbed by the rumble of carts which they learn are disposing of the bodies of victims of yellow fever.[107] Their disillusionment is increased when the innkeeper tells them, "all you people from the old world think money is made for nothing here—but it is all a farce."[108] Their decision to leave Philadelphia is simultaneous with the appearance of "a thin man," who, prating about his "desire to serve all mankind" and "to prevent the schemes of impostors," sells them a thousand acres of land in backwoods Kentucky—just the place for an ideal community.[109] Here the author certainly had Imlay in mind.

En route to the haven, they are beset by high prices, imperti-

[104] Page 161. Cf. *Berkeley Hall*, III, 236 ff.; Mesick, *English Travellers in America*, pp. 55 ff.
[105] Pp. 162-163.
[106] Page 163.
[107] Page 163. The 1793 epidemic attracted much attention in England; see *Gentleman's Magazine*, LXIV[1] (1794), 293-294; *Monthly Review*, XIV (Second Series, 1794), 187 ff.
[108] Page 164.
[109] Pp. 164-166.

nent innkeepers, and dysentery, "which . . . was very usual to new comers."[110] In Kentucky they find their land already in the possession of tenants who have a title from Virginia, and, what with this and their despair at finding lawyers and lawsuits even here, they buy another tract 150 miles ahead and set out for it. They are tormented by "millions of insects," snakes, and "prodigious large frogs and toads wallowing in every little tank of stagnant water"; the weather is "insufferably hot," and, instead of blooming orchards, sugar groves, and velvet meadows, they find only native grass several feet high, "matted so as to be almost impassable, and too rank for any use." Their own property is

covered with prodigious large trees, which seemed to bid defiance to human labour. A thick cane brake over-ran half the surface, and was so matted and entangled with the trees, that they could not even clear a path through. The ground, which was not thus covered, was apparently so barren, that the black heaths of England were a sort of comparative garden.[111]

As Alogos curses the day he set foot in the new world, they settle down to a miserable existence. When another family dies of overwork, our adventurers buy the property, only to find that the surface, which is composed of rotten vegetable matter, gives off deleterious vapors. Alogos and Frederick each have a severe fit of ague. In the manner of Sourby with Polly Macguggerty in *Berkeley Hall*, Stupeo forms a liaison with the maid Susan— an event no doubt meant to satirize Imlay's theories of marital freedom. Susan becomes pregnant, and since, when she gives birth to the child, she has only the help of an ignorant old woman, "the poor wretch expired in agony"--a very different picture from that in *Disobedience*.[112] Stupeo insists that the

[110] Page 169.

[111] Pp. 170-172.

[112] Pp. 174-175. In *Disobedience*, Mary faces the birth of her first with equanimity and even jollity. "The event justified Mary's hopes; it was not long before she embraced, without undergoing any uncommon evil, her first born. . . ." (IV, 147). Within nine years she produced, almost nonchalantly, "six sprightly and blooming children" (IV, 161).

child be brought up in a hardy, natural manner, with the result that it also dies. Then a tribe of Indians steals all their goods and kidnaps Laura; pursuing, the Englishmen get badly lost and wander long in the woods, finally to be themselves captured by savages, who torture Stupeo to death.[113] Even Alogos has completely lost faith:

The Deity does not act by evils, nor are the consequences of our headstrong passions, our follies, and our crimes, to be laid to his charge. Rousseau was a fool, with all his rants and declamations, and many of his followers shew their long ears.[114]

The Indian difficulties, plus an earthquake, complete the reform, and the radicals hasten back to

the land of genuine liberty, where there is not *one* man so obscure as not to possess a right, nor *one* man so high, as not to be subject to the laws.[115]

At one point their own experiences are temporarily sidetracked when they come across a sequestered community which is a parody of the idea of the French Revolution and of every other radical philosophy which Walker does not like, ridiculed through the grotesque effects of a literal application of principles. The people are all naked because they have no one to make clothes. The first man they meet addresses them in Hebrew; he says that he is "studying the public good."[116] The next man they meet is striking a tree with his fist and his head, explaining, "I am endeavouring to drive this idea out of my path." In the construction of buildings laborers work lackadaisically in one-half-hour shifts, thus practicing equal division of labor. Nothing is ever accomplished because each man spends all his time debating how his half-hour of application will best serve the public good. A cicerone explains the history

[113] Pp. 176 ff., 221 ff.
[114] Page 179.
[115] Page 227.
[116] Page 187. For a complete account of the community, see pp. 187-212, from which citations are here made in order.

of the community, which is substantially that of the French Revolution. After "all laws, sacred and civil, were abrogated," no one would work, as a result of which the city is covered "by the most disgusting filth"; there is much disease because physicians have forgot their skill; and "the very cares of connubial affection are become burthensome." Except for indolence, the violence already existing would wipe out everybody. An orator stands on a tub haranguing the naked people on the deception of the senses. Most works of art have been destroyed because their subjects concern a god whom the philosophers have decided the people were to forget. A moral relapse is the result of the loss of religious belief; the moralizing orator tries to rape a woman and kills the young man who tries to defend her. The general availability of liquor fills the streets with drunks, and when sex limitations are withdrawn, "in one week there was scarcely a maid above fourteen." Stupeo, principled to the last, loves this place, but Alogos and Frederick are glad to be out of it.

So much for Walker's satire of the ideal existence in America, which has been presented at some length because, although the intention of curing an illusion leads to grotesquely bitter extremes, the sincerity and conviction and disinterestedness are outstanding. Walker is less a humorist and less an artist than the author of *Berkeley Hall*, but, even if he seems less effective, his beliefs are even more inflexible. Although these are the last works in our period, we may, by way of summary, refer to Charles Lucas's *The Infernal Quixote* (1801), which includes, among its divisions of philosophers, the "Virtuosos." These, according to Miss Whitney,[117]

are apparently the primitivists lumped together with the enthusiasts for classical models in politics. . . . "These are continually telling us what has been. . . . All *modern* customs and laws they abominate. . . . The Virtuosos hate the Government because it is a *modern* fabric and use all their might to overturn the State, that they may revive the bless-

[117] *Op. cit.*, p. 307.

ings of primeval times. All their writings in Divinity, Science, or Politics, are in praise of the Golden Age."

The Virtuosos whom we have seen have attempted a reconciliation of modernity with antiquity by re-establishing the Golden Age in America; and their opponents have attacked social and political panaceas, imaginary or actual, in the American wilderness. The former emphasized the variegated produce and the fecundity of the new world; over this they cast the enchantment of exotic appeal or the soothing charm of a rich, quiet, benevolent, maternal nature; they expelled the vices of civilization and extolled the encouragement to man's natural virtue and consequently to the growth of social and political forms in which, although there were a maximum of liberty and a minimum of restraint, all was amity, generosity, and happiness. Against the picture of an infinitely beneficent herbarium, on the other hand, the opposition stressed the discomforts and hardships of weather, climate, and an uncultivated land where a luxuriant growth, subduing man instead of aiding him, turned the dream of easy subsistence into a nightmare of bitter reality; they argued that such conditions, ameliorated by neither institutions nor traditions, brought out the worst in man and produced a true primitivism in which there predominated not a roseate excellence but a barbaric catch-as-catch-can existence.

In the former, the last gasps of what originally must have been sincere idealism are marked by sentimentality, lushness, the pretentiousness of futility, self-pitying retreatism, and what we now know to have been the ulterior motive of advertising real estate. In the latter there is a quest for realism, leading at times to an ineffective satirical exaggeration; an effort to see life straight, with humor, intellectual vigor, and intolerance of visions; and, above all, an impression of complete integrity.

The conclusion is that utopian novelists, prolonging the myth of America, were, in spite of a slight numerical superiority, arguing a doomed case. In the first place, the opposition was doing a more forceful, a more artistic job. In the second place, the reviews, of whatever political color, aimed a running fire at the Arcadians, rising in intensity. In the third place, and most important, here was the first real body of opposition to the idealization of America that literature shows.

To put it in other words: here, in the period of the American Revolution, were the first manifestations of the critical realism in the English attitude to America which, we have seen, was not characteristic of preceding centuries, but which is clearly discernible in the nineteenth and twentieth centuries. Here is the first microscopy, the first effort to reason things out. Doubtless it can never be proved that the war was the major cause of a changed point of view. The coincidence, however, is impressive.

That coincidence may not be the sole explanation is argued by phenomena in the novels. In the first place, it appears that the war, bringing about a further intimate knowledge of the Indian, casting more serious doubts on his excellence, and suggesting stories of atrocities and cruel captivities, dealt a death-blow to the Noble Savage. Once he was accepted as a part of the primitive ideal, but by 1797 he was repudiated even by that most romantic picture of the Golden Age, *Disobedience,* which says in praise of Kentucky that it has no Indians. Thus the integrated primitive ideal is broken down, vulnerability is admitted, and a gaping inconsistency weakens the argument. In the second place, the democracy which grows out of the war is by no means regarded unanimously as utopian, and freedom arouses no more praise than it does hostility. The Garden of Eden with a Congress may be cheered by liberals, sneered at by Tories, but the causes do not matter. What is important is the difference of opinion, which alone can make for a reasonable interpretation instead of a visionary idealization. In the third place, it is to be noted that the post-war Arcadias are all placed in the tramontane regions—even as far west as the Mississippi. The inland was relatively untouched by even the American civilization of the seaboard, and one could therefore regard it more hopefully; what is more, that inland, since it was little touched by the war, still retained the quality of being unknown, which is essential for the construction of a dream-world.

Hence I think it reasonable to argue that the war had some influence on the growth of the new realism. The war took away the grounds for easy maternal pride and for sanguine expectations; it brought the intimate acquaintanceship which destroys sentimental idealism. It is clear, at any rate, that the old concept of America is being deflated, that the early buoyant hopefulness is subsiding into a dubious and skeptical counting of chicks.

iv

All the glorification of America shows a strong sense of its material potentialities; especially as the century grows old do the press-notices make less play to the soul than to the bank-account. The Golden Age fades into the Land of Promise. In the former, utopianism was essentially of the spirit; in the latter, of the body. The seeker of the Golden Age was fleeing society; the seeker of the Land of Promise was merely shifting to a scene with a better economic outlook. The former pursued an ideal; the latter was doubly conscious of realities. The former sought ease in a company made up entirely of mirrors of himself; the latter expected to work hard in what society he found and to make the most of it. If the former expected to dream about friendship, love, or virtue, the latter wanted only to escape poverty and create a more comfortable material existence. He represented, as I have said, the middle class of emigrants.

That literature should reflect the conception of the Land of Promise follows chiefly, of course, from the fact of the great emigrations, but also from the hopes of America cherished by various literary figures. Sir Walter Raleigh's aspirations and attempts are well known, and Sir Philip Sidney also had an eye on America. Burns contemplated the West Indies; Goldsmith twice considered bettering his fortunes in the new world. Possibly his hopes are represented in *The Vicar of Wakefield* (1766), in which George Primrose had some dealings with a Mr. Crispe, who ran a sort of employment agency for emigrants, and who promised George

that there was at that time an embassy talked of from the synod of Pensylvania to the Chickasaw Indians, and that he would use his interest to get me made secretary. I knew in my own heart that the fellow lied, and yet his promise gave me pleasure, there was something so magnificent in the sound.[118]

Perhaps something "magnificent in the sound" had seduced the impecunious Oliver. John Lowe, the Scotch poet, "doubtful of success" in the church, went to Virginia, where he became a tutor in the family of George Washington's brother.[119] Mrs. Anne Grant (1755-1783), the poetess, spent some years in America because her father, Captain Macvicar, after being in the English army during the Seven Years' War, had settled on the east bank of the Hudson in what is now Vermont.[120] John Keats's brother George went to America "to push the family fortunes."[121]

Promises were not always fulfilled. Hazlitt's father had great hopes of a ministry in New England.

But Channing had not yet made New England a paradise for Unitarian ministers, and Hazlitt was obliged to return to England for lack of a flock.[122]

John Wesley saw the American vision collapse before his eyes. After noting in Georgia, July 23, 1737, that he was "in a condition which I neither desired nor expected in America—in ease and honour and abundance,"[123] he got into various diffi-

[118] (4th ed., 1770), II, 20.
[119] "Lowe, John," *D. N. B.*
[120] "Grant, Anne," *D. N. B.*
[121] "Keats, John," *D. N. B.*
[122] Brinton, *op. cit.*, p. 108.
[123] *Journal*, ed. Nehemiah Curnock (London: Robert Culley, [1910]), I, 371 and note.

culties over a mismanaged love affair and fled home. Next year he made this entry in his journal:

> . . . on *Saturday,* Sept. 2, about eleven, came to Cologne, which we left at one, and between seven and eight reached a village, an hour short of Neus. Here we overtook a large number of Switzers—men, women, and children, singing, dancing, and making merry, being all going *to make their fortunes in Georgia.* Looking upon them as delivered into my hands by God, I plainly told them what manner of place it was. If they now leap into the fire with open eyes, their blood is on their own head.[124]

These instances, noted down at random, show the widespread anticipation of economic betterment in America, unsupported by the philosophical machinery of the searchers for a Golden Age.

Novels make less of this as a motif than one might expect. Besides *The Vicar of Wakefield* three of these appear in the '60's. A rather roundabout approach to the Land of Promise is that in Charles Johnstone's *Reverie* (1762), in which a Jesuit is made to explain his order's intention "to establish an independency in some part of the world."

> We . . . turned our eyes to America, where the weakness of the possessing powers was a temptation as strong as the riches and fertility of their possessions.[125]

There they have hopes "of erecting an empire in some part" of the Spanish dominions. Much more to the point is the decision of Colonel Rivers in Mrs. Brooke's *Emily Montague* (1769) to move to Canada because,

> I cannot live in England on my present income, though it enables me to live *en prince* in Canada.[126]

There he hopes to

> become lord of a principality which will put our large-acred men in England out of countenance,[127]

---

[124] *Ibid.,* II, 62. For a customary sneer, see Bishop Warburton's *Doctrine of Grace* (3rd ed., 1763), p. 180.
[125] II, 196-197.
[126] I, 179-180.
[127] I, 3.

a pleasure enhanced by the fact that "America is in infancy, Europe in old age."[128] This last idea is carried to a logical conclusion in *Private Letters from an American in England* (1769):

These letters are supposed to be written towards the end of the eighteenth century, by a young American, who is stimulated by curiosity to pay a visit to the country of his ancestors. The seat of government is transferred to America; and England is an almost deserted depopulated nation.[129]

But Promise is usually only personal expectation, as in *Humphry Clinker* (1771), the first of a quartet of novels which concern us in the '70's. When Lismahago speaks of making a permanent return to America, Matt Bramble,

. . . understanding that Lismahago's real reason for leaving Scotland was the impossibility of subsisting in it with any decency upon the wretched provision of a subaltern's half pay, began to be warmly interested on the side of compassion.[130]

Lismahago might well have enjoyed high hopes, for he had profited well from "a little traffic he drove in peltry, during his sachemship among the Miamis" and was able to present his bride with "a fur cloak of American sable, valued at fourscore guineas."[131] Another story of economic salvation in America is that of James Neville in *Emma* (1773); his

mother's jointure being a very large one for the estate, he was glad to accept of an American government to enlarge his income, and embarked for that country, where he still resides. . . .[132]

In Brooke's *Juliet Grenville* (1773) there is a story of a French boy of somewhat romantic imagination who, when Moors demand a large ransom for his captive father, prepares to raise

---

[128] I, 48. As a matter of fact, sentimental reasons later dictate his return.
[129] From the "Advertisement," copied by J. M. Clapp, in Professor Greenough's Catalogue.
[130] *Works*, IV, 151.
[131] IV, 284, 289.
[132] (New ed., 1787), II, 164.

the funds by selling himself into service in the French colonies in America.[133] No doubt he hopes to share the fortune of many who shook off their shackles and prospered in more lucrative activities. The story of one Richard in *Edward* (1774), which might have been modeled on that of Mrs. Anne Grant's father, Captain Macvicar, has a more substantial basis than hope:

. . . his regiment had been in America for many years; and when the time for his return to England came, it found him happy in the bosom of a most excellent wife, for whose sake (as well as the dislike he had taken to it from family reasons) he procured a change, and was quite settled in that country.[134]

"Quite settled" is understatement, for, revisiting England, he can refuse a proffered estate:

. . . he protested he had more money than he knew what to do with, and more land in America than could be purchased here for many thousands.[135]

The clouds of war produce a low visibility that frustrates the flights of hopefuls; perhaps for that reason the next fifteen years grant only two glimpses of the Land of Promise. Both are Bage's. The story of the old soldier in *Mount Henneth* presents an unusually balanced view, since the bright horizon produced by Bage's strong sense of the possibilities of America is dimmed by the facts in the individual case; the veteran's loss of an arm makes him not only unable to profit from the potentialities but also unusually conscious of the disadvantages:

They treated us very well here [Williamsburg, Va.]; we had plenty of fresh provisions, and some money when we chose to earn it. I liked the country so well, that I began to care but little about old England, and toward the spring actually hired myself in a tobacco plantation; . . .

The missing arm makes him lose this and other positions.

. . . this want of success, and the flies that tormented me, and the

133 (Philadelphia, 1774), II, 70-71.
134 II, 138.
135 II, 221.

snakes that frightened me out of my senses, made me weary of the finest country I had seen, and turned my desires again to old England.[136]

The "finest country" was properly receptive to Mr. Melton's grandfather, who had migrated to Rhode Island,

bought a great deal of land for a very little money, and pursuing the beaten track of industry, in twenty years became a man of wealth and estimation.[137]

Bage blossoms twice again in the '90's. An incident in *Man As He Is* (1792), however, represents America as the place where financial losses are recouped rather than as the scene of future gain; the new head of a bankrupt "house at Bordeaux"

has been in America; has recovered much supposed to be lost; and has restored the full credit of the house. . . .[138]

Hermsprong's father in *Man As He Is Not* (1796), Lismahago-like, had engaged in the fur-trade with the Nawdoessies and become "affluent to his own satisfaction."[139] The experience of Richard in *Edward* is duplicated by that of a whole regiment in Mrs. Lennox's *Euphemia* (1790), who protest against being shipped back to Chelsea Hospital, saying that

. . . we have . . . spilt our blood for Old England and this here America, which is all one as our native land to us now. We married wives here, and have children and grand-children, and great-grand-children; and all we love is here, and we are used to the climate; so that it is a great hardship to be sent to die from our friends.[140]

There is just a hint of another kind of affluence in *Wanley Penson* (1791), which thus breathlessly reports the return of Melinda Bountly, supposedly drowned:

'Twas Linny, indeed.—That Linny for whose loss he had so often accused the waves; but they were guiltless of her death.—They wafted

[136] Page 191.
[137] Page 198.
[138] III, 146-147.
[139] III, 28.
[140] III, 41.

301

her to a sand-bank;—A French American took her up, and bore her with him to Louisiana.—He had estates on the Mississippi.[141]

Imlay, as we have seen, is one of the most vociferous prophets of a material millennium in America. The advantages are suggested in the episode of P. P—— in *The Emigrants* (1793):

> I had seen much of America during the last war with the French, and as our family continued to increase, I determined to migrate to this Continent, and to live in these back settlements where land is cheap.[142]

Like the James Neville of *Emma,* a Mr. Truman in Mrs. Hedgeland's *Madeline* (1794) finds his problems solved by a tutorship in America, though the position is not permanent.[143] But teaching is an important rung in the ladder of success in *Berkeley Hall* (1796), which, hostile though it is to the romantic idealization of America, concedes without question its material advantages. Dutton, a Cambridge graduate, who has been sold as an indentured servant in Virginia, is learned enough to attract the attention of a Mr. Cookson, who buys his liberty and sets him up in teaching. He makes out well and even becomes prosperous,[144] enough so to buy the liberty of a former fellow-slave and aid him financially to go to a settlement in western Pennsylvania. The latter, after various difficulties, is reported as having both land and hope.[145] Besides these incidents there is a paragraph of praise by Dr. Sourby, who here evidently has the approval of the author. America, he says,

> promises fair to rival, if not excel, her mother, in every thing that can bless and adorn human life. She has every variety of soil and climate. She has no neighboring nation to dread. . . . The necessaries and conveniences of life are more abundant, and property more equally diffused. Plenty is the certain reward of industry.[146]

[141] III, 277.
[142] II, 81.
[143] III, 173.
[144] I, 50-52.
[145] I, 54-57.
[146] I, 302-303.

In Helena Wells's *Step-mother* (1798) is a story of villagers who, their homes destroyed by fire, "declared their resolution of embarking for America."[147] Miss Wells uses the same idea in *Constantia Neville* (1800), in which a Mr. and Mrs. Clayton "had met with misfortunes in England, which induced them to embark as adventurers for North America."[148] Finally, in *Tales of Truth* (1800), there is a reference to

the favored and hospitable land, and which [*sic*], tho' desolated, seems*
like the Phoenix, to be springing up from the ashes of its former
greatness, and promises, in futurity, to be the wonder and admiration
of the world.[149]

Thus the unknown E. H. appropriately concludes the history of the Land of Promise as seen in prose fiction, a history brief enough. Perhaps the "success story" had not yet achieved its later vogue, and readers still preferred the pompous hero who spoke in periods to one who went out into the world and "made good." Perhaps, if there were to be foreign scenes, the public preferred the exotic to the prosaic account of rising fortunes in a store or on a farm. Perhaps the dreamers of a Golden Age were more articulate than those who dreamed only of easier times in America. More of these, however, will appear in later sections.

As for the concept of America, this element in it appears to remain practically constant during the forty-year period, uninfluenced by the war. The hopes now are less grandiose than in the early years when the new world seemed to be chiefly an exaggerated gold mine. Visions of boundless wealth are gone, but economic opportunities are plain; in fact, they were never doubted before the post-1929 raising of eyebrows. Hard sense is the note, and the blunt materialism, as long as it stays on this

[147] II, 59. A Goldsmithian Major, resenting emigration, got up a theatrical "benefit" to help keep them in England.

[148] I, 94. They are driven back by a "pestilential fever," possibly another reflection of the yellow-fever epidemic of 1793.

[149] II, 85-86.

side of feverish expectation, is consistent with the realism that is becoming a more important part of the English attitude to America. Even enemies of democracy and opponents of Arcadias could read the significance of plentiful raw materials, cheap land, and a relatively small population. As for those who doubt even these benefits, they, obviously, are making a still stauncher effort at realism.

v

Mr. Shandy's admirable concern for the welfare of his children naturally was directed also toward their education. That of Bobby, Tristram's elder brother, was to have been financed "with the first money that returned from the second creation of actions in the Mississippi-scheme. . . ."[150] The reference is to Law's Mississippi Bank, a minor counterpart of the South Sea Bubble:

> The collapse of the South Sea ramp, as well as of Law's Mississippi Bank, had taught an elementary if necessary lesson that capital, if it is to bring in permanent profits, must do real work in creating fresh wealth, and can in no way be increased by the inflation of shares on the stock exchange.[151]

Nothing in the latter part of the century gives quite so convenient a toe-hold for the moralist.

The Bubble and the Bank symbolize very clearly the illusions about the sudden material prosperity to be derived from an America that for a long time had been almost synonymous with *gold*. In the days of the sonneteers, such dreams were so unalloyed and so unquestioning as almost to achieve a certain grandeur. Then grandeur declined into greediness; the ventures of valiant pirates begot a mere grab-bag. Hence such benevolences as the Bubble and the Bank, the product of a get-rich-quick psychology.

[150] Lawrence Sterne, *Tristram Shandy* (New York: Modern Library, n.d.), p. 299 (Bk. 4, Chap. 31).
[151] Esmé Wingfield-Stratford, *The History of British Civilization* (New York: Harcourt Brace, 1930), p. 736.

At the tail end of the gold-rush we have the third class of emigrants to, or else mere dreamers about, America, the demos whose objectives are not only exclusively material, but are to be realized with the utmost rapidity. Unlike the Golden-Age group, they are moved by no abstractions; unlike the Land-of-Promise aspirants, they have no conception of a stable position in a new society. They are not alone in seeking financial improvement, but their distinguishing quality is their failure to envisage permanent residence in America. If a prospective emigrant expected to become a part of the new community, if he definitely burned his bridges behind him and considered himself thenceforth an American, he may be said to have sought the Land of Promise. If, on the other hand, his stay was to be brief, if it existed only for what could be got out of it at the time being, he was merely a modern version of the earlier buccaneer who plundered and sailed away. It is this Get-Rich-Quick type, as it appeared in the novel, that we are to examine here.

The category, with its broad definition, is an omnibus. First we have the army man, who sees an American campaign as a source of prizes and a promotion; here the idea of the land of gold has been considerably reduced, but the principle is the same. Second, there is a series of stories dealing with South American ventures, which show the eighteenth-century limitation of a sixteenth-century conception. Third, we have a set of characters whose wealth is a *fait accompli;* the authors' assumption is that readers accept wealth as a concomitant of life in America. Finally, there are a few instances of the direct, limited get-rich-quick attitude, leading to several amusing satires of the idea. The four groups are unified by the central theme of what can be got out of America.

The first case of an army man's getting on in the world is that of Captain Standard in Johnstone's *Chrysal* (1760-1765), who has often been heard to "wish to go there [America], in hopes of rising, when they come into action."[152] In Graves's *Spiritual Quixote* (1772) no details are given about the late Captain Townsend, who "had made a small fortune in America."[153] Lieutenant Vernon, in Pratt's *Pupil of Pleasure* (1776), thus explains his acceptance of a commission in a regiment bound for America: "The half-pay of a Lieutenant, you know, Sir, is not sufficient to, even a man of moderation."[154] Love of gain gives way to love of adventure in *The Travels of Hildebrand Bowman* (1778), the hero of which begins his career on the quarter-deck of the frigate *Mermaid,* plying between England and Newfoundland, but gives it up as too dull.[155] Neville, in Mrs. Lennox's *Euphemia* (1790), always in debt and out of favor with his wealthy uncle, decides to solve his problems by securing a lieutenancy in a company bound for New York.[156] Horton, in Mrs. Rowson's *Mentoria* (1791), needed only an ensign's commission in a regiment going to

America, where he had raised himself to the rank of Captain, and was just now returned to England.[157]

It is an annuity provided by fellow-officers, however, rather than the customary prowess, which accounts for the comfortable circumstances of Captain Eringham in Lathom's *Men and Manners* (1799), who had purchased the inevitable commission in an American regiment.[158] Finally, of all the strange places in which to find a story of this sort, there is *Horrid Mysteries* (1797), translated by P. Will from the German of the Marquis of Grosse. James wanted a military career because it offered most splendor and gain:

Fortune assisted me sooner than I could have expected. A fermentation in New Spain obliged our monarch to send some troops to America,

[152] I, 128.
[153] (London: Peter Davies, 1926), I, 92.
[154] II, 51.
[155] Pp. 7-8.
[156] I, 147.
[157] I, 42.
[158] I, 103-104.

and a regiment that was garrisoned at Madrid was ordered to embark for that purpose. I obtained a company in that regiment. . . .[159]

James carries us across conveniently to the second type of success-in-America story, that dealing with South American scenes. The hero of *Adventures of Alonso* (1775) goes to Rio de Janeiro to make his fortune, finding the people very "affluent and rich," especially the Count de B——, who appoints Alonso

to an employment in the diamond mines, which promised the most flattering prospect, for, independant of a large addition of salary, there occurred such opportunities of gain, that those who had the address to profit by them, never failed to acquire a great and rapid fortune.[160]

Alonso has "the address" and engages in a little diamond-thievery which leads off into other adventures. Harrison's *New Novelist's Magazine* (1786) contains a short story, "The Unfortunate Lovers," attributed to Smollett, in which Alcanor sought wealth in Vera Cruz, and "fortune so prospered his endeavors, that in a few years he was master of forty thousand pistoles."[161] Mrs. Smith's *Wanderings of Warwick* (1794) introduces the history of the Conde de Villanova, including the facts

that my family were noble and rich, and that, during the time that my father occupied a public station at Brasil, he acquired a great addition to his family property by purchases in the New World.[162]

The last tale in this group is found in Godwin's *St. Leon* (1799), the hero of which makes it possible for his son Charles to marry Pandora, by providing her with the needed dowry through the fiction of an inheritance from an uncle who died treasure-hunting in Peru.[163]

In these stories, few though they are, there is a significant use of such magniloquent words as *treasure* and *fortune;* the

[159] (London: Holden, 1927), I, 35.
[160] I, 145.
[161] I, 25.
[162] Page 116.
[163] (3rd ed., 1816), IV, 315.

grand and the vast in wealth are now associated with South America, which, unlike the northern continent, is still little enough known to be the center of fairy-tales. The tradition first represented in Raleigh's hopes of Guiana, echoed by Donne, hangs on tenaciously; Mexico and Peru are conjurers, appearing again and again in such phrases as "far more precious to me than the mines of Golconda or Peru"[164] and "for all the gold in Mexico."[165] Their frequency must have been tiring, for Edward Du Bois remarks in *St. Godwin* (1800), another of that excellent cluster of satires at the end of the century which are the reward of the patient,

there is a kind of irreconcilable insociability between the heights of Parnassus and the mines of Peru. . . .[166]

It is well said.

In a third group of novels wealth in America is a *fait accompli* rather than an object of effort. In *The Female American* (1767) William Winkfield had had some Indian adventures which made him "more suddenly rich than he could have done by an infant plantation";[167] marrying an Indian princess, he received "a great quantity of gold dust and precious stones. . . ."[168] In *The Fortunate Sisters* (1782) a young Mr. Oliver and his bride have to go to Virginia,

for as they had large plantations in Virginia, the presence of one of the partners was indispensibly necessary.[169]

He invites poor relatives to come "and share with him his ample fortune";[170] later we learn about his father, who "was a gentleman of great wealth, and had large plantations."[171] The

164 *The History of Lord Stanton* (1774), II, 82-83.
165 Dr. John Moore, *Zeluco* (Boston, 1792), p. 99.
166 Page 126.
167 Page 8.
168 Page 24.
169 II, 28.
170 II, 37.
171 II, 82.

author has land enough for everybody; another hero, Horatio Villars, goes to Virginia, tutors in the family of a "gentleman possessed of large plantations," nurses the son during a fatal illness, becomes a second son to the surviving father, and, at the latter's death, inherits the fortune.[172] Here we find illustrated the difference from the Land-of-Promise concept, for our heroes will not stay in America; instead, "disposing of their plantations on the best terms they could get, they hastened back to England."[173] There is a clear attitude, too, in the phrase, "presence was necessary," which occurs again in the story of Mrs. Conway in Catherine Parry's *Eden Vale* (1784):

. . . my aunt had a brother, who early in life went over to America; had gained a considerable property there in trade; . . . we received news of his death, and his having bequeathed his fortune to my Edward, whose presence was necessary there to secure his effects.[174]

The gentlemen, that is, gladly collect their prizes but scamper back to civilization as rapidly as possible. Mrs. Hedgeland's *Madeline* (1794) brings in a very admirable Quaker, Josiah Primrose, whose father had "left Pennsylvania with an immense fortune."[175] The one instance we have of an Englishman's having wealth in America and apparent willingness to stay there is in *Jemima* (1795), in which Major Jones tells about his rich uncle, Davison Jones, in New York:

Davison Jones came over from New York . . . and proved to be a kind relation. He gave his brother ten thousand pounds to begin the world with, and me five thousand to buy me a commission in the army. . . .

My uncle Davison having settled all his affairs, and left his brother in a place of trust and honour far beyond his years, took leave of us and re-embarked for New York, for the declared purpose of marrying a young lady to whom he had presumed to engage himself without his

[172] II, 145 ff.
[173] II, 234.
[174] I, 55.
[175] I, 65.

father's sanction, though it . . . would prove a mortal stab to his interest. . . .[176]

Of the young men "on the make," the first is the picaresque Gabriel Outcast in Trusler's *Modern Times* (1785). Having seduced the daughter of Dr. Slashem, at whose school he was an usher, Gabriel

acquainted the Doctor, that I should now be no longer troublesome to him, that I was going to America in a merchant's family, as tutor to his son, a lad of twelve years of age, for which I was to have a handsome salary.[177]

He was, as a matter of fact, working for an auctioneer, but the fiction must have seemed plausible. In contrast with Gabriel is the young man in Mrs. Bonhote's *Parental Monitor* (1788), who

had spent many years in our American conquests, in laboriously acquiring a fortune of 600 l. per annum.[178]

On the same pattern is the story of "a fine young gentleman" in *Twin Sisters* (1788), who, though

he had not now any great matter, would soon do very well; for he was fighting his way in the world, through America; and after that was coming home, with a great fortune. . . .[179]

Finally there are the satires, of regrettable sparseness and brevity. William Beckford, whose *Modern Novel Writing* (1796) takes a fling at many literary conventions, laughs at the custom of conveniently bringing in a wealthy relative from America; he says, in one episode, "Now though a rich grandmother on the maternal side was but just returned from Canada. . . ."[180] Jane Austen, whose juvenilia presage *Northanger Abbey* and *Sense and Sensibility*, wrote one skit pointedly entitled "The Generous Curate," in which there was an eldest son who had become a seaman and gone to Newfoundland,

[176] I, 84-86.
[177] (2nd ed.), I, 33-34.
[178] I, 221.
[179] II, 149.
[180] I, 5.

where his promising & amiable disposition had procured him many freinds [*sic*] among the Natives, & from where he regularly sent home a large Newfoundland Dog every Month to his family.[181]

Here is a splendid antidote to the tales of charming young men whose irresistible personalities produced wealth and friends wherever they went. While the hilarity of Beckford and Miss Austen is inspired by the dullness of novelists, George Walker's satire is directed at illusions; he is moved not by fun-making but by conviction, and he digs harshly rather than prods gently. When his social experimenters in *The Vagabond* (1799) are sailing for America, it will be remembered, they are full of enthusiasm for their future.

The rest of the passengers were mechanics and countrymen, going over to make their fortunes, and the praises of America bounded from one mouth to another.[182]

Their admiration for Washington, and the tremendous commerce there, leads the captain to remark, with rude realism, that the city's main advantage is its being "contiguous to the estate of the President," and to proceed with a long debunking speech beginning, "I am amused with the golden dreams of emigrants. . . ."[183]

The total of novels accepting economic myths about America is not very great, and their power, such as it is, is being broken down by satires. The Get-Rich-Quick idea, like the Golden-Age idea, is going into a decline; that is to say, a realistic attitude is gaining strength. To what extent the phenomenon is due to the war is debatable. It is certainly safe to say that the separation of America from England made the former much less a happy hunting ground than before. There was no longer hope of a rise to fortune in the army; one could not start digging up a neighbor's yard as well as one's own; and perhaps some

[181] *Volume the First* (Oxford, 1933), p. 135.
[182] Page 155.
[183] Page 156.

degree of pride would restrain the attribution of great wealth to inhabitants of a former dependency. This point of view is not inconsistent with the fact that the Land of Promise maintained a fairly steady, if not too impressive, vogue; the new world was still wide open to emigrants who chose to make permanent residence there. They were concerned with economic facts, which could not be shaken by a war that could seriously damage illusions, of whatever kind.

As a magician's hat, as a cornucopia of all good things, concrete and abstract, America was fading. Along with the decline of the casual acceptance of her in this role should be recalled the conclusion of Chapter VII: that toward the end of the century fiction censuring the flaws of Europe made less use of America as an agent of satire, a function implying, however faintly, some degree of excellence. In this phenomenon there is a dim undertone of support for the theory of deflation. The razing of a dream-castle, naturally, is not accomplished by a single puff. All supporters did not desert, but many continued to buttress up the fantasy. Some penmen continued to depict a ready-made Golden Age, others to echo Renaissance exclamations over an El Dorado. But this school of artists was on the wane, and a new class of hearty scorners was increasing in voice. Doubters and skeptics, they made a powerful attack on one aspect of Romantic primitivism even before Romanticism reached its apex.

The war, one may conjecture, had something to do with it. America became closer and better known and therefore less ideal. Uncivilly independent, it raised doubts about primitive virtues; it was no longer a convenient appendage whose excellences flattered the main body. To change the figure, it was no longer a spacious backyard in which one could play all sorts of games. So people began to see it as a backyard and to recall that that was the place where the wash was hung and the garbage kept. That was the first lesson in realism, with the eighteenth century palpably somewhere between Renaissance hopefulness and later disillusion. Authors, inhabiting a microcosm then largely compounded of fancies, were beginning to stretch their feet toward a solid foundation. Midnight was bearing down on Cinderella, and the story was looking forward to the morning after.

CHAPTER X

## THE LESSER EVIL

### i

The newcomers to America described in the preceding chapter risked the voyage because of their expectation of some definite, positive advantage. Not all migration, however, was drawn by the magnetism of the goal; on the contrary, many travelers were not drawn, but impelled, not spurred by hope, but driven by circumstances. Even the romantic idealists in such books as *Disobedience* received their initial impetus from the unpalatability of life in England; but, once en route, they were forward-looking and turned back only to deliver a parting kick or two. To them, the picture of America was different from that seen by a set of gloomy emigrants who were choosing the lesser of two evils. These thought not of search and experiment, but of flight and escape; their motto was *Morituri*, not *Excelsior*. To them America had the negative value of a last resort, a desperate remedy, an expedient compelled by the goading of emotions, poverty, or the law. A refuge may look comparatively comfortable, but it is not an absolute ideal. Among the refugees were many Lot's wives, loving the cities of the plain, and often making for them again as soon as they could.[1]

So America becomes no more a lure than a *pis aller*, no more a great hope than an outer darkness, chosen reluctantly at the

[1] Cf. Thomas J. Mathias, *Pursuits of Literature* (13th ed., 1805), pp. 376-377:

> When Transatlantic Emigrants can roam
> But to return, and praise *our* English home. . . .

He adds an equally scornful footnote: "See Mr. Cooper of Manchester's Account on his return from America, and the Letters of some wandering Journeyman Weaver or Carpenter, I forget which, &c. &c. Impudens liqui patrios Penates, &c." (p. 377).

instance of the sinful, the vengeful, and the unjust. Many a paragraph describes the unwelcome allopathy of emigration. In 1765 Colonel Barré told the House that the Americans "fled from your tyranny";[2] in 1782 Samuel Peters, the picturesque historian, wrote:

It seems that England's intent was to afford an asylum to the republicans who had been a scourge to the British constitution. . . .[3]

In 1795 Charles Pigott printed such definitions as these:

*Emigrant* (English),—one who, like Dr. Priestley or Thomas Cooper, is compelled to fly from persecution, and explore liberty in a far distant land, probably America. . . .[4]
*Refugees,*—English Patriots, as Dr. Priestley and family, Mr. Cooper, of Manchester, &c. &c. who . . . were obliged to quit a country pregnant with bigotry and persecution. . . .[5]

The very printer of these definitions, Daniel I. Eaton, and at least two other members of his profession, had to flee to America.[6] Priestley is one of the most eminent of victims. William Cobbett left England, ultimately arriving in America, after he had "endangered his personal liberty" by the espousal of agitation afoot for the increase of soldiers' pay.[7] Then there were Alexander Wilson, who

on account of republican sentiments inspired by the French revolution, . . . emigrated to America, where he won lasting fame as an ornithologist,[8]

and Hazlitt's father, who fled because of his "increasing unpopularity" after he had

[2] *Parliamentary History*, XVI, 39.
[3] *A General History of Connecticut*, pp. 374-375.
[4] *A Political Dictionary*, p. 17.
[5] *Ibid.*, p. 113.
[6] The others were James T. Callender and Gales, editor of the Sheffield *Register;* for Eaton and Callender, see articles on them in D. N. B.; for Gales, "Montgomery, James (1771-1845)," D. N. B.
[7] D. N. B. Paine's experience was roughly similar.
[8] C. H. E. L., XI, 261.

aroused the suspicions of the townspeople [at Bandon, County Cork] by an apparently too great devotion to the cause of the American soldiers in Kinsale prison.[9]

Less well known of the men in flight were John Craig Millar, an Advocate,[10] and James Tytler, of the Edinburgh literati.[11]

Of all the refugees, the one who conformed most closely to the laws laid down by fiction was William O'Brien, the actor: having married a young lady "of family" without her parents' approval, he found it expedient to go to America. He, also, was among those who came back.[12]

ii

Fiction failed almost completely to take advantage of the good drama resident in the many stories of political refugees, possibly because even those novels which idealized America went in for soft sentimentality rather than anything really robust. Henry Summersett's *Probable Incidents* (1797) tells about a Frenchman and his daughter who, captured in flight from Revolutionary Paris, are transferred, through the agency of their cousin, to a boat which takes them to America. Thence they return, like nearly all of those for whom America is a makeshift.[13] Much the same thing is the story of the hero of Du Bois's satirical *St. Godwin* (1800), who is afraid of being guillotined:

I therefore resolved to go to America. In this resolution, however, I was deceived, and instead of visiting America, I was compelled, by the *omnipotence of necessity*, to visit England, but in such a way as man never visited it before.[14]

Actor O'Brien's life provides a model more frequently used. Not that we have many unwelcome sons-in-law making geta-

[9] *Ibid.*, XII, 182.
[10] Thompson, *A Scottish Man of Feeling*, p. 267 note.
[11] *C. H. E. L.*, XI, 259.
[12] *D. N. B.*
[13] II, 143-145.
[14] Page 212.

ways; rather, people are in difficulties, either because of their own weaknesses or because of some outer force, and they head off across the sea. In most cases they are fundamentally good people, temporarily "down on their luck." The unfortunate-marriage motif is actually found in Mrs. Smith's *Young Philosopher* (1798), in which Glenmorris's family disapprove of his choice. His friends register

abhorrence of the tyranny and injustice that had deprived their friend of affluence, and driven him from society he was so well calculated to adorn, to the wilds of America.[15]

Other tales are vaguer. In Mrs. Parsons' *Voluntary Exile* (1795) a Frenchman says merely that misfortunes had driven him to seek an asylum in America.[16] In *Memoirs and Opinions of Mr. Blenfield* (1790) a mysterious stranger, after behaving obstreperously at an inn, being arrested, and going scot-free, tells the narrator that

he had been in England but a few days; that he was in London about a year since, but should leave it in the following week, in order to go to America, from whence he believed he should never return. . . .[17]

The intolerable family appears as the agent of ejection in Walker's *Theodore Cyphon* (1796), the hero of which plans to flee because he sees "no end to the vindictiveness of my father, or the nefarious practices of my uncle."[18] Instead, however, he kills his uncle, whereupon the friendly Shechem proposes to Theodore's father,

. . . I've a great itch to travel. I intend going to America; now suppose I carry over Theodore and settle there, you will be forever freed from him, and I will answer no tales are told.[19]

"Follies of youth" sometimes lead to a financial state which

[15] I, 247.
[16] V, 96.
[17] I, 33.
[18] I, 253.
[19] II, 207. For the reverse, a flight to England after a supposedly fatal duel in America, see *Berkeley Hall*, III, 267-268.

can be solved only by expatriation, as in the case of George Woodford in *Agitation* (1790):

> Had it not been for his dying mother's injunctions, he would immediately have gone a volunteer to America; but that put a stop to all thoughts of that kind.[20]

Female relatives, although they often pleaded, were seldom so effective; in six other stories dissipation and resultant economic incompetence are the prelude to an American journey.[21] Poverty may be only one of a set of complicating circumstances; in *Idalia* (1800) Mme. St. Croix thus explains her coming to Canada:

> In a few years Monsieur St. Croix died, and left me in a wretched intricacy of situation. I had formerly a relation who had all his life resided here; and after mourning, with a mother's agonized pangs, the loss of one sweet darling, I, with the other, came in quest of my unknown relative.[22]

Emotional upsets are a popular reason for sailing to foreign shores. Following the traditional course of becoming a hermit,[23] Kelan, in *Edward* (1774), is in America because of the unmotivated villainy of one Varnish, the incredible false friend whom one runs across periodically. Varnish's attempt to rape and his murdering Kelan's wife lead Kelan into a twenty-seven-year sojourn in the American woods, ended only by a belated sense

[20] (New ed., n.d.), II, 82.

[21] Mrs. Parsons, *Voluntary Exile* (1795), II, 25 ff., 153 (story of Biddulph); II, 85-86 (story of Osborne); Imlay, *Emigrants* (1793), I, 1-2; *Berkeley Hall* (1796), I, 49; Walker, *Cinthelia* (1797), for which see *Critical Review*, XXIII (New Arrangement, 1798), 353; *Idalia* (1800), II, 11 ff.

[22] II, 184-185.

[23] Several more American hermits, finding relief from Europe, will appear. Professor Greenough's Catalogue lists eighteen titles between 1760 and 1800 which appeal to the general love of hermits. Most popular was James Buckland's *The Remarkable Discovery of an American Hermit*, which in 1786 was published in Portsmouth, New Haven, Middletown, Boston, Pittsburgh, Norwich, and in 1787 in "Pittsburg, Virginia." In 1819 appeared *The Hermit in America*. See *The Rambler*, March 31, 1750, for Samuel Johnson's comment on hermits in "the fictions of the last age."

of duty to his son, who had been unprotected in the meantime.[24] Likewise Mr. Melton's grandfather in Bage's *Mount Henneth* (1781), after his wife had eloped with his best friend, migrated to Rhode Island, where he solaced himself, however, not by eschewing all associations, but by becoming rich.[25] Grief for the loss of his wife and child partly motivate Biddulph's American voyage in Mrs. Parsons' *Voluntary Exile* (1795); in America he meets the hermit Routier, recovering from "despair" at the loss of his fiancée through family interference.[26] The fact that such excursions were considered temporary, as I have contended, is illustrated by Biddulph's happy return, at the end of five volumes; likewise the word *Exile* in the title is very significant. The death of a wife appears for the last time in Surr's *George Barnwell* (1798), again the cause of the widower's trip to America.[27] In *The Solitary Wanderer* (1800) Mrs. Smith, differing from all others, apparently sees aberration as a cause of sudden vanishings:

You have heard of some eccentric man of fortune in England, who, without giving his family or friends the least intimation of his intentions, made it a practice to disappear for some weeks, and the first letters they received from him were dated from the wilds of the American continent, or from the interior parts of Asia.[28]

The most prolific single motive for flight is the bruised heart. When a lady is faithless or cold, when family interference or some other cause wrecks an affair, the lover seeks the consolation of different scenery. The geographical remedy proves the force of his passion, which is as nothing if it does not produce hyperbole of word and deed. Sometimes the mere plan is as convincing as the performance. In *The Relapse* (1779) Lady Scudamore writes of her amorous satellite, Mr. Eveling:

[24] II, 84 ff.
[25] Page 198.
[26] II, 153-154.
[27] I, 175.
[28] III, 1.

He is still determined on his American scheme: he talked of it last night, till I was much too softened.[29]

Happily, Sir Benjamin Scudamore dies, a rare convenience. When Rivers returns from America to find his old love married, in Susanna Keir's *History of Miss Greville* (1787), a friend of his writes:

Rivers must soon return to America. . . . From time, from absence, much may be expected. In him inconstancy would be a virtue.[30]

Rivers agrees:

I will embark for America in the very first Transports; and, since life can be no longer enjoyed, seek relief in an honourable death.[31]

There is a new complication in Ann Thomas's *Adolphus de Biron* (1794). Augustus Margrove, first intending to hunt a father believed to be somewhere in America, is really driven to action by suspicion of his wife's infidelity:

I have been a Dupe to a polished designing Villain, who has forever destroyed my Peace. Henceforth my Enquiries shall be among such as are distinguished by the Name of Savages. I will traverse uncultivated Wilds to find a wretch superior in Vice to the Monster Bromley.[32]

We can dispense with further examples of this and similar themes, which appear in nine other stories.[33]

In all the stories thus far summarized there are two unifying elements: the departures are voluntary (in the last analysis, the characters do not *have* to leave), and the fugitives are sympathetically presented. Whether driven by emotions or by material difficulties, the emigrant is largely at the mercy of circumstances.

[29] II, 144.
[30] III, 40.
[31] III, 58.
[32] I, 187.
[33] Harrison's *New Novelist's Magazine* (1786), I, 276 ("The False Alarm"), 25 ("The Unfortunate Lovers"); Mrs. Smith, *Wanderings of Warwick* (1794), pp. 125 ff.; Mrs. Parsons, *Voluntary Exile* (1795), IV, 60; Walker, *Vagabond* (1799), pp. 30, 225; *Magnanimous Amazon* (1796), pp. 18-19; Harriet and Sophia Lee, *Canterbury Tales* (1799), III, 31-32 ("William Cavendish"), 246-247 ("Henry"); E. H., *Tales of Truth* (1800), III, 91.

In some cases, it is true, the trouble lies in his own weaknesses, but the reader is given to understand that his basic virtue has merely been in temporary eclipse. He leaves approval behind him, and the reader is not to condemn.

### iii

Another group of refugees also depart voluntarily, but, unlike the others already surveyed, they are getting out of hot water of their own manufacture. They have committed wrongs, and they are pursued by obloquy and revilings. They are trying to save their skins, like the other runaways, but they have to go abroad because home soil is too uncomfortable and inhospitable.

Whereas in the preceding section we found flights from unsuccessful love affairs, here we have flight from sexual difficulties. Implications rather than actual troubles are significant in *The Vicar of Wakefield* (1766), in which Arabella Wilmot, explaining her temporary desertion of George Primrose for young Squire Thornhill, cries,

. . . how have I been deceived! Mr. Thornhill informed me for certain, that this gentleman's eldest son, Captain Primrose, was gone off to America with his new-married lady.[34]

This is mild enough; the point is that behind such an allegation lies the suggestion of faithlessness or a bad match or some mistake which makes a move desirable. We advance to actualities, however, in Graves's *Spiritual Quixote* (1772), which tells the story of Joseph Tugwell, who,

having violated the chastity of the justice's maid (who was known to be common to all men), rather than marry her, listed for a soldier; and was supposed to be dead in America.[35]

A good deal more serious is the episode of R. Loyd in Anne Meades's *History of Sir William Harrington* (1771); he deserts his wife, elopes with his mistress, and, in company with Tom

[34] II, 196.
[35] I, 25.

Craven and his mistress, goes to Carolina, where Tom has "bought into" a regiment. For some time they lived "in a state of greater harmony and happiness than their evil deeds had merited," until the

extravagant course of life the men pursued, even there, made it necessary for them to take flight,

and they were never heard of again.[36] The Portuguese hero of *Adventures of Alonso* (1775) elopes with the young wife of the old Don Pedro, and, after much nervous scurrying around in southern Europe, considers a more permanent means of safety:

Of the different projects that run [*sic*] at that time in his head, none appeared to him so advantageous as to get out to the Spanish colonies in America. . . .[37]

The same motif occurs a number of other times.[38]

Sometimes flight has an element of the penitential. Brecknock, a character of fascinating recalcitrancy in *Berkeley Hall* (1796), had shown his scorn for his family by marrying his mistress, had been thrown out of his regiment for generally disreputable conduct, had joined the Pretender to vex his father and brother, and, when fortunes were low, deserted and fled to America. There follow twenty years of penance in a cave where he lives as a hermit.[39] Harry Trevor in *Constantia* (1770) had led a rakish life in Paris and gambled away nine thousand pounds.

This made me act in the Manner I have done, being fully resolved not to see any of my Friends, till every Thing was prepared for my

---

[36] (2nd ed., 1772), IV, 254-255.

[37] I, 36.

[38] *The Relapse* (1779), II, 146, 190; Bage, *Barham Downs* (1784), p. 323; Mrs. Rowson, *Fille de Chambre* (1792), pp. 171 ff.; Thomas Bellamy, *Miscellanies in Prose and Verse* (1794), I, 218-226; Harrison's *New Novelist's Magazine* (1787), II, 17-18.

[39] III, 19 ff.

Departure; then to take a sudden, an everlasting Farewell, and retire to some sequestered Corner of *America*.[40]

Dissipation as the cause of a flight to America appears a number of times.[41] Complete loss of social approval is given as the cause of departure in a letter in Charles Lloyd's *Edmund Oliver* (1798):

> My cousins are about to embark for America; their character is so completely ruined here, that they can no longer make this place their scene of action; . . .[42]

The ruined character is sometimes due to debts which are most easily avoided by a trip to America.[43] The distraught state of mind of debtors must have been appreciated by "Thomas Thoughtless, Jr.," who, in his *The Fugitive of Folly* (1793), helpfully adds a scholarly note on "WHERE they are safe from the Effect of British Debts and WHERE NOT." The latter, he says, includes,

> the East.—West-Indies, or North America, where Powers of Attorney are constantly sent out after the Debtor and he is imprisoned for the same, *on the first Process* as in England.[44]

The possession of this useful information might have made several authors a shade more realistic.

Another type of story is that in which the villain cheats, robs, or leads other people astray and then, when the plot thickens, makes off to America. The conduct of de Charmes in *Edward* (1774) is of a very old pattern; very much a man of the world, he makes love to Louisa, fights with her brother Richard, and ruins her brother Henry by leading him into gambling. In America he runs into Richard; they duel, he repents, and, with

[40] Page 197.

[41] *Elfrida* (1786), II, 111 ff.; III, 129; *Memoirs and Opinions of Mr. Blenfield* (1790), I, 222; Mrs. Parsons, *Voluntary Exile* (1795), V, 69, 116.

[42] (Bristol), II, 235.

[43] *Adventures of an Author* (1767), II, 41; *The Liberal American* (1785), I, 103, 116, 136, 149; Imlay, *Emigrants* (1793), II, 105.

[44] Pp. 127-128 note.

the ease customary among sentimentalists, they become firm
friends.[45] Francis Lathom's *Men and Manners* (1799) tells the
story of how Attorney Blackman, after fleecing Sir Gilbert
Oxmondeley, had fled to America and met death "for some
crime he had there committed."[46] Another fleeing embezzler is
Mr. Potts in *Henry Willoughby*[47] (1798); safety first in America is sought twice after the discovery of robbery,[48] twice after
forgery.[49] A case different from the ordinary is *The House of
Marley* (1797), in which, after a shooting-affair, a servant

Walter with his brother having acknowledged every thing, and sued for
mercy, were with their own consent conveyed to North America. . . .[50]

Finally there is an appropriate summary in Isaac Disraeli's
*Flim-Flams* (1797), which turns America into a sort of wastebasket for all types of *"desoeuvres,* or nothing-to-do gentlemen,
a turbulent and numerous race":

In ages less philosophical than the present, they opened a vent for these
boiling geniuses, by pouring them into some newly discovered island;
the Canaries, or Virginia, or the Moluccas, where they soon exhausted
their souls and bodies.—These newly-discovered islands served as empires for political-justice-mongers! bishopricks for curates! regiments
for disbanded officers! and estates for younger brothers![51]

It is obvious what Disraeli thinks should be done with mal-
contents.

Not all of the expatriates here treated, it is true, were viewed
with complete antipathy, but it is clear that we have come a considerable way from the mere hard-luck story. From unfortunates
we have traveled to undesirables, and many of our passengers

[45] I, 194; II, 138-139.
[46] III, 39; IV, 341. There is also an interesting comment by Lady Varney:
"They send a vast number of stolen trinkets to America, I am told" (I, 318).
[47] I, 102.
[48] Maria Hunter, *Fitzroy* (1792), II, 198-199; William F. Williams, *Fitzmaurice* (1800), II, 189.
[49] Harrison's *New Novelist's Magazine* (1787), II, 130; Surr, *Barnwell,*
(1798), III, 167.
[50] II, 288.
[51] (1805), I, 97.

are potential convicts. When society as a matter of course ships its disturbing members off in one direction, the conception of the destination, naturally, is a picture far different from that which emerges from the minds of those who are utopia-bound. We are at the other extreme of an interpretative spectrum, trying to resolve the many colors in which America appears. Likewise the Elizabethan age had held a multiplex view. But one fact is easily apparent: at the end of the eighteenth century, as fiction interprets it, a great many more derelicts than constructive adventurers were going to the new world. The implied view is not a flattering, but a hard one.

iv

As the gradual transformation of types in the preceding chapter and sections moves on to its logical extreme, we come to a final type of expatriates—those who went abroad involuntarily, either by due process of law or by some simulation or equivalent of it. These include convicts, victims of press gangs, or the prey of abductors and kidnappers; some were bona fide criminals, others innocent victims. For our purposes, the distinction can be ignored, since the essential fact is that those shipped off were not wanted, either by society or by individuals. America, then, was considered a good dumping ground for those whom it was convenient or comfortable to have out of the way.

Since transporting convicts to America was a regular thing from early colonial days, it is hardly surprising to find *The Female American* (1767) saying of Virginians that

many of the colony were not only persons of desperate fortunes, but most of them such whose crimes had rendered them obnoxious in their native country.[52]

And since in the years before the war England was thus getting rid of some two thousand criminals annually,[53] one finds an

[52] Page 25.
[53] Jules de la Pilorgerie, *Histoire de Botany-Bay* (Paris, 1836), p. 5.

325

ironic reference in *The Ants* (1767) not entirely without truth:

> . . . a vile race of vagabonds, the off-scourings of the colony, wretches whom the humanity of our laws alone have [*sic*] exempted from a most shameful and ignominious death. . . .[54]

*The Travels of Hildebrand Bowman* (1778) speaks of the "determined rupublicans [*sic*]" being "yearly reinforced with such a virtuous set of recruits from every jail in the kingdom."[55] Goldsmith, we have already seen, considered fallacious the belief that the "refuse" was populating America, charging that England was losing her best citizenry.[56]

The American adventure in Mackenzie's *Man of the World* (1773) starts with Annesley's being transported for twenty years. The very similar scene in Elizabeth Helme's *Duncan and Peggy* (1794) begins with Captain Grant's being "kidnapped into a vessel" carrying convicts to America, and, by means of forged papers, being sold into slavery with the rest of them at Williamsburg.[57] In Sadler's *Wanley Penson* (1791) there is the story of one Snell:

> Sometime after, having received my unjust sentence, I, with many others, was conveyed to, and put on board a ship destined for South-Carolina. We were heavy ironed, and confined under the hatches, according to custom. . . . We were, generally speaking, a society of miserables, excluded from the participation of every thing, save one another's complaints. Some of us, to be sure, took on strangely when the ship was in motion, and we found we were quitting dear old England.[58]

With this appropriately goes a passage in George Keate's *Sketches from Nature* (1779):

> . . . we lay a-long-side of a Transport-vessel, that was at anchor off that place [Gravesend], and was conveying upwards of *four score* felons to AMERICA.—Two gentlemen, who had accidentally been my

---

[54] II, 24.
[55] Pp. 292-293.
[56] *Citizen of the World*, I, 57.
[57] II, 182-183.
[58] III, 3.

companions in the Hoy, had the curiosity to step into the Transport; and declared to me at their return, that their humanity was most sensibly touched, at seeing so many unfortunate wretches of all ages, from sixteen, to sixty, whose hardened deportment too strongly testified, that even the sense of shame, which often outlives the nobler virtues of the mind, in appearance, excited no sentiments in theirs.

—Heaven protect the country, said I, whither they are going to be transplanted!—for they are weeds that must disgrace every soil!—It is a melancholy reflection, that necessity forces us every year to expel from the kingdom, such numbers of our fellow-creatures, with whom there is no living but at the risque of our peace, and safety,—and against whose fraud and villany, it requires more art to fence ourselves, than against the most savage animals that ravage the world.[59]

Two facts are noteworthy: in the first quotation, the regret at leaving England; in the second, the phrase, "Heaven protect the country," which gives a pretty fair clue to the picture of America which must have been created by such events as those here described.

*Berkeley Hall* (1796) takes a fling at American democracy by having a harangue on liberty

delivered by an attorney's apprentice, transported from London for defrauding his master, but now a principal land-jobber.[60]

In another episode, involving false arrest, the author is indifferent to improbability. In London an old soldier (by way of making pathos doubly sure) picks up a dropped bundle and runs after the owner to return it. He is arrested for theft, convicted, and sentenced to death, but his life is saved when his sentence is commuted to transportation.[61] Reform rather than emotional effect is the purpose of a passage in Walker's *Theodore Cyphon* (1796) which inveighs against the penal system. A young man tells how, after he had got drunk and began playfully to uproot trees,

[59] II, 205-207.
[60] II, 386. For a similar thrust at American character, see Mrs. Parsons' *Voluntary Exile* (1795), IV, 215.
[61] I, 34-46.

I and two others were transported to Virginia, which I thought a little hard for pulling up a tree. . . .[62]

He escapes, returns to England, and lives by thievery.

Another type of transportation is by some private agency, growing not out of statutory offenses but out of somebody's nefarious designs of one sort or another. The kind of possibility existing in the reader's mind is shown in *The History of Miss Sommerville* (1769), in which Lord Kennington is trying to seduce Patty Price, a milliner's assistant. When he writes proposals to her, she pretends that it was not he who wrote the letter, but someone using his name:

> The snare is intended less for my virtue than person; he must be an arrant kidnapper, and would sell me to some of the plantations.[63]

This bit of wisdom makes it not surprising that Patty later turns out to be of noble birth. In *Anecdotes of a Convent* (1771) Miss Jenny Homes is in the hands of a couple of sharpers who are trying to make off with her property. Mrs. Wilder, their agent, says that she'll find Jenny a husband, or

> . . . mark me, Miss, if you don't follow my directions circumstantially for the future, I will, I vow to God, either sell you to some old bawd, or transport you to *America*.[64]

The desertion of roman type marks the horror of the threat, which guarantees unquestioning obedience. The threat almost becomes an actuality in the life of the picaresque Gabriel Outcast in Trusler's *Modern Times* (1785). After a duel with Lord S. over an *affaire de coeur*, Gabriel is kidnapped by the peer's henchmen, taken aboard a boat, and informed that his destination is Nova Scotia. The dire possibility comes to naught when the ship is wrecked off the west coast of England.[65]

---

[62] II, 128.

[63] I, 165-166. A note in the Harvard Library copy attributes this work to "Mrs. Inchbauld."

[64] II, 168.

[65] III, 130-146.

Finally, we may note an apparently related incident in Richard Graves's anti-Methodist *Spiritual Quixote* (1772):

. . . the lawyer's clerk interposing, said, they had too many of them [Methodists] in Bristol; 'but, thank God!' says he, 'two of them were shipped off for North America yesterday morning. . . .'[66]

Literary references to legal transportation, though they do not disappear entirely, tend to thin out after the war. This fact is what one would expect, since the war took away from America the role of penitentiary.

It was a source of worry and annoyance to Londoners that the felons, who could no longer be transported to the American colonies, were imprisoned in hulks on the river.[67]

After extensive discussion, the government finally decided to establish a penal colony at Botany Bay, and the first fleet sailed May 13, 1787.[68] The whole business was no doubt partly responsible for stimulating the interest in penology shown in fiction. Godwin's *Caleb Williams* contains the best known commentary, and Walker's *Theodore Cyphon* unblushingly holds up its action for a discussion of the penal system.[69] Dr. Pemberton, in Davies' *Elisa Powell* (1795), comments,

. . . we are now sufferers by the bad policy of our ancestors, in ablegating their poor to till the wilds of America; and in maintaining them there at an enormous expence, while so much remained to be done at home.

He likewise objects to "supporting a colony among the very antipodes," and Mr. Powell agrees that he "had never entertained a very high opinion of the Botany Bay scheme."[70] The only narrative use of transportation to Botany Bay that I have

[66] II, 45.
[67] Trevelyan, *George the Third and Charles Fox*, II, 312.
[68] Pilorgerie, *op. cit.*, pp. 8-9, 19.
[69] II, 130 ff.
[70] I, 128-129.

come across is in Hannah More's *Cheap Repository Tracts*[71] (1793-1798).

V

The preceding sections suggest a number of conclusions. In the first place it is apparent that novelists using America as a not very welcome refuge for the troubled or as the land of exile for the unwanted were writing as journalists rather than artists. They seized upon a fact without transmuting it into effective literature. Possibly this was because in almost no case was the fact of the departure a cardinal element upon which the drama turned. Rather it was an incident thrown with other staples, by a stock recipe, into the usual hash of the melodramatic and the sentimental. The result is insipid. Like the war itself, another type of action connected with America made only a superficial contribution to the novel.

In the second place, the relation of this material to the war is apparent in two ways. When the war brought to an end the old English custom of dispatching criminals to America, the literary reflection of the custom definitely slackened; the few late-century books using the theme are naturally referring to an earlier period. Further, in a number of novels such as *Elfrida, The History of Miss Greville, The Voluntary Exile,* and the tale "Henry" in *The Canterbury Tales,* the war in America was the secondary objective for which the character sailed from England; he was interested not in the fighting for its own sake, but for the relief which it would afford from the troubles motivating his exodus. These represent the definite influence of the war.

As for the others, they are conjectural. The stories which ship off to America fundamentally good and desirable characters escaping from difficulties or unpleasant circumstances increase gradually in number throughout the forty years: 1761-1770: 1; 1771-1780: 2; 1781-1790: 5; 1791-1800: 18. The ascending

71 (New revised ed., New York: American Tract Society, n.d.), VI, 65.

curve may indicate the growth of a fad, the cumulatively greater use of a motif well adapted to the sentimental novel which could make copious tears of departure and renunciation. It is possible, too, to argue that the war, in separating America from England, made America still more remote and therefore to the popular mind still more conducive to breaking from and for-getting the past. Material to be presented in the next section adds some strength to this proposition. The causal chain be-tween evidence and conclusion, however, is so brittle that there is probably greater logical safety in relying on the theory of literary habits. The same hypothesis may best account for a gradual increase, barring a slight drop in the '80's, in the stories in which a fundamentally undesirable person is escaping the consequences of misdoing. On the other hand, an America which was no longer a part of the British Empire was legally farther away and to that extent promised somewhat greater safety.

The picture of America which emerges from the tales here summarized is consonant with that drawn in the preceding chapter, where we saw a decline of idealization and a growing satirical attitude to inflated hopes about America. As the Golden Age began to fade, a new realism became apparent, and that is what we find here in examining additional types of travelers and further reasons for travel. If we have nothing which did not exist in the seventeenth century, we may at least conclude, from the large number of novels cited, that there is a new widespread matter-of-fact-ness. When people escape from an intolerable England to America, that fact does not argue an idealization of America, but merely an elementary knowledge of psychology. "Change of scenery" is an ancient prescription for many ailments, and to see America merely as different, not as intrinsically better, is realistic enough. Often the realism leans toward the grey view of later disillusionment. Mrs. Par-sons entitles her hero's stay in America an *Exile*. In none of these travelers have we found enthusiasm; in many, resignation

331

and even self-pity. America was a second best, and newcomers went away again as soon as they could. Even convicts were gloomy at leaving "dear old England." And there were many comments about the quality and the unhappy state of a nation made up, to no inconsiderable extent, of "offscourings." Here is a much different view from that of the Renaissance.

vi

The exodus to America, to seek a Golden Age or to avoid jail, and the accompanying interpretations of America, as a roseate utopia or as a grey dumping-ground, have common elements. In both panels of the picture there are escape and riddance, and these in turn are dependent, basically, upon the three thousand miles which separate America from Europe. It was vast distance which supported the long tenure of the most golden illusions about America, which, with better acquaintance, began to droop. It was distance which made America the most healthful place for those who were psychologically disturbed, the most comfortable place for those who had fallen into disrepute, the safest place for those who were running away from the sheriff. And, from the English point of view, it was safest for those whom the sheriff had caught. If America had been one hundred miles west of Ireland, none of these points of view would have been tenable.

The consciousness of the distance of America joins the belief in inexhaustible gold mines as the oldest element in a literary tradition of which we are examining a small part. When Marlowe and Spenser and Milton wanted to suggest vast reaches of space, they made use of the new world; Temple's "from China to Peru" has become colloquial. Two centuries of increasing intercourse did little to diminish the English idea that tremendous space separated the new world from the old.

Before 1765 the preoccupation of Englishmen with their own affairs had resulted in a general indifference to America and an ignorance of her problems. . . . Comparatively few Englishmen ever visited America; few cared to travel in that distant land.[72]

The three thousand miles made a twofold impression on the novel.

In the first place, America was a very handy place to drop characters whom, for the sake of the plot, it was necessary to have temporarily out of the way. America is "off-stage," and, when characters are there, the action is changed accordingly. The plots fall into several rather obvious patterns: the character returning from America may be a *deus ex machina* or else a bringer of catastrophe; the absence of father, husband, or brother may bring other members of the family into the distress upon which the action or a part of it depends; when a lover is in America, there may be all sorts of difficulties in the love affair which is central in most novels; the author may conveniently send an unwanted lover to America, or he may harass a mistress by thus depriving her of her "protector." Once again there is evidence for a conclusion previously stated: authors using America seldom displayed either originality or artistry. They added the new world to an old situation, and then they proceeded to use it unmercifully until, like the old soldier about whom it often revolved, it was worn out.

Happily the well-worn scheme of hatching major events when menfolk are off in America did not persist indefinitely without being satirized. It is again Jane Austen who laughed merrily at the hackneyed, again in a skit in her juvenilia. The heroine of "Henry and Eliza," in dire circumstances, meets Sir George and Lady Harcourt, the latter of whom promptly claims her as a daughter. Sir George speaks to his wife in the most agitated surprise.

"You know you never even was with child. Explain yourself, I beseech you."

"You must remember Sir George, that when you sailed for America, you left me breeding."

"I do, I do, go on dear Polly."

[72] Clark, *British Opinion and the American Revolution*, p. 2.

"Four months after you were gone, I was delivered of this Girl, but dreading your just resentment at her not proving the Boy you wished, I took her to a Haycock & laid her down. A few weeks afterward, you returned, & fortunately for me, made no enquiries on the subject. Satisfied within myself of the welfare of the Child, I soon forgot I had one, insomuch that when, we shortly after found her in the very Haycock, I had placed her, I had no more idea of her being my own, than you had, & nothing I will venture to say would have recalled the circumstance to my remembrance, but my thus accidentally hearing her voice, which now strikes me as the very counterpart of my own Child's."[73]

America is off-stage in twenty-three plots,[74] which are distributed as follows: 1760-1775: 6; 1786-1795: 15; 1796-1800: 2. The plot-type was most popular in the years when the war novel was most popular: indeed, of the fifteen novels in the period after the war, eleven secured the necessary absence of a character by sending him to the war. In other words, here is a further influence of the war, which, concerned in the vicissitudes of love affairs that were the chief stock-in-trade of popular novelists, made a definite contribution to the discoveries, reversals, and catastrophes that most effectively seized upon the emotions of the readers.

The distance of America is less important, however, in this contribution to plot-mechanics than in its influence on the concept of America which appears in novels. Like their ancestors

[73] *Volume the First*, pp. 71-72.

[74] Graves, *Spiritual Quixote* (1772), II, 232; *Edward* (1774), I, 95; II, 44-45; Harrison's *New Novelist's Magazine* (1787), II, 216; *Elfrida* (1786), III, 17, 39, 235; *Wanley Penson* (1791), III, 277-279; Johnstone, *Chrysal* (1760-1765), I, 175; Elizabeth Griffith, *The Delicate Distress* (1769), I, 115; Mrs. Smith, *Emmeline* (1788), II, 58 ff., 95; *Agitation* (1790), I, 102; The Misses Purbeck, *William Thornborough* (1791), III, 66-72; Mrs. Gunning, *Anecdotes of the Delborough Family* (2nd ed., 1792), I, 59-60; Mary Charlton, *Rosella* (1799), I, 83; Mrs. Griffith, *History of Lady Barton* (1771), III, 63, 94; Susanna Keir, *History of Miss Greville* (1787), II, 218, 262; *The Fatal Effects of Deception* (1773), I, 65, 111; Bage, *James Wallace* (1788), p. 446; H. Scott, *Helena* (1790), II, 37; *Argus* (1789), I, 210; Mrs. Hedgeland, *Madeline* (1794), I, 201-202; Mrs. Smith, *Old Manor House* (1793), III, 99; *Memoirs and Opinions of Mr. Blenfield* (1790), II, 108-109; W. F. Williams, *Fitzmaurice* (1800), I, 58.

in Elizabethan and Caroline poetry, our romancers continually show consciousness of the distance of America. From it they draw certain conclusions about the new world, either directly or by a clearly perceptible process of association, and their resultant emotional state is definitely established. First, their notations on mileage are to be observed.

Like Spenser's Britomartis, Thomas Amory's Miss Melmouth has so great love that she could go even to America: "Sir, . . . if you required it, I would go with you to *Hudson's Bay*. . . ."[75] Four other books have similar expressions, with Nova Scotia most often playing limbo.[76] Goldsmith sneers at Anglo-French disputes about "some lands a thousand leagues off"[77]—no doubt the ultimate condemnation. *The Birmingham Counterfeit* (1772) alleges that the Royal Academy at Paris is going to hold "the grand assizes" in the Valley of Jehoshaphat and explains ironically,

. . . because, forsooth, it is the middle of the world, and consequently more convenient for a general rendezvous, than if it had been appointed in Mexico or Japan.[78]

Bage tells the story of a Lord Winterbottom, who, having been rescued from a brawl by an Irishman, is unwilling to have him lost in far corners of the world:

. . . my lord took a liking to Mr Gregory Wycherley, procured him a commission, caused him to sell it for half pay, rather than he should go into America. . . .[79]

In *Emily Herbert* (1786) Lord Sommerville writes Charles Dalton:

You may possibly have seen this lady, heard of her you certainly

[75] *The Life of John Buncle, Esquire* (1766), I, 509.
[76] *The Unexpected Wedding* (1768), p. 4; Pratt, *Miscellanies* (1785), III, 214; Mrs. Smith, *Desmond* (1792), II, 236; Frances Moore, *Rosina* (1793), V, 123.
[77] *Citizen of the World*, I, 55.
[78] I, 258-259.
[79] *Barham Downs* (1784), p. 267.

must, since her marriage with that old dotard Lord Stanley made so much noise, that even I heard of it though at that time in America—[80]

William Renwick, the naval surgeon, assures his wife of infinite fidelity, even though his ship has been assigned to so remote a scene as Newfoundland.[81] The Chevalier de Clairville in *Adeline* (1790) resolved "to visit every part of the habitable globe" to find a lost relative, even "travelled through the continent of America."[82] Priscilla and Theodore, the heroine and hero of the mistitled *Authentic and Interesting History of Miss Moreton* (1791), have a terrifying experience when they are at the mercy of an untrustworthy sea captain who has designs on Priscilla:

. . . and Grenville became uneasy for our safety, often wishing we were landed upon English ground; but we then found ourselves at a greater distance. In short, from what we could learn from the sailors on board, we were upon the borders of America.[83]

This tragic note gives way to the satirical when Miss Hannah More piously assails the international benevolences of Tom Paine, represented as Fantom, who loves the world in general but nobody in particular. The contrasting Trueman says, ". . . I had as lief help Tom Saunders to freedom as a Pole or a South American. . . ."[84] G. Hadley, the author of *Argal* (1793), complains, in very Pauline tones,

I was once very near embarking for America, three times obliged to comply with avaricious demands of sordid pawn-brokers, besides a variety of presents to chimney-sweepers, pastry-cooks, grocers, and other shop-keepers. . . .[85]

—all, it appears, equally unpleasant experiences. On the other

---

[80] (Dublin, 1787), p. 17. Cf. *Helena* (1790), I, 91-92.
[81] *Solicitudes of Absence* (1788), pp. 187-188.
[82] III, 170.
[83] (Birmingham, n.d.), p. 235.
[84] *Cheap Repository Tracts* (1793-1798), II, 22.
[85] (n.d.), I, xxi.

hand, the conquest of space may be exhilarating, as in an enthusiastic passage in Disraeli's *Flim-Flams* (1797):

I abominate libraries!—exclaimed the sublime pedestrian.—There's a mist in a library! all verbal ideas! I have sought for real ideas in things themselves. I have run through the forests of North America; I have swam in the Mississippi; I have strode on the top of Mont Blanc. . . .[86]

Such adventures may confer distinction, as in Lathom's *Men and Manners* (1799), in which Jacob Lamb is spoken of as one "that has travelled so far," and Tom Smith is "all longing to hear you talk about foreign parts." Finally Jacob consents, and, having given the company a short description of such matters

as had excited his own admiration, he returned home, leaving Tom Smith fast asleep on his elbow-chair, and his sister the proudest woman in the village; for her brother had been to Meriky, and she herself had heard all about foreign parts.[87]

Intellectual curiosity, however, is rare. As we have already seen, the idea of distance was seldom treated with neutrality, but, on the contrary, with distaste or apprehension. The result is that America connotes the opposite of the comfortable and the familiar, and it tends to become identified with the uncouth, the wild, the savage, and the barbarian. It is the end of the world. This idea has naturally been prominent in such works as *Berkeley Hall* and *The Vagabond,* which set out to satirize idealized primitivism, but in others with no such bias, and even in novels viewing America quite favorably, such a word as *wilderness* appears regularly. In many novels already quoted the uncultivated, desolate character of American land is practically taken for granted. If one was looking ahead flushed with optimism, he could ignore this objection, but in many others uncheered by illusions there was sharp consciousness of the hardships inseparable from a faraway and uncivilized land. The

[86] II, 223-224.
[87] I, 121-122.

hostility of rude nature, unassuaged by the long touch of humankind, figures importantly in the whole picture of America which we see evolving.

*Uncultivated, wild,* and *hardships* appear outside of fiction.[88] Novels too show a plentiful array of phases suggesting that America is the essence of wildness and therefore of undesirability; these appear fairly regularly to the end of the century:

1761-1762: "a country cold, desolate, and hideous"; "the prowling bear or insidious tyger"; "this desolate country"; "the desarts of America" (Goldsmith, *Citizen of the World,* I, 55-57, *passim*).

1767: "the savage wilds of America? Horrible!" (Young, *Adventures of Emmera,* I, 10).

1772: "the most primitive little damsel . . . [as] if bred in the wilds of America" (*Feelings of the Heart,* I, 6).

1785: "the frightful woods and gloomy deserts of America"; "this prodigious wilderness . . . numberless swamps, and lakes and rivers" (R. E. Raspe, *The Surprising Travels and Adventures of Baron Munchausen,* n.d., pp. 155-156).

1786: "the Wilds of America" (Harrison's *New Novelist's Magazine,* I, 406).

1797: "the horrors of an American wilderness" (Miss De Acton, *Disobedience,* IV, 111).

1798: "penetrated the forests of America" (Henry Summersett, *Aberford,* p. 28).

1799: "the deserts of America" (Harriet and Sophia Lee, *Canterbury Tales,* III, 67).

And in 1800 appeared *Singular Sufferings of two Friends Lost in an American Forest.*

Any American vista found at least one humorous onlooker. Here, as often, it is Jonathan Corncob, who gives vent to a bit of Munchausen-like grotesquerie. En route from Massachusetts Bay to Boston, he is lost for two days in a forest that "seemed to have no end." In search of food, he sees nothing but "blue-tailed jays, that, chattering and hopping from branch to branch,

88 See Barré's speech to the House, *Parliamentary History,* XVI, 39; *The Batchelor* (1766-1768), II, 121; *Baratariana,* p. 173.

338

seemed to make game of me." He saves himself from starvation by hopping from a tree aboard a moose, stabbing it to death as it runs, and slicing a hot steak from its flesh.[89] In *Fanny Vernon* (1788) the deadly serious again rules, what with the death of the heroine and her children in the American woods, into which Fanny, deserted by her husband, plunges in the hope of reaching the coast and finding a ship to England.

The wildest scenes that ever drew tears from a lost traveller now lay before her, and no trace of any human path presented itself.[90]

Exposure, wolves, snakes, and a thunderstorm contribute horrendous effects as the story moves on to its required trio of deaths.[91]

Even admirers of America could not escape the habit of referring to it as though it were in a barbarous state. Imlay's *Emigrants* (1793), three volumes of advertising of America, falls into such words as these:

torn from the bosom of their friends and dear relations,—banished from their country into the wilds of a desart;[92]

family beggared . . . suffering all the tortures of disappointment, with the accumulated evil of being exiled into a wilderness. . . .[93]

Mrs. Smith, almost invariably quite friendly to America, has Colonel Chesterville, in *Ethelinde* (1789), speak of having "traversed the desolate wilds of America."[94] Her *Old Manor House* (1793), very sympathetic with Americans, produces such comments as these:

. . . France, contrasted with his banishment in America, seemed to him to be part of his country. . . . (IV, 5).

. . . he almost wished himself among the cypress swamps and pathless

[89] *Adventures of Jonathan Corncob*, pp. 25-27.
[90] Page 66.
[91] Pp. 78-121.
[92] I, 6.
[93] I, 61.
[94] III, 29.

woods of uncultivated America, that he might fly from the legal crimes to which such scenes were owing (IV, 139).

. . . amidst the most dreary hours he had passed in the wilds of America, and among men who have little more rationality than the animals of their desert, he had never suffered such wretchedness as he now felt (IV, 149).

. . . little apprehensive of the inconveniences that could in this country befall a man accustomed to traverse the deserts of America (IV, 196).

. . . that spot in the wilderness of America where all my happiness was buried (IV, 227).

One of Imlay's plaints is the absence of accommodations; he urges the establishment of a series of inns,

which would be an inducement for people to emigrate and consequently tend to enhance the value of the waste land belonging to the federal empire.[95]

What inns there were did not satisfy. We have seen, in the preceding chapter, how George Walker's *Vagabond* (1799) satirized the wretched service of a Philadelphia hostelry, although primarily he wanted to show the deteriorating effects of democracy. *Tales of Truth* (1800) remarks, referring to the the war-period,

At that time, in America, there were no comfortable inns, as in this cultivated land, where the weary traveller enjoys the independence it offers, when his well stored pockets can command its comforts.[96]

*Berkeley Hall* (1796) does the most complete description of an unsatisfactory inn, criticizing gruffness, bad manners, impolite curiosity, loud and vulgar company, poor food, and beds swarming with bugs.[97]

Since America was thousands of miles away, and since one could expect at best a crude and at worst a barbarous existence there, the prospect of life in America was a very chilling one

[95] *Emigrants,* I, 56.
[96] III, 19.
[97] II, 236-244. Cf. Peters's *History of Connecticut,* p. 120, a possible source.

indeed. The outlook brought forth loud outcries, and a stay was to be cut to the minimum. Mrs. Brooke had lived in Canada, and although she does not give way to the horrified flutterings of the uninitiate, her *Emily Montague* (1769) betrays no enthusiasm. Colonel Rivers can stand America only if his Emily loves him:

. . . if she loves, . . . Canada will be no longer a place of exile; if I have flattered myself, and she has only a friendship for me, I will return immediately to England, and retire with you [his sister] and my mother to our little estate in the country.[98]

But although Emily does love him, she objects to Canada, and the result is a wholesale return to Europe. Arabella Fermor, momentarily left behind by the rest of the apostate adventurers, makes several illustratively gloomy remarks:

I have been seeing the last ship go out of the port, Lucy; you have no notion what a melancholy sight it is: we are now left to ourselves, and shut up from all the world for the winter: somehow we seem so forsaken, so cut off from the rest of human kind, I cannot bear the idea. . . .[99]

. . . I cannot think with patience of continuing in America, when my two amiable friends have left it; I had no motive for wishing a settlement here, but to form a little society of friends, of which they made a principal part.[100]

The Villarses, in *The Fortunate Sisters* (1782), have estates in Virginia which demand their presence. But

Mrs. Villars had received so disagreeable an account of Virginia from Mrs. Oliver, that she had no inclination to visit that place from any motives of pleasure. . . .[101]

The theme is unconsciously expanded in the *Euphemia* (1790) of Mrs. Lennox, who also knew whereof she spoke. When the heroine, now Mrs. Neville, announces that she is to live in

[98] II, 84.
[99] I, 201-202.
[100] III, 101.
[101] II, 158-159.

America, her best friend, Miss Harley, exclaims, ". . . doomed to waste your days in America! I cannot bear to think of it!"[102] and ". . . to traverse an immense ocean, and live in unknown regions, far from your country and all you love!"[103] Her husband has deferred announcement of the trip, "doubtless foreseeing the opposition I should make to this scheme,"[104] and Miss Harley does not help matters with continued lamentation about "the wilds of America."[105] Miss Bellenden, who is going along, dreads "this terrible voyage."[106] Although New York itself turns out to be much less painfully primitive than expected, the worst news is Neville's being appointed to command the fort at "Schonectady." Mrs. Neville mourns "this worse than banishment," although she is reconciled to the fortress because of its security "in this wild country, and among these savage inhabitants."[107] As for their daughter, she is taken to New York every summer to counteract the influences of life "among a rude and unpolished people."[108] The final note, before a happy legacy, approaches despair:

My condition is more truly pitiable now than ever. I am here in this wild country, without friends, without society, without comfort; for my frequent cruel disappointments have even banished hope, the last resource of the afflicted.[109]

Even a round trip just touching America can arouse alarm. When Augustus Margrove in Ann Thomas's *Adolphus de Biron* (1794) decides to search for a father presumably secreted somewhere in the backwoods, he is greeted by shocked disapproval chorusing "hazardous Voyage" and "uncultivated Wilds

[102] I, 5.
[103] I, 48.
[104] I, 148-149.
[105] I, 167.
[106] I, 178.
[107] III, 186.
[108] IV, 7.
[109] IV, 186-187.

of America."[110] The step courageously taken, Antoinette Ville-roi writes,

Poor Margrove! no Account from him. Ah! why did he take such a long and dangerous Voyage?[111]

The efforts at tragedy evoke another pleasant bit of mockery in Beckford's *Modern Novel Writing* (1796), which, with Jane Austen's works, picks on most of the foibles of the age. Mrs. Maltrever assures Lucinda Howard of an interest in her welfare:

. . . I am only actuated by the interest I take in what concerns you, for I made no objection to their cutting down Hadleigh Grove, nor did I wish you to go to America, even at a time when your poor father was such a martyr to the gout.[112]

The love of the familiar underlying most of these woebegone murmurings is sometimes almost magnified into patriotism. Two novels using *American* in their titles stress nostalgia for the past rather than the misery of the future. The narrator in *The American Wanderer* (1783) prays "to feast, once more, my eyes with the chalky cliffs of Albion,"[113] regretting his Ovidian susceptibility to the "taper leg" and other female charms, which has banished him from "a country prodigal of simple beauty."[114] America, as a matter of fact, turns out to be less repellent than he expected. In *The Liberal American* (1785) Sophie Aubrey has to accompany a relative, Mr. Villars, to America, whither business calls:

Think, my dear Louisa, of being torn from my native land, from every youthful friend, from every dear attachment. . . . My aunt . . . is extremely averse to leaving England, and has endeavoured to prevail on Mr. Villars to leave us here, and return as soon as he can settle his affairs; but he declares himself determined to reside in America, as his connexions there render it highly necessary; so there is an end of hope. . . .

[110] I, 193-196, *passim.*
[111] I, 250.
[112] I, 201.
[113] Page 3.
[114] Page 140.

. . . now I find I shall most likely spend my whole life there, it makes me truly unhappy. What can be more distressing to a feeling mind than to be removed from every dear connexion, and placed in a land of strangers![115]

*Berkeley Hall* (1796), though not unfriendly to America, is "strongly pro-British," as Miss Whitney remarks.[116] The following remark is typical of Dr. Homily, the exiled non-juror:

. . . though I bear in my bosom the scars of the injustice of my country, or rather of her infatuated rulers, her image will never be torn from my heart, which has not known peace since absent from my native shore. Happy island![117]

Of Homily and his daughter Matilda, the author assures us:
Here [New Jersey] their days might have glided away in sweet tranquillity and oblivion of care, had not their strong attachment to their native country, and the remembrance of their dear friends and relatives left behind, embittered their pleasures, and tinctured their minds with melancholy. They would often forget together the feast of happiness which nature spread before them, and derive greater transport from the imaginary prospect of one day landing again in England, recovering their paternal estates, and passing the evening of their days in the circle of their old neighbours and friends.[118]

Thus ends the parade of involuntary expatriates and unwilling voyagers, whose grumblings and groanings are imbedded in novels distributed thus: 1761-1770: 5; 1771-1780: 2; 1781-1790: 13; 1791-1800: 16. Turned into percentages, these figures show that the attitude to America here displayed remained fairly constant throughout the forty-year period, even becoming a bit stronger after the war. The variation, however, is negligible. Here, it seems, the war is conspicuously without influence; although it brought about an increased familiarity with America which greatly weakened a flamboyant utopianism, it did not succeed in turning the new world into a comfortably close

---

[115] I, 116-118.
[116] *Op. cit.*, p. 276.
[117] I, 15.
[118] I, 67-68.

neighbor whose home would offer a life not intolerably different from that in one's own. Familiarity bred some signs of contempt without breeding ease. America had always seemed inaccessible, and it still seemed inaccessible; though inaccessibility once meant freedom from contamination, it now meant rather absence of civilization. To many minds, at least, the discomforts and the dangers remained paramount.

Throughout the preceding chapter and the present one we have seen widely varying interpretations of the ultramundane existence. At one extreme there is the experimental, hopeful, dreaming spirit; at the other, stay-at-home contentment, satisfaction with the present, nostalgia for the familiar. Hence America becomes either a new and better world, or merely the end of the world. Toward the end of the eighteenth century the brighter side seemed definitely to be passing out of sight, for, though some starry-eyed gazers still shouted that they saw Arcadia, skeptics became more vociferous and damned such a spectacle as visionary. El Dorado, too, became increasingly a picture visible only to the eye of memory.

To the matter-of-fact, the other hemisphere was the lesser of two evils; it was not a tempting invitation, but a convenience to be utilized by the distraught and the unhappy and the bankrupt and the outlawed. Gloomily they made off to a scene of which the chief virtue was that it was out of reach. This virtue was an evil to those for whom the old country had not become emotionally or socially or legally untenable. They faced a trip there with misgivings, a visit there with distaste, and a protracted stay there with dread; the voyage was risky, the land inhospitable, and the social life non-existent. While they mourned the loss of England, they clamored, vigorously or pitifully, about the uncultivated, wild, desolate land, and the uncivilized and even barbarous life.

This view of the antipodean life is important in connection with the visions of a Golden Age, for the former shrinks from the remoteness and the primitive conditions that the latter con sider essential to virtue and happiness. The contented are antagonistic to the very conditions most praised by the proponents of a backwoods utopia. This ideal called forth many skeptics. To the professional satirists we must add the large segment of the public to whom there never occurred even the thought of a sylvan idyl, but who disliked and feared the milieu in which, according to the manifestoes, it was to flourish. In the aggregate, then, the novelists, and the large public to and for which they spoke, appear growingly hostile to an America conceived of in romantic terms.

The main thesis, that of a growing realism in the English concept of America shown in prose fiction, gains support from the evidence here summarized. Perhaps the last section, with its emphatic insistence on the wildness and desolateness of America, does not argue a realistic spirit in the best sense. The parts of America to which most of the voyagers were going were neither particularly wild nor particularly desolate; Mrs. Lennox even admits that her family of emigrants considered three months a year in New York City sufficient to give their daughter a modicum of polish. Novelists may not have made distinctions between cities and backwoods, or they may have played up savagery for dramatic effect. That does not particularly matter. What does matter is that these pictures of America, veracious or not, are obviously not seen through rose-colored spectacles. Some of the observers may even be going to the other extreme and wearing dark glasses. Very well; so much the further, then, from the breezy optimism of the Renaissance, and so much the closer to the spirit of later periods. We are apparently seeing the final stage of the transition.

# CHAPTER XI

## THE AMERICANS

### i

America, as we have seen, collected a miscellaneous assemblage of social and political idealists, prospective good citizens, gold seekers, political refugees, victims of circumstance, grief-stricken or lovesick beings in need of a change, debauchees, forgers, embezzlers, and convicts. If its populace was not yet of widely cosmopolitan origins, America was none the less a melting pot. Here we are looking for the end-product, the composite man who was "American." What was his character, or at least how is it interpreted by the novelists who collected such diverse ingredients?

Just when the medley of seekers and sought who composed America were conceived of as transformed into an independent national entity with a character of its own is debatable. For a long time, naturally, the new country was simply a branch of England, and the people were conceived of as English, probably little different from the stay-at-homes. But when generation after generation had been abroad, a sense of separation, and with it a sense of difference, would grow up, although all the talk, late in the eighteenth century, about a "civil war" naturally implies that the sense of Anglo-American identity is not altogether lost. One may argue, on the other hand, that the equally plentiful talk about "American spirit" suggests consciousness of a distinct, integrated national body.

One automatically, if too hastily, makes the war a dividing line between the transplanted Englishman and the new American. Beginning her study of travelers' accounts with the year 1785, Miss Mesick concludes,

347

The American character was considered . . . to be something distinct, and belonging peculiarly to the country.[1]

Fiction, as we shall see, appears to parallel non-fiction, which was prolific in comment on American character.[2] Actually, however, the creation of the "American type" appears to have begun long before. Swift's *Modest Proposal,* which appeared in 1729, contains two pungent comments on the new-world dweller:

> I have been assured by a very knowing American of my acquaintance in London, that a young healthy child well nursed is at a year old a most delicious, nourishing, and wholesome food, whether stewed, roasted, baked, or boiled. . . .[3]

> . . . for as to the males, my American acquaintance assured me from frequent experience, that their flesh was generally tough and lean, like that of our school-boys. . . .[4]

Cannibalism, of course, belongs to the conception of the *Homo Americanus* proper, but the reference certainly indicates a white man rather than a redskin, and the irony, to be effective, had to keep within bounds beyond which popular fancies could not possibly go. But if Swift in his fury still seems to outstrip the most fevered imagination, we can consider a definition made by Francis Grose in his *Classical Dictionary of the Vulgar Tongue* in 1785:

> *Gouge,* to squeeze out a man's eye with the thumb, a cruel practice used by the Bostonians in America.[5]

Apparently anything could be believed of Americans. Imlay, on the other hand, insisted that Americans were marked by simplicity, naturalness, sincerity, and

[1] *English Travellers in America 1785-1835,* p. 299.

[2] *Ibid.,* pp. 299-320.

[3] Jonathan Swift, *Prose Works,* ed. Temple Scott (London: Bell, 1925), VII, 209.

[4] *Ibid.,* VII, 211.

[5] Quoted by M. M. Mathews, *A Survey of English Dictionaries* (Oxford, 1933), p. 27.

too much hospitality and suavity of manners to inform him [the Englishman] that they have neither sentiments nor religion.[6]

The idea of American character which is created by the novels appears somewhat sketchily in the comments on the colonial spirit shown during the war, already summarized in Chapter V. A few English thought Americans were pusillanimous, stubborn, or self-seeking, but a vast majority appears to have conceived of the rebels as spirited, independent, unflinching, honest, and brave; in a few novels they were even characterized as considerate, polished, suave, and sensitive to the demands of rank and fortune. Whatever the details, the portrait was predominantly favorable. Here, however, the artists were working under special conditions; they were not so much depicting a nationality as a body of fellowmen struggling under serious handicaps against injustices which their creators themselves attacked; and they were often excited in their portraiture by their own Phaëthon-like rhetoric. Peace-time characterization is another matter, and it remains to be seen whether Americans who had turned swords into ploughshares remained as fine as the underdogs who appealed powerfully to sensibility. A few other less flattering comments, even in war-time, are yet to be recorded.

In fiction as in non-fiction, the question, What is an American? appears to be more insistent and to receive more definite answer after the war. In other ways, too, the novel follows the travel-books. Miss Mesick comments:

> The number of Englishmen who made any real attempt at analysis of American character is relatively small. Incidental and local comments of course are more numerous, but one feels the lack of a complete and philosophical discussion.[7]

Similarly in fiction the composite at which we arrive has to be pieced together from snapshots here and there, though occasional generalizations appear. Likewise the novel offers

[6] *Topographical Description*, p. 179.
[7] *Op. cit.*, p. 320.

conflicting evidence, presenting, as it does, "the diversity of character met with on a long journey."[8]

## ii

At any time the novel could unapologetically act as a travel account, becoming a *pasticcio* of odds and ends of no general significance. Mrs. Brooke's *Emily Montague* (1769) devotes a good deal of space to a decidedly adverse picture of French Canadians,[9] whom, of course, she knew by personal contact, and whom she considered largely indolent and dirty. *Caroline* (1790) talks about the pride of those Canadians who are conscious of relationship with or descent from noble settlers.[10] Mrs. Lennox's *Euphemia* (1790), another guidebook, refers caustically to "the boorish manners of the men, and the awkward ignorance of the women" among the Dutch in New York.[11] These, however, are all special cases and can be dismissed accordingly.

War-stories make frequent notes on American character. What has already been said of Americans during the fray has dealt specifically with their "spirit," that is, with their attitude toward the dispute with England, toward England, toward actual warfare; with their being scared or brave or, as Jonathan Corncob's brother Jeptha put it, "full of fight." They were considered exclusively as combatants, and as combatants in an unequal struggle. What else the novelists said about Americans, even while dealing with the war, is more general or appears to have more general implications. The distinction is between the mood of the moment and the whole character. Often the distinction is anything but clear-cut; the comments which follow, however, appear to me to represent an intention to indicate more permanent traits than those evinced particularly under the stress of conflict, and to suggest the author's belief that he

[8] *Ibid.*, p. 299 *et seq.*
[9] I, 23 ff., 127 ff.; II, 55-56, 202 ff.; III, 58, 106 ff.
[10] II, 8.
[11] III, 97-98; see also III, 33, 123, 147-148.

is characterizing a people, not merely describing their emotions at a given moment.

Americans fare quite badly at the hands of several authors who were either convinced of their barbarism or played it up with commercial intent. When Pleydel in *The School for Fathers* (1788) was arrested in Boston for his obstinate loyalism, colonial officers "inhumanly" refused his wife information about him; with "unpardonable barbarity" they told her that he would in some way as yet undetermined be put to death; on the streets she was "reviled and insulted by the rabble," and those whom she had charitably helped "were among the foremost to insult and ill-treat her."[12] The account burns with such phrases as "severities of his treatment," "barbarous insults," "tyrannic power," "victim to their revenge," "taunts and acrimonious insults."

. . . he was heavily ironed, and chained to the tail of a cart, decorated with the thirteen stripes, branded with infamous titles, and exposed to a licentious mob—those sacred patrons and preservers of liberty![13]

When a jailer expresses willingness to help him escape, Pleydel replies with heavy irony,

Pardon me . . . if from the instances I have so lately received of the turpitude of human nature, when degenerated by treason, I, for a moment, question a zeal so very exalted.[14]

In H. Scott's *Helena* (1790) Americans raid and fire the house of General D——; his sister dashes into the woods with her infant nephew, and his wife runs out screaming, is cut by a bayonet, and swoons.[15] On another still livelier occasion Lucinda Franklin is almost "frozen with horror" as she observes "atrocious actions": colonials seize a Mr. C——, suspected of communication with the enemy, and drag him around Philadelphia in a cart. In the presence of his wife and children he is

[12] I, 215-217, *passim.*
[13] II, 6-9, *passim.*
[14] II, 13.
[15] I, 65-66.

351

insulted by the rabble, in every way they could devise, and it was with difficulty he was preserved from being torn to pieces by the enraged multitude. . . .[16]

Mrs. C—— dies, but C—— is ultimately pardoned, provided he move fifty miles away from Philadelphia.[17] These Tory tales, it is to be noted, both use the word *rabble* and stress American savagery; the author gives the impression of a very Swiftian conception of all Americans, who only require such an occasion as the war to show their true nature.

Otherwise Americans fare better. In *Slavery* (1792) Mrs. Mackenzie is wroth with them for their failure to protect the property of General St. Leger, but consistency is the least of her troubles, for a little later she has her hero subsisting

upon the bounty of those generous Americans who knew him only as an unfortunate sufferer, emancipated from confinement by their humane intercessions.[18]

Two other tales similarly praise American hospitality.[19] Unlike Mrs. Mackenzie, Mrs. Smith is conscious when she presents varying pictures. When the hero of *Wanderings of Warwick* (1794) and his family are captured by an American frigate, he refers to his captors as a "crowd of ruffians," but, as a matter of fact, they treat him much more decently than he had expected.[20] Later he is sent to help defend Stony Point.

Here I was made prisoner by General Waine with about five hundred British. I cannot say I had any particular cause of complaint against the Americans, whose treatment of me was as good as circumstances allowed. . . .[21]

Again he is taken prisoner, this time by a French ship with a

---

[16] I, 268-269.
[17] I, 281-282.
[18] Page 225.
[19] Eugenia De Acton, *Disobedience* (1797), IV, 145; E. H., *Tales of Truth* (1800), II, 123; cf. Mesick, *op. cit.*, pp. 315-317.
[20] Page 15.
[21] Page 36.

crew composed largely of Americans, and again he is surprised, since

in general they behaved much better than I expected, for the Captain was a man of decent manners.[22]

Finally he records that during all their American difficulties he and his family had the aid of a "faithful American woman."[23] The relative balance of these interpretations gives way to a strong pro-American bias at the hand of Mrs. Parsons, whose partiality is stronger than Mrs. Smith's. When Osborn in *The Voluntary Exile* (1795) is taken prisoner, he notes, with reference to the colonel

and several other American commanders, whom I occasionally met with in my several expeditions, that their civility and humanity to those in their power, could not be exceeded by the most benevolent and polished Englishman.[24]

The note of surprise is clear.

In Bage's *Mount Henneth* (1781) the independence generally attributed to the colonies in war is transferred to the heroine, Camitha Melton, in personal experiences. She has been held in durance vile by Captain Suthall of the British navy, who has no good intentions.

Miss Melton . . . asserted her claim to independency and freedom, (for she is an American,) with great spirit and force of language; not without mingling certain innuendoes, by no means agreeable to the elegant ears of Mrs. P—— [her jailer]. The captain swore she was his property by the laws of war: he had a better title from the lady's poverty and want of friends. Several gentlemen had been introduced to her; some she laughed at; others she abused; according to the mirthful or splenetic mood she happened to be in.[25]

Obviously unlike the tearful heroine who has met the usual experience of abduction, she speaks up vigorously:

[22] Page 73.
[23] Page 241.
[24] IV, 81.
[25] Page 129. Cf. Mesick, *op. cit.,* pp. 306-308.

Take care, Mrs. P——; though born in a distant country, without the knowledge of a single person to support, assist, or protect me; without knowing, if I was out of your walls, which way to procure myself a morsel of bread, or lodging for a night, I demand my liberty. Deny it me at your peril. Destitute as I am, I may one day find means to call you to account for these outrages.[26]

Clarissa Americanized is indeed a new creature. Another of the suffering sisterhood is Anna Middleton, daughter of an American senator in *Francis the Philanthropist* (1785), who, in trying to escape from America to her lover in England, falls into the clutches of her "old persecutor, the hated, detested, infamous, Major Singleton."[27] But here the significant person is not Anna, but Captain Singleton, for he is a pillar, not of the British, but of the American army. Not all of the villainy in amorous intrigues was English.

What is American about Captain Singleton, however, is only the label, for he belongs to a type that flourishes in nearly every sentimental novel. Here we run into the standard literary device of putting old pictures into new frames; we have seen it before—the transference of familiar plots and characters to the American scene. Very recognizable is the American Villars in *The Liberal American* (1785), who first appears as the probable second husband of Sophia Aubrey's aunt, Mrs. Summers, and whom Sir Edward Hambden, Sophia's beloved, charges with "consummate art, vanity, and selfishness."[28] Mrs. Summers is completely taken in, and Villars treats her "with great unkindness."[29] He turns out to be a bigamist; his first wife was a Miss Hunter, who says,

. . . he had often told me he had not a relation in England, nor any acquaintance but with a few people in trade, whose intimacy was not worth my cultivating; but, as soon as possible, he should take me to America.[30]

[26] Page 138.
[27] Page 250.
[28] I, 71.
[29] I, 166.
[30] II, 78.

Discovery of his duplicity, inspired by financial difficulties, leads
to his suicide. Before his death he had plotted a final piece of
stock villainy: fearing a revelation of his past through the
intimacy of "Miss Hunter" and Sophia, he had had the latter
kidnapped by the worthless Captain Colville.[31] The whole plot
is decrepit, and Villars is a type, with nothing American except
the designation; what the story proves, if anything, is that
Americans could plausibly be classified in the same way as
English. Others presented are Mrs. Dalton, "rather tall, remarkably thin, and her face such as I can say nothing favourable about"; her pupil, educated in England, having "an air
and manner the most haughty and forbidding I ever saw";[32] an
objectionable old bachelor, Mr. Henshaw, who reminds Sophia
of Will Honeycomb:

I never liked that man. He is really troublesome with his overstrained
politeness, and has teized me into a horrid ill-humour. . . . I have
often been inclined to shut my eyes to avoid the sight of his long
visage, which has been within a finger's length of mine the whole day;
and he grins most horribly by way of shewing what pains he takes with
his few remaining teeth.[33]

In the accumulation of objectionable characteristics, there is
some individuality, of course, but there is no effort to represent
the combination as specifically American. The same holds true
of the more acceptable Mr. and Mrs. Mo[u]ntague:

I never was happier since I left England. . . . Mr. Montague is . . .
very agreeable in person, but infinitely more so in manners. An excellent understanding, a benevolent heart, and a politeness I never saw
exceeded. . . . His lady is . . . a most lovely little woman . . . not
beautiful, but . . . truly amiable . . . but I think the qualities of the
mind so much more important, that I seldom bestow encomiums on
the most beautiful outside.[34]

Americans, it is clear, can have all the virtues of the English.

[31] II, 227.
[32] I, 144-145.
[33] II, 7-8.
[34] II, 9-10.

Nowhere is this more apparent than in the title-hero, Mr. Elliot, who, although he is called "the most accomplished man in America,"[35] is only Grandison again, with American citizenship patently unproved. He combines all the elegances and the proprieties, with no transatlantic variations. Sophia meets him in America, refuses him because she is in love with Sir Edward Hambden, but ultimately is talked into marrying him because of his appalling limitless virtues. Elliot soon sees that he does not possess her heart, and then he dies, with this helpful benediction:

I saw two virtuous hearts struggling with an unhallowed passion, and I have bore a part in your sufferings, because I considered myself the cause of them. But, why are you thus distressed, my Sophia? Be assured I rejoice to find that your affections are bestowed on one so worthy. Look forward to happier days. You must reward the deserving Hambden; it is my dying request.[36]

An Englishman asks, "Who . . . can refuse the tribute of a tear to the memory of this liberal American!"[37] Liberal no doubt he is, but the reader never feels that he is American.

A similar failure to grasp any essentially national element and to compel the reader to recognize it as such appears in the characterization of several Americans in *The Young Widow* (1785) of H. S. Here, however, there is a more perceptible individualization; the author writes with more circumspection, more firmness, and less of the skimming facility and generalization of the sentimentalists. And on occasion she shows decided neatness of phrase:

The old gentleman was one of that kind of men, whom all speak well of, because he could never enter into a competition with themselves. His abilities were of the plainest kind—or rather he had no abilities at all;—his head would not suffer him to do mischief, nor his

[35] I, 170.
[36] II, 257-258. Moderns will recall a similar scene in Mr. Charles Morgan's *The Fountain*.
[37] II, 265.

heart to do good: in short, he was harmless for want of the power to be otherwise.

His wife was much of the same kind, and as *he* was called a *worthy man, she* had gained the appellation of a *good kind of woman,* though neither, that I could ever discover, were possessed of any one good quality, or ever did a generous action; but it was to their insignificancy alone they were indebted, as none ever thought it worth their while to speak ill of them.

Their son was very unlike them in every respect; so much, that I was almost tempted to believe there must be a mistake in his birth that was then undiscovered.

With regard to their daughter. . . . She affected to be a wit, but could never reach higher than a flippant pertness, which at times amounted almost to rudeness; and if it had not been for her very great aptitude at mischief, I should, without hesitation, have pronounced her dull and stupid.

. . . nature had bestowed upon him [the son] all that sprightliness which his sister seemed so desirous to possess. His understanding was more showy than solid, yet was by no means despicable. His temper was a remarkably good one, and regularly the same; he had strong passions, but little sensibility, and was besides wild and inconstant.[38]

With them was another young American who

had a good flow of spirits without running into those extravagances, which was too frequently the case with young Levingstone.—Mr. Nugent's understanding kept him within proper bounds, and he diverted without wearying.[39]

In describing the parents, the author is doing a very competent job of character-writing, and her Rochefoucauldian observations on nonentities, sharply put, show better than average perception. Though, like her contemporaries, she is describing types, they are not abstractions. Nor, however, are they in any way national; she makes no point of "American mediocrity," as well she might. The three young people are real individuals, sketched rather deftly, and with a much more precise vocabulary than usual, but they, again, might just as well be English or

[38] I, 89-92.
[39] I, 93-94.

French or Polish. They happen, as a matter of fact, to be rather like those West Indians who were more favorably characterized in the literature of the day.

If any national character is emerging by now, it is possibly that of the young lady, who appears to have a basis of sprightliness, vivacity, and independence. In *The Liberal American* she is merely "haughty and forbidding," and in *The Young Widow* she has "flippant pertness." In Bage's *Mount Henneth*, however, liveliness appeared at its best. Camitha in that book has somewhat of a counterpart in the Julia Franklin of Mrs. Rowson's *Charlotte Temple,* "a girl of lively disposition, and humane, susceptible heart." Her uncle

had too high an opinion of her prudence, to scrutinize her actions so much as would have been necessary with many young ladies. . . . she was . . . the life of society, and the universal toast.[40]

Her appearance suggests her nature:

. . . her eyes, full, black, and sparkling, darted their intelligent glances through long silken lashes. . . . there was an air of innocent gaiety that played about her countenance, where good humour sat triumphant.[41]

The "American girl" that is coming to life, if she does not prove her creators to be startlingly inventive, at least shows that at times they can drop the lilies and roses of sensibility.

One of the few efforts at direct appraisal of Americans is that in Mrs. Lennox's *Euphemia* (1790), which, besides its despairing notes on the rustics, makes some analysis of New York City society. Mrs. Lennox's travelers expect the worst of America in every way; since they are in that frame of mind, they naturally discover unforeseen graces. Houses, furnishings, and other equipment are elegant, and the inhabitants are civilized and even polished. The governor's wife (it would not be fiction if the characters were satisfied with a lesser social achievement)

[40] Page 92.
[41] Page 95.

is gracious; there is a "succession of visits, balls, and entertainments"; the officers live in a "style suitable to rank," and the governor, although he maintains "proper state and dignity," is affable.[42] The snobbishness, which was essential if the novel was to have any appeal to the pit, does not obscure an unusually favorable estimate. There is not much of American character, of course, but there are at least implications about the nature of a country in the admission that it has created a society acceptable to the English palate.

A different social plane comes under the eye of the author of *Berkeley Hall* (1796). En route to utopia, Dr. Sourby and Tim stop at East Town (Easton), Pennsylvania, where they discover some surprising realities:

Instead of that simplicity of manners, and peaceable demeanour, which they expected to find in those sequestered retreats, they were surrounded with crafty, bold, enterprising *mutineers;* hackneyed in all the stratagems, evasions, and collusions of the old world, and indeed the florid excrescences of its too luxuriant population, and the aggregate of those whom idleness, want of employment, discontent, or an itch of rambling, or worse causes, would not permit to remain in their own country.[43]

Here American character is an outgrowth of the conception of America as a wastebasket for European undesirables. No such influence, however, can account for a unique picture of higher education in America in the same novel. Timothy Tickle had gone to a college in New Jersey—one may speculate whether the author had Princeton in mind—which is described in terms that at times seem plausible, at others grow out of spleen or sheer fantasy. He found

all the honours of the institution, and the favours of the learned body, lavished partially on a few insolent coxcombs; who had nothing to recommend them, but the enormous landed estates of their fathers, or their seats in the provincial assemblies or councils. These mock noblesse

[42] II, 220 ff.
[43] II, 293-294.

had more family pride and aristocratical spirit, than the wealthiest and most ancient of the European nobility.[44]

Here the author's anti-leveling spirit comes to the fore, as it does further in his depiction of Squire Aaron Forester, "the most arrogant of these mimic *lordlings*." Tim alleges that the faculty showed him all kinds of favors, even to the extent of providing him with advance copies of the questions to be asked in public examination.

He was savage in his form, manners, temper, and amusements. He delighted in confining animals of various kinds in his room, which resembled a menagerie, for the sake of torturing and executing them himself in various modes, or to fatten them in the daintiest manner for his voracious palate. He would travel at any time forty or fifty miles, to be entertained with the spectacle of a wretch expiring on the gallows; and has frequently been known to curse the lenity of his government for reprieving a criminal, and robbing him of the pleasure of an execution. He was mean, penurious, and irascible; and, confiding in his acknowledged superiority of influence, insulted all around him with impunity.[45]

This fascinating amalgamation of the epicure and the savage, epitomizing unmercifully a parvenu society, represents the most caustic exercise in the characterization of Americans as little removed from barbarism.

Such a delineation aroused the ire of Mrs. Smith, who in *The Young Philosopher* (1798) satirizes narrowness and bigotry in the person of vulgar and gossipy Mrs. Crewkherne. This beldam, learning that a neighbor, Mr. Armitage, is entertaining in his home an American woman, chooses to put the least favorable construction on the circumstances:

Marry an American girl, who may be a stroller for aught he can tell! nothing can be worse than for great families to demean themselves by low alliances, and especially with folks not born according to the laws of England—and then an American too!—a race that for my part seem not to belong to Christian society somehow, and who, I understand, are

[44] I, 132.
[45] I, 134-135.

no better than atheists; . . . But I am assured that they are excessive bad people, and that it is a dangerous thing to have any communication with them. . . .[46]

Mr. Armitage, it happens, is merely befriending a Mrs. Glenmorris and her daughter Medora, "the little wild Caledonian-American," formed on a primitive mold already discussed. George Delmont is in love with her; his coarse brother, the major, jocosely suggests rivalry but finally assures George that he need not be jealous.

She who has been brought up among the strait-laced, lop-eared puritans of the United States, will look with no predilection on a being like me.[47]

This is an early reference to a subject most easily identified with America in all literatures at all times; the early novels associate puritanism with New England and religion, which will receive attention in the next chapter.

After attacking the bourgeois conception of Americans as wild men and good-for-nothings, Mrs. Smith goes on to establish an ideal American type in *The Solitary Wanderer* (1800). Mr. Warren had seen

a great deal of the world, about which he had now been wandering some years, partly for his own amusement and partly on the public affairs of America, for he was a native of that continent. His mind was the most enlightened I had ever observed. Considering himself as a citizen of the world, and all mankind as his brethren, his whole business seemed to be to counteract the ill effects of all those prejudices which teach them only to tear and destroy each other. Speaking several languages with equal facility, and having made the general forms of government as well as the passions of individuals his study, he was possessed of the means of doing a great deal of good, and no occasion to do it ever escaped him.

A typical opinion of his is the following:

. . . thanks to the spirit of inquiry, the parent of all that is good and laudable, the fetters so long patiently endured are every day falling off!

[46] I, 131-133.
[47] III, 26.

Mankind will hourly become more enlightened, and therefore more free, and priestcraft will soon be as little an instrument of tyranny as witchcraft.[48]

The description unmistakably suggests Franklin, who, we shall see, constantly evoked the admiration of novelists. The definition of an American, established on intellectual rather than romantic or sentimental grounds, is the most flattering we find. Against the urbane cosmopolite we have the romanticized backwoodsman in Luke De Eresby in Helena Wells's *Constantia Neville* (1800), who, flashing forth from an Indian background, hints the Algeresque with the successful study of English law. "When called to the bar, the young American gave the most convincing proofs that he had not mistaken his talent."[49] Eminent as a barrister, he is admired in private life for the freedom and frankness with which he discusses his background and the supposed ignorance of his parents. But, like Bage's Hermsprong, whom he resembles, he turns out to be no American at all.[50]

Returning to the war and starting off in another direction, we find other characterizations which, like these which have appeared to be largely emanations of current conventions, extend to the American scene another tradition—the picaresque. There is an example of this in *The Adventures of Anthony Varnish* (1786); Anthony, in the course of his travels,

joins a begging soldier and his doxy. The former, with many oaths and digressions, tells how he fought at Bunker Hill and found his wife in Boston, as clever a girl as ever pillaged a battlefield. Among other tricks, he feigns the falling sickness with soap under his tongue.[51]

A like scheme appears in Richard Sickelmore's *Mary Jane* (1800). At Brighton several of the principal characters give alms to a beggar who thus appeals to them:

I am American born . . . and have no legal claim on the buildings

48 I, 186-187.
49 III, 22.
50 III, 320-321.
51 Chandler, *The Literature of Roguery*, II, 334.

362

constructed and appropriated for the reception of the poor in this island, or you had not seen me in this distressed situation.[52]

The suppliant is a bent and withered old man. Later in the day our charitable party sees another group of vacationers being panhandled by a maimed sailor, who addresses them thus: "I am American born . . . and have no legal claim. . . ." Although the rest of the speech is identical with that previously heard, the speaker, who is no longer tremulous, looks fifty years younger. When he sees his former dupes, his crippled leg comes to life, and he makes off at top speed. Radmill, the principal philanthropist, remarks, "Rot it, may I never die, if I once suspected the old rascal of an American was an impostor."[53] If the impostor was not actually an American, he was thought to be so, and it is clear that an American could be thought of not only as gouger of eyes but also as cozener.

Of course the best picaresque hero was Jonathan Corncob, whose *Adventures* shed enough illumination on acceptable ideas of America to merit some quotation. Jonathan was the son of

an excellent woman: she bred like a rabbit; scolded all day like a cat in love; and snored all night as loud as the foreman of a jury on a tedious trial.[54]

His father was

troubled with the green sickness ever since a disappointment in love, he met with at the age of two and twenty.[55]

His aunt, who was "a plague to every body in the house," met her death one day when she was arguing with Jonathan's father about her age. She shouted "forty-eight" and Corncob shouted "fifty-two" alternately until she, "with a determination of having the *last word,* called forty-eight, and expired."

At this time I was only seven years old, and when I heard the news, I

52 I, 55.
53 I, 63.
54 Page 8.
55 Page 10.

came jumping and laughing into the room, "Old Bathsheba is dead,"
said I *ha! ha! ha!*

Whereupon his mother beat him soundly,

though I did not very well understand why I was obliged to cry at the
death of a person, whom every body in the house had wished dead a
thousand times a day.[56]

Jonathan recounts his education, designed to make him useful
in his father's shop,

or as it is called in New England, his *store,* for he was not only farmer,
but merchant, and sold butter, cheese, spike-nails, rye meal, shuttle-
cocks, New-England rum, hartshorn shavings, broad cloth, gunpowder,
and yellow basilicon. Besides the inferior parts of education, such as
reading, writing, and arithmetick, I studied latin, and at the end of
seven years made very tolerable nonsense verses. I was considered, in
Massachusset's [*sic*] Bay, as a prodigy of learning, and was not less
distinguished for my address in all the fashionable exercises and amusements of that country. I excelled in walking in snow shoes, driving a
sled, shooting squirrels, and bobbing for eels; but of all my amusements none had such charms for me as *bundling.*[57]

Jonathan's proficiency in bundling leads his associate in the art,
Desire Slawbuck, into difficulties; the town council meets and
sentences Jonathan to marriage; and he, procuring funds by
selling some of his father's rum to British soldiers, leaves town
in haste, with the British forces in New York as his objective.
After numerous adventures, he establishes himself in New York
and proceeds to seduce his landlady's daughter, Diana Done-
well, a venture which makes it necessary for him to have the
services of Dr. Bullock, a quack. Bullock resembles the in-
efficient medico who later appears in Mrs. Parsons' *Voluntary
Exile;* apparently America was considered a likely place in
which to find professional incompetence. After some of Bullock's treatment, Jonathan complains,

[56] Pp. 13-14.
[57] Pp. 18-19. The anticipation of bundling accentuated Frederick's advance
enthusiasm for America in Walker's *Vagabond.*

I had almost all the symptoms of the present Columbus made to Europe: such as gonorrhea, phymosis, paraphymosis, bubo, fistula in ano; carnositates in uretere, nodi, tophi, gummata, corona veneris, caries ossium, &c. I thought it high time to change my surgeon, and had the good fortune to recover tolerable health, after a long course of frictions, injections, fumigations, scarifications, purgations, salivations, and the like.[58]

Later in New York a drunken revel leads Jonathan into the arms of his old fellow-bundler, Desire Slawbuck, now married to a Scotch officer named Seeclear, but no more inhibited than before. Jonathan is soon in a brawl with the captain,

and . . . as he was a strong powerful fellow, a Scotchman, and a little brutal, he knocked me down. This was the most critical situation I ever found myself in in my life; nobody but little Jeptha [Jonathan's young brother] was in the room, and if I returned the blow, I was sure of getting soundly pummelled to no purpose—on the other hand, if I did not resent the injury on the spot, I was convinced that my character for courage would be totally lost. In this perplexing business I fortunately found an expedient, which insured my person and reputation. As a man is supposed to be blinded by rage, I pretended to mistake my little brother Jeptha for my antagonist; I fell upon him, knocked him down, and continued threshing him in good earnest, and abusing him for an overgrown Scotch rascal, till his cries brought half the family from the next room: I then discovered my mistake, and as soon as I found myself held by the arms, wanted to attack the captain. . . .[59]

Jonathan's whole family, obviously, are in town—his father Habakkuk, his mother Charity, his brothers Zedekias, Hannaniah, Melchisedeck, and Jeptha, and his sisters Supply and Increase, names clearly satirizing New England nomenclature. Habakkuk's flight to New York has been caused by the furore aroused by his having passed a forged $100 bill, which was of course not his work, since he could not write. Jonathan's sister tells him that he has grown handsome.

"Handsome is that handsome does," said my good old mother Mrs.

[58] Pp. 57-58.
[59] Pp. 112-113.

Charity. This I suppose was meant as a little hint of my depredations in the *store*.[60]

Jonathan, however, does not possess all the beauty in the family.

As my youngest sister was extremely pretty, I was soon after this affair [with Seeclear] appointed acting purser of a frigate going to Barbadoes.[61]

Then follow the West-Indian adventures, chiefly significant in that Jonathan's apparently sincere sympathy with the slaves gives him momentarily a greater depth of character than that of the average picaresque hero. Little more is learned about him in subsequent escapades, which end with his landing in England and arguing, by way of finale, that more truth can be found in novels than in any other kind of reading. Here, of course, the truth is largely that of the picaresque tradition. Still, a genuine effort is made to place Jonathan in an American background, the specific details of which suggest that the author had more than a literary acquaintanceship with his scene. If Jonathan makes no major contribution to the conception of an American type, he is not totally un-American; his shrewdness is consistent with a New England character that appears also in *Berkeley Hall* and later fiction. And the outstanding characteristic of his whole family is hypocrisy, which, justly or unjustly, has been prominent in many a portrait of Uncle Sam.

With *Jonathan Corncob* go several other novels not very favorably disposed to Americans. When the subject of innkeepers comes up, Imlay, of course, is laudatory, extolling their hospitality;[62] but *Helena* (1790) contrasts the elegant English innkeepers with their inferiors in America.[63] Mrs. Smith's *Ethelinde* (1789) imputes graspingness to an American ship-captain. Charles Montgomery, the hero, was shipwrecked on the Isle of Bourbon and finally got back to England by way of America

---

60 Page 105.
61 Page 115.
62 *Emigrants*, I, 26 ff.
63 I, 97-98.

on an American ship. When he first bargained for passage, he found that

the master, who was a species of animal I had never seen before, would not receive me without money, of which, though I had saved my purse, I had now very little left. I was obliged, therefore, to agree to work for my passage; and in that situation I arrived at Boston, after a long voyage, in which I suffered some fatigue and hardship. . . .[64]

Then there are a number of comments on the American attitude to slavery. *The Fashionable Tell-Tale* (1778) recounts the surprise of an American when Sir William Gooch returned the salute of a negro, saying, "I cannot suffer a man of his condition, to exceed me in good manners."[65] Mrs. Smith's *Wanderings of Warwick* (1794) makes a reference to negro-beatings:

. . . the continental Americans, like those of the West Indies, consider such things as mere matters of course—though it is said that they are less severe in their treatment of that unhappy race of people.[66]

*Berkeley Hall* (1796) does the subject vigorously and draws inferences about American character. The sight of a "haughty Carolina planter" whipping a negro and otherwise acting imperiously produces this observation:

These petty great men in this country, you must have observed, are prouder bashaws and tyrants than any of the noblesse in Europe. He eyed us all with a look of ineffable contempt; and as we proceeded in our passage, frequently made the captain alter his course, at his pleasure.[67]

A Mr. Lumeire argues for a hereditary nobility because

those who have been longest acquainted with power certainly use it with most moderation. It is observable that the *negro-drivers* are infinitely more oppressive to their fellows than any others; and a mush-

[64] V, 314.
[65] I, 103. Gooch was Lieutenant Governor of Virginia, 1726-1737 (Beatson, *Political Index,* III, 464).
[66] Page 56. Cf. Mesick, *op. cit.,* pp. 309-310.
[67] I, 52.

room planter, or *mandamus* counsellor, has more pride and insolence than the first peer in Britain.[68]

The arrogance of newborn power is exemplified in a Colonel Beekman, who, in proposing marriage to a girl,

was so self-important from his immense wealth, and held in such high veneration for it by his associates, that he had no conception that the honour of his hand could be refused in an American colony.[69]

The strictures on the American upper class are in line with the author's already quoted account of higher education. Just or unjust, what he says is highly interesting because of the rare interpretation of character with reference to the formative influences of a young country without traditions.

Finally, there are some relevant notes on language. Pye's *Democrat* (1795) says of Jean Le Noir, a Frenchman, that

his long and early residence in America had made him so perfect a master of the English language, that even by his pronunciation he could hardly be distinguished from a native.[70]

Unfortunately it is far from clear whether Pye had the "American language" in mind and whether he distinguished between American and British English. Such a distinction, however, is plainly made in *Jonathan Corncob,* which presents the only Americanisms and the only phonetic spellings of American pronunciation that I have come across. Among the former are "blaze away," which appears three times,[71] and "I snore" or "I snort,"[72] both obviously so used as to indicate that they were transatlantic peculiarities. Still clearer is the intention of eccentric orthography in such phrases as *"blaaze away like daavils"*[73] and "get *aloong,* let me *alo-one."*[74] The author's use of italics

[68] II, 74.
[69] II, 90.
[70] I, 14.
[71] Pp. 16, 30, 111.
[72] Pp. 30, 106.
[73] Page 31.
[74] Page 52.

makes doubly sure that the reader will notice what the Americans are doing with the language. The word *daavils* apparently shows a qualitative change. Otherwise, *Jonathan Corncob* is making among the earliest notes on what is today called the "Yankee drawl." The differences in speech imply the existence of a different nation with a character of its own, and, since the author, a satirist rather than a scientist, was presenting the linguistic variations as ludicrous, it follows that Americans were conceived of as at least mildly uncouth and outlandish.

The label *American* has been attached to a conglomeration of diverse characteristics of which it is impossible to make a satisfactory synthesis. The effort to fuse the ingredients, however, and to establish a recognizable composite can be simplified by the elimination of much that is without real import. One can safely discount the barbarism attributed to Americans in such war stories as *The School for Fathers* and *Helena*, not to mention the muddled antipathy which Mrs. Mackenzie shows in *Slavery;* nor is there a serious contribution in the purely picaresque elements in *Anthony Varnish* and *Jonathan Corncob*. Here is largely typical fiction material, as there is in the standardized portraits of human excellence and evil which flourish in *Francis the Philanthropist* and *The Liberal American*. All these show is that good and bad, pleasant and unpleasant people, as conventionally conceived, flourished on both sides of the Atlantic. *The Young Widow* makes a satisfying transformation of types into individuals, but the author fails to convince the reader that they are of any particular nationality. Is there, then, any sound conception of American character?

Not all the novelists are technically adolescent, and there are a few notes of authenticity. The war episodes in *Wanderings of Warwick*, for instance, contrast the unfavorable anterior ideas about Americans with their actual tolerableness. *Euphemia*, likewise proceeding by contrasts, praises the urbanity of New York society. *Mount Henneth, The Young Widow,* and *Charlotte Temple* agree on a certain vivacity and inde-

369

pendence in young ladies, though none of them has a very strong air of reality. The most flattering portrait of an American is that of the Franklin-like cosmopolite in *The Solitary Wanderer.*

On the other hand, from the traditional rogueries of *Jonathan Corncob* emerge some notes on New Englanders which are more than conventionalities. The speech indicates provincialism; various episodes signify shrewdness and hypocrisy, the same characteristics possessed by the New Englanders in *Berkeley Hall. Ethelinde* presents a grasping American captain. *Jonathan Corncob* and *The Voluntary Exile* both cite examples of professional incompetence. Several novels comment on the crudeness of American innkeepers, several others on callous acceptance of slavery. Although *The Vagabond* and *Berkeley Hall* are doctrinaire in conservatism, their strictures on American bumptiousness cannot be entirely discounted. The latter book especially, despite its bias, impresses one with a certain reasonableness and mature intelligence; its censure of favoritism in higher education and of crudity in the new "aristocracy" is moderately convincing.

The defense and the prosecution are very close to a deadlock, and the case is such that one can hardly count points and reach a decision by a convenient mathematics. The final impression created by this section as a whole is that enthusiasm about Americans is fairly well restrained and that here as in few other aspects of the treatment of America is there a fairly consistent tendency to judge adversely. If one combines what is said here with all the shudders about a "wild" and "desolate" America, one finds, in a rather indecisive, inchoate fashion, the makings of the pioneer tradition later to become platitudinous. Its sins are crudity and bumptiousness; its virtues, those of the "diamond in the rough." But to achieve this view, one has to use fairly strong magnifying glasses on the meaningful interlinear spaces. A conclusion which requires much less inference is that the whole attitude to American character involves hardly a trace of vapid idealization, for the romantic imagination which dreamed a Golden Age or a republican utopia simply does not function here. Insofar as there is a genuine effort to interpret the new nation, it is fundamentally realistic; the approximate balance of approval and disapproval shows the absence of any predominant illusions or disillusionment which would be an obstacle against valid interpretations. And the rather considerable skepticism, though from the viewpoint of absolute values it may be too gimlet-eyed, is quite significant in its anticipation of the unhesitatingly analytical attitude of later generations.

The relation of the war to the struggles toward a conception of American character is twofold. In the first place, and rather superficially, the search for definitions grows out of war stories in eleven of the twenty-three novels here quoted. A more fundamental matter is that all but one of these novels were written after 1781, that is, after the war. It is of course logical enough that the first efforts to analyze American character, however fumbling and immature they may be, come after the Revolution. Before it, strictly speaking, there was no America; there was only a vast amount of land which was really a branch of England. The war crystallized an amorphous population into a political entity, and, once conceived of as a nation in itself, America would by the nature of things have a character of its own.

### iii

Where did novelists find the prototypes for their Americans? Except Mrs. Brooke and Mrs. Lennox, who had been abroad, they may seem to have been enjoying an unrestrained exercise of the imagination, and no doubt many did extract their impressions from thin air. But any writer in search of an American would not have had to travel three thousand miles, for not all Americans were stay-at-homes. From the West to the East there was traveling a constant stream of students, artists, diplomats, "practical tourists," and "philanthropic travelers."[75] Further,

[75] Spiller's *The American in England* discusses these types in successive chapters.

copious secondhand information could have been, and no doubt was, secured from thousands of returned soldiers. The war, indeed, was often thought of in personal terms, and in many a novel we have found the king, his ministers, and his generals Cornwallis, Howe, and Burgoyne.[76]

The remaining problem is to see what the novel did with personalities on the American side, which, in the broadest sense, included not only Americans but also radical Englishmen such as Paine, Price, and Priestley. Paine, who evoked many a storm in England,[77] was naturally called to task by several novelists who included among their duties the defense of the old order. The most interesting of these is Ann Thomas, whose *Adolphus de Biron* (1794) had this to say:

Foremost in this daring Attempt [the French Revolution] is Thomas Paine, who began his political Career by publishing *Common Sense,* a Book which is as much a Libel on the Title it assumes, as his *Rights of Man* is on the Constitution of his Country. It was this seditious and inflammatory Book, which incited our Fellow-subjects in America to shake off their constitutional Dependence on the Parent State, and to dismember the British Empire.[78]

From here Miss Thomas launches into a long diatribe against his revolutionary activities and his "diabolical Publications." The pious Hannah More devotes a story, "The History of Mr. Fantom, the New-Fashioned Philosopher, And His Man William," to the destruction of Paine and other liberals.[79] *The*

---

[76] None of these stimulated fiction as did Wolfe, who appeared in *A Collection of Scarce, Curious and Valuable Pieces, Both in Verse and Prose* (Edinburgh, 1773), pp. 18 ff.; *Memoirs of an Unfortunate Queen* (1776), pp. 246-247; Pratt, *Pupil of Pleasure* (1776), II, 62; Rev. Everhard Ryan, *Reliques of Genius* (1777), pp. 22-23; Sir Herbert Croft, *Love and Madness* (1780), pp. 57 ff.; *Adventures of a Hackney Coach* (1781), pp. 11-13; *Argus* (1789), I, 191; *The Bastile* (1789), II, 113; Scott, *Helena* (1790), II, 8; Beckford, *Modern Novel Writing* (1796), II, 136; Harriet and Sophia Lee, *Canterbury Tales* (1799), III, 246 ff.

[77] See Cairns, *British Criticisms of American Writings 1783-1815,* pp. 56 ff.; Thompson, *A Scottish Man of Feeling,* pp. 257-258.

[78] II, 66. The topic continues to II, 79.

[79] *Cheap Repository Tracts,* II, 5 ff.

*Neighbourhood* (1800) sneers at Young Callico, who had learned, according to Dr. Singleton,

> to abuse the laws and constitution with all the petulance of Tom Payne, or to cavil at them with the flippant sophistry of the author of 'Political Justice:' . . . and his religious notions have since improved by the writings of Dr. P——y, and he is become a *philosophical necessitudinarian.*[80]

The defense is shocked into action, it is worth noting, less by the American than by the French Revolution.[81]

Mrs. Smith's *Banished Man* (1794) tells the story of the acquisition of a country place, formerly the property of a rich button manufacturer, by a wealthy Nabob just back from India. The redecoration gives a good clue to the associations in the minds of different social classes:

> Franklin and his round-heads were swept away for ever. Instead of pictures of Price and Priestly, the aspiring Pagoda was represented on the painted sattin that covered the walls. . . .[82]

Lady Ellesmere, of a neighboring estate, disliked the innovation because of the enviable grandeur, and its predecessors because of their social inadequacy:

> . . . the bust of Franklin, and the prints of Priestly and of Price . . . could not, in point of respectability, be compared with all the noble personages who had borne for three centuries the name of Ellesmere.[83]

Franklin and Washington monopolized the interest in individual Americans. There is one reference to Arnold—in Mrs. Parsons' *Voluntary Exile* (1795), which introduces a character whose name was Arnold, (but not related to the General of that name,

[80] II, 214-215.

[81] Edward Sayer's *Lindor and Adelaide* (1791) has this informative subtitle: "A Moral Tale. In which are Exhibited the Effects of the late French Revolution on the Peasantry of France. By the Author of 'Observations on Doctor Price's Revolution Sermon.' "

[82] IV, 38-39.

[83] IV, 40.

whose subsequent conduct was deservedly despised by both friends and foes).[84]

Novels, however, give almost no attention to American military figures except Washington, who, in England, was "spoken of with respect, and often with admiration";[85] who aroused enthusiasm in Germany;[86] and who even "became the perfect copy of virtue, an example of the way man developed away from civilization."[87] In contrast with this primitivistic view is a more realistic analysis by Godwin, who begs to doubt whether Washington's career was entirely free from a "personal motive."[88]

In the novel, it is neither primitivists nor psychologists, but sentimentalists, who get hold of Washington. Before presenting their incongruous views, however, we may note several fairly straightforward references. Even the pro-English *American Wanderer* (1783) can remark, with reference to the hillside location of a monastery, "General Washington exhibits not more skill in chusing his ground."[89] And the widespread interest in Washington is evidenced by the introduction of a Frenchman with great "curiosity relative to General Washington, the Congress, &c."[90] Washington receives incidental praise in a passage in *Reveries of the Heart* (1781):

> After the ladies were gone, I viewed the room; but of this, as clumsy a large solid piece of architecture as ever Vanburgh designed, I shall give you no description. To descend to it, after mentioning its furniture would be in the words of my friend, as great a fall as after Franklin to mention a North; or after Washington a Germaine.[91]

Another passage, very realistic, makes the point that the English are less liable to defeat by Washington, able as he is, than by "Generals mountain, river, forest, desert, climate, fever, sickness,

[84] IV, 210.
[85] Cairns, *British Criticisms 1783-1815*, p. 41.
[86] Weber, *America in Imaginative German Literature*, pp. 3, 27, 69.
[87] Brinton, *Political Ideas of the English Romanticists*, p. 26.
[88] *Enquirer*, pp. 313-314.
[89] Page 164.
[90] Page 175.
[91] I, 88.

famine, and tempest."[92] From such scientific observations we cross worlds to the amazing rhapsodies of Pratt, who, unembarrassed by the slightest sense of the ridiculous, turns Washington into a man of sensibility. When Emma, who, in *Emma Corbett* (1780), has been pursuing her lover, a British soldier, is captured, together with her guardian, Raymond, by the Americans, Raymond tells Washington about the purpose of Emma's trip to America:

> The General heard the story of her love as I related it. I concealed no part from him. . . . I brought the narrative down to the moment of reciting it. The soldier's cheek was not without the graceful dignity of a tear. He wept.
>
> Sacred, said he, be the rights of hospitality! I am not at war with the *affections*. Ever privileged be their *emotions*. I feel them all. The beauteous prisoner is at liberty, Sir Robert, to go where she pleases. I shall appoint persons to attend her, who may prevent all interruptions and insult, but *you*, methinks, Sir Robert, should continue to follow her fortunes as a *friend,*—you are *both* free.[93]

What Pratt is doing is what most of his fellow-scribblers do: honoring a character, not by discovering what is admirable in him, but by bestowing upon him, without regard to plausibility or appropriateness, such characteristics as the temperament and prejudices of the writer demand. This is highest praise. The unconscious process is this: "I prefer weeping; you are an admirable person; therefore you weep." Mrs. Parsons' mind, as exhibited in *The Voluntary Exile* (1795), works in about the same way, except that here Washington is made to share, not her tears, but her profound respect for her hero. In fact, any American could prove his essential acceptableness by granting the hero an interview for which there was no reason at all and in that interview showing exaggerated esteem for the rather patronizing and fatuously complacent young Englishman. Here, Biddulph

[92] I, 176-177.
[93] III, 69-70.

was one evening invited to the General's tent, if it could be called such, being very little superior to the common huts erected for the troops. . . . The General received him with a polite affability that banished reserve. . . . The conversation was free and unreserved, without at all reverting to political subjects, or any thing that could offend the feelings of an Englishman.

Biddulph was extremely sensible of this delicacy, and, charmed with the amiable manners of Washington, he remarked . . . the involuntary effusions of love and confidence mingled with admiration [of the soldiers]. He returned to his quarters highly gratified with beholding a man so generally esteemed, even by those whose principles differed from his own, and who reprobated the cause in which he was engaged.[94]

On another occasion Washington is made to demonstrate a rather windy and self-conscious humanitarianism. When he was evacuating Philadelphia, he was advised to destroy it.

He shuddered at the proposal.—"What! cried he! (indignantly) would you have me *ruin my friends*, that I may injure my enemies? No, the English are generous; I confide in the honour and humanity of their General. The day of triumph is now with them—shortly it may be ours; and when I enter this city again, it shall be to receive the *congratulations* of the inhabitants, unmixed with reproaches for having destroyed their property myself, or having provoked the enemy to make reprisals to the ruin of individuals."[95]

Mrs. Parsons is most effective in establishing the regard in which Washington was held by his soldiers. At Brandywine

they fought to distinguish themselves under the eye of a Washington, and to deserve his approbation, they fought like lions with the greatest intrepidity.[96]

At Valley Forge

the attachment to their General, which pervaded throughout the whole American camp, evinced . . . unshaken determination to bear with every inconvenience, and struggle through every difficulty under his command, whom they looked up to as a father and a preserver. . . .[97]

Even a Quaker

[94] III, 134-135.
[95] II, 165.
[96] II, 163.
[97] III, 127.

had quitted . . . the olive-branch which distinguishes his sect, and repaired to the Jerseys, that he might have the glory to command under General Washington.[98]

Whatever they made of him, the novelists assuredly withheld no praise.

Though Franklin had less of the dramatic appeal of the soldier, he received even more attention than the commander-in-chief. By the nature of things he was better known in Europe, and his vogue, both as personality and as writer, was great in England, Germany, and France.[99] His scientific work stirred the imagination; not only is he mentioned frequently in Erasmus Darwin's *Botanic Garden* but also in still more minor poetry.[100] On February 1, 1780, Mackenzie's *Mirror* quoted a "Professor" as saying:

What a pity it is, that the illustrious Dr. *Franklin*, the discoverer of electricity, and the author of so many inventions in the sciences, should descend from the sublime heights of philosophy, to employ his time and study in directing the trifling and unimportant contentions of nations![101]

From his life, too, are drawn suitable conclusions for such a didactic work as Dr. Thomas Percival's *A Father's Instructions to His Children*,[102] written during the '70's.

We have already had two references to Franklin in novels, one in *Reveries of the Heart* (1781), the author of which says that to mention North after Franklin is anti-climactic; the other in Mrs. Smith's *Banished Man* (1794), in which Franklin's bust is equally revered with the pictures of Price and Priestley. In this story the Ellesmeres are quite irked by a Presbyterian neighbor who had got rich on buttons. He had built a large house,

[98] III, 129-130.

[99] See Cairns, *op. cit.*, pp. 53 ff.; Weber, *op. cit.*, pp. 2-4; Mantz, *French Criticism of American Literature*, pp. 5 ff.

[100] See, for instance, Peter Pindar [John Wolcot], *Works* (1794), II, 119 ff.; Thomas Mathias, *Pursuits of Literature*, p. 220.

[101] II, 88. Cf. Mackenzie's *Lounger*, I, 270 ff.

[102] (Dublin, 1790), pp. 30, 91-92, 94, 240-242.

placed a bust of Franklin in his vestibule; (a vestibule in the house of a mechanic!) had Ludlow among his books, quoted Milton to his companions and drank to the rights of man.[103]

This array of idols was evidently considered typical of bourgeois liberalism. Usually Franklin is thought of as a man of science, as in *The Philosophical Quixote* (1782), which tells how the hero Wilkins evolved a scheme to keep dry in the rain by having himself charged, the theory being that all raindrops are positively or negatively charged and hence can be repelled by a body similarly charged. His enemies deride him, but his friends defend the experiment warmly, "justifying its likelihood by a late similar one of the illustrious Dr. Franklin."[104] The name is talismanic. One of the characters in Mrs. Lennox's *Euphemia* (1790) writes,

> I am to set out in a few days for Philadelphia. . . . I shall then be able to give you some account of that celebrated city; whose founder, in my opinion, is not much inferior to Solon, or any of the wise lawgivers of antiquity.[105]

Disraeli's *Flim-Flams* (1797) makes two references to Franklin.

> To point out some beautiful instances of what is called popular philoso-phy. FRANKLIN, (an experimentalist of the obsolete school,) exulted in drawing down *fire from heaven;* my Uncle prided himself in *sending the smoke there,* by curing chimnies.[106]

Then Franklin enters incidentally into an attack on Godwin:

> We find in "POLITICAL JUSTICE" (two strangely-coupled words!) this memorable observation:
> "FRANKLIN, a man habitually conversant with the system of the external universe, and *by no means propense to extravagant specula-tions,* conjectured that MIND will one day become omnipotent over MATTER. In *whatever sense* HE understood this expression, WE *are certainly at liberty to apply it in the sense* WE THINK PROPER."

103 IV, 37-38.
104 II, 33-34.
105 IV, 41.
106 I, 76-77.

In plainer English, Franklin made use of a certain expression, which ought to be understood in an obvious sense, because he never indulged extravagant ideas.—But we, in using his *own expression,* are not to attend to his *own meaning*—but give it *any signification* we may take a fancy to![107]

Here is a keener critical sense than we usually come across. Less abstract are several references by Miss Edgeworth. Intoxication plus a hazy memory of Franklin almost results in the drowning of Clarence Hervey in *Belinda:*

. . . and instantly Hervey, who had in his confused head some recollection of an essay of Dr. Franklin's on swimming, by which he fancied that he could ensure at once his safety and his fame, threw off his coat and jumped into the river—luckily he was not in his boots.[108]

Two of the *Moral Tales* (1801) pay more positive tribute to the American. The hero of "Forester" changes from enthusiasm for the primitive to an acceptance of civilization by reading the life of Franklin and by reflecting upon Franklin's patience in difficult circumstances.[109] As preparation for the cleaning of chimneys, Howard in "The Good Aunt" buys a copy of Franklin's essay and studies it. Laughed at for his research by M. Supine, a pedant, he points out the name of the author, which his critic had not seen. Then Supine changes his tone: ". . . to be sure I must bow down to *that.*"[110]

Bowing down characterized nearly everyone who mentioned Franklin. Washington, who was more distant and less striking, evoked only slightly less veneration. The chief point to be made is that the war did not inspire hostility to Americans, especially those who were conspicuous in the American victory; the personal virtues shone through whatever fog of antipathy might have influenced the English view. Only in Godwin's comment, which lies outside of fiction, is there a trace of postwar skepticism which appears in relation to other American

[107] I, 152 note. Cf. Mathias, *Pursuits of Literature,* p. 220.
[108] *Tales and Novels* (New York, 1836), XI, 87.
[109] *Ibid.,* II, 68-71.
[110] *Ibid.,* II, 183.

matters. Here, however, it is not a case of illusions which needed to be broken down, but of matters of fact to be perceived, facts of human abilities and achievements. The war appears in no way to have effected that distortion of view which is an expected concomitant of armed hostilities. Instead of influence, there was absence of influence. The situation is the same that we saw in discussing the English attitude to and criticism of the war, their admiration for American spirit, and their humanitarian sympathy for the "oppressed."

The war, of course, made Washington; it certainly did not un-make Franklin. While one writer regretted his concern in petty politics, the others treated him exclusively as a thinker, practical, scientific, and moral. The admiration for both is in contrast with the uncertainty about Americans in the mass, perhaps because one could not treat personages of distinguished accomplishments with the suspicion reserved for types. In the attitude to both, however, there is observable the effort to get at truth. Again the novel-world is attempting to identify itself with the actual world.

# CHAPTER XII

## AMERICAN INSTITUTIONS

i

The American Revolution, we have been reiterating, was not only of interest to novelists in itself, but it also changed the geographical and political map which perennially illustrated fiction; the war created a new nation which inspired study and criticism. Hence its cardinal position, which we assumed at the outset. While on the one hand the new world excited greater interest after 1783, on the other hand it became less a dumping ground, less a fertile soil for gold diggers, less a dreamworld for theorists. The dreamworld and the dumping ground, however, false or true, were simply versions of a depersonalized America, a mere formless continent, a vast territory without specific social or political systems. What was going on was imaginative transformations of raw material.

In discussing English interpretations of American character, however, we left behind the country and the land in itself and advanced to the human values developed in America. We now go a step further to examine the society composed by the individuals, or, more specifically, the institutions through which the people collectively expressed their faiths and their convictions. The human establishments did not have the same latitude of speculative possibilities as the country per se because in them there was already definiteness of form, if not actual rigidity. They had neither the vastness nor the virginity which could transform them, like the country in which they flourished, into gods or monsters according to the predilections of the observer; they partook too much of the nature of matters of fact. That is not to say that matters of fact could be presented only in an uncritical monotone, for, in truth, there is palpable difference of opinion about American institutions. Republicanism, we have already seen, won both plaudits and hisses.

Republicanism, the political principles and machinery of the United States, is one of the subjects to be examined here, since novelists had a great deal to say about the new style of government and its implications. They were scarcely less backward in dogmatizing about a related matter—religious democracy, which, already mentioned, will also have a section of this chapter. Other institutions were treated less fully. The paragraphs on college life in *Berkeley Hall* are the extent of the criticism of higher education. The character of Americans, by no means passionately admired, suffered somewhat in English opinion because of their tolerance of slavery, which received from prose fiction the attention which one might expect in the years of intensifying abolitionism.

ii

Slavery can be dealt with rather cursorily here, both because the stories in question were concerned largely with a West-Indian locale, and because another work discusses completely the literary treatment of slavery.[1] What is especially interesting from the viewpoint of the present study is that the attack on slavery first becomes strong in the 1780's, as if the reforming energies evoked by the war and the humanitarianism manifested in discussion of it here combined for the first time in an effective crusade. In the '80's the slave trade began to exact considerable attention from Parliament;[2] Klingberg entitles a chapter, "The Attack on the Slave Trade, 1783-1793. Aggressive Humanitarianism."[3] The stress on political liberty after 1776 must have stimulated a demand for another kind of independence. If the correspondence in dates is an accident, at least that accident

[1] Dr. F. Wylie Sypher, *The Anti-Slavery Movement to 1800 in English Literature* (Thesis, Harvard University, 1937).
[2] See *Parliamentary History*, XXIII ff.
[3] *The Anti-Slavery Movement in England*, p. 59.

happens more than once. Crèvecoeur, glorifying America in 1782, included a horrified description of slavery,[4] and half of the *Gentleman's* review of his book was devoted to quoting such a passage.[5] In 1784 Richard Price, continuing in his enthusiasm for American activities, termed the slave trade "shocking to humanity, cruel, wicked, and diabolical."[6] In 1792 Imlay likewise mingled extravagant praise of America with an attack on slavery.[7] Early travelers after the war noted the anomaly of slavery in the land of the free.[8]

Any thesis that one may want to press about the influence of war-time on peace-time humanitarianism gains some support from the fact that before and during the war, novels dealt with slavery only sporadically, whereas afterward the subject became a frequent one.[9] Ignoring the large number of stories about slavery in the West Indies, which are outside our province, we find that nearly all of the few referring to slavery on the continent were written after 1780. Unfavorable notes on American character as shown in relations with negroes were made, we have seen, in *The Fashionable Tell-Tale* (1778), Mrs. Smith's *Wanderings of Warwick* (1794), and *Berkeley Hall* (1796). Three books in the '80's deal with the negro. Most interesting is Sir Herbert Croft's *Love and Madness* (1780), a long section of which is a piece of literary research that in modern university parlance would be entitled "The Influence of *The Town and Country Magazine* on William Chatterton from January, 1769, to His Death." Examining the material that Chatterton had probably read, Croft recoils with the same horror that he at-

---

[4] *Letters from an American Farmer* (New ed., 1783), pp. 216 ff.

[5] LII (1782), 440-441.

[6] *Observations on the Importance of the American Revolution*, p. 83.

[7] *Topographical Description*, pp. 221-231.

[8] Mesick, *op. cit.*, pp. 122 ff.

[9] Miss Tompkins remarks that American scenes in the novels "are mostly connected with the war or with slavery" (p. 184). There are, as a matter of fact, many episodes connected with neither. For a discussion of the climax of the whole literary movement in the '80's see Dr. Sypher's Chapter 5, "Full Attack, 1787-1789," *op. cit.*, pp. 563-664.

tributes to the "genius of Rowley" on finding an article in the issue of July, 1769, p. 389 (correctly annotated!), citing the number of slaves shipped from Africa to the various European countries and America.[10] Bage's *Mount Henneth* (1781) is less exclamatory; it drily describes how an ex-soldier lost his job on an American tobacco plantation because, having only one arm, he could not whip the slaves satisfactorily.[11] In Moore's *Zeluco* (1786), which deals at length with slavery in the West Indies, a doctor makes a relevant comment:

Let the proprietors of estates in America and the West India islands consider how far their treatment of the negroes is agreeable to his [Christ's] doctrine and conduct. . . .[12]

In the '90's Mrs. Lennox's *Euphemia* (1790) enters the scene with a terrifying report that the slaves in New York are bent on rebellion.[13] Usually faithful to fact, Mrs. Lennox is here probably enjoying the luxury of a thrill without regard to fact. The same thrill is sought in a different way by Mrs. Mackenzie's *Slavery* (1792), which sentimentalizes the preternaturally noble Zimza out of all recognition. As this paragon is a West-Indian product, America enters only adventitiously through his connection with General St. Leger, who had been in the Revolution. The raised eyebrows that one expects appear most clearly in Walker's *Vagabond* (1799), in which one Adams, who wants to "cut up popery root and branch," is thus answered by Master Ketchup, the tradesman:

So you would establish liberty by religious prosecution? That would be like the Americans fighting for freedom with one hand, and rattling the whip over their slaves with the other.[14]

Mrs. Smith's *Solitary Wanderer* (1800) tells of a West Indian who on his death left behind many writings

10 Page 224.
11 Page 191.
12 Page 87.
13 III, 195.
14 Page 46.

on the condition of the Africans and their state of slavery in the American colonies.[15]

The only full-length treatment of slavery is that of *Berkeley Hall* (1796), which, exemplifying the usual method of the sentimental novel, gives a watery picture of the incredibly harmonious relationship between whites who are invariably kind and sympathetic and blacks who therefore ask only to die for their masters. As that nonpareil in servitude, Sancho, puts it,

I ask no other *liberty*, than that of *choosing* whom I may serve. I shall be a slave indeed, if I am not to be permitted to attend on and live with old and young massa.[16]

In view of this defense and of the small number of attacks on slavery on the mainland, we have inadequate evidence here of the actual movement in fiction. More to the point, however, is the rise of activity after the war, a fact which leads one to suspect a carry-over of the humanitarianism brought to the surface by the war into another kind of social protest. Certainly there was a new passion for liberty, and the efforts to make it more widely effective may well have been stimulated by one dramatically successful *coup d'état*.

The few comments on slavery make no very clear contribution to the picture of the United States, but they do exemplify further the realistic attitude which we have seen gaining strength. The search for truth appears more fully and clearly in the long series of comments on ecclesiastical and political matters in America.

[15] II, 281.

[16] III, 169. Sancho nobly suffers unjust accusation of theft and the consequent punishment (II, 97 ff.), gives a description of Heaven which anticipates *Green Pastures* by a century and a quarter (III, 176 ff.), and details at wearisome length the life of his father, Pangoleen, beginning with slave-ship scenes (I, 86 ff.) and continuing with Munchausen-like fantasies in South America, Mexico, and California (I, 191 ff.). The saga has very much the air of being borrowed; the adventures include, for instance, the story of the hollow idol which amplifies sounds within it (I, 209 ff.) that embellishes *The Female American* and *Henry Lanson*.

iii

Whenever English fiction-readers turned their minds from elopement and seduction to the religion or the churches of America, they were following their authors in a kind of transition which was no more difficult for those hardy men and women of letters than any of the other feats of literary prestidigitation with which they overwhelm the modern reader. By now, however, nothing surprises. That these pen men, most of them unprincipled hacks, should have discussed God's business is logical enough in view of their profession of catering to the *bourgeoisie*. "Religion" was one of the most constant headings in the periodicals, not only because of the temper of the public but also for a special cause, the Methodist furore. And the association of religion and America needs no explanation, for God and gold were the first subjects that the new world suggested in the Renaissance; gold faded, we have seen, but the kingdom of God remained a vital issue. The search for religious freedom had so long a history that, as a subject of interest, it was not crowded out entirely even by the newer and much more startling quest for political independence.

In the seventeenth century, literary reflections on religion in America were concerned roughly with three subjects: conversion of the Indians, the future of the church in America, and the character of the Puritans in New England. With variations and additions, the same interests appear in the novels of the late eighteenth century.

Evangelical efforts, the first of these subjects, make little stir in the novel. We have already noted the surprising, and successful, devotion of William Winkfield and his daughter Eliza, leading spirits of *The Female American* (1767), to establishing Anglicanism among the heathen, but otherwise noble, savages among whom they lived.[17] Except for these episodes, we come across only verbal references to Christianizing the ungodly.

[17] Pp. 16, 24, 35, 73 ff. *Henry Lanson* (1800), based on either *The Female American* or its source, has the same story (pp. 10 ff.).

Most interesting of these is the ironic contention in *The Batch-elor* (1766-1768) that religious fervor alone motivated foreign conquests by Europe:

It was that alone which induced the Spaniards to conquer Mexico and Peru, and not the gold and silver mines, as some have vainly imagined . . . nor did we possess ourselves of such vast tracts of country in America for any other purpose. This might sometimes have been attended with some circumstances of injustice, not to mention cruelty; such as depriving the natives of their natural rights, and butchering, perhaps, three fourths of them; but then we must allow that they were savages who were thus treated, and it was entirely for their good.[18]

George Primrose in *The Vicar of Wakefield* (1766), it will be remembered, was once promised the secretaryship of "an embassy . . . from the synod of Pensylvania to the Chicka-saw Indians."[19] Humor of a different kind appears in an anecdote from *The Fashionable Tell-Tale* (1778) about Count Zinzendorf's efforts to convert a tribe of North-American In-dians "who were distinguished by the character of the Knowing-ones"; when he asked them whether they had heard of Jesus Christ, they replied,

Yes surely . . . we knew Jesus Christ very well: Jesus Christ was a Frenchman, that was murdered by those rogues the English.[20]

Finally, the '90's produce two brief references to missionary activities. Mrs. Mackenzie's *Slavery* (1792) introduces a Mr. Hawkins, of "angelical sweetness, mixed with a melancholy cast," who thus accounts for himself:

Engaged for two years in a mission among the Canadians, and with tolerable success: I thought not of returning to Europe, till a letter, explaining Mrs. St. Leger's death and the necessity of my presence at Port-Royal, occasioned me reluctantly to quit the honest creatures, who

[18] II, 120.
[19] II, 20.
[20] I, 94-95.

distinguished the moment of my departure with tears of unfeigned esteem.[21]

The record closes with *Henry Somerville* (1798), which states literally what *The Batchelor* had said ironically thirty years before, that voyages of discovery had been

calculated for the noble purpose of enlightening the minds of ignorant nations—diffusing christianity, and rendering mankind therefore more happy.[22]

*The Batchelor's* sneer at the conquistadors is an indirect hit at Catholicism in America, which, early taken to task in Marvell's *The First Anniversary of the Government under Oliver Cromwell,* was later satirized, as we saw in Chapter VII, in Johnstone's *Chrysal, The Adventures of Alonso,* and Cullen's *Castle of Inchvally.* With their perennial fear of papists, the English were never tired of shuddering at conversion by the sword. The omnivorous author of *Berkeley Hall* (1796) also seized upon this morsel, telling how Pangoleen, the negro, was tortured by the Spanish in California to make him confess the true faith, and sentenced to the silver mines for suggesting that his soul was as white as those of his persuaders.[23] A rare note on the other side is the account by William Hayley in his *Essay on Old Maids* (1785) of a remarkable Mexican nun, Juana Inez de la Cruz, distinguished equally by piety and dialectical skill.[24] This is the last note on the subject of missions as it appeared in prose fiction. Not a very indicative contribution, it shows, if anything, a sense that, what with the need of Christianity and the regrettable tactics of the Catholics, America was not all it should be. Nor, as I have said before, was there a Golden Age resurrected in America; Arcadia could scarcely have needed the institution of Christianity.

The future of the Christian church in the West, the second

21 Page 30.
22 Page 179.
23 II, 4-7.
24 III, 98 ff.

of the ecclesiastical matters to draw comment from novelists, was first described optimistically by Alexander, Davenant, and Herbert, who foresaw America not only as the inheritor of the Christian tradition, but also as the reviver of a moribund faith. Such fond hopes were not for the Age of Reason, which had few dreams left about America. Novelists did speculate about the religious outlook in America, not without admiration, and they were mildly concerned about the status of Anglicanism. But they kept their feet on the ground.

Moore's *Zeluco* (1786) speaks of

a Physician who sometimes reads the Bible: There are, it would appear, some of that kind in America.[25]

Did the Doctor mean "even in America" or "only in America"? Whatever his intention, he made one of the few general references to the religious state of a country which was thought of rather in terms of its tolerance, and, as a side issue, its variety of ecclesiastical organizations. The religious tolerance which Price praised so enthusiastically[26] received attention chiefly from the Golden-Age group of novels, here closer to fact than in some other matters. In *Man As He Is Not* (1796) Bage, with Hermsprong as mouthpiece, stresses American hospitality to new opinions:

It is true, they dispute there very much, grow animated sometimes, and sometimes indulge in personal abuse; but this is evanescent. To your polite hatred for opinion, generally they are strangers. I imagine they owe this to their diversity of religions, which, accustoming them to see difference of opinion in a matter of the greatest importance, disposes them to tolerate it on all subjects, and even to believe it a condition of human nature. Their Government too embraces all sects, and persecutes none; and when there is no reward for persecution, and no merit attached to it, I suppose it possible for men to refrain from it.[27]

[25] Page 121.
[26] *Observations on the Importance of the American Revolution*, pp. 7, 20 ff.
[27] III, 237.

In *Disobedience* (1797) Mary's mother offers, among others, the following objection to going to America:

. . . how can I consent to forego my religion? I have been told that there are no bishops, no regular church in America. Think you I will associate with fanatical baptists and gloomy presbyterians?

Mary reassures her:

. . . I am neither a baptist nor a presbyterian;—and if you recollect that you used to ridicule me for my piety, you may rest contented that I should not be happy in *any* country where I could not regularly serve my God in the way I preferred. . . . I verily believe, where there is one person in Europe under the influence of a religious sentiment, there are ten in America.[28]

The last statement may provide the clue to *Zeluco's* note on religious physicians in America. Still more advanced claims are made for America in *Henry Willoughby* (1798), in which the ideal community, Anachoropolis, practices "the utmost latitude of scepticism." The prevalent "philosophy and liberal enquiry" have partly given up the doctrine of revelation "as the only touchstone of moral rectitude." Yet the community found it difficult to "dispel the fanaticism that rankled in the hearts of a few" who "openly lamented the defeat of superstition, and secretly fomented measures for its re-establishment." Ultimately, however, the "illusions of bigotry were dissipated"; "cheerless gloom," "inspiration of the spirit," and "groans of self-tormentors" all disappeared.[29] The spirit which made the Bermudas "safe from the . . . Prelat's rage," in Marvell's phrase, is exemplified dramatically in *Berkeley Hall* (1796), in which Dr. Homily, the central character, is a religious exile, moderately happy in New Jersey.

To be plain, his father had been a rigid nonjuror; and if report err not, derived full episcopal authority from Archbishop Sancroft; and his son (our worthy host) had similar powers and principles.[30]

Homily is not lonely:

28 IV, 214-215.
29 II, 239-241.
30 I, 59.

Our family also had many other respectable friends . . . whom religious persecutions or misfortunes had driven from England, to seek an asylum in the new world.[31]

Ultimately Homily gives up his intransigence and is restored to his Lancashire estate.

When Mary's mother in *Disobedience* feared that a bishopless America would be uncongenial, she must have spoken for many of the Anglican faithful, though they made only a small noise in fiction. In a more serious world, enough was said. While Berkeley wanted to found a Christian university in the Bermudas, Swift would have installed the Anglican church in America.[32] Granville Sharp (1735-1813), better known as an abolitionist, was interested in the same end.[33] Richard Price, on the other hand, hoped fervently that there would never be an establishment in America.[34] Trevelyan discusses the efforts to impose an establishment, the influence of the church in the Revolution, and the coming to an end, through the war, of the establishment in the South.[35]

In the realm of story-writers, the only serious proponent of an episcopacy is Mrs. Brooke, who argues, first in *Lady Julia Mandeville* (1763), that Canada will be a valuable province if, among other things, the inhabitants

are allured to our religious worship, by seeing it in its genuine beauty, equally remote from their load of trifling ceremonies and the unornamented forms of the dissenters. . . .[36]

She amplifies and extends her proposal in *Emily Montague* (1769):

As therefore the civil government of America is on the same plan with that of the mother country, it were to be wished the religious establish-

[31] I, 69.
[32] *Cambridge History of the British Empire*, I, 623.
[33] *D. N. B.*
[34] *Observations on the Importance of the American Revolution*, p. 46.
[35] *The American Revolution*, Part II, II, 280-329.
[36] Pp. 156-157.

ment was also the same, especially in those colonies where the people are generally of the national church; though with the fullest liberty of conscience to dissenters of all denominations.

I would be clearly understood, my Lord; from all I have observed here, I am convinced, nothing would so much contribute to diffuse a spirit of order, and rational obedience, in the colonies, as the appointment, under proper restrictions, of bishops: I am equally convinced that nothing would so much strengthen the hands of government, or give such pleasure to the well-affected in the colonies, who are by much the most numerous, as such an appointment, however clamored against by a few abettors of sedition.[37]

The "abettors of sedition" won the day, of course, and henceforth the pious Mrs. Brooke's idea comes in for only attack or scorn. Bage speaks up, inevitably. In *Mount Henneth* (1781) James Foston, listing the eligibles for a hypothetical society at Henneth Castle, includes

Any bishop, who can demonstrate to the general conviction of America, that the pastoral staff was made for the benefit of mankind.[38]

The Quakeress Miss Carlill speaks for Bage in *Man As He Is* (1792), in which Mr. Holford argues the need of a national religion.

"I pray thee, . . . which is the national religion of America?"

"Pshaw!" says the parson, rather angrily; "they'll come to nothing for want of it."

"When they do, the argument will be in thy favour," answered Miss Carlill.

"But if they do flourish," says Mr. Holford, "they must have one; they must have a chief magistrate; one or many. This chief must have a religion; he must prefer his own, and the very preference will soon give a decided majority; and a national religion follows of course."[39]

The proponent of a fantastic colony in *The Twin Brothers* (1787) holds forth on the advantage which his colony derives from its lack of religion:

[37] II, 207-208.
[38] Page 224.
[39] I, 89-90.

Mine, he adds, is not likely to prove so troublesome as some others have been. A colony without religion, is at least free from the jealousy and murmuring respecting modes of worship, which, it has been asserted, contributed to the revolt of our old colonies.[40]

The final comment is a jibe at believers in an establishment. The ignorant and vulgar Mrs. Crewkherne in Mrs. Smith's *Young Philosopher* (1798) characterizes Americans as

a race that for my part seem to me not to belong to Christian society somehow, and who, I understand, are no better than atheists; for I am told there are no clergy in America, as our's are, established by law, to oblige and compel people to think right; but that all runs wild, and there are no tithes, nor ways of maintaining that holy order, as we have, but every body prays their own way, if indeed such free-thinkers ever pray at all, which I dare say they do not.[41]

From tolerance and an establishment it is scarcely a step to the third subject about which cluster fictional discussions— dissent; of the various Protestant groups in America, the Methodists, Moravians, and Quakers attract some attention, but strongest appeal to the imagination was made by the Puritans of New England, who could always be turned handily to the use of the picturesque and the grotesque. Nearly two centuries before, Thomas Carew had spoken of New England as having

purged more virulent humours from the politic body, than Guiacum and the West-Indian have from the natural bodies of the kingdom.[42]

The "virulent humours," popular butts on the Restoration stage, continued in the same way to evoke the same kind of laughter in an age much less gay. Once, at least, they are criticized seriously—in Bage's *Mount Henneth* (1781), which has the distinction of being the only novel to base an episode on witchcraft. At a witchcraft trial in Boston Mr. Melton had

[40] Page 16 note. In 1776 there appeared in London a pamphlet, *Hypocrisy Unmasked; or, a short Enquiry into the religious Complaints of our American Colonies* (see *Gentleman's Magazine*, XLVI, 225-226).

[41] I, 132-133.

[42] *Poems, ed. cit.*, p. 205. For anti-Puritan ballads, see Firth, *An American Garland*, p. xxvi.

succeeded in saving the defendant, an old lady who later went to his house as sanctuary.

His life, as well as hers, was threatened. Once the tumult rose so high as to set some out-buildings on fire. Mr Melton claimed assistance from the officers of the militia, by whom the mob was at length dispersed.

Mr. Melton wrote against the belief in witchcraft; "this brought upon him a severe persecution, from which he was obliged to fly," but in three years toleration was legally established.[43] Toleration is seldom mentioned in these books, which regularly treat New Englanders as narrow, doleful, enthusiastic, and hypocritical. We have already seen how *Disobedience* and *Henry Willoughby,* in picturing their ideal communities, inveighed against gloominess and fanaticism—no doubt an assurance to prospective emigrants who might not properly distinguish between Boston and backwoods. *The Fashionable Tell-Tale* (1778) has a story of the commander of a British ship stationed at Boston, who, for kissing his lady publicly, was publicly whipped; in return for this treatment, he invited all the magistrates of Boston on board, gave them a dinner, and then had them whipped by the sailors.[44]

Rollicking satire of Puritans contributes to the liveliness of two books already seen to be adept at fun-making—*Jonathan Corncob* (1787) and *Berkeley Hall* (1796). The former gives this introductory description of Jonathan's father, a Massachusetts storekeeper:

Mr. Habakkuk Corncob was a rigid presbyterian; he considered any man who played at cards as irrevocably d—n'd, as well as any man who walked out on a Sunday. He employed every part of the day, that was not spent at the meeting-house, in reading the book of Leviticus, for the instruction of his family, and thought himself peculiarly indulgent, when, by way of amusement, he favoured us with the history of

43 Page 199.
44 I, 36-39.

Shadrach, Meshach, and Abednego, or a few pages of the Pilgrim's Progress.[45]

He was superstitious to the extent of being unorthodox, for he thought that the soul of his dead sister Bathsheba had entered a "large black wild turkey" which he met while hunting.[46] In New York, Jonathan enjoys the society of his landlady, the daughter of a Presbyterian parson, who was

particularly well versed in the Old Testament, she was acquainted with all its personages, from Abishag the Shunamite, who lay with old David to keep his feet warm, to Bildad the Shuhite, who was a greater plague to Job than all his misfortunes. As I was always of a pious turn, I was exceedingly fond of her conversation, only I thought she made somewhat too free with respectable characters. She said Lot was a nasty old dog. King David stood pretty high in her good graces; she approved very much of the abhorrence he showed of adultery, by the speedy means he used to divorce Bathsheba from her husband. She did not scruple to say that Solomon was *stark nought:* a man who was not satisfied with three hundred wives, all princesses too, but kept seven hundred mistresses, could have no conscience.[47]

Her niece was "of the same religious turn," but that did not prevent her rather easy seduction. Afterward,

giving me a kiss, she exclaimed, *"behold thou art fair, my beloved, yea thou art pleasant; also our bed is green."* I found this ejaculation so happily applied, that I could not help lamenting that we had only seven or eight songs remaining of the thousand and five written by King Solomon.[48]

When Jonathan subsequently found himself diseased and complained to the aunt, that lady, always apt in texts, replied that if her niece really had

. . . the complaint you mention, it is not her fault, poor thing, somebody has given it to her, and I have no doubt that it is one of those

[45] Pp. 10-11. It may be noted here that in his prefatory verses to the Second Part Bunyan speaks of his book's receiving, in New England, "so much loving Countenance."
[46] Page 16.
[47] Pp. 45-46.
[48] Page 54.

British officers who, according to the words of Ezekiel, are *captains and rulers, clothed most gorgeously, horsemen riding upon horses, and all of them desirable young men—whose flesh is as the flesh of asses, and their issue as the issue of horses.*[49]

The trio, however, continue to live amicably together, whiling away long winter evenings with "a kind of religious conundrums," which generally had to do with the aberrations of Biblical characters from the strictest code of sexual morality.[50]

*Berkeley Hall* has more diversified satire, first using religiosity as a cloak for swindlers. We have already seen how Dr. Sourby, in attempting a new Golden Age at Independent Hall in the mountains of Pennsylvania, had been grossly cheated by a pair of pious New Englanders, Deacon Phineas Chauncey and the venerable Mr. Truby. These two appear later to Dr. Homily as fervid nonjurors, showing great interest in his projected abridgement of Hooker; one of them claims to be "a relative of the celebrated George Hicks." Under the circumstances it is not surprising that the good Doctor gives them ten pounds toward their fund for building a meetinghouse, and that he resents the attitude of a neighbor who says that they are only "New-England-men, and he believed no better than a couple of swindlers."[51] Ultimately Homily learns that this is the truth and that

they retreated, covered with shame, from the colonies where they were known, to practice their arts in Canada.[52]

Another incident is of the *Jonathan Corncob* variety; it concerns a company of sailors who, drunk, "proposed to sacrifice also to the *Cyprian goddess.*" In their company are the sanctimonious Deacon Liptrap and Mr. Mawworm, who were

the most forward in promoting this expedition; whether the fumes of the wine had laid reason asleep, and given their dormant passions a

49 Page 55.
50 Pp. 59 ff.
51 III, 300-303.
52 III, 359.

fillip; or whether the curtain being drawn, discovered only what their hypocrisy and art concealed from the public eye.

The leaders of the expedition, seeing the excitement of the neophytes, decide to hunt amusement rather than love; so they take Liptrap and Mawworm, not to their expected destination, but instead to the house of a

Puritanical preacher, whose wife took in a few country boarders, and kept a day school. Nathan Sackbut, for this was his name, was a man of the most inflexible muscles, a famous holder-forth, and eminent for chamber consolation, and soul searchings, among the sisterhood and devout brothers. He was much visited for this purpose, and had pocketed no little filthy *lucre* by dispensing his spiritual nostrums.

Liptrap and Mawworm are told that Sackbut's place is a house of pleasure, but that they are to be periphrastic in their approach and to pay no attention to the verbal piety of the proprietor, who is "jealous of the decorum and character of the house." The plan works to perfection, and the ensuing scene is in the manner of the best Smollettian farce; the final result is a free-for-all, and Liptrap and Mawworm are jailed.[53]

A direct reference to Puritans comes in the tale of Brecknock the hermit:

I then travelled through the middle colonies, and resolved to settle in New England; but the fanatical strictness and prejudices of the inhabitants disgusted my *philosophy;* while my licentious opinions and conduct drew on me the odium, and even persecutions, of the pious and orthodox. Thus *hating, and hated* by all, I found no satisfaction in their conversation, nor in a country where no public amusements or entertainments were admitted to divert the mind from its cares.[54]

Finally, Mrs. Smith's *Young Philosopher* (1798) contains an incidental reference to the "strait-laced, lop-eared puritans of the United States."[55]

Of all ecclesiastical bodies, the Methodists were objects of

[53] II, 178 ff.
[54] III, 27-28.
[55] III, 26.

severest satire in the eighteenth century. Their American activities receive mention in only two novels, both dealing with
outstanding personalities. One section of *Adventures of a
Hackney Coach* (1781) makes a vicious attack on John Wesley, the "disciple of iniquity" and "hypocritical impostor," to
quote only two of the author's copious epithets. Wesley is
accused of peculation, about which he soliloquizes:

If the satirical author of Sketches for Tabernacle Frames should get
the most distant information of this affair, I should be hunted with the
same terriers, that led me such a perilous chase when Warburton attacked me about my affair of *crim-con* in America.[56]

It was probably George Whitefield and his successful preaching tour through the northern colonies which led to the caustic
account of an itinerant evangelist in *Berkeley Hall*. Traveling
through western New Jersey, Dr. Sourby and Timothy Tickle
find, at an unnamed small town, that

the celebrated itinerant, Mr. Cantwell, was expected, it seems, that day,
which had created an universal uproar. By his pulpit oratory, and
maddening doctrines, he had spread the most extraordinary epidemical
enthusiasm among the deluded people. This *mania* spared neither age
nor sex. All aspired to the gift of preaching, and the blacks quitted
their spits and pans in the kitchens, to listen to his rhapsodies, or attend
little parties of *feelers, seekers,* and *ghostly grunters,* and *groaners.*[57]

At an inn the travelers can get no service because of the presence of Cantwell, who finally comes to the expected sermon,
after he had

ranted forth a prayer, more adapted to the humours and prejudices of
his hearers, than the solemnity of the place. He then poured forth a

---

[56] Page 117. This is a libelous reference to Wesley's badly managed affair
with Sophia Hopkey, treated at disproportionate length by most of the biographies. *Sketches for Tabernacle Frames* was a 36-p. quarto satire of 1778.
For an answer to charges of misappropriation, see Abram Lipsky, *John Wesley:
A Portrait* (New York: Simon and Schuster, 1928), p. 247. The reference to
Warburton is to *The Doctrine of Grace,* which re-tells the Hopkey story as
suggestively as possible (*ed. cit.,* pp. 176 ff.).

[57] II, 252-253.

discourse, consisting of a flood of ribaldry, vulgar, and even *indecent* comparisons, and wild mystical declamations. . . .

At one time he set his hearers in a roar, with a *facetious story* or *anecdote,* in which he abounded, and, to do him justice, could tell with singular humour.[58]

Excitement rises, and the outcome is a medley of a country fair and a drunken orgy. For interrupting, Dr. Sourby is tarred and feathered. Cantwell works up the women to such an extent that they start throwing their finery into the flames, but he restrains them, persuades them to sell the articles and turn the proceeds over to him. Here the author footnotes: *History of Connecticut,*[59] presumably referring to the work by Samuel Peters, which makes a number of references to Whitefield.[60] Tim and Sourby move on, finally stopping in a Pennsylvania town at an inn where the neighboring room is occupied by enthusiasts just returned from Cantwell's harangue. When Tim protests at their noise, a general fight results. Then another group of converts comes to apologize for the actions of the others "and to administer some ghostly advice and instruction." They drone on

till the Irishman and our hero, no longer able to restrain themselves, sprang from bed, seized the two pharisees by their asses ears, dragged them to the passage, and urged them rapidly down stairs, by repeated applications of their feet to the seats of honour of these recreant reformers.[61]

Warned by the host, they leave in the middle of the night and on the road are attacked by robbers, whom they repel, capturing one of them. When they come to East Town (Easton), they find their prisoner to be one of the exhorters. But here

[58] II, 257.

[59] II, 274.

[60] *Ed. cit.,* pp. 211, 303 ff. Whitefield seems the most likely subject for the portrait in *Berkeley Hall,* though Peters is less unfavorably disposed toward him. Peters speaks of his having made "wisemen mad" and tells anecdotes about his bringing about a fanatical application of religion in actual life (pp. 306-312).

[61] II, 283.

399

they are again attacked and arrested, brought to trial, and jailed, finally to gain their release by pretending adherence to one of the contending parties in a local election.[62] The thoroughness of the satire, which is the most vivid commentary we find on American religion, is to be interpreted in the light of the high-church bias of the book, which, Miss Whitney believes, "was apparently written to counteract current criticisms of the English government and church."[63]

Except for brief references to Quakers,[64] attention was otherwise directed chiefly to the Moravians, who had a mild run in the fiction of the '90's. *Wanley Penson* (1791) praises them for making

no national distinctions; an European, an African, and an American, they reckon only as three brothers born of the same parent, in different climes.[65]

The Americans thus admitted to universal fellowship had their chief settlement at Bethlehem, Pennsylvania, where Moravian College is a present-day reminder of early history. *Berkeley Hall* gives a description of the settlement,[66] but most detail is contributed by Mrs. Parsons' *Voluntary Exile* (1795), in which Biddulph, who never has to attend to business for very long at a time but can deviate in accordance with the whims of his creatrix, stops at Bethlehem, looks about him, and passes his

[62] II, 286 ff.
[63] *Op. cit.,* p. 276.
[64] As individuals, they are almost always treated favorably. In *Henry Willoughby* (1798) they receive credit for founding the free-thinking Anachoropolis, distinguished by its pedagogical innovations. *The Fashionable Tell-Tale* (1778) tells about the severe treatment of Quakers by Lord Howard of Effingham, Governor of Virginia from 1682 to 1692 (Beatson, *Political Index,* III, 484). When, protesting but unrelieved, they say, "Well . . . the Lord's will be then done," the Governor replies, "Yes, by G-d, . . . and the lord's (meaning himself) will shall be done, I give you my word" (I, 104).
[65] II, 349. The book also praises their discipline, which it says is observed uniformly in all nations (II, 31). In 1793 the Klosterpresse at Ephrata issued *Anonymus's Travels from Europe to America . . .* (Professor Greenough's Catalogue).
[66] II, 319-320.

gleanings on to the reader. He describes the systematic, virtuous, and industrious life of a society organized on a partially
communal basis, which "he had scarce ever heard of." One
commendable aspect of Moravianism is the courtesy of the
"manager," who, like all Americans, is obsequious to the English gentleman, and who

> very politely conducted him through the establishments, both of the
> men and women; every thing bore the face of industry and regularity;
> he was particularly charmed with the neatness and air of content that
> seemed diffused among both sexes. . . .[67]

When Biddulph returns to Bethlehem later, this manager, Mr.
Colyer, discourses again:

> No human institution can be perfect . . . nor am I by any means an
> advocate for innovations or alterations in general established religions;
> I trust, however, our institution here, if not perfect, and liable perhaps
> to many objections, yet is such as inculcates religion, morality, and
> benevolence: charity and industry are its basis.[68]

The novelists' history of religion and the church in the new
world clearly has less relation with the war than any other
aspect of American life that found a niche in fiction. A decline
of interest in missionary endeavor is possibly due to the separation of the colonies, which is of course responsible for the
end of the rather feeble cries for an establishment. Otherwise
chronological distinctions cannot be made. The whole ecclesiastical picture presents an anomaly: although most Englishmen, as we see them here, approve the American principle of
tolerance, they find difficulty in approving what the Americans
tolerated. True, the Quakers get by, and the Moravians are
not significant enough to attack; but the Catholics are excori-
ated, the Methodists sneered at, and the Puritans damned. Of
course, authors are here continuing and extending an old
English custom, for the Catholics are treated no more harshly

[67] IV, 16-18.
[68] IV, 69.

than by Marvell and Oldham, the Methodists than by Foote and Graves, and the Puritans than by the Restoration stage. On the other hand, it may be remarked that the voyage across the Atlantic did not wash away the sins of papists, dissenters, and new-light brethren; hence America gained no character from their presence. Of all of them, the Puritans come closest to being identified with Americans, who, whether they were New Englanders or not, were likely to be conceived of as gloomy, fanatical, and, above all, formalistic and hypocritical. It was possible that any American might quote scripture and flog the mildly indecorous, and then thieve or lie. There was, of course, some belief in a genuinely religious spirit in America and a good deal of belief in a generally healthful ecclesiastical situation. But there were few signs left of the great seventeenth-century hopes of a renewed and revivified Christianity across the Atlantic. Here again is the skepticism which we have seen more than once toning down the bright-eyed European glances toward the freshest spot on the map.

iv

In 1931 Democracy said to George Bernard Shaw:

My name is Demos; and I live in the British Empire, the United States of America, and wherever the love of liberty burns in the heart of man.[69]

To which the philosopher replied, in part:

I don't believe your name is Demos: nobody's name is Demos; and all I can make of your address is that you have no address, and are just a tramp—if indeed you exist at all.[70]

What was mildly prophetic in 1931 would at the time of the eighteenth-century revolutions have been as reactionary as Burke's opposition to the "metaphysical rights" of the insurgent French. In those days Democracy was not only a reality, but a

[69] Preface to *The Apple Cart, ed. cit.,* p. xvi.
[70] *Ibid.,* p. xvii.

reality either thrilling or very disturbing, and its home address was the United States. No one alive to the current world was indifferent to it, and it was at the center of political speculation; as Professor Laski puts it, "The American War and the two great revolutions brought a new race of thinkers into being."[71] And Professor Dunning:

. . . the entrance of American conditions and institutions . . . [was] an influential element in political philosophy. . . . In the search for principles adapted to political liberty the American systems were studied by many European thinkers.[72]

Such audible voices as those of Crèvecoeur and Price cried up the admirable innovations, the formation of the new republic being, in the latter's view, second only to Christianity as "the most important step in the progressive course of human improvement."[73]

Prose fiction followed the hue and cry, just as it trailed nonfiction in voicing its stand on slavery and religious matters; in fact, as many citations have suggested, it seldom opened its mouth without issuing some emphatic pronouncement on the life political. Such getting out of bounds aroused some protest, ineffective though it was. As early as 1775 the *Critical* said of *The Adventures of Alonso* that it contained "too much political matter, . . . to render his book a favourite with the readers of novels."[74] Mrs. Westbury in Sarah Burney's *Clarentine* (1796) is made to restrain the expression of her political knowledge:

Upon *Revolutions, Government, &c. &c.* fortunately for her fair auditor,

[71] Harold J. Laski, *Political Thought in England from Locke to Bentham* (New York: Holt, 1920), p. 23.

[72] William A. Dunning, *A History of Political Theories* (New York: Macmillan, 1902-1920), III, 80-81.

[73] *Observations on the Importance of the American Revolution,* p. 6.

[74] XL, 163. Joseph B. Heidler, *The History, from 1700 to 1800, of English Criticism of Prose Fiction* (University of Illinois Studies in Language and Literature, Vol. XIII, No. 2, Urbana, 1928), pp. 110-111, referring especially to the novels of Bage, Holcroft, Godwin, and Mrs. Smith, says that in general the reviews were unfavorable to the propagandistic character of the works.

she wholly forbore touching, knowing well that Mrs. Denbigh . . . had an insuperable aversion to them, and wisely suspecting, that with the modest Clarentine it might be the same.[75]

From which one might deduce that Miss Burney was jealous of Mrs. Charlotte Turner Smith; and perhaps Robert Bage equally irked William Linley, who, in the preface to his *Forbidden Apartments* (1800), expresses certainty that "the reader is better pleased when he has not political discussions intruded upon him."[76]

Judging by their frequency, such intrusions must have met at least tolerance. In their simplest form we find them simply recognizing the existence of certain political characteristics across the Atlantic. *Berkeley Hall* (1796) indicates the tolerance of America in the fact that it harbors Dr. Sourby, whose "political liberty bordered on licentiousness and anarchy";[77] and then, since its purported composition in days of happy colonyhood eliminates discussion of the existent situation, the book has recourse to prophecy, making a concession which, in view of the author's Tory leanings, is generous enough:

They [the colonies] will improve, perhaps, on their parent, and spread the same language, spirit of liberty, and industry, over this continent! over *one half the world!*[78]

"The same spirit of liberty" in mother and child draws only sarcasm in Mrs. Eliza Hamilton's *Translation of the Letters of a Hindoo Rajah* in the same year:

Benevolent people of England! it is their desire, that all should be partakers of the same blessing of liberty, which they themselves enjoy. It was doubtless with this glorious view, that they sent forth colonies to enlighten, and instruct, the vast regions of America. To disseminate

[75] III, 25-26.
[76] I, vi-vii.
[77] I, 69.
[78] II, 36-37. Here Dr. Homily stops to quote passages from Seneca and other classical writers which he considers anticipations of the new world and of its contribution to the future greatness of Britain (II, 45 ff.).

the love of virtue and freedom, they cultivated the trans-Atlantic isles. . . .[79]

The first use of the phrase "the United States of America" that I have found is in Hayley's *Essay on Old Maids*[80] (1785), and the most recent in Erskine's *Armata* (1817), which concludes with praise for

the United States of America, the foundation of which I have always considered to be the most auspicious aera in the history of the world, and vindicated by the principles of our own revolution.[81]

The interim produces Mrs. Smith and Bage as the staunch defenders that one would expect. In the former's *Desmond* (1792) Montfleuri says that the war has been advantageous to America,

now recovered of those wounds, which its unnatural parent hoped were mortal, and in the most flourishing state of political health.

What then becomes of the political credit of those who prognosticated, that her productions would be unequal to her wants; her legislature to her government.—I know not how far the mother-country is the worse for this disunion with her colonies—but, I am sure, they are the better; and, nothing is more false than that idea of the veteran statesmen, that a country, under a new form of government, is destitute of those who have ability to direct it.—That they may be unlearned in the detestable chicane of politics, is certain; but, they are also uncorrupted by odious and pernicious maxims of the unfeeling tools of despotism; honest ministers then, and able negociators will arise with the occasion.[82]

Bage describes the ideal government in *Man As He Is Not* (1796), an ideal which America, if she does not entirely realize it, at least comes very close to. Montfleuri's "unlearned in the detestable chicane of politics," in the citation above, is paraphrased by Hermsprong in explaining why the American system would not do in England:

[79] (Dublin, 1797), I, 14.
[80] I, xviii.
[81] Page 211.
[82] I, 154-155.

A simple government, without money to buy men, is little adapted to people who will do nothing till they are bought.[83]

Another trouble with England is that she has not learned to be comfortable with differences of opinion, whereas in America there is genuine tolerance.[84]

The Whig chorus is less well manned than that of the Tories. Although the War itself had brought forth a preponderance of pro-American opinion, which extended into much later discussion of the conflict, the subsequent developments meet a pendulum swinging in the other direction. It is probably not so much a case of the court of public opinion reversing itself as it is of a well-known rise of reaction after a panicky sense of instability had been created by the French Revolution. Danger now seemed real, for the Channel was somewhat narrower than the Atlantic. Still there is no wholesale anti-republicanism, but the apostles of liberty do meet perceptibly greater opposition.

Doubts about the American panacea for political ills first appear in an essay on "Taxology" in Richard Graves's *Lucubrations* (1786), in which a plaint to the demon of taxation includes the assurance that, ". . . if we cross the Atlantic, thou ragest with tenfold fury in the Utopian states of America."[85] The same year produces a more general attack; in her *Juvenile Indiscretions,* the pious Mrs. Bennet sneers at a Mrs. Downe for her political liberalism:

. . . now in the centre of politics, [she] is employed in writing down Monarchy; and it is rumoured, she means to visit America, the fame of her talents having reached the wise body of people there, who, it is said, wish to have the assistance of the learned Mrs. Downe, in framing a certain code of laws for the use of the commonwealth.[86]

In his *New Tale of a Tub* (1790) John Pinkerton, if not hostile

[83] II, 164.
[84] III, 237.
[85] Page 90. For the opposing belief, that government cost less in America, see Smith, *Priestley in America,* p. 92.
[86] V, 264.

to democracy in the abstract, doubts its workability in large nations:

> Yet pedants apply their maxims to modern states. . . . Holland and Venice are not republics but aristocracies, Switzerland the same. America consists of federative republics; perhaps it may be one republic, but it is not yet tried.[87]

Walker's *Vagabond* (1799) has a similarly worded criticism which, however, not so much questions practicability as attacks all the supposed virtues of republics:

> 'This [the French] is a philosophical republic,' said Alogos; 'the ancient republics were fighting republics;—the Americans and Hollanders are trading republics, but man seemed neither better satisfied, better governed, or better fed in any of them; nor in fact, do they enjoy so many benefits as in a limited monarchy.'[88]

Reference has already been made to Walker's wrathful conception of the results of democracy; in a Philadelphia inn his travelers were treated in the most insulting fashion by menials possessed of the new democratic spirit.[89] A final skeptical note on democracy takes a completely different tack, seeing not the impracticability or the undesirability of democracy, but its break-up; reviewing Mrs. Smith's *Young Philosopher* (1798), the *Critical* makes an elegiac note on "those simple republican principles which were once characteristic of the Americans."[90]

As the quoted observations on republics show, America did not make an isolated entry into the European political forum, but instead had several almost inevitable companions. American political problems were taken in by the same glance which was directed at the domestic situation, for there was a close liaison. Not only did the demand for governmental reform, allied with the issues of the war, grow more vigorous after 1781, but it also "extended itself into an appeal for religious toleration, a free

[87] Page 23. Cf. Dunning, *A History of Political Theories*, III, 98.
[88] Page 204.
[89] Page 161.
[90] XXIV (New Arrangement, 1798), 79.

press, free platform, free right of petition."[91] The linking of the American question with other contemporary problems has already been observed in the account of political satires in Chapter VII. It appears specifically in Bage's *Barham Downs* (1784), in which Sir Ambrose Archer writes Mr. Wyman:

I am returned from a meeting, called an association, the object of which is, as you know, to call upon Parliament with a loud voice to redress our grievances. And what are your grievances? says a well-pensioned gentleman, Mr T'otherside. That the Crown hath acquired too much influence by the worst of all possible ways—corruption. That our representatives endanger their health—by too long sitting. That as we never saw the least prospect of benefit from engaging in the American war, we see as little from its continuance.[92]

Liberalism extended to an endorsement of "political liberty" in Ireland and France, often thought of in conjunction with American success.[93] Nowhere is the connection more clearly demonstrated than in *Baratariana,* the patriotic essays by Irishmen during the '70's, which constantly make common cause between America and Ireland, and of which the first six are letters "From a Native of Barataria to his friend in Pensylvania."[94] The relationship gains expression in two novels. In *Reveries of the Heart* (1781) the English government is addressed thus:

. . . did you cherish them [the Irish] as fellow-subjects? no! on the contrary every means which fraud and cunning, wearing the mask of law could devise, and real power could execute, were put in force against the miserable natives; who were universally stripped and proscribed as Americans would be, had many, I am afraid too many, of our rulers the power.[95]

[91] Fraser, *English Opinion of the American Constitution and Government,* pp. 67-68. Cf. Laski, *op. cit.,* pp. 204-205.

[92] Page 294.

[93] See Laski, *op. cit.,* p. 204; Fraser, *op. cit.,* pp. 72-73. In one of his frequent asides in *The Botanic Garden,* Erasmus Darwin describes the advent of Liberty in Columbia, and her travels thence to Hibernia and Gallia (Book I, Canto II, 361-394).

[94] See *ed. cit.,* p. 2.

[95] II, 91-92.

To return to Bage's *Barham Downs*, we find the following in a conversation between Sir George Osmond and Captain O'Donnel:

Well, says Sir George, your country is going to recover her lost rights; America restores them to her.

And I thank her with all my soul; and I wish her good luck for it, by sea and land, and every other country too that deserves it.[96]

Still closer was the common association of the American and the French Revolution, not only because Frenchmen kept a watchful eye on America,[97] but especially because of the parade of prominent Englishmen who espoused, in one way or another, both causes: Charles Fox, whose "logic" at the time of the American war led "inevitably to his support of the French Revolution";[98] Paine, who received more opprobrium than any radical of the day; Priestley, whom persecution drove from England; Price, who drew down the wrath of Burke with the famous sermon of November 4, 1789, in which he said,

After sharing in the benefits of one Revolution, I have been spared to be a witness to two other Revolutions, both glorious.[99]

Whether because conservatism was gradually getting tuned up to strenuous literary activity, or because a feeble novel lacked courage to follow daring political theorists in the days when the government could risk treason trials and other repressive

[96] Page 363.

[97] Dunning, *History of Political Theories*, III, 84.

[98] John Drinkwater, *Charles James Fox*, p, 162.

[99] *A Discourse on the Love of Our Country* . . . (2nd ed., Dublin, 1790), p. 55. The customary association of the characters here named is shown in a report of a parliamentary debate on December 17, 1792, when Mr. Grey made a "Complaint of a Libel intituled 'One Pennyworth of Truth, from Thomas Bull to his Brother John.'" Grey was defending dissenters, against whom he quoted the following "libellous invective" from the pamphlet: "Our national debt, for which we are now paying such heavy taxes, was doubled by the troubles in America, all brought upon us . . . by the dissenters. . . . Did not Dr. Price write for them? And did not that Birmingham Doctor . . . encourage them, and write mob-principles of government to justify them?" Grey contended that riots are produced not by Paine's work, but by pamphlets against dissenters, none of whom was safe (*Parliamentary History*, XXX, 128-130).

measures, prose fiction no longer vents fierce opposition as in the relatively free '70's and '80's. For the *bourgeoisie*, revolution is now more cried down than talked up. During the '90's the two experiments in liberty find as real defenders only two liberals, and one of these is a sentimentalist rather than a freethinker. That is Mrs. Mackenzie, in whose *Slavery* (1792) General St. Leger and the Rev. Mr. Hawkins are locked up in a French prison during the Revolution. Hawkins reassures the General's weepy daughter, ". . . should your father be known, his situation in America would exonerate him from suspicion,"[100] and the daughter throws herself before a French officer: "He has fought and bled in the cause of *liberty*, what would you have more?"[101] The case conveniently turns out to have been one of false arrest. Twice Mrs. Charlotte Smith speaks up, first in *Celestina* (1791), in which the Count de Bellegarde is glorifying the events in France:

> But my residence among the Americans, has awakened in my mind a spirit of freedom. The miseries, the irreparable injuries I had received from ill-placed and exorbitant power, prompted me to assert it. . . . In this disposition, it may easily be imagined, that if I possessed the power, I was not without inclination to add fewel to that fire, which immediately after the end of the war in America, was kindled, though it yet burnt but feebly in France. I wrote—I acted upon my newly-acquired principles, with the energy of a sufferer, and with the resolution of a martyr.[102]

In *Desmond* (1792) Mrs. Smith appears a little less enthusiastic, discussing rather than praising. Desmond remarks that the English are rejoicing in French troubles thus: "Oh! the French deserve it all for what they did against us in America." Montfleuri interrupts to argue that French intervention was

---

[100] Page 289. Here Mrs. Mackenzie makes the egregious slip of permitting the general to confess that he fought only to save his property, and, too, the reader recalls that his part in the war was chiefly showing the better part of valor.

[101] Page 291.

[102] IV, 290-291.

. . . the act of the cabinet, not of the people, who had no choice, but went on to be shot at for the liberties of America, without having any liberty at all of their own. However, our court has found its punishment; blinded by that restless desire of conquest, and their jealousy of the English, which has ever marked its politics, our government did not reflect that they were thus tacitly encouraging a spirit subversive to all their views; nor foresee, that the men who were sent out to assist in the preservation of American freedom, would soon learn that they were degraded by being themselves slaves; and would return to their native country to assert their right to be themselves free.[103]

Against these rather tremulous arias of approbation, the chorus of reaction roars self-confidently throughout the decade. After noting, by way of preliminary, Pinkerton's assurance in his *New Tale of a Tub* (1790) that a republic in France will succeed not a whit better than one in America,[104] we run into two burly satires of Priestley—and incidentally of Price: *Flights of Inflatus* (1791) and *The History of Sir Geoffry Restless* (1791), both apparently by Henry Man, whose point of view may conceivably have been conditioned by his position in the South Sea House.[105] The former we can dismiss, since its excitement is chiefly over Priestley's theological disputes. The latter takes up various aspects of his career, but we are interested only in the references to his political theories. Satire is achieved through Sir Geoffry Restless, a sort of latter-day de Coverley, except that, far from being unwaveringly Tory, he is subject to such whims as an enthusiasm for "one Selim Slim, a presbyterian parson, who formerly had distinguished himself as a philosopher. . . ."[106] With Slim goes Slug, obviously Price:

His [Sir Geoffry's] ideas upon civil government were no less extravagant and absurd than Slim's, or Slim's friend Slug, who has pes-

[103] I, 151-153.

[104] Pp. 23-24.

[105] The title page of each novel says, "By the Author of the Trifler," which Man published in 1770 (*D. N. B*). Lamb gives an interesting description of him in "The South-Sea House"; the author of the novels is fitted by the description of Man as intensely interested in politics and as having a wit unfitted for "these fastidious days."

[106] I, 106. "In person Priestley was slim. . . ." (*D. N. B.*).

tered the world so much about the American revolution, and the pure democratic form of its present government, as a circumstance of all things to be wished to take place in this or any other country, at the hazard of any commotions whatever, notwithstanding the constitution of England, establishes the freedom of its inhabitants upon the firmest basis.[107]

As a result of the Slim-Slug influence, Sir Geoffry addresses the county court:

The misfortune is, gentlemen . . . that you will not pay that attention to the natural and unalienable rights of men, which my friend Mr. Selim Slim the presbyterian parson has so repeatedly offered in his writings to your serious consideration. . . .

If you would allow them to live in a perfect state of civil liberty, or according to the tendency of my friend's arguments upon this subject, to leave them to their own free will, to do what they pleased, without any restraint or check upon their actions, you would deprive them of the only means of doing mischief, and of every excitement to the commission of crimes.[108]

Price-Priestley terminology drips from the passage, which goes on to become a hodge-podge of nearly all newfangled ideas of the day as the knight argues for the Golden Age, the relaxation of marriage laws, the abolition of the judiciary and the priesthood, and many other proposals, and concludes with a plea that people

agree with the whole truth of innovations, with respect both to civil and religious liberty, which, as from the penetrating eye of a demi-god, my friend Mr. Selim Slim has so lavishly offered to your consideration.[109]

[107] I, 107. Price's papers on the American Revolution have already been frequently cited.

[108] I, 111.

[109] I, 124. Price's Revolution Sermon in 1789 inspired Burke's *Reflections on the French Revolution*, which in turn brought forth Priestley's *Letters to Burke* (Birmingham, 1791). Priestley makes the point that America flourished with complete religious liberty (pp. iv-vi). Of Burke he says, ". . . I must now no longer class him among the friends of what I deem to be *the cause of liberty, civil or religious*"; see Anne Holt, *A Life of Joseph Priestley* (Oxford, 1931), p. 147.

Sir Geoffry arouses only a laugh, and, on returning home, finds Slim and Slug writing furiously, the latter

poring over his calculations, in all the stupidity of feature conceivable, for the purpose of proving by them the ruin of this most flourishing country.[110]

Finally the knight recovers from his infatuation and orders the philosophers out, whereupon Slim calls him

a vile cowardly apostate from the sublime principles of civil and religious liberty, and the natural and unalienable rights of men.[111]

A fight follows; Slug sneaks off, and Slim narrowly avoids a severe beating.

Then the author takes time out to discuss Slim, admitting that he is really a distinguished philosopher except for his incessant religious disputes and

his self-sufficient propagation of his levelling principles respecting civil government, and reducing all things to a state of democratical anarchy at the risk of any commotions whatever. . . .[112]

This comment leads naturally to the expected attack on the French Revolution, with a scornful comment on America:

With respect to the American states, they are composed of a set of emigrants from this kingdom.—They fondle over their plebeian indistinction, because there never was any nobility among them; and their admirers on this side the atlantic, vainly imagine, that a nation like France, whose sons have been bred up with the highest notions of rank and precedence, will as tamely fall into the same measures (which a terrible convulsion has forced upon them) as the states of America

[110] I, 128. Price's writings on national finances were so well-known that they became the subject of a contemporary study, William Morgan's *A Review of Dr. Price's Writings of the Finances of Great Britain* (2nd ed., 1795). On October 6, 1778, the American Congress resolved to ask Price to assist in the management of colonial finances; see Roland Thomas, *Richard Price: Philosopher and Apostle of Liberty* (Oxford, 1924), pp. 86-87.

[111] I, 142. Cf. T. E. Thorpe, *Joseph Priestley* (New York: Dutton, 1906), p. 116: "His [Priestley's] controversies, . . . were carried on with temper and decency."

[112] I, 156.

have done: whose levelling principle of government has not the least shadow of a precedent to oppose it; but flows naturally in upon them from their origin, or first existence in that country.[113]

For once the two revolutions are not lumped together indiscriminately. The spirit and intention, however, are those of the suspicious decade, prolific in satirists, which offers *Berkeley Hall, The Vagabond,* and *The Anti-Jacobin* as its best work.

By comparison, Ann Thomas's *Adolphus de Biron* (1794) is very doleful indeed. M. de Biron views the wreckage with horror:

> Our Interference in the American War poisoned our Loyalty, and taught us to be ungovernable. These latent Principles of Faction and Infidelity have been silently fermenting together for some time; but little did we suspect, that all Orders and Establishments, that all Government and Religion would so soon be blown up by the Explosion.[114]

Gloomier still, and proportionately long-winded, is Monsieur D——, who, writing to an English friend, pleads that England do not fight against France:

> How different was our Conduct, when we lately saw you weakened by intestine Divisions, and engaged in an unfortunate War with your Colonies, which terminated in the Dismemberment of your Empire! . . . At the Moment we were renewing the most solemn Promises of Friendship, we were secretly assisting your American Subjects; till at last, in Violation of every Principle of Honour, and the most sacred Obligation of Treaty, we threw off the Mask, and commenced your open Enemies. . . .
>
> But what was the Consequence of our Treachery to ourselves? Alas! all the Misery we now groan under originated from our unjust and unprovoked Interference in that War. It was in America that our People were first possessed with the Spirit of Liberty, or rather with the Demon of Licentiousness. This evil Genius, imported to France, and uniting with Infidelity (the spontaneous Production of our Country) has engendered a pernicious Brood of Evils, that are the Bane of Social Happiness, and the natural Offspring, of such a Connexion.—

[113] I, 171.
[114] I, 5.

For my own Part, I cannot help considering our present Calamities as the just Judgment of Heaven for our Perfidy.[115]

The lovers of the new masses viewed these phenomena somewhat differently.

Such dismal cringing, implausibly foisted upon an improbable Frenchman by a very virtuous English spinster, one is glad to give up for the somewhat merrier anti-sans-culottism of Pye's *Democrat* (1795), which satirizes French participation in the American struggle in a different way. The French forces, and indeed the doctrine of leveling and the spirit of liberty, are personified in picaresque Jean Le Noir,

one of those that were sent by the court of France to assist the Americans against Great-Britain. During the voyage he was encouraged by his comrades to extend his notions of equality beyond the narrow limits of private property. The French officers . . . considering themselves now as champions of universal liberty, all the doctrines of equality and freedom . . . were impressed in full force on their eager and frivolous imaginations.

As for his conduct during the war:

It is sufficient to say, that however his theory of equalization might be enlarged, he was not forgetful of the practical scheme he had formerly adopted; and in the execution of this, he exercised the strictest impartiality; omitting no opportunity of making a more equal division of the property of those to whom fortune had given a larger share than himself, without at all regarding whether they were on the side of Great-Britain or France.

Thus the new Franco-American view of life. After the war he decides to stay in America, which, since

new forms of government and new regulations of law were going to be tried, offered more brilliant scenes to his imagination than the established code of his country; he embraced therefore the earliest opportunity of asserting his natural right to independence, by deserting his regiment.

Because it is Boston where "opposition to the power of England

[115] II, 88-89.

had originally broke [*sic*] out," he fixes on it "for his asylum."
There he

soon rendered himself conspicuous by his violent declamations in
favour of universal liberty, and his avowed determination to quit for
ever a country submitted to the yoke of monarchal and aristocratical
despotism, for the happier regions of independence and equality: professions which flattered both the natural and political prejudices of his
hearers, and which strongly prepossessed them in favor of a youth,
who . . . soon got to be domesticated in some of the best families of
Boston. Nor did he suffer either his principles or his practices to lie
dormant.

He stayed

till the seeds of republicanism, sown among the French army while on
that continent, produced so abundant an harvest in their own country,
to which he then eagerly returned, as to a proper theatre on which he
might display his natural talents, now so greatly improved by the many
civic conversations he had held with the enlightened inhabitants of
New-England.[116]

Pye's sarcasms, relatively restrained, make clear his feeling that
the distinguishing French and American trait is gullibility in
the presence of false prophets. Ultimately Le Noir gets to
England, where he is amazed to discover that a popular election
may choose the most able and disinterested candidate,

as he had been informed by the most respectable authority, both in
France and America, that there were seldom above three or four voters
in any place, who were either obliged to chuse whoever the Minister,
or some great lord nominated; or, if they were left to their own
choice, always put the seat up to public auction, and sold it to the best
bidder.[117]

And an old story crops up once again when the Count de
Tournelles complains that the French, after the war in America,

along with our laurels, brought back the seeds of those principles
which have overspread our country with calamity and ruin.[118]

[116] I, 5-10.
[117] I, 27.
[118] I, 66.

Novelists do not abate their fury as the century goes out but continue to belabor libertarians. *Berkeley Hall* and *The Vagabond,* with their onslaughts on primitivistic theories, have already been quoted amply; the latter, it is to be recalled, flays the French Revolution more bitterly than any of the standpatters. Finally there is Mary Anne Burges's *The Progress of the Pilgrim Good-Intent* (1800), which, in the same way in which Surr revamps *Barnwell* to illuminate contemporary evils, adapts Bunyan for the task of quelling Jacobinism. There is little, however, specifically to our purpose. Miss Burges draws a vivid picture of *Liberty* overthrowing the tower of SOCIAL ORDER and producing a lake of blood "whence presently flowed a stream, which deluged all the country round,"[119] but she avoids geographical specifications. Then there is a group of people loaded with chains, the result of practicing the doctrines of RIGHTS-OF-MAN.[120] The Pilgrim has to ascend the Hill *Difficulty,* but this is easy in comparison with the alternative, the mountain of *Revolution.*[121] The author's agitation, however, is largely a result of the French Revolution.

So ends the intrusion of novelists' noses into politics. The olfactory venture, it must be recorded, proceeds from a tentative sniffing to a very considerable suspicion, and from suspicion to continual growls of antagonism. Not always, of course. The heralds of a new order, who subsequent history was to show had the better sense of the world's direction, recognized a new nation, praised its tolerance, admired the honesty and excellence of its political system, hailed warmly its contribution to political reform in England, Ireland, and France. But the believers in the "progress of civil society," as that laborious versifier, Richard Payne Knight, called it, were numerically in a minority. The doubters, the leaners-backward, the staunch souls to whom all political virtue rested eternally in the English Constitution—

[119] (2nd American, from 5th English, ed., Charlestown, 1801), p. 49.
[120] Pp. 54-55.
[121] Page 57.

417

they thought taxes were high in America, sneered at American wisdom, considered a republic impracticable, and viewed Demos with passing great suspicion. Barring major disturbances, their outcries might soon have subsided into negligible whispers. But the Bastille fell, and their whole world seemed to be clattering about their ears. Then they gained voice, and often wit, and, when they viewed the spectacle of a Franco-American combination assaulting the old order, threatening, it seemed, all dependable institutions, they clamored against an onrushing world; grubbily morose at times, they were mostly sharp and agile in a spirited offensive, laying about them lustily with satirical weapons often of no mean order. So in the '90's the novels picture America as a rascally disturber of the peace, at times merely wrongheaded, at others deliberately bent on overturning a satisfactory world. In so doing, they were creating the political novel.

Novelists' views of American institutions—slavery, the church, the political system—though not all of a piece, have something in common. All the problems cluster, in greater or less degree, about the war. The attack on slavery, first achieving maturity after the war, possibly found vital stimulation in the humanitarianism which the war called forth. The war probably put an end to the interest in Christianizing Indians, and it naturally put an end to the hopes for an established church in America; it certified, too, the religious tolerance which many Englishmen lauded highly. And, of course, all political questions were a result of the war, without which there would have been no American system to discuss. Many novels would not have existed or would have been considerably different but for the Revolution, the state of affairs which it brought about, and the consequent repercussions in Europe. This is the final service of the war to the novel.

The picture of America which emerges from the various discussions is a fairly unified and consistent one. There are usually two panels, which reflect two kinds of artistic temperament, the conservative and the liberal. The adherents of new thought do not like slavery; but they realize that an established church in America is out of the question, they wholeheartedly approve of religious tolerance, and they point with pride to America's political experiment. "Civil and religious liberty" is their slogan. The defenders of the old order, on the other hand, present at least one tableau of an ideal relationship between slave and master; they suspect America of substituting religiosity for religion, for they incline to interpret Puritanism and Methodism as pretentious shams; and in politics America is, they sincerely believe, a mere subverter of genuine law and order.

Two conclusions appear. In the first place, derogation is markedly more voluble than praise, and the attitude of the liberals to slavery, combined with the suspicion of the conservatives of the ecclesiastical and political situation in America, makes anything but an appetizing picture of the new world. It is hardly thinkable that prospective emigrants could have been inspired by such reading matter as that here quoted, and yet, in this, the most popular form of literature, they found more attacks than defenses. In other words, skepticism sets the dominant tone in the descriptions of American society, and once again we find the loss of faith which we have already seen influencing the concept of America. To repeat the initial thesis, there is unquestioned progress toward the hard analysis, the quest for the factual, which is central in European discussions of America until today. Now it may be argued that all the adverse criticism of America is not to be taken too seriously or to be conceded the value of a reasoned estimate, because it represents not a consistent attitude but only a flurry, an unreasoning snappishness of a momentarily frightened England. It may be said that it has, therefore, a disproportionate volume, which must be reduced in drawing conclusions.

In that case, a second interpretation is to be made: what is to be stressed here is the importance of the difference of opinion, regardless of which side seems to predominate. There is the same clash that we have seen before, and it is this clash which convincingly demonstrates the increasing realism in the attitude to America. Neither of the debating teams may have been very near metaphysical truths, but at least there was a debate, and not a unanimous genuflection before an unquestioned, shining ideal, as there virtually was in the Great Dawn. The Everlasting Yea of the Renaissance may not be completely negatived, but the hecklers have gained courage and assertiveness. Hecklers, if not always completely admirable in themselves, sometimes prevent too easy hoodwinking. And the hoodwinking by the believers in El Dorado and Utopia, whether deliberate or accidental, is about finished. The attacks have opened the way for clearer analysis.

# CONCLUSION

This study has been divided into two main parts: the first, Chapters III to VII, discusses the influence of the American Revolution on the contents of English prose fiction; the second, Chapters IX to XII, describes apparent changes in the English concept of America as expressed in prose fiction, with notes on the probable influence of the war in bringing about those changes. These two aspects of the study, however, are neither parallel nor consecutive, but interlocking; and separation for convenience' sake should not lead to an ignoring of interrelationships. When one reads stories about the war, he learns considerable about the English attitude to America and the English idea of Americans; as one goes through books discussing the promise or the people or the politics of America, he automatically infers some relationships with the war, or else he notes a direct connection with a narrative of the war. On the one hand, Pratt's war story, *Emma Corbett,* shows great sympathy with and admiration for Americans, and Mrs. Smith's *Old Manor House* a lively appreciation of American spirit and ideals; on the other, Pye's *Democrat* founds its satire of political liberalism in a story of the war, and Mrs. Smith's *Celestina* comments on the political situation brought about by the war. Again, *Jonathan Corncob* is, from one point of view, a war-story; from another, a treatment of American character. It remains to make a few more such cross references.

The direct influences of the war on the novel, as outlined in the earlier chapters, were an apparent lowering of the production of novels during the war; an increase of American material of all kinds in the novel; the appearance of about seventy-five stories dealing with the war in one way or another; the introduction into about two score of novels of favorable or unfavorable discussions of the principles and management of the war; many discussions of colonial and economic problems leading up to the war, and the economic implications and results of the war; and the use of American themes in satirizing various aspects, most notably the government, of life at home.

Here, the function of the war was primarily the provision of material about which to write; in finding subjects, however, the writers were not merely being neutral storytellers but were already giving clues to the interpretation of America. In creating stories or in discussing theories about the conflict, novelists were establishing a concept of American character, which, in all the events from the Stamp Act to Yorktown, is alleged to show spirit and independence, or else crudeness, selfishness, and even barbarism—the same elements which appear later in discussions not related to the war. The constant stress on the oppression of Americans and on the desolation of America implies a certain excellence in both the people and the country. The wailing and the gnashing of teeth about the economic consequences of the war show a sense of the material advantages resident in the new country, and fall into line with the treatment of America as the Land of Promise. The intertwining of American affairs in criticism and satire of English government and methods again implies something admirable in America and Americans, who, as a nation, were best praised by the portraits of Washington and Franklin. On the other hand, America as a point of departure in satire appears much less frequently in years in which the existent order in England is felt to need defense, and, indeed, situations are then reversed.

When we pass over to those books and passages which are introduced primarily in their interpretative function, we find that many of them have a connection with or a starting point in the war. The ideal community in *Henry Willoughby* is the result of a flight from the war; that in *Disobedience* is, as it were, guaranteed by the war, the safeguard of American integrity. The type of plot in which the success of the young man is important often sends him to the war to make a name for himself. In the popular story in which a character, meeting misfortune in love or finance, seeks sanctuary in America, he most frequently goes to the war. When America is conceived of as off-stage, a convenient place in which to have an actor while other events are taking place on the stage, that actor is often sent to fight. At least half of the discussions of American character have their genesis in war stories. Finally, in the commentaries on American institutions, those concerned with politics and government inevitably start with or refer to the war.

Thus there is constant interaction between the two main divisions of the material, neither of which is fully significant in isolation. The two parts must be considered jointly, also, in evaluating finally the contribution of the American subjects to the technical development of the novel. Perhaps the reader is struck most sharply by a lack of influence—the failure of the war-material, immediate and dramatic as it was, to inject any real vitality into the novel. There is no effective realism of the sort produced by the World War. The novel of adventure had little to do with America, and it is only in the specialized picaresque form that we find mild distinction—for example, in *Jonathan Corncob*. The less robust writers, the sentimentalists, introduced transatlantic scenes most regularly, but they fitted them into old patterns with tearful intent. That of the parted lovers will do as a reminder. In the later chapters, dealing with the concept of America, we have seen further typical episodes introduced without freshness or effort at innovation—the trip to America for fame and fortune, the flight from disgrace, the journey in behalf of the broken heart, the convenient disappearance while complications pile up at home. The growing consciousness of America, then, appears to have done little more than provide another name to be carelessly substituted for the Scotland or France or Italy which was used just as much and would do just as well.

There is, on the other hand, a less negative conclusion. In

423

the realm of satire American subjects produced, if nothing new, at least relative excellence in the popular novel—action, zest, traces of character, and highly entertaining farce. Besides these, there are at least two contributions to new types. The heterodox treatment of the war, not as a glorious crusade but as futile horror and cruelty, and the related attack on all war, with its suggestion of modern pacifism, provide the first intimations of the humanitarian novel. Superficially sentimental, various such novels have some authentic concern for mankind, manifesting what today is called "social consciousness." With them must be considered a group in reality much larger than it has been possible to demonstrate here—the anti-slavery novels, expressing a movement to which the war in various ways probably gave impetus. The two causes are recognizably established in fiction that was still much concerned with the elegant remarks of Lord This and Lady That, and they lay the foundation for a type that, with the addition of many themes, is of first importance today. The spirit of reform in humanitarian works carries over into another aspect of prose fiction. We saw, in Chapter V, a great deal of criticism of the government because of the war; in Chapter VI, equally extensive criticism of the management of colonial affairs; in Chapter VII, use of American material in criticism of English politics and government; in Chapter XII, somewhat the converse, a defense, direct or implied, of the English political system by way of attack on American democracy, especially when coupled with that in France. All these elements, whether liberal or reactionary in tone, unite to lay the foundation of the political novel, which, with characters, plots, and other equipment of fiction, is beginning to take over the functions of the pamphlet. The new form, neither mature nor polished, yet clearly existent, is almost never throughout this period separated from America and American issues.

In content and form, then, the debts of prose fiction to the war and allied events are these: a number of subjects which

CONCLUSION

were used with surprising frequency and disappointing monot-
ony; new scenes and names to fit into old plots and forms,
among which only the satirical and the picaresque made rather
good reading of the material presented; the stuff from which
the humanitarian novel began to take form; a wealth of excellent supplies from which to construct the political novel.

There remains the question of interpretation and attitude—
the concept of America. The war stories, if not unanimous,
show a startling preponderance of sentiment favorable to Americans; the attacks on North are equalled by praise for the
courage and tenacity of the rebels, who emerge in the end, not
merely victims of oppression, but plumed knights utterly devoted to a high cause. America becomes the land of the free
and the home of the brave. Now, against this we have seen, in
Chapters IX to XII, a quite different point of view, a strong
tendency to examine more closely, to doubt and even deny, the
virtues attributed to America, Americans, and American society.
Not that the new world is without defense and even praise, but
it no longer has a majority; there is a balance of pro and
con, with the skeptical opposition achieving, at century-end, an
almost complete control of fiction. Was the support of the
revolutionaries, then, only a passing enthusiasm, to disappear
on sober reflection? Is there an inconsistency in the interpretation, an irreconcilable contradiction in attitudes? Does the novel
flit hither and yon, so blown about by various winds of feeling
that it provides no trustworthy key to the period?

Before answering the questions, it may be well to summarize
the less ecstatic comments on the American scene. In these days
when the pseudo-cultural flight from America to Europe is
becoming somewhat less a spiritual necessity than it was once
supposed to be, it is interesting to look back to the last days
of the anti-cultural flight from Europe to America. In the eyes
of the late eighteenth-century fiction, America as the home of
a new Golden Age was becoming less and less plausible, and
Europe more habitable after all. Professed believers there still

were, but they appear to have been as much dollar-minded drummers as true acolytes at the altar of the American ideal. The stuff that dreams are made of was being torn to shreds by shrewd unbelievers. The Land of Promise still held on, but this was less a vision than simple economics. The land of gold, however, that glittering creation of the Renaissance, and its various transformations were passing; to cross the Atlantic no longer made one an Aladdin with an omnipotent lamp. In fact, the creatures of the fiction-world were making the long voyage less because they wanted to than because they had to, glumly leaving civilization because of censorious eyes or the condition of their hearts or pocketbooks or because America was preferable to jail. It is no very cheerful world that is created from their stories, and anything but an idealized one, anything but the glorious land where liberty made a leonine struggle against tyranny. As America grew older and less stimulating to the imagination, it no longer suggested glorious adventure and heroic quest. In spite of improvements in communications, America was felt to be far away, and the journey was uncomfortable and dangerous. As the century came to an end, there was continued emphasis on the uncultivated backwoods, the hostile wilderness, "the desolate wilds of America." Arcadia was forgotten, and instead there was the end of the world. Its inhabitants ranged between astonishing virtue and astonishing villainy, seldom as characters in fiction becoming very plausible; awkwardness in portrayal aside, the important thing is the failure of Americans as citizens to evoke the wide admiration which came to them as fighters. Their attitude to negroes was anything but praiseworthy. Their latitudinarianism in religion was commendable, most observers thought, but in actual practice they leaned regrettably toward intolerable dourness, freakishness, pretentiousness, and hypocrisy. As for their republicanism, to some it seemed the last word in political achievement; to still more, a sad commentary on the decline of true civil order, an indulgence of the worst in human nature, a deceptive prelude

426

to anarchy. So America reached 1800 pretty much without make-up, still beautiful to some, to others plain and even repellent. She was no longer the Renaissance belle, and romance was about over.

Now to return to the apparent contradiction between the glorified war-time America and the debatable peace-time United States. The first picture was of course colored by the sympathy which naturally evaporated when the underdog won and became more comfortably established than could have been expected. Then English patriotism grew less critical and resumed a normal defensiveness, coupled with a characteristic suspicion of foreigners. Further, there was a difference between the '70's and '80's, when liberalism was coming into the ascendant, and the '90's, when Robespierre and then Napoleon played into the hands of reaction. Even with all the changes in circumstance, however, I do not think that the novel underwent a fundamental change in its attitude to America, but that, on the contrary, it was consistently as realistic as it was capable of being. Admitting that the praise of the fighting Americans was at times hyperbolical, even hysterical, the fact is that English disapproval of the war, as manifested in the novel, was anything but romantic or enthusiastic. It grew out of economic fact: the English were losing money. It grew out of political fact: the middle classes were seriously concerned about the preservation of their own liberties. It grew out of psychological fact: apparently most of the nation sensed that the government was mismanaging affairs badly from almost every point of view. Hence the pro-Americanism, which, when it appears with violent emotionalism in the novels, is merely being decked out, quite ineptly, for popular consumption.

The near-apotheosis of Americans was not absolute, but only relative to the specific circumstances. Once the war was out of the way, the realistic tendency, the sense of fact, began to retouch the portrait of America and Americans, and the new product was much more somber, suggesting even a disillusioned brush. Here one is aware of realism in a more exact sense. It may be argued, perhaps, that there was no realism because nowhere can one find a single sound, balanced interpretation of America. In a sense that is true. But, if as yet we find no middle ground of unbiased evaluation, we can derive a workable mean from difference of opinion. Of that we have a sufficiency, and there is the important fact. Certainly there is a safer avenue to truth through diversity of views than through unanimous adulation. Real insight, of course, comes neither from an aggregate of differences nor through a sort of average of conflicting judgments, but from skilled, modulated individual analyses. These are prepared for by debate.

The new realistic attitude to America appears in its best light by comparison with earlier periods when the new world with its size and freshness and potentialities overwhelmed the old world and made balance and rationality impossible. El Dorado, Utopia, individual and social excellence, a new political order, a fulfilled Christianity, a scene of heroic endeavor—such ideas flew together in a shining, breath-taking muddle which was America. Such an expansive hope was bound to be deflated, and no one could tell what America really meant until the glitter of gold, real and metaphorical, had stopped blinding the sight. Today most reasoned critiques at least have perspective. Before scenes could be reported truly, mirages had to go, and there is the service of these once-popular novels. Biased, perhaps, and never very clear-eyed at best, many of them no doubt reacted too far and thus went way beyond fact, but at least they debated, and, in so doing, they punctured illusions and cleared the ground for dispassionate criticism.

When the novel first began taking serious account of America at the time of the Revolution, it took over, as a matter of course, most of the myths and legends which had grown up from the sixteenth century on. There had never been major or consistent dissent. When the novel passed America on to the nineteenth century, it handed over a vitally changed saga, practically denuded of heroic and faery accoutrements. As a mere matter of chronology, the war appears to mark the dividing line between the early and the late America. It both provided the first sharp break in the continuity of an idealizing tradition and compelled a protracted acquaintanceship with actualities that, better known, were less susceptible of exaltation. Wildernesses responsible for defeats were little suitable for idyls, and untrustworthy and barbarous redskins, rated disgraceful allies even by Parliament, were poor models for noble savages. The basic, incontrovertible fact, however, is that the war created a new entity, a new order, a new nation, in place of a dependent and virtually unbounded continent. There could not fail to be a new perspective and new meanings. All America's wonderful possibilities alienated, the country began to seem distant and uncivilized after all. People could remember all the convicts sent there, and the once courageous pioneers began to look like very ordinary and unpleasant levelers. So it appeared in an impressive number of novels. This literary microcosm may not be fully representative, but its apparent movement insistently suggests, and for its own duration unmistakably coincides with, the sweep and the complete transformation of an idea between Elizabeth and Victoria.

If America did the novel somewhat of a service by providing it with much to talk about, the novel did America an equal service by initiating her rescue from a false and essentially untenable position. Neither America nor any other country was up to a 365-day role of Great World Hope. In making this point, the popular novel was showing a characteristic unwillingness to play along unquestioningly with Romantic developments. True, in espousing the call for reform in the '70's and '80's, it was carried ahead by the rising tide of the new worldsentiments. Then it held back. In making the first sharp attack on Romantic primitivism and in registering a profound suspicion of democracy, it refused to adopt positions which, in either proposals or poems, were countenanced by Southey, Coleridge,

Wordsworth, Shelley, Campbell, and, fleetingly, even Byron. The last words of the Age of Prose, though spoken by no one of any consequence, were, in a small way, ahead of their times. They made the first serious effort to view America rationally. Novels had their illusions, of course, plenty of them, but grasping also at facts, they approached a balance, a realistic interpretation.

The American Revolution secured a surprisingly large place in the contemporary English novel. The novel, interpreting the Revolution for the middle classes, showed a scarcely anticipated penetration of the fundamental issues, an understanding which expressed itself in a hearty pro-Americanism. The same sense of fact led later to a growing skepticism of the values which were distinctively American. America had long held a place in English literature, but it was a pleasantly vague, ill-defined place, created rather by an unfettered imagination than by knowledge or a real urge to interpret. Then came the war, and the era of stimulating generalities was clearly doomed. The novel adapted current events to its own use; reading them, it made the initial efforts toward a real insight.

# APPENDICES

## AND

# BIBLIOGRAPHY

THE DEVELOPMENT OF THE GOTHIC NOVEL, THE HISTORICAL
NOVEL, SCANDINAVIAN INFLUENCE, THE CELTIC REVIVAL,
ANTIQUARIANISM, AND THE ORIENTAL TALE

The following tables illustrate the rise of the historical novel and
the Gothic novel.[1]

| Period | Number of Works | |
|---|---|---|
| | Historical | Gothic |
| 1760-1769...... | 3 | 1 |
| 1770-1779...... | 3 | 1 |
| 1780-1784...... | 3 | 2 |
| 1785-1789...... | 7 | 8 |
| 1790-1794...... | 25 | 10 |
| 1795-1799...... | 29 | 45 |

No argument is necessary to show that the first substantial increase in
the number of novels of both types occurs in the half-decade after the
conclusion of the war; the parallel development is more significant than
would be a marked increase in either genre alone at the time concerned.
With regard to the Gothic novel, Professor Heidler finds the period
1778-1789 one of increased interest:

Decidedly, the critical attitude towards romantic fiction had changed.
The times were indeed favorable for Mrs. Radcliffe's romances. . . .[2]

The statistics shown above gain value if added to others of similar
import. An interesting phenomenon of the time was the development
of interest in Norse mythology and literature. If measurable at all, it

[1] The figures represent my own count of the entries in the subject-file in
Professor Greenough's Catalogue. Usually an entry denotes a historical or
Gothic novel, sometimes a novel with a predominant or large historical or Gothic
interest. Works such as *The Recess*, where the two types coalesce, are counted
in each group.

[2] Heidler, *op. cit.*, p. 145.

433

can be gauged by Professor Farley's chronological list of English works showing Scandinavian influence,[3] from which I have drawn up the following tables:

| Period | Number of Works |
|---|---|
| 1700-1760...... | 13 |
| 1761-1770...... | 14 |
| 1771-1780...... | 7 |
| 1781-1790...... | 20 |
| 1791-1800...... | 12 |

Here is to be noted not only the increase of works after the war, such as we have already seen, but also an important concomitant, the apparent decline of interest during the decade in which most of the war was fought.

A related subject is that of the new interest in things Celtic, which has been examined in the period 1760-1800 by Professor Snyder. The material which he finds between 1760 and 1770 is "by no means rich";[4] in the next decade the Celtic influence is "more pronounced";[5] the final decade of the century "shows the Celtic Revival in full swing."[6] The intervening decade I have purposely taken out of chronological arrangement in order to throw emphasis upon Professor Snyder's conclusion with regard to it:

As one looks back over the decade from 1781 to 1790, it is evident that the Celtic-English poetry produced amounted to more, in both quality and quantity, than that of the previous twenty years.[7]

Once again the decade in which the war ended shows a significant increase in literary production.

Another tradition was that of the new antiquarianism most familiarly exemplified in Percy's *Reliques.* Professor Jensen's "List of Works

[3] Frank E. Farley, *Scandinavian Influences in the English Romantic Movement* ([Harvard] Studies and Notes in Philology and Literature, Vol. IX, Boston, 1903), pp. 229-231. As in all these lists, the count is my own.

[4] Edward D. Snyder, *The Celtic Revival in English Literature 1760-1800* (Cambridge: Harvard University Press, 1923), p. 105.

[5] Page 128.

[6] Page 188.

[7] Page 162.

Published between 1765 and 1802 Illustrating the Revival of Interest in the Study of the Early Literature of England and Scotland"[8] shows the following distribution of such works:

| Period | Number of Works |
|---|---|
| 1761-1770...... | 12 |
| 1771-1780...... | 20 |
| 1781-1790...... | 30 |
| 1791-1800...... | 28 |

Here the tabulation is less striking than previously, since there is a notable increase in the '70's; in the next decade, however, the rate of increase is higher and the peak is reached.

Finally, to examine another genre familiar in the eighteenth century, the Oriental tale, we find in Miss Conant's list[9] of English works reflecting an interest in the Orient the following distribution:

| Period | Number of Works |
|---|---|
| 1760-1770...... | 19 |
| 1771-1780...... | 12 |
| 1781-1790...... | 23 |
| 1791-1800...... | 27 |

The decline during the war-years and the subsequent increase are closely perceptible.

[8] Arthur E. Jensen, *The Revival of Early Literature in England and Scotland from Percy to Scott 1765-1802* (Doctoral Dissertation, University of Edinburgh, 1933), II, 472-486. Dr. Jensen's list up to 1770 includes only ten titles, to which are added, in my count, two works earlier in the decade whose existence he has called to my attention.

[9] Martha P. Conant, *The Oriental Tale in England in the Eighteenth Century* (New York: Columbia University Press, 1908), pp. 279-291. The rather complicated assemblage of new editions and reprints makes it difficult to secure a dependable count. I have found, however, that the resultant curve is much the same whether one counts only first editions or all editions. In order to provide the most comprehensive view of the interest in the form, I have done the latter, including, for instance, all the editions of Voltaire's works, but not counting separately the individual Oriental tales except when they were published separately.

In summary, we observe that the production of historical novels increased rapidly in the second half of the '80's, that Gothic novels likewise suddenly became more numerous in these years, that the interest in Scandinavian material dropped during the '70's and then underwent a marked rise during the following decade, that the Celtic influence first really began to flower in the '80's, that antiquarian interests showed a slight increase in the same years, and that the Oriental tale, the only one of these literary elements to have a long life before this period, appeared less frequently during the '70's, and then underwent a renewal of popularity in the next decade. In other words, of the half-dozen literary streams here examined, those which existed before the war all tended to become restricted during the war-years, and those which were just coming into existence made a scarcely audible splash before 1781; then, after the outcome of the American controversy was clear, all broadened out into currents of sufficient strength and importance to affect permanently the literary geography of the period. As already acknowledged, the figures and tendencies give no definite proof of a war-influence. The combination of decreases and subsequent increases, however, offers some probability, as has been set forth in Chapter II, that the war exerted a temporary check upon literary development.

# APPENDIX B

## NEGATIVE RESULTS

The following list includes novels in which I have found no references to America, the West Indies, or the East Indies. See Chapter III. Titles are listed under year of publication. A few works, such as those of Jane Austen, are included under presumptive dates of composition.

1761. William Hawkesworth, Almoran and Hamet; Mrs. Charlotte Lennox, Henrietta.

1762. A History of the Matrimonial Adventures of a Banker's Clerk; John Langhorne, Solyman and Almena.

1764. Horace Walpole, The Castle of Otranto.

1765. Nutrebian Tales.

1766. The Adventures of Jack Wander; Samuel Johnson, The Fountains; Margaret and Susanna Minifie, The Picture.

1767. The History of Julia; James Boswell, Dorando; Mrs. Frances Sheridan, The History of Nourjahad.

1768. Flagel; The History of Miss Emilia Beville; The Vanity of Human Wishes; Thomas Mulso, Callistus.

1769. The Fruitless Repentance; The Happy Discovery; The Masquerade; Treyssac de Vergy, The Lovers, The Mistakes of the Heart.

1770. Belinda; Letters between an English Lady and her Friend at Paris; The Maid of Quality; Anne Dawe, The Younger Sister; Richard Griffith, The Koran; Janet Timbury, The Male Coquet.

1772. The Precipitate Choice; C. H., Genuine Memoirs of Miss Harriet Melvin and Miss Leanora Stanway.

1773. The Mercenary Marriage; 'Twas Wrong to Marry Him; William Duff, The History of Rhedi.

1775. Sophronia; The Tender Father; Maria S. Cooper, The History of Fanny Meadows.

1776. Alexander Bicknell, The History of Lady Anne Neville.

1777. Clara Reeve, The Old English Baron; A. Rogers, The History of Miss Temple.

1778. Alexander Bicknell, Prince Arthur; Frances Burney, Evelina.

1779. Georgiana Cavendish, Duchess of Devonshire, The Sylph; Thomas Scott, The Force of Truth.

437

1780. Dorothy Kilner [?], Memoirs of a Peg Top.

1783. School for Majesty; John Murdoch, Pictures of the Heart.

1784. The Distressed Lady; William Beckford, Vathek (tr. Henley); John Potter, The Virtuous Villagers.

1785. The Rencontre; Susanna H. Keir, Interesting Memoirs; Lucy Peacock, The Adventures of Six Princesses of Babylon.

1786. Mrs. M. Harley, St. Bernard's Priory.

1787. Blenheim Lodge; The History of the Unfortunate Sisters; William of Normandy.

1788. Powis Castle; Mrs. Burke, Emilia De St. Aubigne; Esther Finglass, The Recluse; Mrs. M. Harley, The Castle of Mowbray; Mary Wollstonecraft, Mary.

1789. The Progress of Love; Rosenberg; Mrs. C——, Belinda; Anne Fuller, The Son of Ethelwolf; Hannah More [?], The Self-Tormentor; Mrs. Radcliffe, The Castles of Athlin and Dunbayne.

1790. Arnold Zulig; Cornelia Knight, Dinarbas; Mrs. Amelia Opie, Dangers of Coquetry; Mrs. Radcliffe, A Sicilian Romance.

1791. Edwy; E. Miles, Violet Hill; Henry Siddons, Leon.

1792. Thomas Beddoes, The History of Isaac Jenkins; S. E. Brydges, Mary De Clifford; Mrs. Mary Robinson, Vancenza.

1793. John Mitchell, The Female Pilgrim.

1794. Argentum; Stephen Cullen, The Haunted Priory.

1795. Jane Austen, Lady Susan [date?]; Mrs. Mary M. Sherwood, The Traditions; Ann Yearsley, The Royal Captives.

1796. Jane Austen, Pride and Prejudice [date?]; Mrs. Inchbald, Nature and Art.

1797. Percy; Austen, Northanger Abbey [date?]; M. Hare, The Bastile; Mrs. Radcliffe, The Italian.

1798. Theopha; Isaac Disraeli, Romances; Sophia King, Waldorf; Charles Lamb, A Tale of Rosamund Gray; Mrs. Eliza Parsons, An Old Friend with a New Face; Mrs. F. C. Patrick, More Ghosts!

1799. Kilverston Castle; Reginald; The Witch; James N. Brewer, A Winter's Tale; Mrs. Cooke, Battleridge.

1800. Henry of Northumberland; Horatio of Holstein; The Libertines; The Mysterious Penitent; Maria Edgeworth, Castle Rackrent; G. A. Graglia, The Castle of Eridan; Mrs. Pilkington, New Tales of the Castle; George Walker, Three Spaniards.

# APPENDIX C

## America in the Novel, 1761-1800

There follows a list of all the novels and specimens of prose fiction between 1761 and 1800 in which I have found references of any kind to America. See Chapter III. All but a few of these works are discussed in the text. Those which appear only here make brief notes on fauna, flora, geography, and so on, which could be omitted painlessly. Novels which I have been able to treat only through the medium of secondary sources or reviews are marked with an asterisk (*).

1761. Oliver Goldsmith, The Citizen of the World (1760-1761); Charles Johnstone, Chrysal (1760-1765); Lawrence Sterne, Tristam Shandy (1760-1767).

1762. Charles Johnstone, The Reverie.

1763. Mrs. Frances Brooke, Lady Julia Mandeville.

1765. Memoirs of a Coquet; Henry Brooke, The Fool of Quality.

1766. The Adventure of a Bale of Goods; Goldsmith, The Vicar of Wakefield; Lady Sarah Pennington, Letters on Different Subjects.

1767. The Adventures of an Author; The Female American; Philip Withers [?], The Ants; Arthur Young, The Adventures of Emmera.

1768. The Unexpected Wedding; The Visiting Day.

1769. The History of Miss Sommerville; *Private Letters from an American in England; Mrs. Brooke, The History of Emily Montague; Mrs. Elizabeth Griffith, The Delicate Distress; Smollett, The Adventures of an Atom.

1770. Constantia; The Fortunate Blue-Coat Boy; Edward Bancroft, *The History of Charles Wentworth; Thomas Bridges, The Adventures of a Banknote; Charles Jenner, The Placid Man; Charles Johnstone, The Pilgrim.

1771. Anecdotes of a Convent; Mrs. Griffith, The History of Lady Barton; Herbert Lawrence, The Contemplative Man; Mackenzie, The Man of Feeling; Anne Meades, The History of Sir William Harrington; Smollett, Humphry Clinker.

1772. The Birmingham Counterfeit; The Feelings of the Heart; Mrs. Elizabeth Bonhote, The Rambles of Mr. Frankly; Richard Graves, The Spiritual Quixote; Richard Griffith, Something New.

439

1773. A Collection of Scarce . . . Pieces; Emma; The Fatal Effects of Deception; Henry Brooke, Juliet Grenville; Mackenzie, The Man of the World.

1774. Edward; The History of Lord Stanton.

1775. The Correspondents; Mr. Digges of Maryland [?], Adventures of Alonso; Thomas Percival, A Father's Instructions to His Children.

1776. Memoirs of an Unfortunate Queen; Thomas Cogan, John Buncle, Junior, Gentleman; S. J. Pratt, The Pupil of Pleasure.

1777. Mrs. Frances Brooke, The Excursion; Lady Mary Hamilton, Memoirs of the Marchioness de Louvoi; Mackenzie, Julia de Roubigné; S. J. Pratt, Travels for the Heart.

1778. The Fashionable Tell-Tale; The Travels of Hildebrand Bowman; A Trip to Melasge; Mrs. Phoebe Gibbes, *Friendship in a Nunnery; Lady Hamilton, Munster Village.

1779. The Relapse; George Keate, Sketches from Nature; S. J. Pratt, Shenstone Green.

1780. Sir Herbert Croft, Love and Madness; Charlotte Palmer, Female Stability; S. J. Pratt, Emma Corbett.

1781. Adventures of a Hackney Coach; Reveries of the Heart; Robert Bage, Mount Henneth.

1782. The Fortunate Sisters; Ways and Means; Helenus Scott, The Adventures of a Rupee.

1783. The American Wanderer; Thomas Day, Sandford and Merton; Theophilus Johnson, Phantoms; William Thomson, The Man in the Moon.

1784. The Ring; Bage, Barham Downs; Catherine Parry, Eden Vale.

1785. The False Friends; Francis the Philanthropist; The Liberal American; "Sir Humphry Polesworth," A Fragment of the History of . . . John Bull; S. J. Pratt, Miscellanies; Eric Raspe, Baron Munchausen; H. S., The Young Widow; John Trusler, Modern Times; B. Walwyn, *Love in a Cottage.

1786. Elfrida; Emily Herbert; Mrs. Agnes M. Bennet, Juvenile Indiscretions; Anne Fuller, The Convent; Harrison's New Novelist's Magazine, Vol. I; Charles Johnstone [?], *Anthony Varnish; Henry Lemoine, *The Kentish Curate; Dr. John Moore, Zeluco; William Richardson [?], *The Cacique of Ontario.

1787. The Adventures of Jonathan Corncob; Bage, *The Fair Syrian; Harrison's New Novelist's Magazine, Vol. II; Susanna H. Keir, The History of Miss Greville.

1788. The Adventures of a Watch; Fanny Vernon; The Ramble of Philo; The School for Fathers; The Twin Sisters [date?]; Bage, James Wallace; Mrs. Bonhote, The Parental Monitor; William Renwick, The Solicitudes of Absence; Mrs. Susanna Rowson, The Inquisitor; Mrs. Charlotte Turner Smith, Emmeline; Mrs. Harriet P. Thomson, Fatal Follies; Mary Wollstonecraft, Original Stories.

1789. The Bastile; Richard Cumberland, Arundel; Sir W——L——, Young Hocus; Mrs. Matthews, Argus; Mrs. Rowson, The Test of Honour; Mrs. Smith, Ethelinde; William Thomson, Mammuth; Helen M. Williams, Julia.

1790. Adeline; Agitation; The Fair Cambrians; Louisa Wharton [date?]; Memoirs and Opinions of Mr. Blenfield; William Combe, The Devil Upon Two Sticks in England; Mrs. Elizabeth Hervey, Louisa; Dennett Jaques [?], Caroline; Mrs. Charlotte Lennox, Euphemia; John Pinkerton, A New Tale of a Tub; H. Scott, Helena.

1791. The . . . History of Miss Moreton; Matilda; "Toby Broadgrin," Book of Oddities; Mrs. Elizabeth Inchbald, A Simple Story; Henry Man [?], Flights of Inflatus, The History of Sir Geoffry Restless; The Misses Purbeck, William Thornborough; Mrs. Radcliffe, The Romance of the Forest; Mrs. Rowson, The History of Charlotte Temple, Mentoria; —— Sadler, Wanley Penson; Edward Sayer, Lindor and Adelaide; Mrs. Smith, Celestina.

1792. Frederica; Jane Austen, Volume the First [date?]; Bage, Man As He Is; Susanna M. Gunning, Anecdotes of the Delborough Family; Thomas Holcroft, Anna St. Ives; Maria Hunter, Fitzroy; Mrs. Anna M. Mackenzie, Slavery; Mrs. Rowson, Fille de Chambre; Mrs. Smith, Desmond.

1793. Jane Austen, Love and Freindship [date?]; Mrs. Gunning, Memoirs of Mary; G. Hadley, Argal; Gilbert Imlay, The Emigrants; Frances Moore, Rosina; Hannah More, Cheap Repository Tracts (1793-1798); Mrs. Smith, Old Manor House; "James Thoughtless, Jr.," The Fugitive of Folly; John Trusler, Life.

1794. Thomas Bellamy, Miscellanies; William Godwin, Caleb Williams; Mrs. Isabella Kelly Hedgeland, Madeline; Elizabeth Helme, Duncan and Peggy; Holcroft, The Adventures of Hugh Trevor; Mrs. Smith, The Banished Man, Wanderings of Warwick; Ann Thomas, Adolphus de Biron; Mary J. Young, The East Indian.

1795. Jemima; Robert and Adela; Edward Davies, Elisa Powell; Mrs. Eliza Parsons, The Voluntary Exile; Henry J. Pye, The Democrat.

1796. Berkeley Hall; The Magnanimous Amazon; Bage, Man As

He Is Not; William Beckford, Modern Novel Writing; Stephen Cullen, The Castle of Inchvally; Mrs. A. Gomersall, The Disappointed Heir; Mrs. Elizabeth Hamilton, Translation of the Letters of a Hindoo Rajah; Mrs. Elizabeth Hervey, *The History of Ned Evans; The Misses Purbeck, Matilda and Elizabeth; Mrs. Smith, Marchmont; Rev. Thomas Stabback, Maria; George Walker, Theodore Cyphon.

1797. Elizabeth; The House of Marley; Eugenia De Acton, Disobedience; Harriet Lee, Canterbury Tales, Vol. I; S. J. Pratt, Family Secrets; Henry Summersett, Probable Incidents.

1798. Henry Somerville; Henry Willoughby; Human Vicissitudes; Samuel E. Brydges, Arthur Fitz-Albini; Sophia Lee, Canterbury Tales, Vol. II; Charles Lloyd, Edmund Oliver; Hannah More, Cheap Repository Tracts (1793-1798) ; Mrs. Smith, The Young Philosopher; Henry Summersett, Aberford; Thomas S. Surr, Barnwell; Helena Wells, The Step-Mother.

1799. Mary Charlton, Rosella; J. B. Louvet de Couvrai, Love and Patriotism (trans.) ; Francis Lathom, Men and Manners; Harriet and Sophia Lee, Canterbury Tales, Vol. III; H. J. Pye, The Aristocrat; Clara Reeve, Destination; George Walker, The Vagabond; W. F. Williams, Sketches from Modern Life.

1800. Idalia; The Life and Adventures of Henry Lanson; The Neighbourhood; The Sailor Boy; Mary Anne Burges, The Progress of the Pilgrim Good-Intent; Edward Du Bois, Saint Godwin; E. H., Tales of Truth; Richard Sickelmore, Mary Jane; Mrs. Smith, The Letters of a Solitary Wanderer; Helena Wells, Constantia Neville; W. F. Williams, Fitzmaurice.

# APPENDIX D

## The West Indies in the English Novel, 1761-1800

The following chronological list includes all novels in which I have found any reference, brief or extended, to the West Indies. See Chapter III.

1761. Charles Johnstone, Chrysal (1760-1765) ; Mrs. Frances Sheridan, Memoirs of Miss Sidney Bidulph.

1762. Johnstone, The Reverie.

1763. Mrs. Frances Brooke, Lady Julia Mandeville.

1764. Edward Kimber, Maria.

1765. Sarah Fielding, The Governess; Mrs. Sarah R. Scott, The History of Sir George Ellison.

1766. Goldsmith, The Vicar of Wakefield.

1767. The Adventures of an Author.

1768. The Perplexed Lovers; Mrs. Susanna Gunning, Barford Abbey.

1769. The General Lover; The History of Lord Clayton and Miss Meredith.

1770. Female Friendship; Thomas Bridges, The Adventures of a Banknote; Charles Jenner, The Placid Man.

1771. Anecdotes of a Convent; Herbert Lawrence, The Contemplative Man; Mackenzie, The Man of Feeling; Smollett, Humphry Clinker.

1772. The Feelings of the Heart; Mrs. Elizabeth Bonhote, The Rambles of Mr. Frankly; Richard Graves, The Spiritual Quixote.

1773. A Collection of Scarce . . . Pieces; The Fatal Effects of Deception; J. and L. A. Aikin, Miscellaneous Pieces . . .; Henry Brooke, Juliet Grenville.

1777. Mrs. Frances Brooke, The Excursion; Mackenzie, Julia de Roubigné.

1778. The Fashionable Tell-Tale; The Unfortunate Union.

1779. George Keate, Sketches from Nature.

1780. Julia Stanley.

1782. The Fortunate Sisters; Frances Burney, Cecilia; Helenus Scott, The Adventures of a Rupee.

1783. Thomas Day, Sandford and Merton; Theophilus Johnson,

Phantoms; Sophia Lee, The Recess [1783-1785]; Clara Reeve, The Two Mentors.

1784. Mrs. Eliza N. Bromley, Laura and Augustus.

1785. Francis the Philanthropist; Mrs. Agnes M. Bennet, Anna; H. S., The Young Widow; John Trusler, Modern Times.

1786. Elfrida; Mrs. A. M. Bennet, Juvenile Indiscretions; Harrison's New Novelist's Magazine, Vol. I; Dr. John Moore, Zeluco.

1787. The Adventures of Jonathan Corncob; Harrison's New Novelist's Magazine, Vol. II; Elizabeth Helme, Louisa.

1788. The Adventures of a Watch; Sophia; Bage, James Wallace; Mrs. Bonhote, The Parental Monitor; Clara Reeve, The Exiles; William Renwick, The Solicitudes of Absence; Mrs. Charlotte Turner Smith, Emmeline; Mrs. Harriet P. Thomson, Fatal Follies.

1789. The Ill Effects of a Rash Vow; The Solitary Castle; Richard Cumberland, Arundel; Mrs. Susanna Rowson, The Test of Honour; Mrs. Smith, Ethelinde.

1790. Adeline; Memoirs and Opinions of Mr. Blenfield; Mrs. Bonhote, Ellen Woodley; William Combe, The Devil upon Two Sticks in England; Mrs. Eliza Parsons, The History of Miss Meredith; H. Scott, Helena.

1791. "Toby Broadgrin," Book of Oddities; Mrs. Elizabeth Inchbald, A Simple Story; The Misses Purbeck, William Thornborough; Mrs. Radcliffe, Romance of the Forest; John Raithby, Delineations of the Heart; Mrs. Rowson, Mentoria; Mrs. Smith, Celestina.

1792. Mrs. Anna M. Mackenzie, Slavery; Mrs. Rowson, Fille de Chambre; Mrs. Smith, Desmond.

1793. Mrs. Gunning, Memoirs of Mary; Mrs. Smith, Old Manor House; Rev. J. Thomson, Major Piper; Mrs. Jane West, The Advantages of Education.

1794. Thomas Bellamy, Miscellanies; William Godwin, Caleb Williams; Mrs. Isabella Kelly Hedgeland, Madeline; Mrs. Smith, Wanderings of Warwick; Mrs. Jane West, A Gossip's Story.

1795. Richard Cumberland, Henry; Edward Davies, Elisa Powell; Eugenia De Acton, Plain Sense; M. G. Lewis, The Monk; Mrs. Eliza Parsons, The Voluntary Exile; Henry J. Pye, The Democrat.

1796. William Beckford, Modern Novel Writing; Frances Burney, Camilla; Sarah Burney, Clarentine; Mrs. A. Gomersall, The Disappointed Heir; Elizabeth Helme, The Farmer of Inglewood Forest; The Misses Purbeck, Matilda and Elizabeth; Rev. Thomas Stabback, Maria.

1797. Rose Cecil; Eugenia De Acton, Disobedience; S. J. Pratt,

Family Secrets; Catherine Selden, The English Nun.

1798. Henry Willoughby; Samuel E. Brydges, Arthur Fitz-Albini; Mrs. Smith, The Young Philosopher; Helena Wells, The Step-Mother.

1799. Josephine; Mary Charlton, Rosella; George Walker, The Vagabond; W. F. Williams, Sketches of Modern Life.

1800. Idalia; The Neighbourhood; The Sailor Boy; Richard Cumberland, John De-Lancaster; E. M. F., Miriam; Catherine Harris, Edwardina; Richard Sickelmore, Mary Jane; Mrs. Smith, The Letters of a Solitary Wanderer; Helena Wells, Constantia Neville; W. F. Williams, Fitzmaurice.

# APPENDIX E

## The East Indies in the English Novel, 1761-1800

The following list includes all the fiction in which I have found any kind of reference to India or the East Indies. See Chapter III.

1761. Goldsmith, The Citizen of the World [1760-1761]; Smollett, Sir Launcelot Greaves.

1762. All for Love.

1763. Margaret and Susanna Minifie, The Histories of Lady Frances S——, and Lady Caroline S——.

1764. Mrs. Phoebe Gibbes, The Life and Adventures of Mr. Francis Clive; Mrs. Susanna Gunning, Family Pictures.

1766. The Conflict; Hugh Kelly, Memoirs of a Magdalen; Arthur Young, The History of Sir Charles Beaufort.

1767. The Adventures of an Author; Arthur Young, The Adventures of Emmera.

1768. The Perplexed Lovers.

1769. The History of Lord Clayton and Miss Meredith; Mrs. Frances Brooke, The History of Emily Montague.

1770. Thomas Bridges, The Adventures of a Banknote; Charles Jenner, The Placid Man.

1771. Anecdotes of a Convent; The Unfashionable Wife; Mrs. Elizabeth Griffith, The History of Lady Barton; Herbert Lawrence, The Contemplative Man; Mackenzie, The Man of Feeling; John Potter, The Curate of Coventry; Smollett, Humphry Clinker.

1772. The Feelings of the Heart; Mrs. Bonhote, The Rambles of Mr. Frankly; Richard Griffith, Something New.

1773. Emma; The Fashionable Friend; The Fatal Effects of Deception; Henry Brooke, Juliet Grenville.

1775. The Adventures of a Corkscrew; Mr. Digges [?], Adventures of Alonso; Elizabeth Draper [?], Letters from Eliza to Yorick; Henry Man, Mr. Bentley; Thomas Percival, A Father's Instructions to his Children; Sterne [?], Letters from Yorick to Eliza; Arthur Young, The History of Julia Benson.

1776. Dr. Thomas Cogan, John Buncle, Jr.

1777. Mrs. Frances Brooke, The Excursion.

446

1778. The Example; The Fashionable Tell-Tale; The Travels of Hildebrand Bowman; A Trip to Melasge; The Unfortunate Union; Lady Mary Hamilton, Munster Village.

1779. Richard Graves, Columella; George Keate, Sketches from Nature; S. J. Pratt, Shenstone Green.

1780. Julia Stanley; True and Affecting History of Henrietta de Bellgrave; Mrs. Charlotte Charke, The History of Charley and Patty; Margaret Minifie, The Count de Poland; Charlotte Palmer, Female Stability; S. J. Pratt, Emma Corbett.

1781. Adventures of a Hackney Coach; Colonel Ormsby; Bage, Mount Henneth.

1782. Helenus Scott, The Adventures of a Rupee.

1783. Memoirs of the Manstein Family; Theophilus Johnson, Phantoms; Clara Reeve, The Two Mentors.

1784. History of Lord Belford and Miss Sophia Woodley; Mrs. Eliza N. Bromley, Laura and Augustus.

1785. Francis the Philanthropist; The Liberal American; Sentimental Memoirs; Agnes M. Bennet, Anna; Richard Graves, Eugenius; "Sir Humphry Polesworth," A Fragment of the History of . . . John Bull; Eric Raspe, Baron Munchausen.

1786. Elfrida; Emily Herbert; The History of Tom Jones in His Married State; Agnes M. Bennet, Juvenile Indiscretions; Harrison's New Novelist's Magazine, Vol. I; Harriet Lee, Errors of Innocence; Dr. John Moore, Zeluco.

1787. The History of Captain and Miss Rivers; The Perplexities of Love; Mrs. Burke, Ela; Harrison's New Novelist's Magazine, Vol. II; Elizabeth Helme, Louisa.

1788. The Adventures of a Watch; The Twin Sisters [date?]; Mrs. Bonhote, The Parental Monitor; William Renwick, The Solicitudes of Absence; Mrs. Rowson, The Inquisitor; Mrs. Charlotte Smith, Emmeline; Mrs. Harriet P. Thomson, Fatal Follies; Mary Wollstonecraft, Original Stories.

1789. The Bastile; The Ill Effects of a Rash Vow; The Solitary Castle; Mrs. Mathews, Argus; Mrs. Smith, Ethelinde; William Thomson, Mammuth; Sir W—— L——, Young Hocus; Helen M. Williams, Julia.

1790. Adeline; Agitation; The Fair Cambrians; Mrs. Bonhote, Ellen Woodley; William Combe, The Devil upon Two Sticks in England; Mrs. Elizabeth Hervey, Louisa; Mrs. Charlotte Lennox, Euphemia; Mrs. Eliza Parsons, The History of Miss Meredith; H. Scott, Helena.

1791. The . . . History of Miss Moreton . . .; "Toby Broadgrin," Book of Oddities; —— Sadler, Wanley Penson; Mrs. Smith, Celestina.

1792. Bage, Man As He Is; W. Holloway, Dovedell Hall; Maria Hunter, Fitzroy; Mrs. Rowson, Fille de Chambre; Mrs. Smith, Desmond.

1793. Louisa Matthews; Mrs. Gunning, Memoirs of Mary; Frances Moore, Rosina; Mrs. Smith, Old Manor House; Rev. J. Thomson, Major Piper; John Trusler, Life.

1794. Mrs. Isabella Hedgeland, Madeline; Holcroft, The Adven tures of Hugh Trevor; Mrs. Elizabeth G. Plunkett, The Packet; Mrs. Smith, The Banished Man, Wanderings of Warwick; Ann Thomas, Adolphus de Biron; Jane West, A Gossip's Story; Mary J. Young, The East Indian.

1795. Robert and Adela; Richard Cumberland, Henry; Edward Davies, Elisa Powell; Mrs. Elizabeth V.-R. Gooch, The Contrast; M. G. Lewis, The Monk; Mrs. Eliza Parsons, The Voluntary Exile; H. J. Pye, The Democrat; Mrs. Smith, Montalbert.

1796. The Magnanimous Amazon; William Beckford, Modern Novel Writing; Mrs. Burke, Adela Northington; Frances Burney, Camilla; Sarah Burney, Clarentine; Stephen Cullen, The Castle of Inchvally; Mrs. A. Gomersall, The Disappointed Heir; Mrs. Elizabeth Hamilton, Translation of the Letters of a Hindoo Rajah; Elizabeth Helme, The Farmer of Inglewood Forest; Mrs. Smith, D'Arcy [author?], Marchmont; Rev. Thomas Stabback, Maria; George Walker, Theodore Cyphon.

1797. Elizabeth; The House of Marley; The Posthumous Daughter; Jane Austen, Sense and Sensibility [date?]; Eugenia De Acton, Disobedience; Catherine Selden, The English Nun; Henry Summersett, Probable Incidents.

1798. Henry Willoughby; Human Vicissitudes; S. E. Brydges, Arthur Fitz-Albini; Sophia Lee, Canterbury Tales, Vol. II; Charles Lloyd, Edmund Oliver; Mrs. Smith, The Young Philosopher; G. Thompson, A Sentimental Tour; Helena Wells, The Step-Mother.

1799. Mary Charlton, Rosella; Miss A. A. Hutchinson, Exhibitions of the Heart; Harriet and Sophia Lee, Canterbury Tales, Vol. III; H. J. Pye, The Aristocrat; Clara Reeve, Destination.

1800. Idalia; The Neighbourhood; The Sailor Boy; Emily Clark, Ermina Montrose; Richard Cumberland, John De-Lancaster; E. M. F., Miriam; E. H., Tales of Truth; William Linley, Forbidden Apartments; Richard Sickelmore, Mary Jane; Helena Wells, Constantia Neville.

# LIST OF CHIEF WORKS CONSULTED

This list excludes periodicals, standard reference works, the volumes of poetry and drama referred to in Chapter I, and primary and secondary works only incidentally referred to. Titles are punctuated uniformly.

## PROSE FICTION

Adeline, or, the Orphan. 3 vols. London. 1790.

Adventure of a Bale of Goods in Consequence of the Stamp Act, The. London. 1766.

Adventures of a Hackney Coach. 3rd ed. London. 1781.

Adventures of an Author, The. 2 vols. London. 1767.

Adventures of Jonathan Corncob, Loyal American Refugee. Written by Himself. London. 1787.

Agitation, or, Memoirs of George Woodford and Lady Emma Melvill. New ed. 3 vols. London. [1790].

American Wanderer through Various Parts of Europe, The. By a Virginian. Dublin. 1783.

Anecdotes of a Convent. 3 vols. London. 1771.

Authentic and Interesting History of Miss Moreton and the Faithful Cottager, The. 2 vols. in one. Birmingham. [1791].

Bastile, The, or, the History of Charles Townly, a Man of the World. 4 vols. London. 1789.

Berkeley Hall, or, the Pupil of Experience. 3 vols. London. 1796.

Birmingham Counterfeit, The, or, Invisible Spectator. A Sentimental Romance. 2 vols. London. 1772.

Collection of Scarce, Curious and Valuable Pieces Both in Verse and Prose, A. Edinburgh. 1773.

Constantia, or, the Distressed Friend. London. 1770.

Devil upon Crutches in England, The. Or, Night-Scenes in London. 4th ed. London. 1759.

Edward. 2 vols. London. 1774.

Elfrida, or, Paternal Ambition. 3 vols. London. 1786.

Elizabeth. 3 vols. London. 1797.

Emily Herbert, or, Perfidy Punished. Dublin. 1787.

Emma, or, the Unfortunate Attachment. A Sentimental Novel. New ed. 2 vols. London. 1787.

Fair Cambrians, The. 3 vols. London. 1790.

False Friends, The. 2 vols. London. 1785.

Fanny Vernon, or, the Forlorn Hope; a Tale of Woe; Containing Scenes of Horror and Distress that Happened during the War in America. London. 1789.

Fashionable Tell-Tale, The; Containing a Great Variety of Curious and Interesting Anecdotes. 2nd ed. 2 vols. in one. London. 1778.

Fatal Effects of Deception, The. 3 vols. London. 1773.

Feelings of the Heart, The, or, the History of a Country Girl. Written by Herself and Addressed to a Lady of Quality. 2 vols. London. 1772.

Female American, The, or, the Extraordinary Adventures of Unca Eliza Winkfield. Newburyport. n.d.

Fortunate Sisters, The, or, the History of Fanny and Sophia Bemont. 2 vols. London. 1782.

Francis the Philanthropist: an Unfashionable Tale. Dublin. 1786.

Frederica, or, the Memoirs of a Young Lady. 2 vols. Dublin. 1792.

Henry Somerville. Dublin. 1798.

Henry Willoughby. 2 vols. London. 1798.

History of Lord Stanton, The. A Novel. By a Gentleman of the Middle Temple. 5 vols. London. [1774].

House of Marley, The. 2 vols. London. 1797.

Idalia. A Novel. Founded on Facts. 2 vols. London. 1800.

Jemima. 2 vols. London. 1795.

Liberal American, The. 2 vols. London. 1785.

Life and Wonderful Adventures of Henry Lanson, The, . . . of . . . the West Indies. London. [1800?].

Louisa Wharton. A Story, Founded on Facts. . . . Wherein Is Displayed some Particular Circumstances which Happened during the Bloody Contest in AMERICA. London. [1790?].

Magnanimous Amazon, The, or, Adventures of Theresia, Baroness Van Hoog. With Anecdotes of Other Eccentric Persons. London. 1796.

Matilda, or, the Adventures of an Orphan. London. [179-].

Memoirs and Opinions of Mr. Blenfield. 2 vols. London. 1790.

Memoirs of a Coquet, or, the History of Miss Harriot Airy. London. 1765.

Memoirs of an Unfortunate Queen. Interspersed with Letters (Written by Herself). London. 1776.

Neighbourhood, The. 2 vols. London. 1800.

New Novelist's Magazine, The, or, Entertaining Library of Pleasing and Instructive Histories, Adventures, Tales, Romances, and Other Agreeable and Exemplary Little Novels. 2 vols. London: Harrison. 1786-1787.

Philosophical Quixote, The, or, Memoirs of Mr. David Wilkins. 4 vols. in two. London. 1782.

Ramble of Philo and His Man Sturdy, The. Dublin. 1789.

Relapse, The. 2 vols. London. 1780.

Reveries of the Heart; During a Tour through Part of England and France: In a Series of Letters to a Friend. 2 vols. London. 1781.

Ring, The. 3 vols. London. 1784.

Sailor Boy, The. 2 vols. London. 1800.

School for Fathers, The, or, the Victim of a Curse. 3 vols. London. 1788.

Sentimental Memoirs. 2 vols. London. 1785.

Sentimental Traveller, The, or, a Descriptive Tour through Life, Figuratively as a Trip to Melasge, in which Is Included the Adventures of a Gentleman in the East-Indies: the Whole, Forming a System of Education, with Instructions to a Young Gentleman, Entering into Life. 2 vols. London. [1778].

Travels of Hildebrand Bowman, Esquire, The, into Carnovirria, Taupiniera, Olfactaria, and Auditante, in New-Zealand; in the Land of Bonhommica, and in the Powerful Kingdom of Luxo-Volupto, on the Great Southern Continent. London. 1778.

Trip to Melasge—see Sentimental Traveller.

Twin Brothers, The, or, a New Book of Discipline for Infidels and Old Offenders. Edinburgh. 1787.

The Twin Sisters, or, the Effects of Education, 3 vols. London. 1788.

Unexpected Wedding, The, in a Series of Letters. London. 1768.

Ways and Means, or, a Sale of the L---S S-------L and T------L, by R---L P--------N. London. 1782.

Amory, Thomas—The Life of John Buncle, Esquire. 2 vols. London. 1766.

Austen, Jane—Love and Freindship and Other Early Works Now First Published from the Original MS. New York: Stokes. 1922.

———. Volume the First. Oxford. 1933.

Bage, Robert—Barham Downs, James Wallace, and Mount Henneth. Ballantyne's Novelist's Library, Vol. IX. London. 1824.

———. Man As He Is. 2nd ed. 4 vols. London. 1796.

———. Man As He Is Not, or Hermsprong. 3rd ed. 3 vols. London 1809.

Beckford, William—Modern Novel Writing, or, the Elegant Enthusiast. 2 vols. London. 1796.

Bellamy, Thomas—Miscellanies: In Prose and Verse. London. 1794.

Bennet, Agnes Maria—Juvenile Indiscretions. 2nd ed. 5 vols. London. 1805.

Bonhote, Mrs. Elizabeth—The Parental Monitor. 2 vols. London. 1788.
——. The Rambles of Mr. Frankly. 2 vols. Dublin. 1773.

"Broadgrin, Toby"—Book of Oddities, or Agreeable Variety for Town and Country. 3rd ed. Dublin. 1791.

Brooke, Mrs. Frances—The History of Emily Montague. 4 vols. in two. London. 1769.
——. Lady Julia Mandeville. Ed. E. Phillips Poole. London: Scholartis Press. 1930.

Brooke, Henry—Juliet Grenville, or, the History of the Human Heart. 3 vols. in two. Philadelphia. 1774.

Brydges, S. Egerton—Arthur Fitz-Albini. 2 vols. London. 1798.

Burges, Mary Anne—The Progress of the Pilgrim Good-Intent in Jacobinical Times. 2nd American from 5th English ed. Charlestown. 1801.

Burney, Sarah H.—Clarentine. 3 vols. London. 1796.

Charlton, Mary—Rosella, or, Modern Occurrences. 4 vols. London. 1799.

Cogan, Dr. Thomas—John Buncle, Junior, Gentleman. 2 vols. London. 1776.

Combe, William—The Devil upon Two Sticks in England. 3rd ed. 3 vols. Dublin. 1790-1791.

Croft, Sir Herbert—The Abbey of Kilkhampton, or, Monumental Records for the Year 1980. London. 1780.
——. Love and Madness. A Story Too True. London. 1780.

Cullen, Stephen—The Castle of Inchvally: a Tale—Alas! Too True. 3 vols. London. 1796.

Cumberland, Richard—Arundel. 2 vols. London. 1789.

Davies, Edward—Elisa Powell, or, Trials of Sensibility. 2 vols. London. 1795.

De Acton, Eugenia—Disobedience. 4 vols. London. 1797.

[Digges, Mr., of Maryland?]—Adventures of Alonso: Containing Some Striking Anecdotes of the Present Prime Minister of Portugal. 2 vols. London. 1775.

Disraeli, Isaac—Flim-Flams! or, the Life and Errors of My Uncle, and the Amours of My Aunt! 3 vols. London. 1805.

Du Bois, Edward—Saint Godwin: a Tale of the Sixteenth, Seventeenth, and Eighteenth Century. London. 1800.

Edgeworth, Maria—Tales and Novels. 18 vols. in nine. New York. 1836.

Erskine, Thomas, Lord—Armata: a Fragment. 2nd ed. New York. 1817.

Fuller, Anne—The Convent, or, the History of Sophia Nelson. 2 vols. London. [1786].

Godwin, William—Saint Leon: a Tale of the Sixteenth Century. 3rd ed. 4 vols. London. 1816.

Goldsmith, Oliver—The Citizen of the World. 3rd ed. 2 vols. London. 1774.

———. The Vicar of Wakefield. 4th ed. 2 vols. London. 1770.

Graves, Rev. Richard—The Spiritual Quixote, or, the Summer's Ramble of Mr. Geoffry Wildgoose. 2 vols. London: Peter Davies. 1926.

Griffith, Elizabeth—The Delicate Distress. 2 vols. Dublin. 1787.

———. The History of Lady Barton. 3 vols. London. 1771.

Gunning, Mrs. Susanna Minifie—Anecdotes of the Delborough Family. 2nd ed. 5 vols. London. 1792.

———. Memoirs of Mary. 5 vols. London. 1793.

H., E.—Tales of Truth. 4 vols. London. 1800.

Hadley, G.—Argal, or, the Silver Devil, Being the Adventures of an Evil Spirit. 2 vols. London. [1793].

Hamilton, Mrs. Elizabeth—Translation of the Letters of a Hindoo Rajah. 2 vols. Dublin. 1797.

Hamilton, Lady Mary Walker—Memoirs of the Marchioness de Louvoi. 3 vols. London. 1777.

———. Munster Village. 2 vols. in one. Dublin. 1779.

Hayley, William—A Philosophical, Historical, and Moral Essay on Old Maids. 3 vols. London. 1785.

Hedgeland, Mrs. Isabella Kelly—Madeline, or, the Castle of Montgomery. 3 vols. London. 1794.

Helme, Elizabeth—Duncan and Peggy: a Scottish Tale. 2 vols. London. 1794.

Holcroft, Thomas—The Adventures of Hugh Trevor. 2nd ed. 6 vols. London. 1794.

———. Anna St. Ives. 5 vols. London. 1800.

Hunter, Maria—Fitzroy, or, Impulses of the Moment. 2 vols. London. 1792.

Hutchinson, Miss A. A.—Exhibitions of the Heart. 4 vols. London. 1799.

Imlay, Gilbert—The Emigrants, &c., or, the History of an Expatriated Family. . . . Written in America. 3 vols. London. 1793.

[Inchbald, Mrs. Elizabeth Simpson?]—The History of Miss Sommerville. 2 vols. London. 1769.

[Jaques, Dennett, of Chelsea?]—Caroline, the Heroine of the Camp. 2 vols. London. 1830.

Johnson, Theophilus—Phantoms, or, the Adventures of a Gold-Headed Cane. 2 vols. London. 1783.

Johnstone, Charles—Chrysal, or, the Adventures of a Guinea. 4th ed. 4 vols. London. 1764-1765.

———. The History of Arsaces, Prince of Betlis. 2 vols. London. 1774.

———. The Pilgrim, or, a Picture of Life. 2 vols. London. 1775.

———. The Reverie, or, a Flight to the Paradise of Fools. 2 vols. London. 1763.

Keate, George—Sketches from Nature: Taken, and Coloured, in a Journey to Margate. 2 vols. London. 1779.

Keir, Susanna H.—The History of Miss Greville. 3 vols. Edinburgh. 1787.

L——, Sir W——, K—— —Young Hocus, or, the History of John Bull during the Years 1783, 1784, 1785, 1786, 1787, 1788, 1789. Vol. I [no more published]. London. [1789].

Lathom, Francis—Men and Manners. New ed. 4 vols. London. 1800.

Lee, Harriet—The Errors of Innocence. 5 vols. London. 1786.

———. (With Sophia Lee) Canterbury Tales. 5 vols. London. 1797 ff.

Lennox, Mrs. Charlotte—Euphemia. 4 vols. London. 1790.

Linley, William—Forbidden Apartments. 2 vols. London. 1800.

Lloyd, Charles—Edmund Oliver. 2 vols. Bristol. 1798.

Louvet de Couvrai, Jean Baptiste—Love and Patriotism. Philadelphia. 1797.

Mackenzie, Mrs. Anna Maria—Slavery, or, the Times. Dublin. 1793.

Man, Henry—Flights of Inflatus, or, the Sallies, Stories, and Adventures of a Wild-Goose Philosopher. 2 vols. London. 1791.

———. The History of Sir Geoffry Restless and his Brother Charles. 2 vols. London. 1791.

Mathews, Mrs.—Argus, the House-Dog at Eadlip. Memoirs in a Family Correspondence. 3 vols. London. 1789.

Meades, Anne—The History of Sir William Harrington. 2nd ed. 4 vols. London. 1772.

Moore, Frances—Rosina. 5 vols. London. 1793.

Moore, Dr. John—Zeluco. Boston. 1792.

More, Hannah—Cheap Repository Tracts: Entertaining, Moral, and Religious. New Revised ed. 8 vols. New York: American Tract Society. n.d.

Parry, Mrs. Catherine—Eden Vale. 2 vols. London. 1784.

Parsons, Mrs. Eliza—The Voluntary Exile. 5 vols. London. 1795.

Percival, Dr. Thomas—A Father's Instructions to his Children: Consisting of Tales, Fables, and Reflections. Dublin. 1790.

Pinkerton, John—A New Tale of a Tub. London. 1790.

"Polesworth, Sir Humphry"—A Fragment of the History of That Illustrious Personage John Bull, Esq; . . . London. [1785].

Pratt, Samuel Jackson—Emma Corbett, or, the Miseries of Civil War. 4th ed. 3 vols. London and Bath. n.d.

———. Miscellanies. 4 vols. London. 1785.

———. The Pupil of Pleasure. 2nd ed. 2 vols. London. 1777.

———. Shenstone-Green, or, the New Paradise Lost. 3 vols. London. 1779.

Purbeck, The Misses—Matilda and Elizabeth. 2 vols. Dublin. 1796.

———. William Thornborough, the Benevolent Quixote. 4 vols. London. 1791.

Pye, Henry James—The Democrat, or, Intrigues and Adventures of Jean Le Noir. 2 vols. in one. New York. 1795.

———. The Aristocrat. 2 vols. London. 1799.

Reeve, Clara—Destination, or, Memoirs of a Private Family. 2 vols. Dublin. 1799.

Renwick, William—The Solicitudes of Absence. London. 1788.

Rowson, Mrs. Susanna Haswell—Fille de Chambre. Baltimore. 1795.

———. The History of Charlotte Temple. 2 vols. in one. New York. 1814.

———. The Inquisitor, or, Invisible Rambler. 2nd American ed. 3 vols. in one. Philadelphia. 1794.

———. Mentoria, or, the Young Lady's Friend. 2 vols. in one. Philadelphia. 1794.

Ryan, Rev. Everhard—Reliques of Genius. London. 1777.

S., H.—The Young Widow, or, the History of Mrs. Ledwich. 2 vols. London. 1785.

Sadler, ———, of Chippenham—Wanley Penson, or, the Melancholy Man. A Miscellaneous History. 3 vols. London. 1791.

Sayer, Edward—Lindor and Adelaide. London. 1791.

Scott, Helenus—The Adventures of a Rupee. New ed. London. 1783.

———. Helena, or, the Vicissitudes of a Military Life. 2 vols. Cork. 1790.

Sickelmore, Richard—Mary Jane. 2 vols. London. 1800.
Smith, Mrs. Charlotte Turner—The Banished Man. 4 vols. London. 1794.
———. Celestina. 2nd ed. 4 vols. London. 1791.
———. Desmond. 3 vols. London. 1792.
———. Emmeline, the Orphan of the Castle. 3 vols. Philadelphia, etc. 1802.
———. Ethelinde, or, the Recluse of the Lake. 2nd ed. 5 vols. London. 1790.
———. The Letters of a Solitary Wanderer: Containing Narratives of Various Description. 3 vols. London. 1800.
———. Marchmont. 4 vols. London. 1796.
———. The Old Manor House. 2nd ed. 4 vols. London. 1793.
———. The Wanderings of Warwick. London. 1794.
———. The Young Philosopher. 4 vols. London. 1798.
Smollett, Tobias—Works. 12 vols. New York: Scribner. 1901.
Stabback, Rev. Thomas—Maria, or, the Vicarage. 2 vols. London. 1796.
Sterne, Lawrence—Tristram Shandy. New York: Modern Library. n.d.
Summersett, Henry—Probable Incidents, or, Scenes in Life. 2 vols. London. 1797.
Surr, Thomas S.—Barnwell. 4th ed. 3 vols. London. 1807.
Thomas, Ann—Adolphus de Biron. A Novel Founded on the French Revolution. 2 vols. Plymouth. [1794].
Thompson, G.—A Sentimental Tour, Collected from a Variety of Occurrences. Penrith. 1798.
Thomson, William—Mammuth, or, Human Nature Displayed on a Grand Scale: In a Tour with the Tinkers, into the Inland Parts of Africa. 2 vols. in one. London. 1789.
———. The Man in the Moon, or, Travels into the Lunar Regions. 2 vols. London. 1783.
"Thoughtless, Thomas, Jr."—The Fugitive of Folly. London. 1793.
Trusler, John—Life, or, the Adventures of William Ramble, Esq. 3 vols. London. 1793.
———. Modern Times, or, the Adventures of Gabriel Outcast. 2nd ed. with Additions. 3 vols. London. 1785.
Walker, George—Theodore Cyphon, or, the Benevolent Jew. Alexandria. 1803.
———. The Vagabond. 1st American from 4th English ed. Boston. 1800.

BIBLIOGRAPHY

Wells, Helena—Constantia Neville, or, the West Indian. 2nd ed. 3 vols. London. 1800.

————. The Step-Mother; a Domestic Tale, from Real Life. 2nd ed. 2 vols. London. 1799.

Will, P., tr.—Horrid Mysteries. From the German of the Marquis of Grosse. 2 vols. London: Holden. 1927.

Williams, Helen Maria—Julia. 2 vols. London. 1790.

Williams, William F.—Fitzmaurice. 2 vols. London. 1800.

Withers, Philip—[?] The Ants; a Rhapsody. 2 vols. London. 1767.

————. History of the Royal Malady, with a Variety of Entertaining Anecdotes. London. 1789.

Young, Arthur—The Adventures of Emmera, or, the Fair American. Exemplifying the Peculiar Advantages of Society and Retirement. 2 vols. London. 1767.

OTHER PRIMARY SOURCES

Baratariana. A Select Collection of Fugitive Political Pieces Published during the Administration of Lord Townshend in Ireland. 3rd ed. Dublin. 1777.

Beatson, Robert—A Political Index to the Histories of Great Britain and Ireland. 3rd ed. 3 vols. London. 1806.

Blake, William—Prophetic Writings. Edd. D. J. Sloss and J. P. R. Wallis. 2 vols. Oxford. 1926.

Boswell, James—The Hypochondriack. Ed. Margery Bailey. 2 vols. Stanford University: Stanford University Press. 1928.

Crèvecoeur, J. Hector St. John de—Letters from an American Farmer. New ed. London. 1783.

Godwin, William—The Enquirer. Reflections on Education, Manners, and Literature. London. 1797.

————. Enquiry Concerning Political Justice. 1st American from 2nd London ed. 2 vols. Philadelphia. 1796.

Graves, Rev. Richard—Lucubrations. Consisting of Essays, Reveries, &c. in Prose and Verse. London. 1786.

Imlay, Gilbert—A Topographical Description of the Western Territory of North America, etc. 3rd ed., with Great Additions. London. 1797.

[Jephson, J., Courtenay, John, and others?]—The Batchelor, or, Speculations of Jeoffry Wagstaffe, Esq. 2 vols. Dublin. 1769.

Mackenzie, Henry—The Lounger. A Periodical Paper Published at Edinburgh in the Years 1785 and 1786. 4th ed. 3 vols. London. 1788.

————. The Mirror: A Periodical Paper Published at Edinburgh in the Years 1779 and 1780. 2nd American ed. Philadelphia. 1793.

Mathias, Thomas—The Pursuits of Literature. 13th ed. London. 1805.

Parker, George—A View of Society and Manners in High and Low Life; Being the Adventures in England, Ireland, Scotland, Wales, and France, &c. of Mr. G. Parker. In Which Is Comprised a History of the Stage Itinerant. 2 vols. in one. London. 1781.

Peters, Samuel—A General History of Connecticut. 2nd ed. London. 1782.

Pigott, Charles—A Political Dictionary: Explaining the True Meaning of Words. London. 1795.

Price, Rev. Richard—Observations on the Importance of the American Revolution, and the Means of Making it a Benefit to the World. Dublin. 1785.

PRINCIPAL SECONDARY SOURCES

Baker, E. A.—The History of the English Novel. 7 vols. London: Witherby. 1924-1936.

Bissell, Benjamin—The American Indian in English Literature of the Eighteenth Century. Yale Studies in English, Vol. LXVIII. New Haven: Yale University Press. 1925.

Brinton, Crane—The Political Ideas of the English Romanticists. Oxford. 1926.

Cairns, William B.—British Criticisms of American Writings 1783-1815. University of Wisconsin Studies in Language and Literature, No. 1. Madison. 1918.

————. British Criticisms of American Writings 1815-1833. University of Wisconsin Studies in Language and Literature, No. 14. Madison. 1922.

Chandler, Frank W.—The Literature of Roguery. 2 vols. Boston and New York: Houghton Mifflin. 1907.

Clark, Dora Mae—British Opinion and the American Revolution. New Haven: Yale University Press. 1930.

Dunning, William A.—The British Empire and the United States. New York: Scribner. 1914.

————. A History of Political Theories. 3 vols. New York: Macmillan. 1902-1920.

Einstein, Lewis—Divided Loyalties: Americans in England during the War of Independence. Boston and New York: Houghton Mifflin. 1933.

Fairchild, Hoxie Neale—The Noble Savage. New York: Columbia University Press. 1928.

Fraser, Leon—English Opinion of the American Constitution and Government 1783-1798. New York. 1915.

Gregory, Allene—The French Revolution and the English Novel. London and New York: Putnam. 1915.

Heidler, Joseph B.—The History, from 1700 to 1800, of English Criticism of Prose Fiction. University of Illinois Studies in Language and Literature, Vol. XIII, No. 2. Urbana. 1928.

Hinkhouse, Fred J.—The Preliminaries of the American Revolution as Seen in the English Press 1763-1775. New York: Columbia University Press. 1926.

Holzman, James M.—The Nabobs in England: a Study of the Returned Anglo-Indian 1760-1785. New York. 1926.

Jones, Howard M.—America and French Culture 1750-1848. Chapel Hill: University of North Carolina Press. 1927.

King, Henry S.—Echoes of the American Revolution in German Literature. University of California Publications in Modern Philology, Vol. 14, No. 2. Berkeley: University of California Press. 1929.

Klingberg, Frank J.—The Anti-Slavery Movement in England: a Study in English Humanitarianism. New Haven: Yale University Press. 1926.

Lowes, John L.—The Road to Xanadu. Boston and New York: Houghton Mifflin. 1927.

McLaughlin, Andrew C.—America and Britain. New York: Dutton. 1919.

Mantz, Harold E.—French Criticism of American Literature Before 1850. New York: Columbia University Press. 1917.

Mesick, Jane Louise—The English Traveller in America 1785-1835. New York: Columbia University Press. 1922.

Mumford, Lewis—The Story of Utopias. New York: Boni and Liveright. 1922.

Nevins, Allan—American Social History as Recorded by British Travellers. New York: Holt. 1923.

Smith, Edgar F.—Priestley in America 1794-1804. Philadelphia: Blakiston. 1920.

Spiller, Robert E.—The American in England during the First Half Century of Independence. New York: Holt. 1926.

Thompson, Harold W.—A Scottish Man of Feeling. London and New York: Oxford University Press. 1931.

Tompkins, J. M. S.—The Popular Novel in England 1770-1800. London: Constable. 1932.

Trevelyan, Sir George Otto, Bart.—The American Revolution. Three Parts. London and New York: Longmans Green. 1899-1907.

———. George the Third and Charles Fox: The Concluding Part of the American Revolution. 2 vols. New York: Longmans Green. 1912-1914.

Weber, Paul C.—America in Imaginative German Literature in the First Half of the Nineteenth Century. New York: Columbia University Press. 1926.

Whelpley, J. D.—British-American Relations. Boston: Little Brown. 1924.

Whitney, Lois—Primitivism and the Idea of Progress in English Popular Literature of the Eighteenth Century. Baltimore: Johns Hopkins University Press. 1934.

INDEX

# INDEX

# INDEX

Bromley, Mrs. Eliza N., *Laura and Augustus*, 444, 447.

Brooke, Mrs. Frances, 41, 66n.; *The Excursion*, 440, 443, 446; *The History of Emily Montague*, 66, 69, 84, 200, 209, 218, 239, 298-299, 341, 350, 391-392, 439, 446; *Lady Julia Mandeville*, 87, 219, 239, 391, 439, 443.

Brooke, Henry, 41; *The Fool of Quality*, 439; *Juliet Grenville*, 299-300, 440, 443, 446.

Brown, Alexander, *The Genesis of the United States*, 22n.

Bryce, James, 29.

Brydges, Sir Samuel E., *Arthur Fitz-Albini*, 60n., 128, 442, 445, 448; *Mary De Clifford*, 438.

Buckland, James, *Remarkable Discovery of an American Hermit*, 64, 318n.

Bunker Hill, 96, 98, 99, 100, 102, 119, 126, 129, 185.

Bunyan, John, *Pilgrim's Progress*, 395n.

Burges, Mary Anne, *The Progress of the Pilgrim Good-Intent*, 417, 442.

Burgoyne, General John, 27, 32, 112, 123, 126, 129, 133, 148-149, 166, 182, 183, 247, 372.

Burke, Mrs., *Adele Northington*, 448; *Ela*, 447; *Emilia de St. Aubigne*, 438.

Burke, Edmund, 1, 2, 27, 31 and n., 49n., 116, 176, 402; *Reflections on the French Revolution*, 412n.

Burney, Frances, 32 and n., 41, 136; *Camilla*, 444, 448; *Diary and Letters*, 32n.; *Cecilia*, 443; *Evelina*, 437.

Burney, Sarah, *Clarentine*, 403-404, 444, 448.

Burns, Robert, 4, 33, 37, 58, 296.

Bute, John Stuart, third Earl of, 205n., 209.

Byron, George Gordon, Lord, 266, 430.

C——, Mrs., *Belinda*, 438.
*Cabinet conference, The, or tears of ministry . . .,* 49.

*Cacique of Ontario, The:* see Richardson, William.

Cairns, William B., *British Criticisms of American Writings 1783-1815*, 12, 15, 34, 372n., 374, 377n.; *British Criticisms 1815-1833*, 15, 34.

Callender, James T., 315n.

*Cambridge History of the British Empire, The*, 166, 264, 391.

*Cambridge History of English Literature, The*, 31 and n., 315, 316.

Camden, Charles Pratt, first Earl, 208n.

Campbell, P., 67n.

Campbell, Thomas, 266 and n., 283, 430.

Canada, 66n., 69, 78, 88-89, 187, 215, 219, 238-239, 298, 310, 341, 350, 391.

Carew, B. M., *Apology*, 65n.

Carew, Thomas, 16-17, 17n., 393.

Carleton, Governor Guy, 122 and n., 133.

Carlyle, Thomas, 4n.

*Caroline:* see Jaques, Dennett.

Carver, Jonathan, *Travels*, 81n.

Catholicism, 237-238, 251, 298, 388, 401.

Cawley, Robert R., 20n., 25n., 34.

Cecil, David, *The Stricken Deer*, 33.

Celtic Revival, 52, 252, 434, 436.

Central America (see also South America), 70, 388.

Cestre, Charles, *La Révolution Française et les Poètes Anglais*, 51n.

Chalmers, George, *An Estimate of the Comparative Strength of Great Britain, etc.*, 60.

Champ d'Asile, Le, 264n.

Chandler, Frank W., *The Literature of Roguery*, 69n., 100n., 362.

Chapman, George, *De Guiana*, 21, 22, 23, 263; *Eastward Ho*, 14, 17n.; *The Masque of the Inns of Court*, 17-18, 18n.

Charke, Mrs. Charlotte, *The History of Charley and Patty*, 447.

Charleston, South Carolina, 82-83, 130n.

Charlton, H. B., 19n.

*Fashionable Tell-Tale, The,* 88, 367, 383, 394, 400n., 440, 443, 447.
*Fatal Effects of Deception, The,* 334n., 440, 443, 446.
Faÿ, Bernard, *The Revolutionary Spirit in France and America,* 5 and n.; *Roosevelt and His America,* 10, 11, 15.
*Feelings of the Heart,* 269n., 338, 439, 443, 446.
*Female American, The,* 63, 66, 70, 84, 175, 236, 268-269, 308, 325, 385n., 386-387, 439.
*Female Friendship,* 443.
Fielding, Henry, 41, 74, 79, 287.
Fielding, Sarah, *The Governess,* 443.
Filson, John, *Discovery . . . of Kentucky,* 81, 85, 269, 273.
Findley, William, *History of the Insurrection,* 216n.
Finglass, Esther, *The Recluse,* 438.
Firth, Sir Charles, *An American Garland,* 34, 393n.
Fitzgeffry, Charles, 25.
*Flagel,* 437.
Fletcher, Phineas, 19.
Flood, Henry (see *Baratariana*), 208n.
Foote, Samuel, 402.
*Fortunate Blue-Coat Boy, The,* 439.
*Fortunate Sisters, The,* 72, 308-309, 341, 440, 443.
Fox, Charles James (see Drinkwater), 27, 31n., 147 and n., 166, 233, 249, 409; *Speeches,* 223n., 249n.
*Francis the Philanthropist,* 71-72, 84, 96-98, 100, 144, 192, 354, 369, 440, 444, 447.
Franklin, Benjamin, 27, 38, 265, 362, 370, 373, 377-380, 422.
Fraser, Leon, *English Opinion of the American Constitution,* 34, 48n., 407-408, 408n.
*Frederica,* 116-117, 441.
Frederick the Great, 137.
French characters, 103, 115-116, 118, 120, 123, 126, 131, 147, 152-155, 162, 171, 188, 299-300, 316, 317, 368, 374, 405, 410-411, 414-416.
French literature, 4n., 5, 6, 33-34, 377.

French Revolution, 5, 6, 35, 55, 56, 57, 62, 65, 67, 77, 78, 85, 116, 120, 126, 152-155, 159-160, 269, 292-293, 315, 316, 372-373, 402-403, 406, 409-418, 424.
Freneau, Philip, 30.
*Fruitless Repentance, The,* 437.
Fuller, Anne, *The Convent,* 103, 147, 440; *The Son of Ethelwolf,* 438.

Gage, Colonel Thomas, 190, 247.
Gales, editor of the Sheffield *Register,* 315n.
Gallipolis, Ohio, 264n.
*General Lover, The,* 443.
Gentleman, Francis, 137.
*Gentleman's Magazine,* 14, 45 and n., 46, 50n., 51n., 63n., 64n., 66n., 83n., 218n., 264, 269n., 290n., 383, 293n.
George II, 69.
George III, 146-147, 150, 152 and n., 163, 169, 213, 245-246, 247.
Georgia, 83n., 297.
*Georgium Sidus,* 152 and n.
Gerard, Alexander, *Liberty a cloack of maliciousness . . .,* 49.
German literature, 4n., 5 and n., 6, 28, 34, 35 and n., 374, 377.
Gibbes, Mrs. Phoebe, *Friendship in a Nunnery,* 64, 83, 84, 139, 166, 191, 440; *The Life and Adventures of Mr. Francis Clive,* 446.
Gibbon, Edward, 33.
Gifford, William, 17n.
*Gilham Farm,* 59.
Glover, Arnold, 18n.
Godwin, William, 78, 378-379, 403n.; *Caleb Williams,* 329, 441, 444; *The Enquirer,* 86-87, 374, 379-380; *Political Justice,* 176, 278n.; *St. Leon,* 307.
Goethe, 5-6, 34.
Golden Age in America (see also Noble Savage, Primitivism), 23-24, 26, 37, 40, 78, 261 ff., 332, 371, 388, 389 ff., 396, 412, 425-426, 428.
Goldsmith, Oliver, 32, 296; *Citizen of the World,* 200, 209, 218, 238-239, 326, 335, 338, 439, 446; *Deserted*

Radicals and radicalism (see also Price, Priestley, Paine, Parliamentary Reform, French Revolution), 27, 49, 67, 78-79, 118 and n., 119, 160, 165, 197, 267, 287-294, 372-373, 404, 407-417.

Raithby, John, *Delineations of the Heart,* 444.

*Rajah Kisna,* 63n.

Raleigh, Sir Walter, 85, 296, 308.

*Ramble of Philo, The,* 151, 441.

Raspe, R. E., *Baron Munchausen,* 338, 440, 447.

Rastell, John, *The Four Elements,* 18, 20, 22, 258.

Reading, Pennsylvania, 110.

Realism in interpretation of America, 15-16, 26-27, 37, 38, 257-258, 259, 312-313, 331, 345-346, 370-371, 402, 419-420, 425-430.

Reeve, Clara, 41; *Destination,* 176n., 442, 448; *The Exiles,* 444; *The Old English Baron,* 437; *The Two Mentors,* 444, 447.

*Reginald,* 438.

*Relapse, The,* 91, 319-320, 322n., 440.

Religion in America (see also Puritans, Methodism, Catholicism, etc.), 18-19, 25, 38, 70, 202, 219, 268, 269, 382, 386-402, 412n., 418-419, 426, 428.

Renaissance, European attitude to America in, 9-11, 14, 16-26, 257, 259, 312, 325, 332, 335, 346, 386, 389, 402, 420, 426-427, 428.

*Rencontre, The,* 438.

Renwick, William, *Solicitudes of Absence,* 104, 150-151, 153n., 181, 336, 441, 444, 447.

*Reveries of the Heart,* 71, 144, 167, 168, 179-180, 192, 223, 246-248, 374-375, 377, 408, 440.

*Revolution, The,* 64.

*Revolutions of an Island,* 245n.

Rhode Island, 99, 115, 301, 319.

Richardson, Samuel, 4n., 41, 47n.

Richardson, William, *The Cacique of Ontario,* 64, 72, 440.

*Ring, The,* 95, 440.

*Robert and Adela,* 441, 448.

Robespierre, Isidore, 427.

Robinson, Mrs. Mary E., 42; *Vancenza,* 438.

Robinson-Morris, Matthew, *Peace the best policy . . .,* 49.

Rockingham, Charles Watson-Wentworth, second Marquis of, 214n.

Rodney, Admiral, 128, 130, 133, 143, 189.

Rogers, A., *The History of Miss Temple,* 437.

Rollins, Hyder E., *Pepys Ballads,* 22n.

Romanticism, 2, 4, 27-29, 34, 52, 78, 189, 197, 261 ff., 312, 429-430.

*Rose Cecil,* 444.

Rourke, Constance, *American Humor,* 73n.

Rousseau, J. J., 4n., 67, 78, 81, 277; *Emilius,* 277 and n., 278n.

Rowson, Mrs. Susanna H., 76n.; *Fille de Chambre,* 76, 124-125, 155-156, 170, 232, 270, 322n., 441, 444, 448; *The History of Charlotte Temple,* 76, 116, 358, 369, 441; *The Inquisitor,* 101, 232, 441, 447; *Mentoria,* 88, 306, 441, 444; *The Test of Honour,* 441, 444.

Rumford, Benjamin Thompson, Count von, 74n.

Rusk, Ralph L., *The Adventures of Gilbert Imlay,* 264n.

Ryan, Rev. Everhard, *Reliques of Genius,* 372n.

S., H., *The Young Widow,* 356-358, 369, 440, 444.

Sadler, ——, of Chippenham, *Wanley Penson,* 155, 301-302, 326, 334n., 400, 441, 448.

*Sailor Boy, The,* 88, 442, 448.

Sailors and the navy in literature (see also Rodney), 24-25, 26, 96n., 104, 113, 124, 130, 131, 133, 159, 188-189, 276, 306, 310-311, 336, 352-353, 366-367, 394.

St. Clair, Foster Y., *The Myth of the Golden Age,* 263.

St. Lawrence River, 270.

Saintsbury, George, 21n., 31n.; *The English Novel,* 69n.
Samson, J., *Oppression,* 265 and n.
Sandys, Sir George, 17.
Saratoga, 129.
Sargent, Winthrop, *Loyal Verses,* 30n.
Sayer, Edward, *Lindor and Adelaide,* 115-116, 153, 373n., 441; *Observations on Dr. Price's Revolution Sermon,* 153n.
Scandinavian influences on English literature, 52, 252, 433-434, 436.
*School for Fathers, The,* 109-110, 149-150, 169-170, 230-231, 255, 351, 369, 441.
*School for Majesty, The,* 438.
Schulze, Konrad, 17n.
*Scots Magazine,* 50n.
Scott, Helenus, *The Adventures of a Rupee,* 63n., 93, 110n., 440, 443, 447; *Helena,* 110-111, 110n., 112, 170, 334n., 336n., 351-352, 366, 369, 372n., 441, 444, 448.
Scott, Mrs. Sarah R., *The History of Sir George Ellison,* 443.
Scott, Temple, 348n.
Scott, Thomas, *The Force of Truth,* 437.
Scott, Walter, 4n., 32, 41.
Selden, Catherine, *The English Nun,* 445, 448.
*Sentimental Memoirs,* 176, 447.
Seven Years' War, 66, 69, 87-89, 240-242, 243, 251, 297.
*Sewanee Review,* 264n.
Seward, Anna, *Monody on Major André,* 51.
Shakespeare, William, *As You Like It,* 21; *Henry VIII,* 24-25; *The Tempest,* 16, 17.
Sharp, Granville, 391.
Shaw, G. B., *The Apple Cart,* 11, 402.
Shebbeare, John, 31; *Lydia,* 69 and n.
Sheffield, John Baker Holroyd, first Earl of, *Observations on the Commerce of the American States,* 60.
Shelburne, William Petty, Lord, 146n.
Shelley, Percy B., 266-267, 430.
Sheridan, Mrs. Frances, *The History of*

*Nourjahad,* 437; *Memoirs of Miss Sidney Bidulph,* 443.
Sheridan, R. B., 31-32.
Sherwood, Mrs. Mary M., *The Traditions,* 438.
Sickelmore, Richard, *Mary Jane,* 362-363, 442, 445, 448.
Siddons, Henry, *Leon,* 438.
Sidney, Sir Philip, 296.
Sime, James, *William Herschel and His Work,* 152n.
*Singular Sufferings of Two Friends Lost in an American Forest,* 65, 132n., 338.
*Sketches for Tabernacle Frames,* 398 and n.
Slave Trade (see also Slavery), 7n., 29, 382-384.
Slavery (see also Humanitarianism), 29, 38, 39n., 175-176, 366, 367, 382-385, 418-419, 424, 426.
Sloss, D. J., 28n.
Smith, Adam, 33.
Smith, Mrs. Charlotte Turner, 42, 67n., 84n., 133, 164, 189, 256, 403n., 404; *The Banished Man,* 84n., 117-118, 129n., 373, 377-378, 441, 448; *Celestina,* 84n., 120, 129n., 221, 232, 410, 421, 441, 444, 448; [?] *D'Arcy,* 448; *Desmond,* 84n., 153, 171, 193, 225, 335n., 405, 410-411, 441, 444, 448; *Emmeline,* 84n., 87, 320n., 334n., 352-353, 383, 441, 444, 447; *Ethelinde,* 84, 181, 271 and n., 272, 339, 366-367, 370, 441, 444, 447; *Letters of a Solitary Wanderer,* 84n., 221, 319, 361-362, 370, 384-385, 442, 445; *Marchmont,* 84n., 126-127, 442, 448; *Montalbert,* 448; *Old Manor House,* 67, 76, 84, 122-123, 156-158, 170, 182-184, 193, 215, 225, 334n., 339-340, 421, 441, 444, 448; *Wanderings of Warwick,* 77, 123-124, 307, 367, 369, 441, 444, 448; *The Young Philosopher,* 67, 77 and n., 127, 159-160, 173, 193-194, 317, 360-361, 393, 397, 407, 442, 445, 448.

N 2